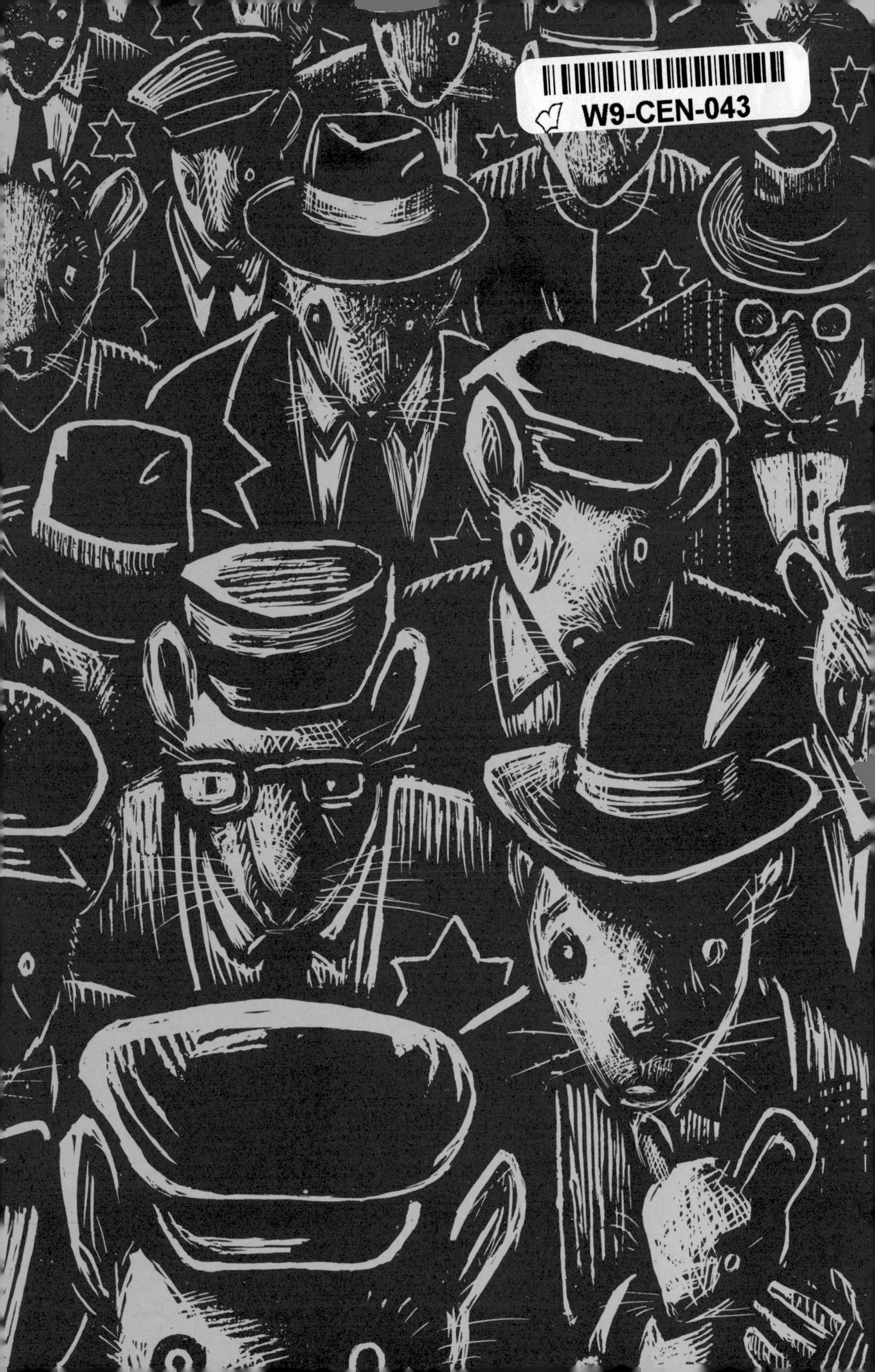

MAUS

A SURVIVOR'S TALE

PANTHEON B

¡AUS

A SURVIVOR'S TALE

I
MY FATHER BLEEDS HISTORY

II
AND HERE MY TROUBLES BEGAN

art spiegelman

OKS NEW YORK

Thanks to Ken and Flo Jacobs, Ernie Gehr, Paul Pavel, Louise Fili, Steven Heller,
Deborah Karl, and Mala Spiegelman, whose appreciation and support
have helped bring this book into the world.

And thanks to Françoise Mouly for her intelligence and integrity,
for her editorial skills, and for her love.

 Published in the United States by Pantheon Books, a division of Random House, Inc., New York, and simultaneously in Canada by Random House of Canada Limited, Toronto.

Chapters one through six of *Maus, Volume I* and chapters one through four of *Maus, Volume II* first appeared, in a somewhat different form, in *Raw* magazine between 1980 and 1991.
"Prisoner of the Hell Planet" originally appeared in *Short Order Comix #1,* 1973.

Library of Congress Cataloging-in-Publication Data
Spiegelman, Art.
Maus : a survivor's tale / Art Spiegelman.
p. cm.
Contents: My fathers bleeds history — And here my troubles began.
ISBN 978-0-679-40641-9
1. Spiegelman, Vladek—Comic books, strips, etc.
2. Holocaust, Jewish (1939-1945)—Poland—Biography—Comic books, strips, etc.
3. Holocaust survivors—United States—Biography—Comic books, strips, etc.
4. Spiegelman, Art—Comic books, strips, etc.
5. Children of Holocaust survivors—United States—Biography—Comic books, strips, etc. I. Title.
DS135.P63S68 1997
940.53'18'0922—dc20 [B] 96-32796 CIP

Printed in China

37 C 36

Rego Park, N.Y. c.1958

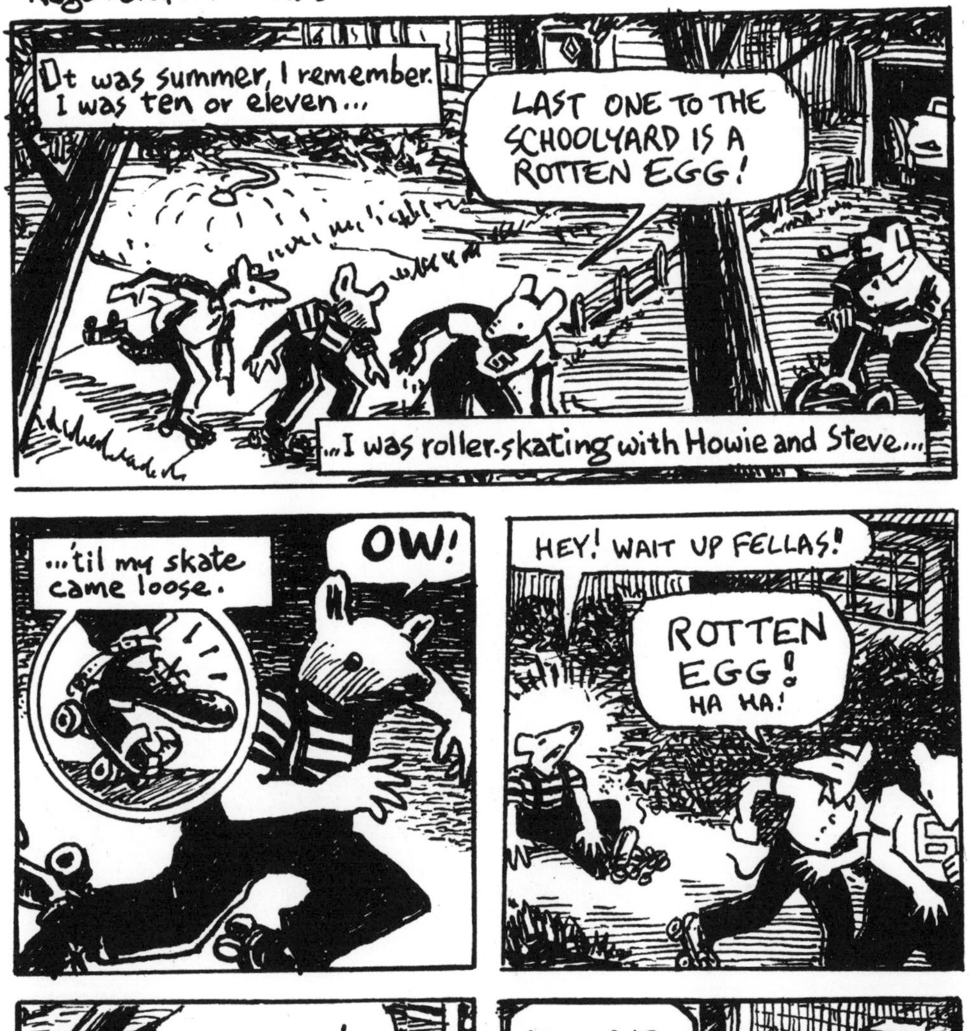
It was summer, I remember. I was ten or eleven...
LAST ONE TO THE SCHOOLYARD IS A ROTTEN EGG!
...I was roller-skating with Howie and Steve...
...'til my skate came loose.
OW!
HEY! WAIT UP FELLAS!
ROTTEN EGG! HA HA!
W-WAIT UP!
SNK, SNF
My father was in front, fixing something...

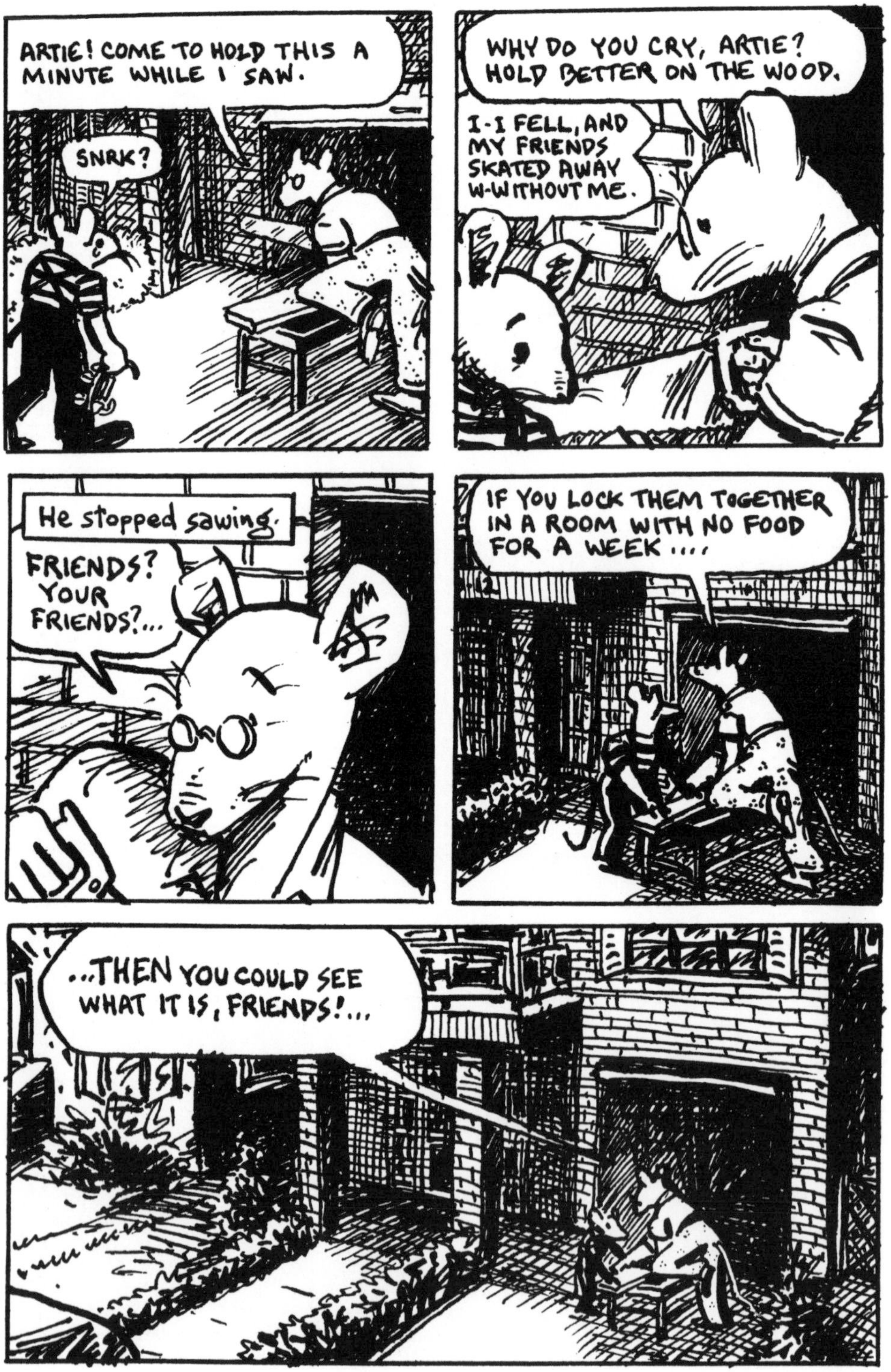
ARTIE! COME TO HOLD THIS A MINUTE WHILE I SAW.
SNRK?
WHY DO YOU CRY, ARTIE? HOLD BETTER ON THE WOOD.
I-I FELL, AND MY FRIENDS SKATED AWAY W-WITHOUT ME.
He stopped sawing.
FRIENDS? YOUR FRIENDS?...
IF YOU LOCK THEM TOGETHER IN A ROOM WITH NO FOOD FOR A WEEK....
...THEN YOU COULD SEE WHAT IT IS, FRIENDS!...

MAUS

I

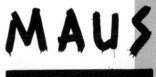

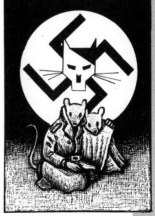

FOR ANJA

MY FATHER BLEEDS HISTORY

(MID-1930s TO WINTER 1944)

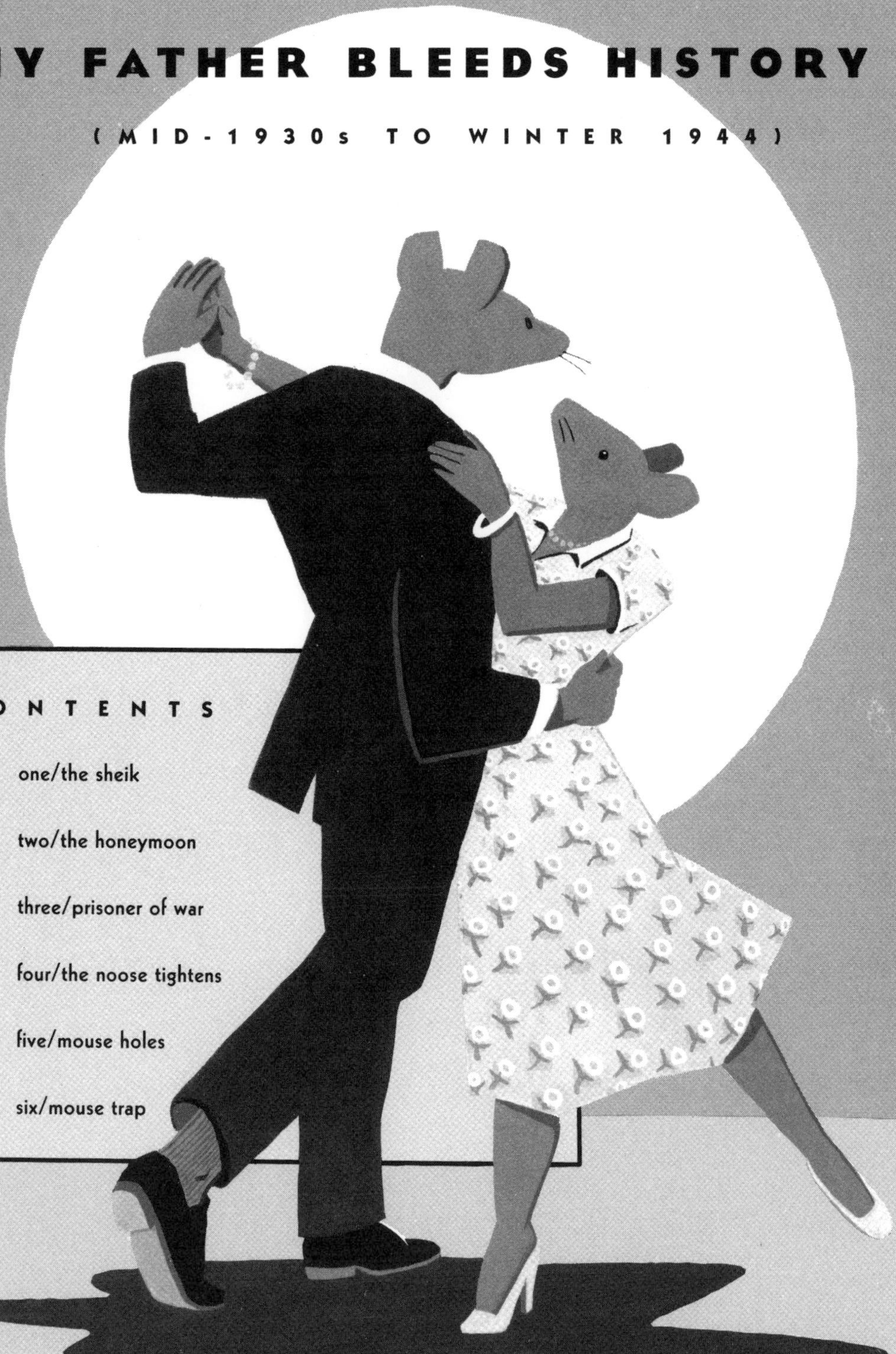

CONTENTS

"The Jews are undoubtedly a race,

but they are not human."

Adolf Hitler

CHAPTER ONE

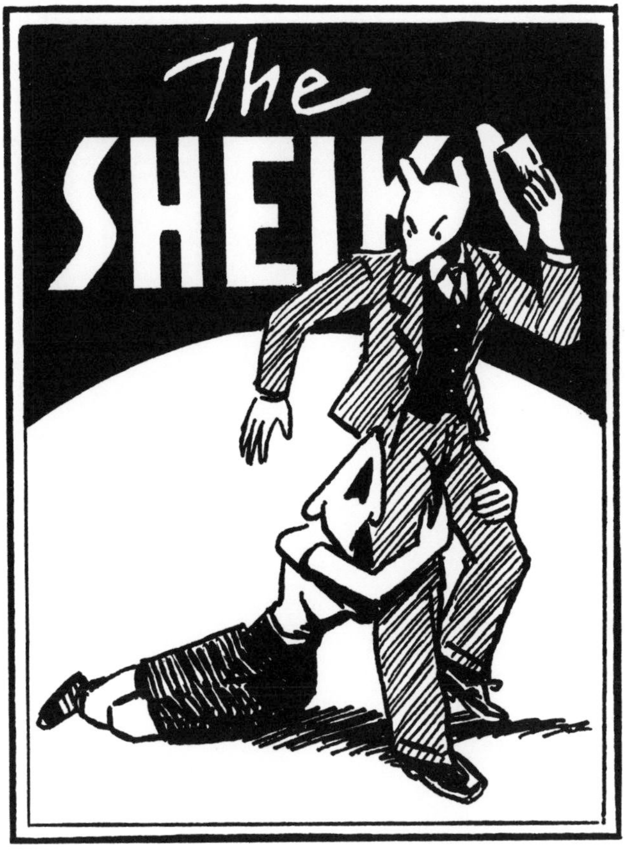
The
SHEIK

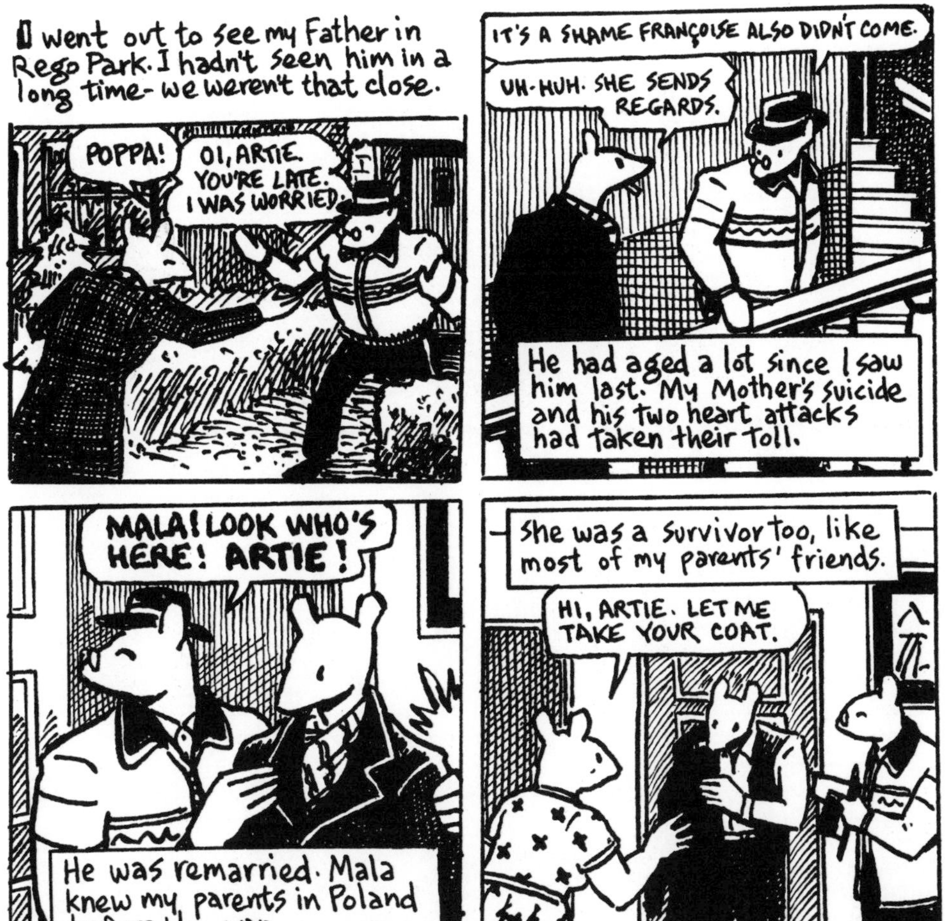
I went out to see my Father in Rego Park. I hadn't seen him in a long time- we weren't that close.
POPPA!
OI, ARTIE. YOU'RE LATE. I WAS WORRIED.
IT'S A SHAME FRANÇOISE ALSO DIDN'T COME.
UH-HUH. SHE SENDS REGARDS.
He had aged a lot since I saw him last. My Mother's suicide and his two heart attacks had taken their toll.
MALA! LOOK WHO'S HERE! ARTIE!
He was remarried. Mala knew my parents in Poland before the war.
She was a survivor too, like most of my parents' friends.
HI, ARTIE. LET ME TAKE YOUR COAT.
THE DINNER IS ON THE TABLE.
ACCH, MALA!
A WIRE HANGER YOU GIVE HIM! I HAVEN'T SEEN ARTIE IN ALMOST TWO YEARS- WE HAVE PLENTY WOODEN HANGERS.
They didn't get along.

After dinner he took me into my old room...

COME—WE'LL TALK WHILE I PEDAL...

IT'S GOOD FOR MY HEART, THE PEDALING. BUT, TELL ME, HOW IS IT BY YOU? HOW IS GOING THE COMICS BUSINESS?

I STILL WANT TO DRAW THAT BOOK ABOUT YOU...

THE ONE I USED TO TALK TO YOU ABOUT...

ABOUT YOUR LIFE IN POLAND, AND THE WAR.

IT WOULD TAKE **MANY** BOOKS, MY LIFE, AND NO ONE WANTS ANYWAY TO HEAR SUCH STORIES.

I WANT TO HEAR IT. START WITH MOM... TELL ME HOW YOU MET.

BETTER YOU SHOULD SPEND YOUR TIME TO MAKE DRAWINGS WHAT WILL BRING YOU SOME MONEY...

BUT, IF YOU WANT, I CAN TELL YOU... I LIVED THEN IN CZESTOCHOWA, A SMALL CITY NOT FAR FROM THE BOR-DER OF GERMANY...

I WAS IN TEXTILES—BUY-ING AND SELLING—I DIDN'T MAKE MUCH, BUT ALWAYS I COULD MAKE A *LIVING*.

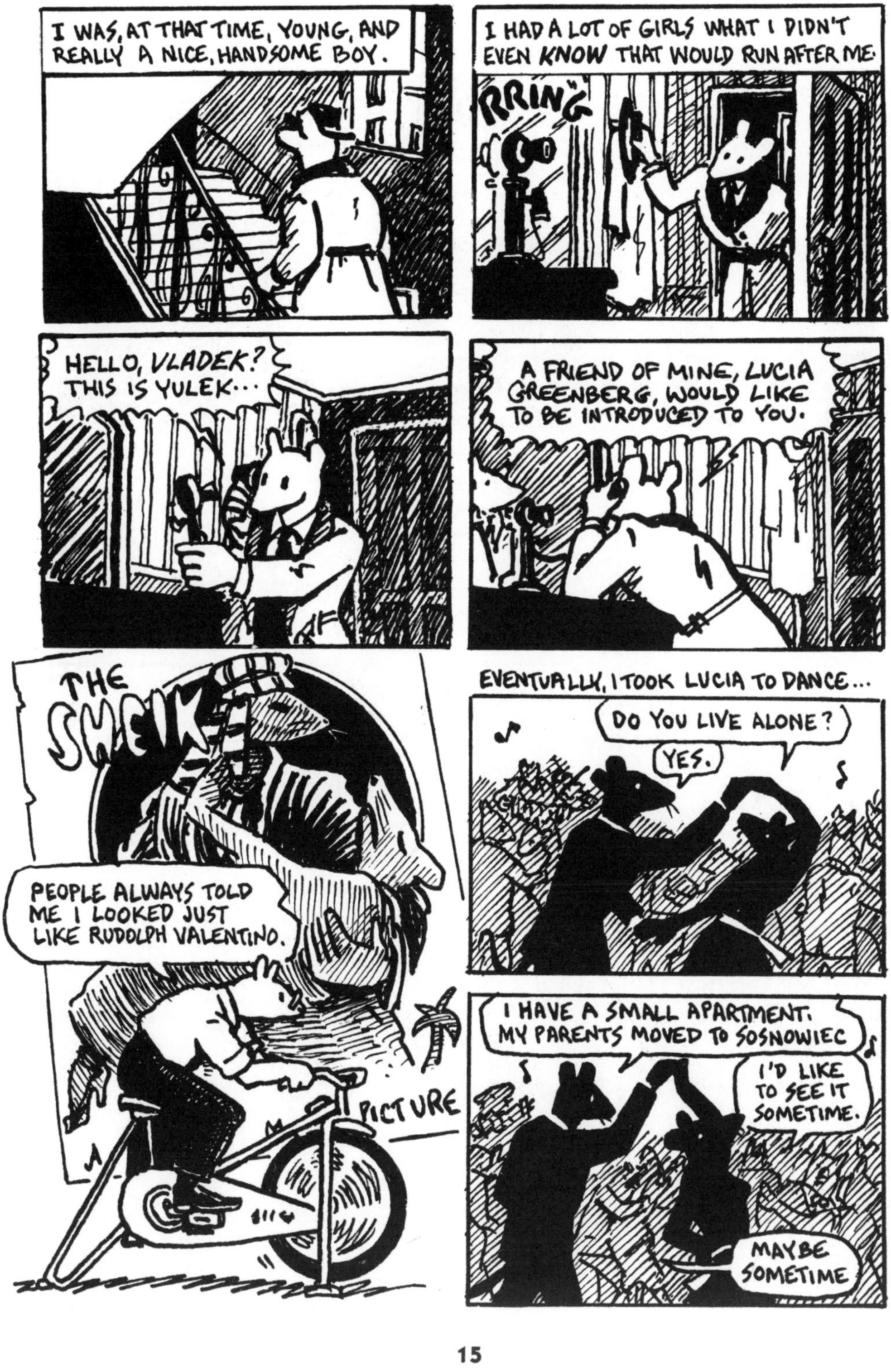
I WAS, AT THAT TIME, YOUNG, AND REALLY A NICE, HANDSOME BOY.
I HAD A LOT OF GIRLS WHAT I DIDN'T EVEN KNOW THAT WOULD RUN AFTER ME.
"RRING"
HELLO, VLADEK? THIS IS YULEK...
A FRIEND OF MINE, LUCIA GREENBERG, WOULD LIKE TO BE INTRODUCED TO YOU.
THE SHEIK
PEOPLE ALWAYS TOLD ME I LOOKED JUST LIKE RUDOLPH VALENTINO.
PICTURE
EVENTUALLY, I TOOK LUCIA TO DANCE...
DO YOU LIVE ALONE?
YES.
I HAVE A SMALL APARTMENT. MY PARENTS MOVED TO SOSNOWIEC
I'D LIKE TO SEE IT SOMETIME.
MAYBE SOMETIME

WHEREVER I WENT - I LOOKED AROUND - AND LUCIA GREENBERG WOULD BE ALSO THERE ...

VLADEK! - WHICH WAY ARE YOU GOING?

JUST TO THE MARKET.

ME TOO - LET'S WALK TOGETHER.

BUT, POP... MOM'S NAME WAS ANNA ZYLBERBERG! ...

ALL THIS WAS BEFORE I MET ANJA - JUST LISTEN, YES?

WHY DON'T YOU EVER INVITE ME TO YOUR HOME? ... ARE YOU ASHAMED OF IT?

SHE KEPT INSISTING ME TO SHOW HER MY APARTMENT...

- SO FINALLY, I INVITED HER...

EVERYTHING'S SO NEAT AND CLEAN!

I LIKE TO KEEP THINGS IN ORDER.

YOU MUST HAVE ANOTHER GIRL-FRIEND WHO CLEANS FOR YOU - NO?

NO.

...I DIDN'T WANT TO BE MORE CLOSER WITH HER, BUT SHE REALLY WOULDN'T LET ME GO.

16

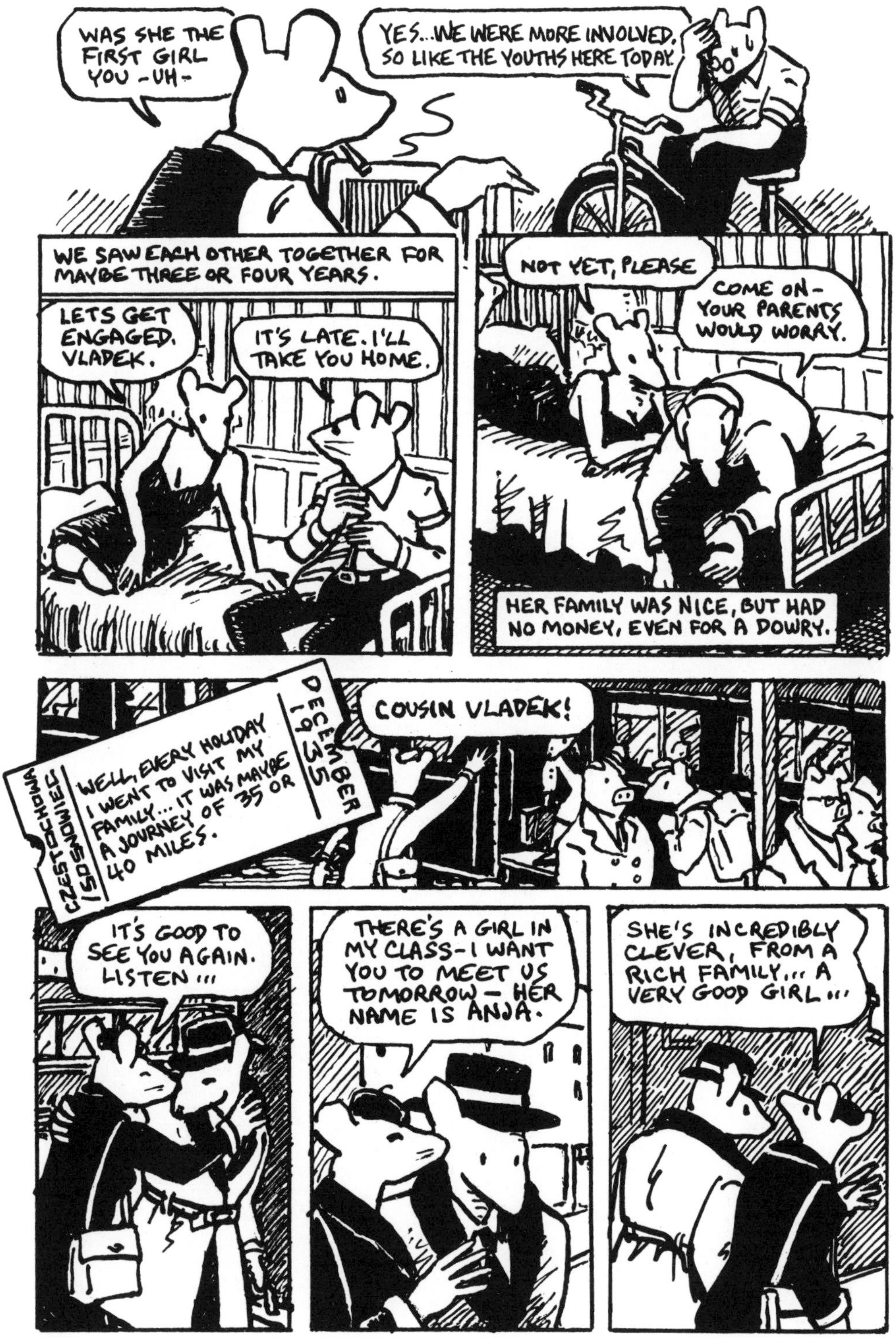
WAS SHE THE FIRST GIRL YOU -UH-
YES...WE WERE MORE INVOLVED, SO LIKE THE YOUTHS HERE TODAY.
WE SAW EACH OTHER TOGETHER FOR MAYBE THREE OR FOUR YEARS.
LETS GET ENGAGED, VLADEK.
IT'S LATE. I'LL TAKE YOU HOME.
NOT YET, PLEASE
COME ON- YOUR PARENTS WOULD WORRY.
HER FAMILY WAS NICE, BUT HAD NO MONEY, EVEN FOR A DOWRY.
CZESTOCHOWA
SOSNOWIEC
WELL, EVERY HOLIDAY I WENT TO VISIT MY FAMILY... IT WAS MAYBE A JOURNEY OF 35 OR 40 MILES.
DECEMBER 1935
COUSIN VLADEK!
IT'S GOOD TO SEE YOU AGAIN. LISTEN...
THERE'S A GIRL IN MY CLASS- I WANT YOU TO MEET US TOMORROW- HER NAME IS ANJA.
SHE'S INCREDIBLY CLEVER, FROM A RICH FAMILY... A VERY GOOD GIRL...

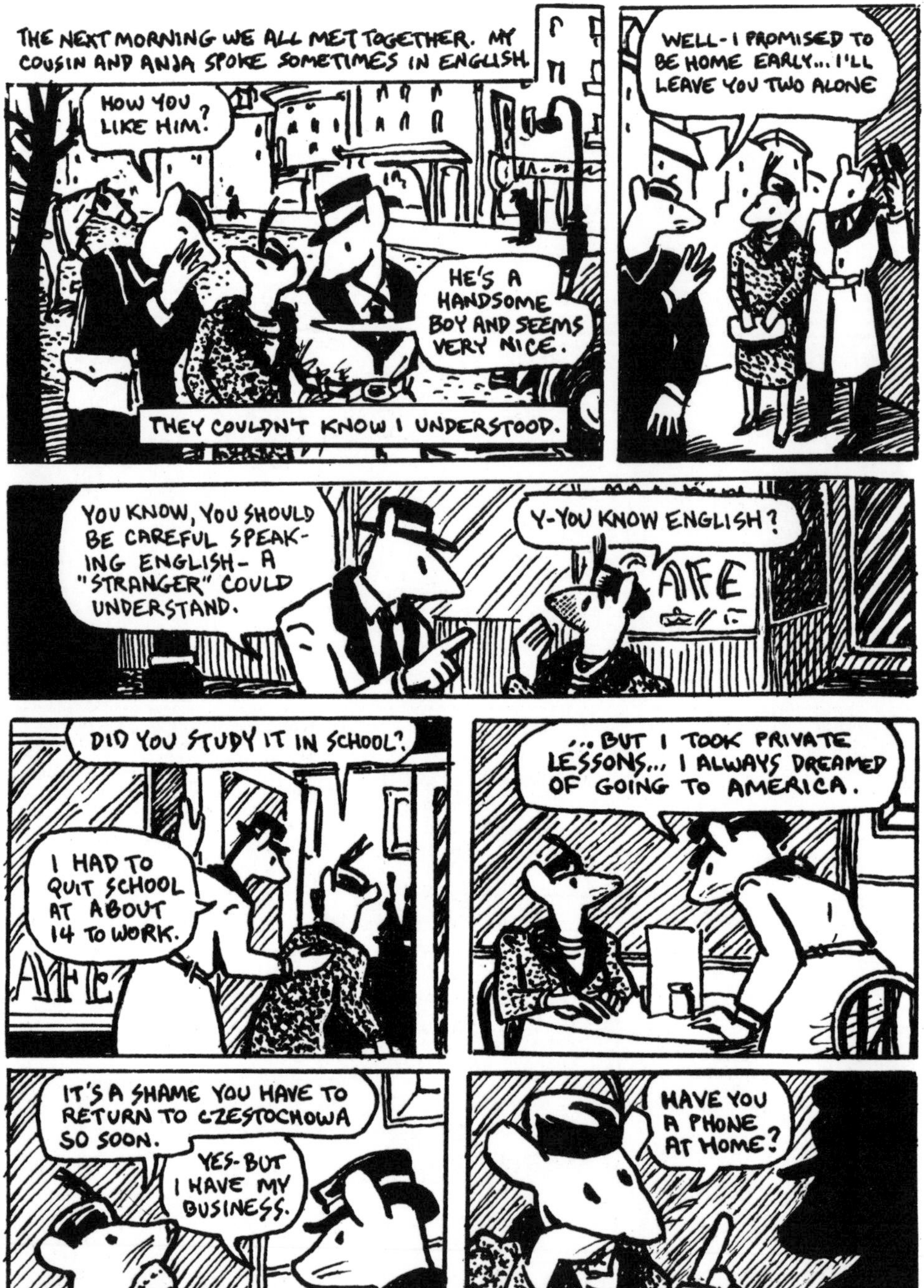
THE NEXT MORNING WE ALL MET TOGETHER. MY COUSIN AND ANJA SPOKE SOMETIMES IN ENGLISH.
HOW YOU LIKE HIM?
HE'S A HANDSOME BOY AND SEEMS VERY NICE.
THEY COULDN'T KNOW I UNDERSTOOD.
WELL- I PROMISED TO BE HOME EARLY... I'LL LEAVE YOU TWO ALONE
YOU KNOW, YOU SHOULD BE CAREFUL SPEAKING ENGLISH- A "STRANGER" COULD UNDERSTAND.
Y-YOU KNOW ENGLISH?
DID YOU STUDY IT IN SCHOOL?
I HAD TO QUIT SCHOOL AT ABOUT 14 TO WORK.
...BUT I TOOK PRIVATE LESSONS... I ALWAYS DREAMED OF GOING TO AMERICA.
IT'S A SHAME YOU HAVE TO RETURN TO CZESTOCHOWA SO SOON.
YES- BUT I HAVE MY BUSINESS.
HAVE YOU A PHONE AT HOME?
AS SOON I CAME BACK TO CZESTOCHOWA, SHE CALLED - ONCE A DAY... TWICE... EVERY DAY WE TALKED.

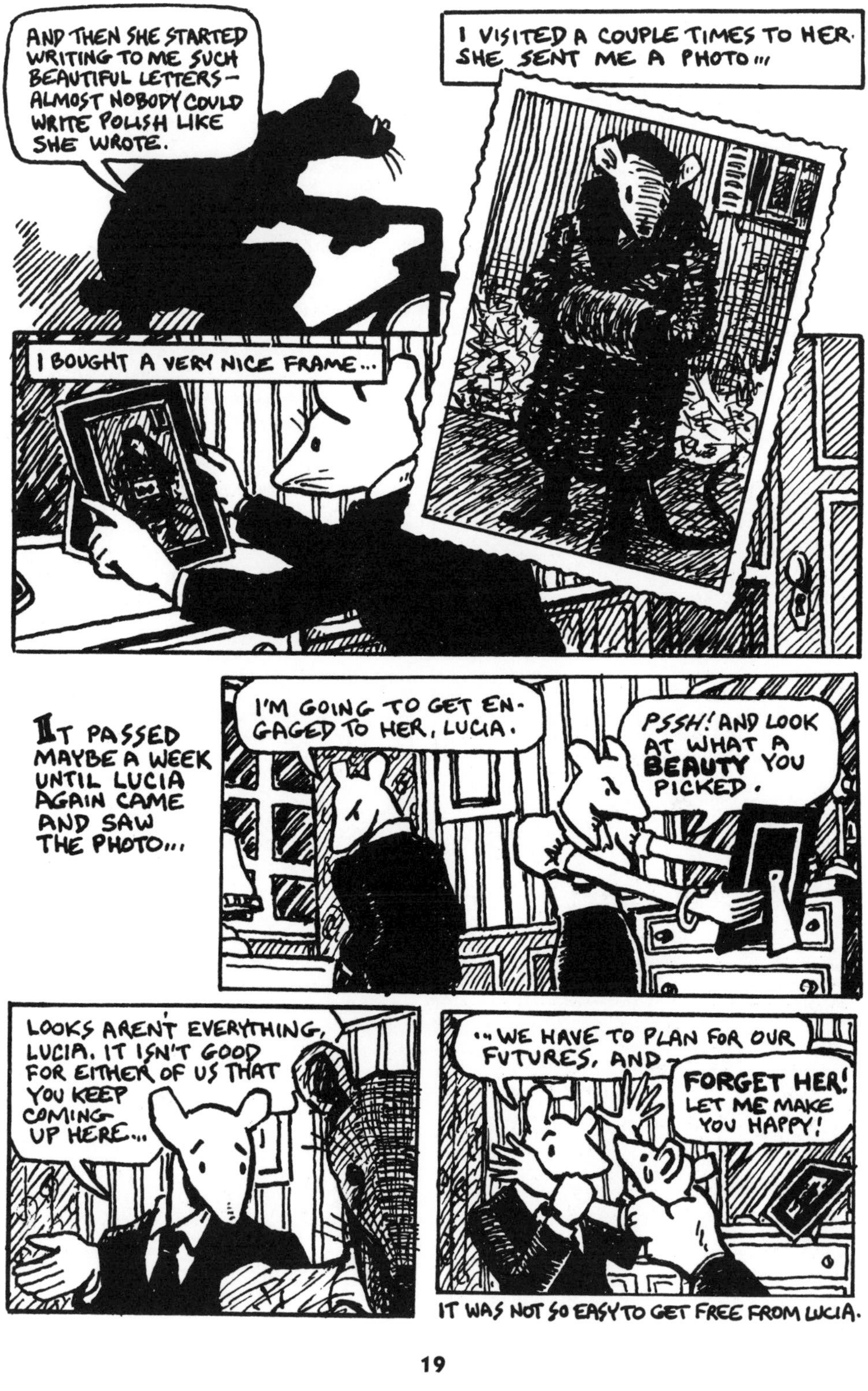
AND THEN SHE STARTED WRITING TO ME SUCH BEAUTIFUL LETTERS– ALMOST NOBODY COULD WRITE POLISH LIKE SHE WROTE.
I VISITED A COUPLE TIMES TO HER. SHE SENT ME A PHOTO...
I BOUGHT A VERY NICE FRAME...
IT PASSED MAYBE A WEEK UNTIL LUCIA AGAIN CAME AND SAW THE PHOTO...
I'M GOING TO GET ENGAGED TO HER, LUCIA.
PSSH! AND LOOK AT WHAT A BEAUTY YOU PICKED.
LOOKS AREN'T EVERYTHING, LUCIA. IT ISN'T GOOD FOR EITHER OF US THAT YOU KEEP COMING UP HERE...
...WE HAVE TO PLAN FOR OUR FUTURES, AND–
FORGET HER! LET ME MAKE YOU HAPPY!
IT WAS NOT SO EASY TO GET FREE FROM LUCIA.

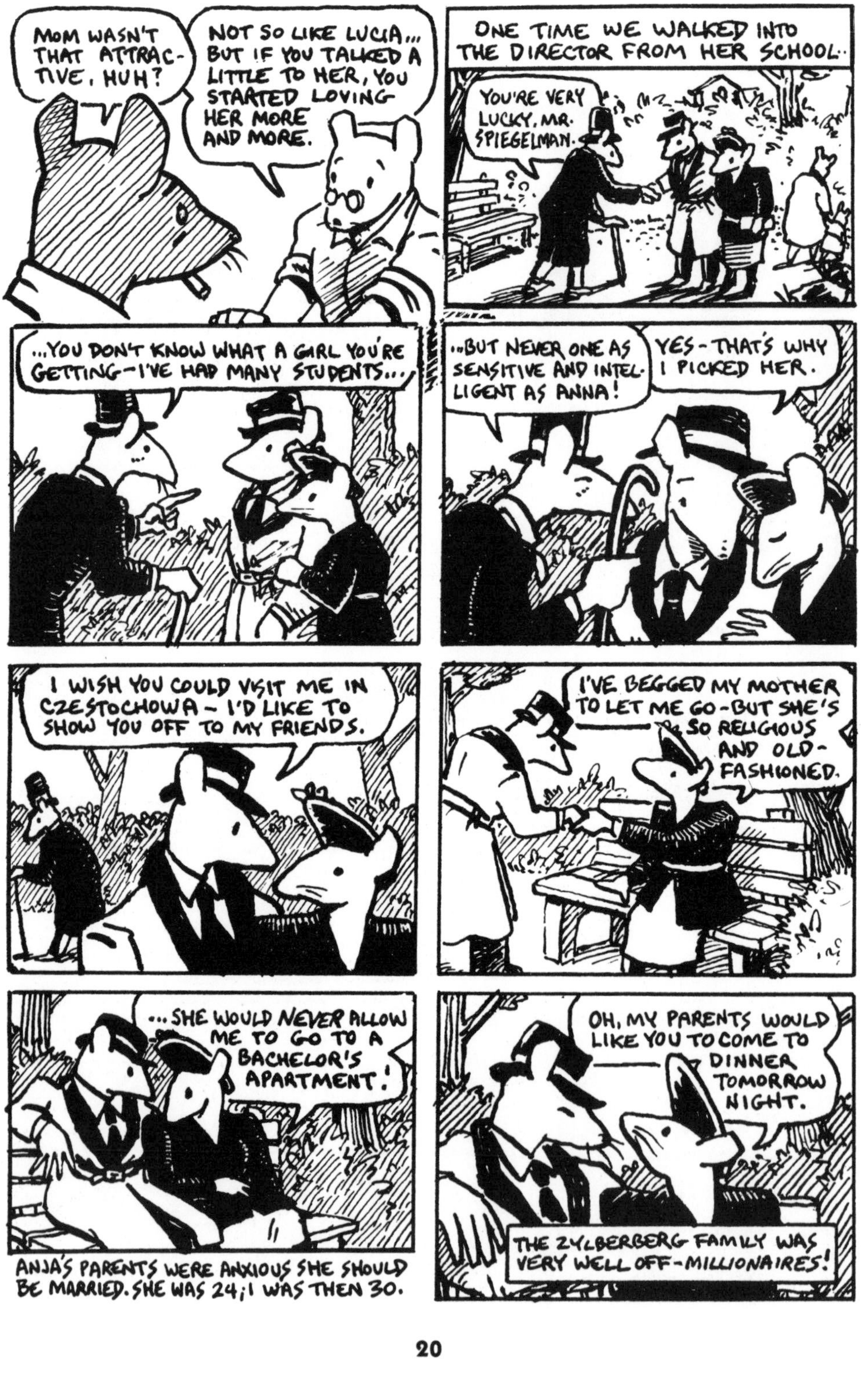

MOM WASN'T THAT ATTRACTIVE, HUH?
NOT SO LIKE LUCIA... BUT IF YOU TALKED A LITTLE TO HER, YOU STARTED LOVING HER MORE AND MORE.
ONE TIME WE WALKED INTO THE DIRECTOR FROM HER SCHOOL.
YOU'RE VERY LUCKY, MR. SPIEGELMAN.
...YOU DON'T KNOW WHAT A GIRL YOU'RE GETTING—I'VE HAD MANY STUDENTS...
...BUT NEVER ONE AS SENSITIVE AND INTELLIGENT AS ANNA!
YES—THAT'S WHY I PICKED HER.
I WISH YOU COULD VISIT ME IN CZESTOCHOWA—I'D LIKE TO SHOW YOU OFF TO MY FRIENDS.
I'VE BEGGED MY MOTHER TO LET ME GO—BUT SHE'S SO RELIGIOUS AND OLD-FASHIONED.
...SHE WOULD NEVER ALLOW ME TO GO TO A BACHELOR'S APARTMENT!
ANJA'S PARENTS WERE ANXIOUS SHE SHOULD BE MARRIED. SHE WAS 24; I WAS THEN 30.
OH, MY PARENTS WOULD LIKE YOU TO COME TO DINNER TOMORROW NIGHT.
THE ZYLBERBERG FAMILY WAS VERY WELL OFF—MILLIONAIRES!

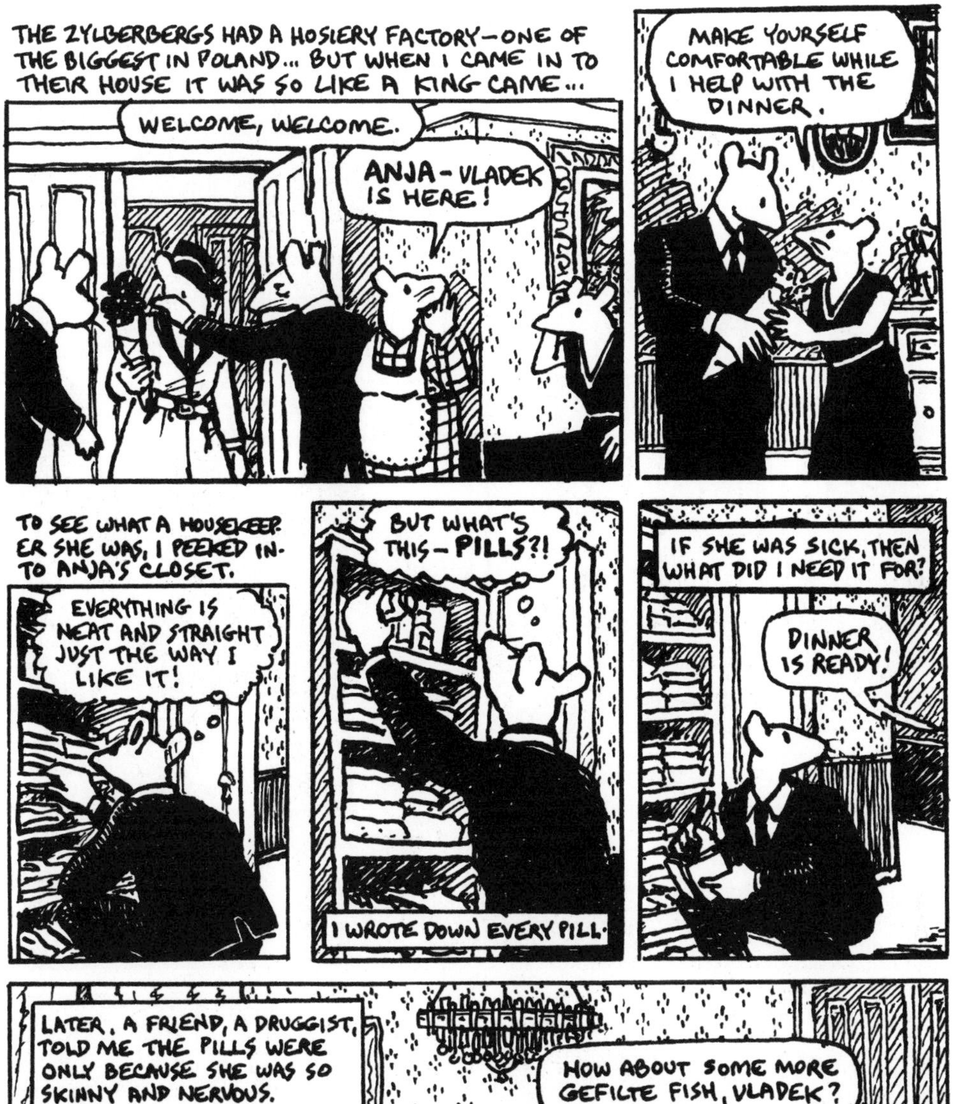
THE ZYLBERBERGS HAD A HOSIERY FACTORY—ONE OF THE BIGGEST IN POLAND... BUT WHEN I CAME IN TO THEIR HOUSE IT WAS SO LIKE A KING CAME...
WELCOME, WELCOME.
ANJA - VLADEK IS HERE!
MAKE YOURSELF COMFORTABLE WHILE I HELP WITH THE DINNER.
TO SEE WHAT A HOUSEKEEPER SHE WAS, I PEEKED INTO ANJA'S CLOSET.
EVERYTHING IS NEAT AND STRAIGHT JUST THE WAY I LIKE IT!
BUT WHAT'S THIS - PILLS?!
I WROTE DOWN EVERY PILL.
IF SHE WAS SICK, THEN WHAT DID I NEED IT FOR?
DINNER IS READY!
LATER, A FRIEND, A DRUGGIST, TOLD ME THE PILLS WERE ONLY BECAUSE SHE WAS SO SKINNY AND NERVOUS.
HOW ABOUT SOME MORE GEFILTE FISH, VLADEK?
SO, TO MAKE A LONG STORY SHORT, BY THE END OF 1936 WE WERE ENGAGED AND I MOVED FROM CZESTOCHOWA TO SOSNOWIEC.

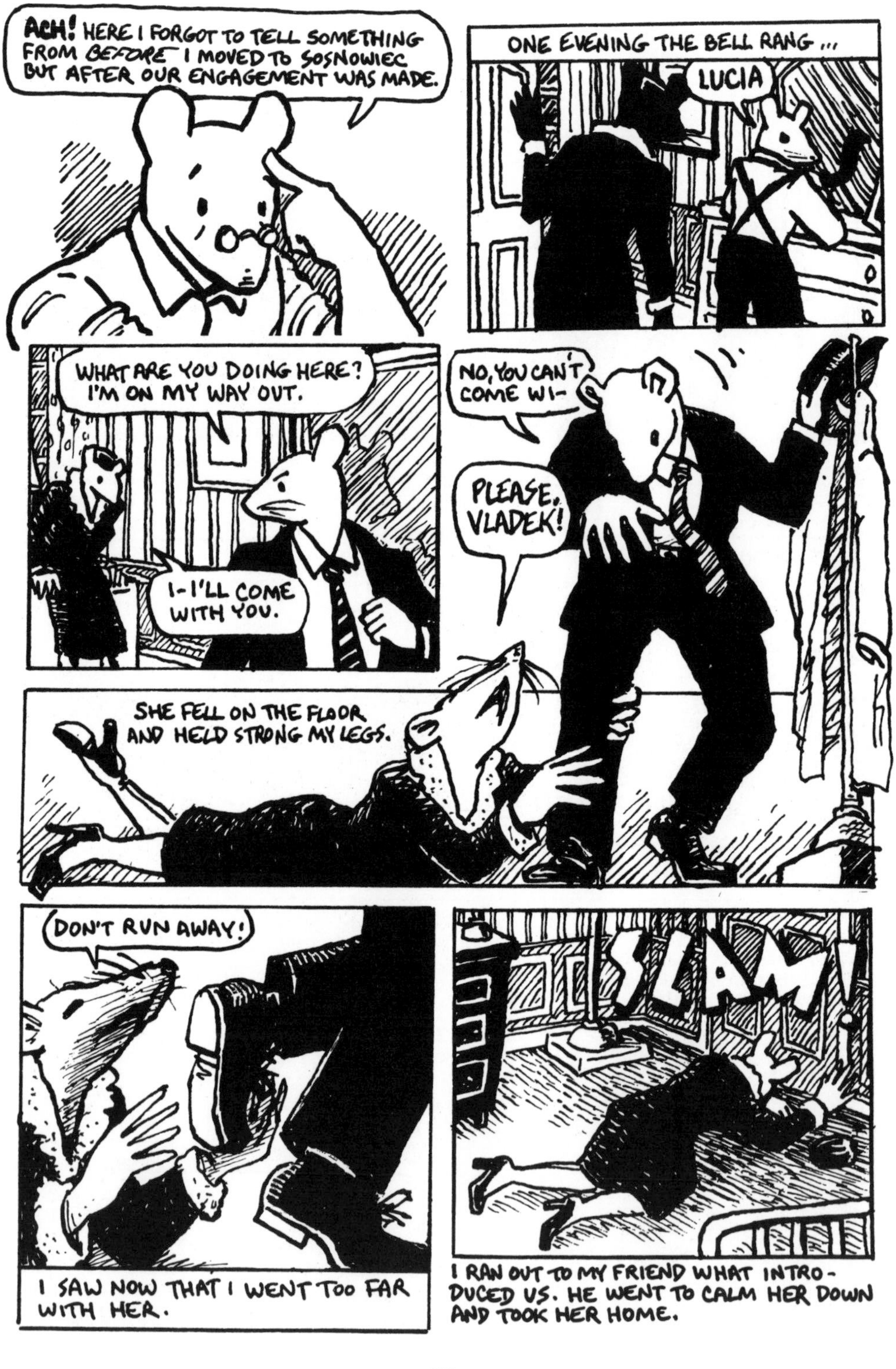
ACH! HERE I FORGOT TO TELL SOMETHING FROM BEFORE I MOVED TO SOSNOWIEC BUT AFTER OUR ENGAGEMENT WAS MADE.
ONE EVENING THE BELL RANG...
LUCIA
WHAT ARE YOU DOING HERE? I'M ON MY WAY OUT.
I-I'LL COME WITH YOU.
NO, YOU CAN'T COME WI-
PLEASE, VLADEK!
SHE FELL ON THE FLOOR AND HELD STRONG MY LEGS.
DON'T RUN AWAY!
I SAW NOW THAT I WENT TOO FAR WITH HER.
SLAM!
I RAN OUT TO MY FRIEND WHAT INTRO-DUCED US. HE WENT TO CALM HER DOWN AND TOOK HER HOME.

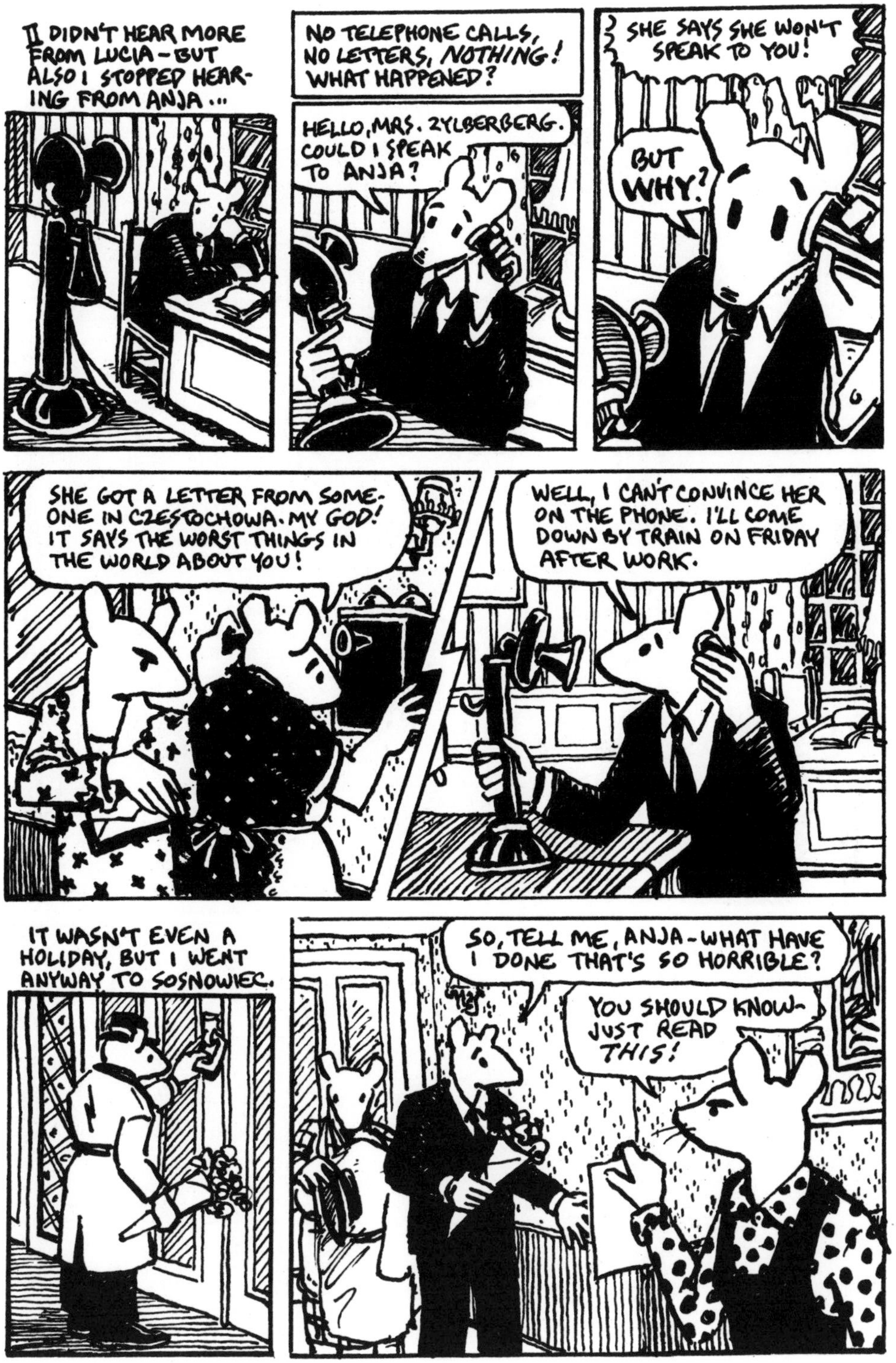
I DIDN'T HEAR MORE FROM LUCIA - BUT ALSO I STOPPED HEARING FROM ANJA ...
NO TELEPHONE CALLS, NO LETTERS, NOTHING! WHAT HAPPENED?
HELLO, MRS. ZYLBERBERG. COULD I SPEAK TO ANJA?
SHE SAYS SHE WON'T SPEAK TO YOU!
BUT WHY?
SHE GOT A LETTER FROM SOMEONE IN CZESTOCHOWA. MY GOD! IT SAYS THE WORST THINGS IN THE WORLD ABOUT YOU!
WELL, I CAN'T CONVINCE HER ON THE PHONE. I'LL COME DOWN BY TRAIN ON FRIDAY AFTER WORK.
IT WASN'T EVEN A HOLIDAY, BUT I WENT ANYWAY TO SOSNOWIEC.
SO, TELL ME, ANJA - WHAT HAVE I DONE THAT'S SO HORRIBLE?
YOU SHOULD KNOW - JUST READ THIS!

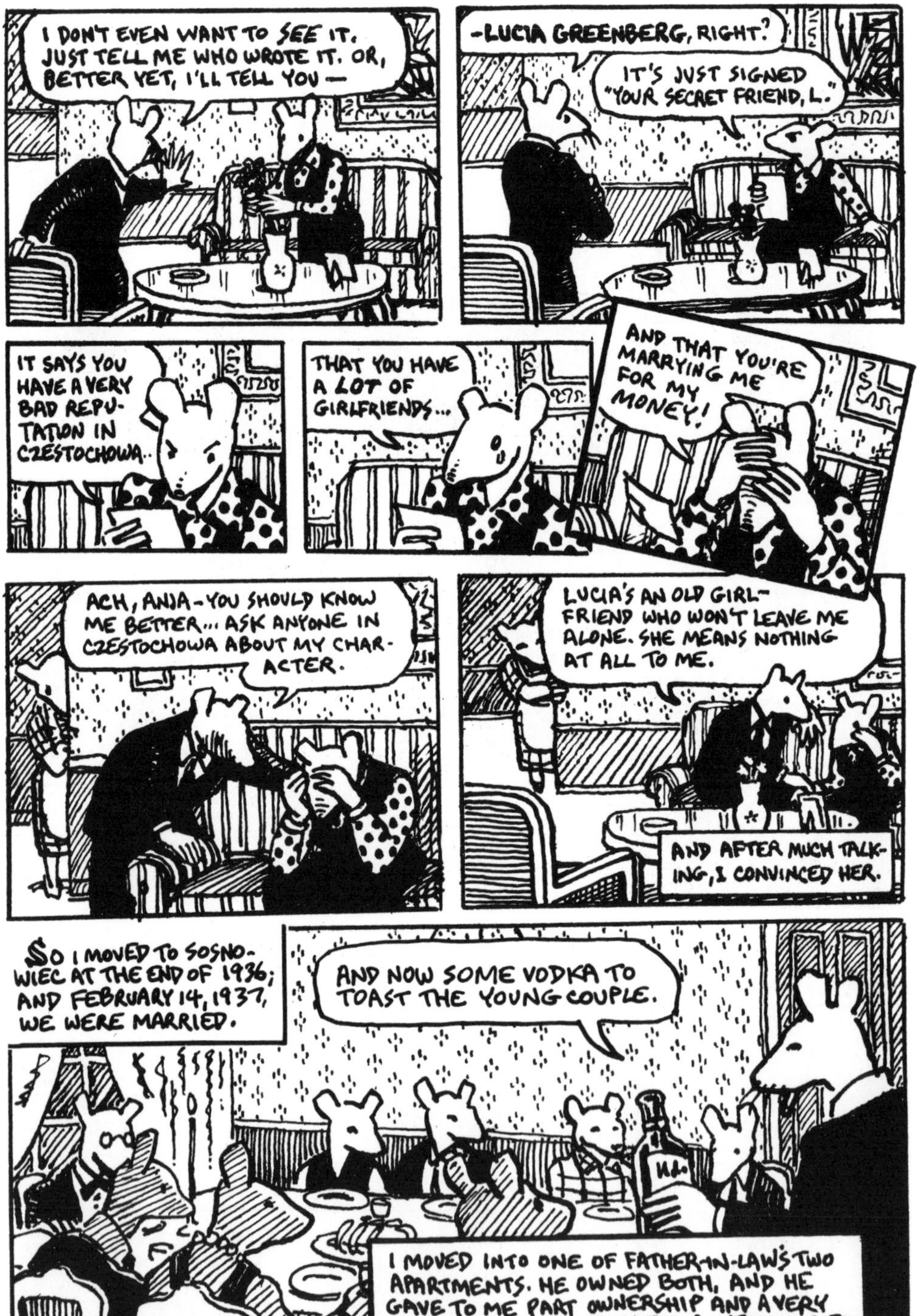
I DON'T EVEN WANT TO SEE IT. JUST TELL ME WHO WROTE IT. OR, BETTER YET, I'LL TELL YOU—
—LUCIA GREENBERG, RIGHT?
IT'S JUST SIGNED "YOUR SECRET FRIEND, L."
IT SAYS YOU HAVE A VERY BAD REPUTATION IN CZESTOCHOWA...
THAT YOU HAVE A LOT OF GIRLFRIENDS...
AND THAT YOU'RE MARRYING ME FOR MY MONEY!
ACH, ANJA–YOU SHOULD KNOW ME BETTER... ASK ANYONE IN CZESTOCHOWA ABOUT MY CHARACTER.
LUCIA'S AN OLD GIRLFRIEND WHO WON'T LEAVE ME ALONE. SHE MEANS NOTHING AT ALL TO ME.
AND AFTER MUCH TALKING, I CONVINCED HER.
SO I MOVED TO SOSNOWIEC AT THE END OF 1936; AND FEBRUARY 14, 1937, WE WERE MARRIED.
AND NOW SOME VODKA TO TOAST THE YOUNG COUPLE.
I MOVED INTO ONE OF FATHER-IN-LAW'S TWO APARTMENTS. HE OWNED BOTH, AND HE GAVE TO ME PART OWNERSHIP AND A VERY BEAUTIFUL GOLD WATCH FOR A WEDDING GIFT.

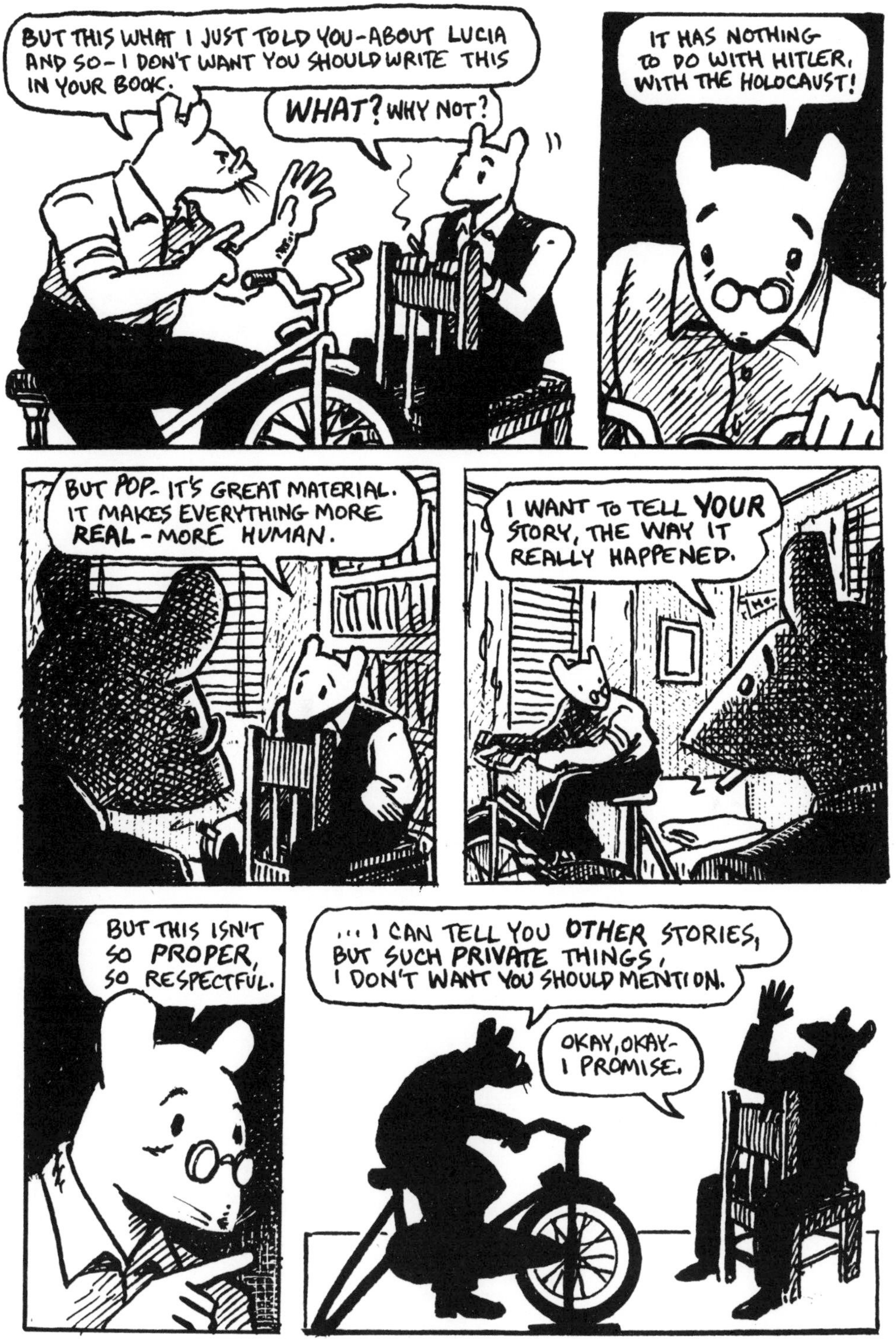

BUT THIS WHAT I JUST TOLD YOU-ABOUT LUCIA AND SO- I DON'T WANT YOU SHOULD WRITE THIS IN YOUR BOOK.
WHAT? WHY NOT?
IT HAS NOTHING TO DO WITH HITLER, WITH THE HOLOCAUST!
BUT POP- IT'S GREAT MATERIAL. IT MAKES EVERYTHING MORE REAL-MORE HUMAN.
I WANT TO TELL YOUR STORY, THE WAY IT REALLY HAPPENED.
BUT THIS ISN'T SO PROPER, SO RESPECTFUL.
...I CAN TELL YOU OTHER STORIES, BUT SUCH PRIVATE THINGS, I DON'T WANT YOU SHOULD MENTION.
OKAY, OKAY- I PROMISE.

CHAPTER TWO

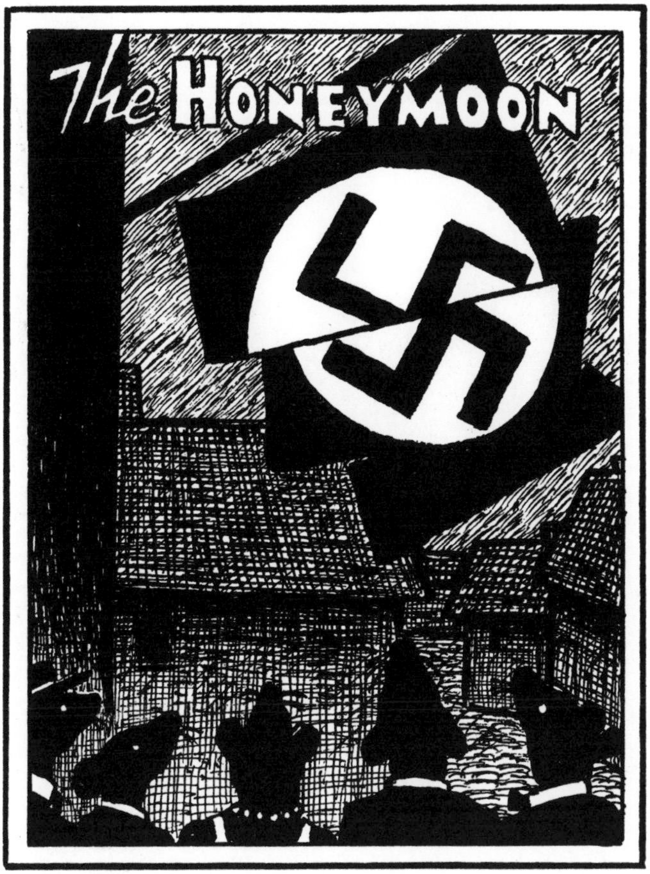

The HONEYMOON

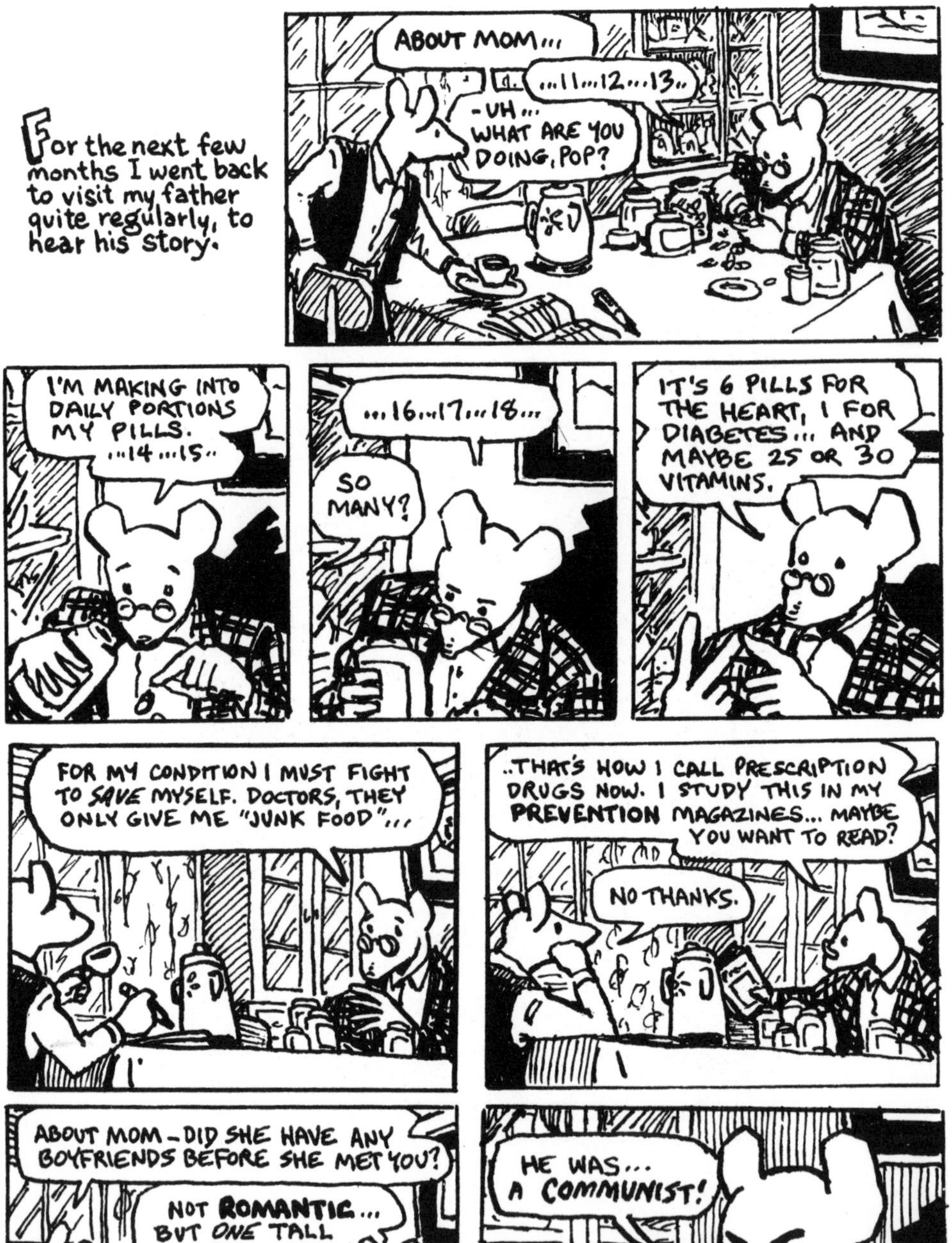
For the next few months I went back to visit my father quite regularly, to hear his story.
ABOUT MOM...
...11...12...13...
-UH... WHAT ARE YOU DOING, POP?
I'M MAKING INTO DAILY PORTIONS MY PILLS. ...14...15...
...16...17...18...
SO MANY?
IT'S 6 PILLS FOR THE HEART, 1 FOR DIABETES... AND MAYBE 25 OR 30 VITAMINS.
FOR MY CONDITION I MUST FIGHT TO SAVE MYSELF. DOCTORS, THEY ONLY GIVE ME "JUNK FOOD"...
..THAT'S HOW I CALL PRESCRIPTION DRUGS NOW. I STUDY THIS IN MY PREVENTION MAGAZINES... MAYBE YOU WANT TO READ?
NO THANKS.
ABOUT MOM - DID SHE HAVE ANY BOYFRIENDS BEFORE SHE MET YOU?
NOT ROMANTIC... BUT ONE TALL BOY FROM WARSAW
HE WAS... A COMMUNIST!

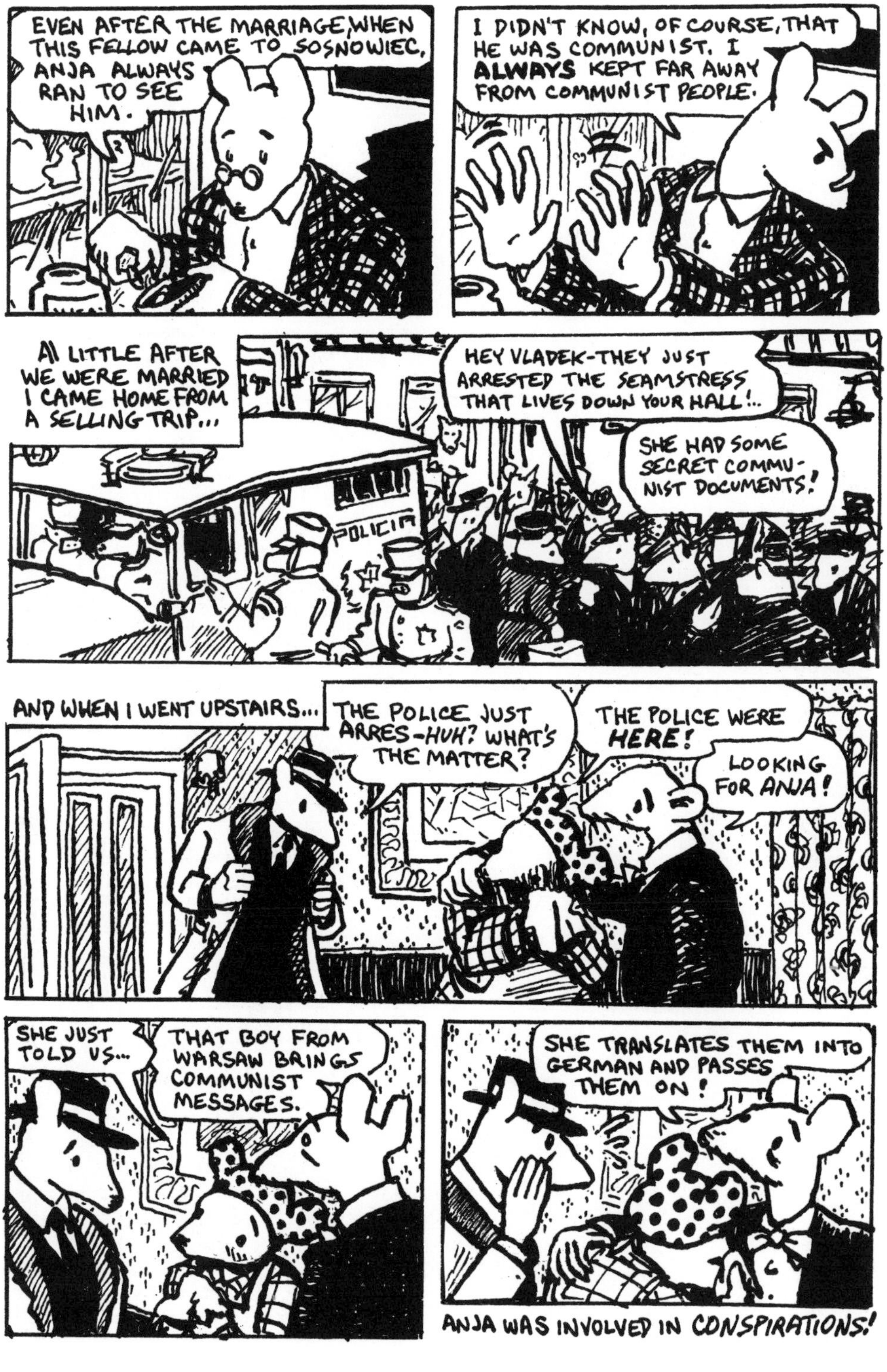
EVEN AFTER THE MARRIAGE, WHEN THIS FELLOW CAME TO SOSNOWIEC, ANJA ALWAYS RAN TO SEE HIM.
I DIDN'T KNOW, OF COURSE, THAT HE WAS COMMUNIST. I **ALWAYS** KEPT FAR AWAY FROM COMMUNIST PEOPLE.
A LITTLE AFTER WE WERE MARRIED I CAME HOME FROM A SELLING TRIP...
HEY VLADEK-THEY JUST ARRESTED THE SEAMSTRESS THAT LIVES DOWN YOUR HALL!..
SHE HAD SOME SECRET COMMUNIST DOCUMENTS!
POLICJA
AND WHEN I WENT UPSTAIRS...
THE POLICE JUST ARRES-*HUH?* WHAT'S THE MATTER?
THE POLICE WERE ***HERE!***
LOOKING FOR *ANJA!*
SHE JUST TOLD US...
THAT BOY FROM WARSAW BRINGS COMMUNIST MESSAGES.
SHE TRANSLATES THEM INTO GERMAN AND PASSES THEM ON!
ANJA WAS INVOLVED IN *CONSPIRATIONS!*

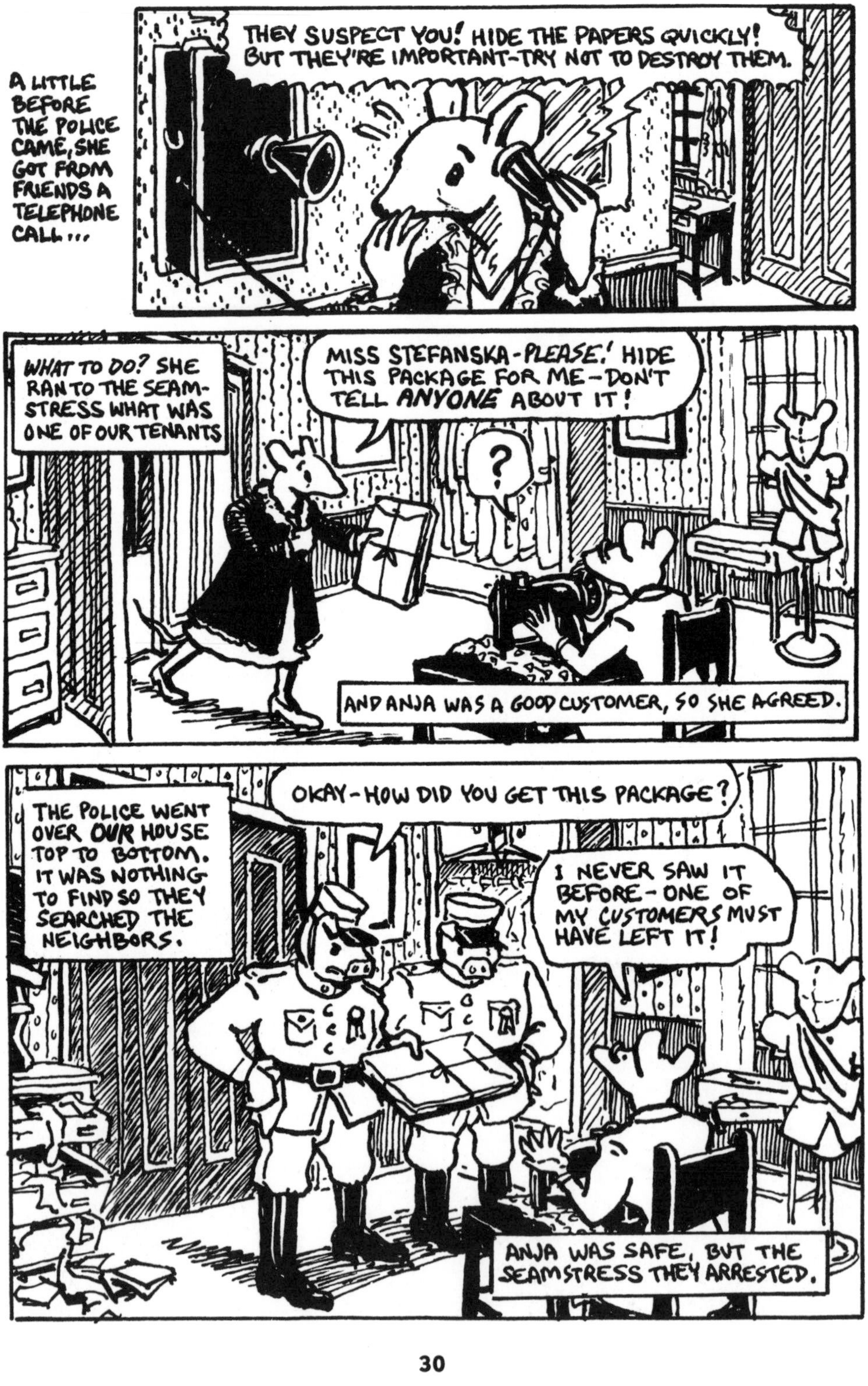
A LITTLE BEFORE THE POLICE CAME, SHE GOT FROM FRIENDS A TELEPHONE CALL...
THEY SUSPECT YOU! HIDE THE PAPERS QUICKLY! BUT THEY'RE IMPORTANT-TRY NOT TO DESTROY THEM.
WHAT TO DO? SHE RAN TO THE SEAMSTRESS WHAT WAS ONE OF OUR TENANTS
MISS STEFANSKA-PLEASE! HIDE THIS PACKAGE FOR ME-DON'T TELL ANYONE ABOUT IT!
?
AND ANJA WAS A GOOD CUSTOMER, SO SHE AGREED.
THE POLICE WENT OVER OUR HOUSE TOP TO BOTTOM. IT WAS NOTHING TO FIND SO THEY SEARCHED THE NEIGHBORS.
OKAY-HOW DID YOU GET THIS PACKAGE?
I NEVER SAW IT BEFORE-ONE OF MY CUSTOMERS MUST HAVE LEFT IT!
ANJA WAS SAFE, BUT THE SEAMSTRESS THEY ARRESTED.

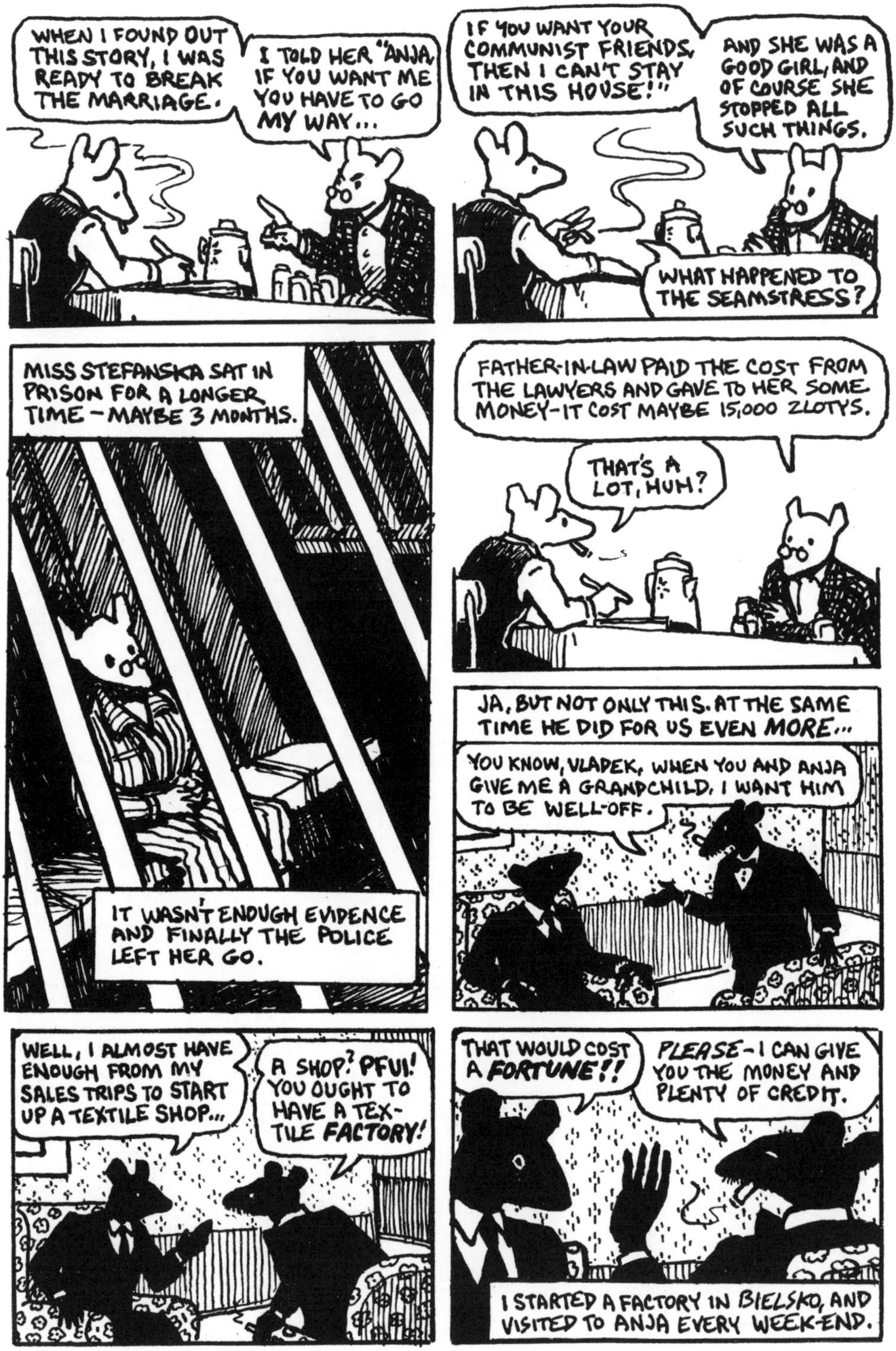
WHEN I FOUND OUT THIS STORY, I WAS READY TO BREAK THE MARRIAGE.
I TOLD HER "ANJA, IF YOU WANT ME YOU HAVE TO GO MY WAY...
IF YOU WANT YOUR COMMUNIST FRIENDS, THEN I CAN'T STAY IN THIS HOUSE!"
AND SHE WAS A GOOD GIRL, AND OF COURSE SHE STOPPED ALL SUCH THINGS.
WHAT HAPPENED TO THE SEAMSTRESS?
MISS STEFANSKA SAT IN PRISON FOR A LONGER TIME - MAYBE 3 MONTHS.
IT WASN'T ENOUGH EVIDENCE AND FINALLY THE POLICE LEFT HER GO.
FATHER-IN-LAW PAID THE COST FROM THE LAWYERS AND GAVE TO HER SOME MONEY - IT COST MAYBE 15,000 ZLOTYS.
THAT'S A LOT, HUH?
JA, BUT NOT ONLY THIS. AT THE SAME TIME HE DID FOR US EVEN MORE...
YOU KNOW, VLADEK, WHEN YOU AND ANJA GIVE ME A GRANDCHILD, I WANT HIM TO BE WELL-OFF.
WELL, I ALMOST HAVE ENOUGH FROM MY SALES TRIPS TO START UP A TEXTILE SHOP...
A SHOP? PFUI! YOU OUGHT TO HAVE A TEX-TILE FACTORY!
THAT WOULD COST A FORTUNE!!
PLEASE - I CAN GIVE YOU THE MONEY AND PLENTY OF CREDIT.
I STARTED A FACTORY IN BIELSKO, AND VISITED TO ANJA EVERY WEEK-END.

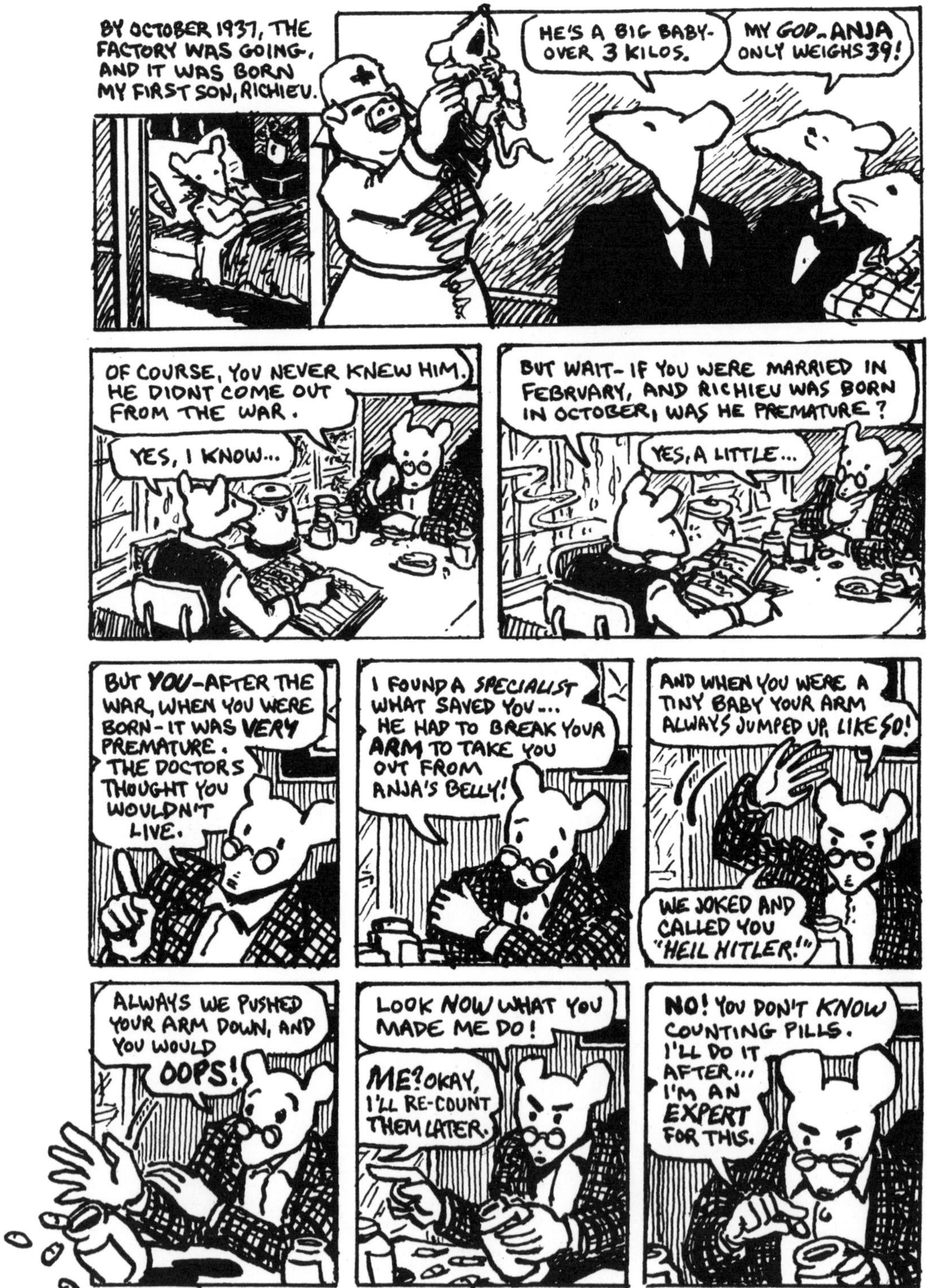
BY OCTOBER 1937, THE FACTORY WAS GOING, AND IT WAS BORN MY FIRST SON, RICHIEU.
HE'S A BIG BABY-OVER 3 KILOS.
MY GOD-ANJA ONLY WEIGHS 39!
OF COURSE, YOU NEVER KNEW HIM. HE DIDNT COME OUT FROM THE WAR.
YES, I KNOW...
BUT WAIT- IF YOU WERE MARRIED IN FEBRUARY, AND RICHIEU WAS BORN IN OCTOBER, WAS HE PREMATURE?
YES, A LITTLE...
BUT YOU-AFTER THE WAR, WHEN YOU WERE BORN- IT WAS VERY PREMATURE. THE DOCTORS THOUGHT YOU WOULDN'T LIVE.
I FOUND A SPECIALIST WHAT SAVED YOU... HE HAD TO BREAK YOUR ARM TO TAKE YOU OUT FROM ANJA'S BELLY!
AND WHEN YOU WERE A TINY BABY YOUR ARM ALWAYS JUMPED UP, LIKE SO!
WE JOKED AND CALLED YOU "HEIL HITLER!"
ALWAYS WE PUSHED YOUR ARM DOWN, AND YOU WOULD
OOPS!
LOOK NOW WHAT YOU MADE ME DO!
ME? OKAY, I'LL RE-COUNT THEM LATER.
NO! YOU DON'T KNOW COUNTING PILLS. I'LL DO IT AFTER... I'M AN EXPERT FOR THIS.

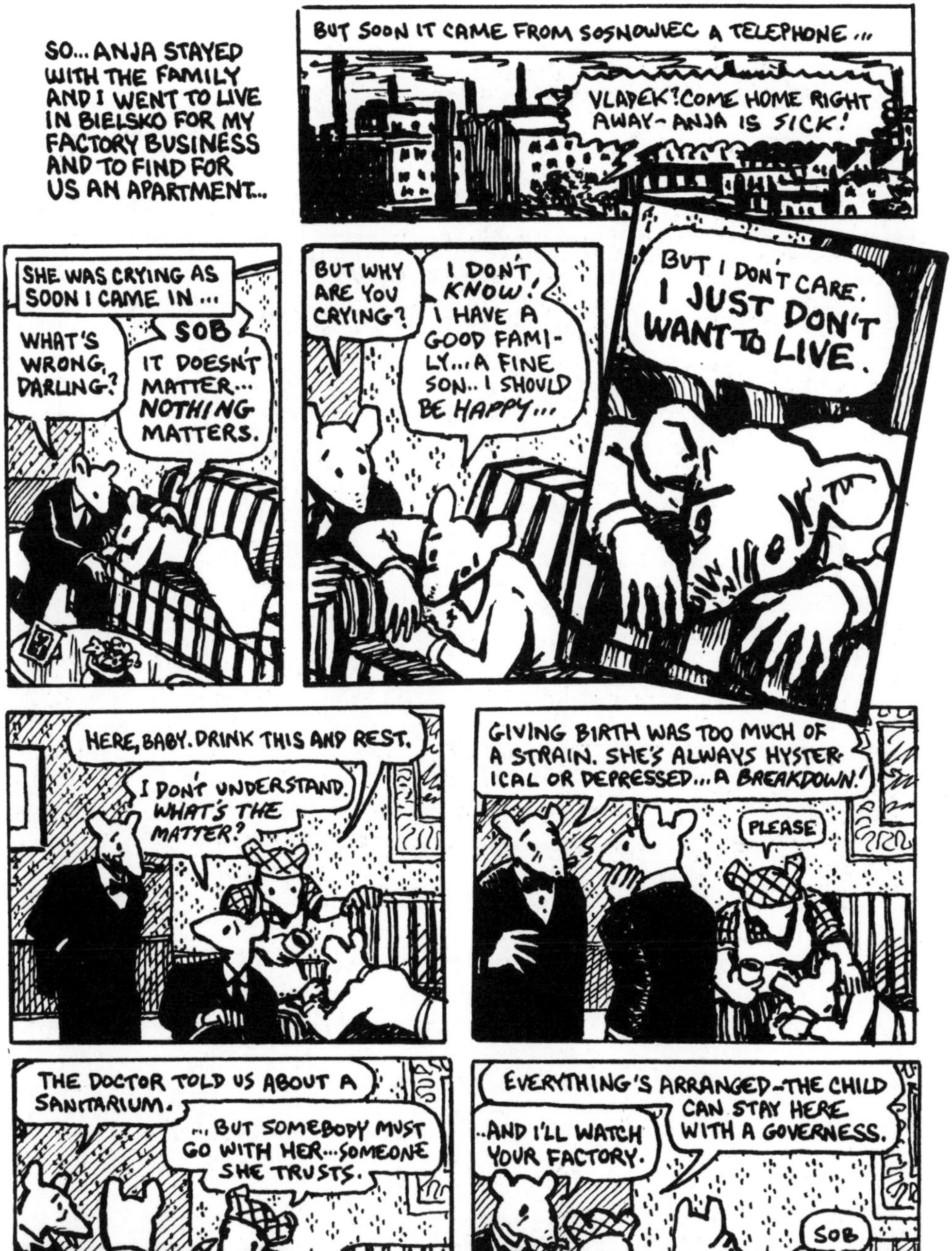
SO... ANJA STAYED WITH THE FAMILY AND I WENT TO LIVE IN BIELSKO FOR MY FACTORY BUSINESS AND TO FIND FOR US AN APARTMENT...
BUT SOON IT CAME FROM SOSNOWIEC A TELEPHONE...
VLADEK? COME HOME RIGHT AWAY- ANJA IS SICK!
SHE WAS CRYING AS SOON I CAME IN...
WHAT'S WRONG, DARLING?
SOB
IT DOESN'T MATTER... NOTHING MATTERS.
BUT WHY ARE YOU CRYING?
I DON'T KNOW! I HAVE A GOOD FAMILY... A FINE SON.. I SHOULD BE HAPPY...
BUT I DON'T CARE. I JUST DON'T WANT TO LIVE.
HERE, BABY. DRINK THIS AND REST.
I DON'T UNDERSTAND. WHAT'S THE MATTER?
GIVING BIRTH WAS TOO MUCH OF A STRAIN. SHE'S ALWAYS HYSTERICAL OR DEPRESSED... A BREAKDOWN!
PLEASE
THE DOCTOR TOLD US ABOUT A SANITARIUM.
...BUT SOMEBODY MUST GO WITH HER... SOMEONE SHE TRUSTS.
EVERYTHING'S ARRANGED-THE CHILD CAN STAY HERE WITH A GOVERNESS.
..AND I'LL WATCH YOUR FACTORY.
SOB

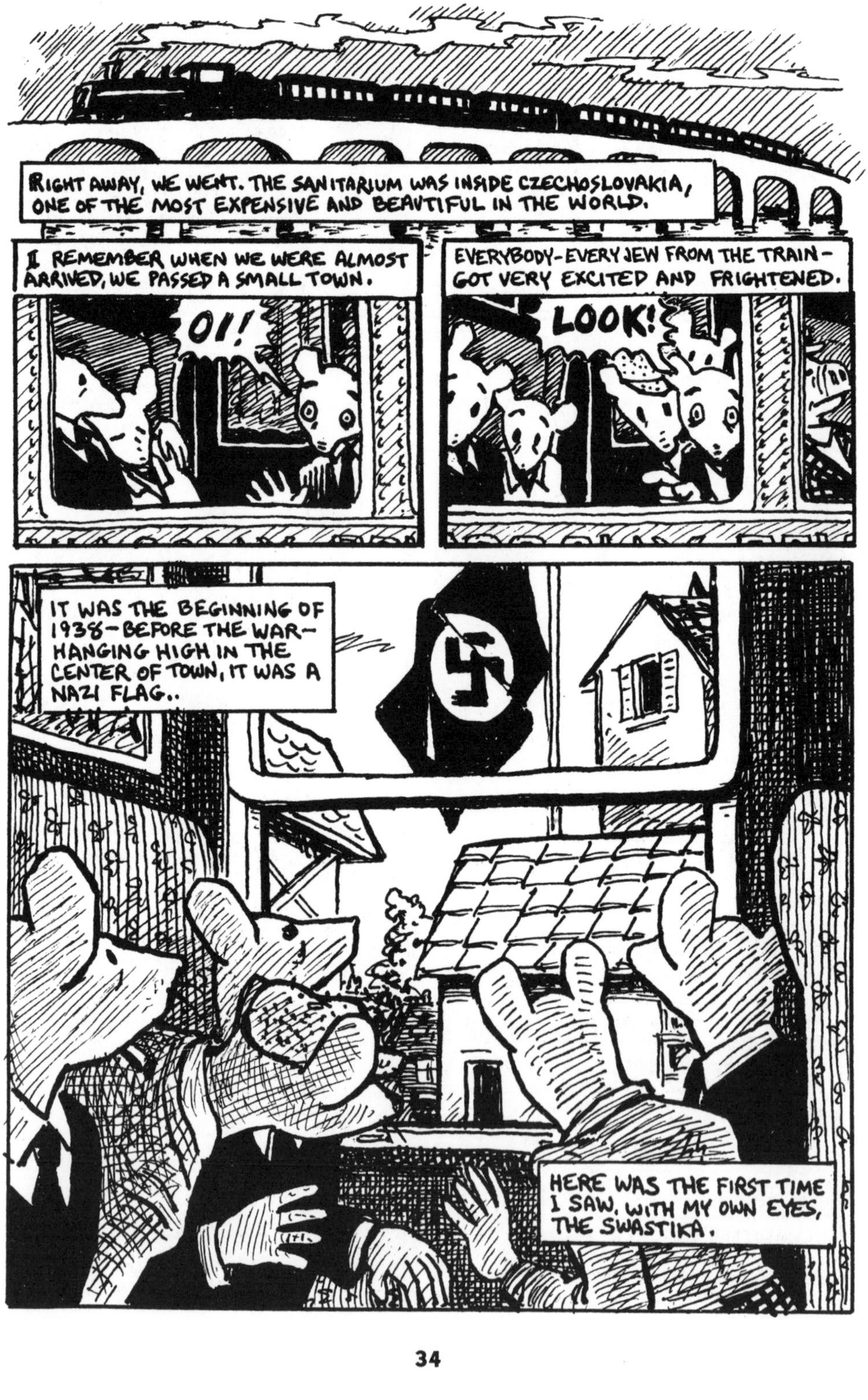
RIGHT AWAY, WE WENT. THE SANITARIUM WAS INSIDE CZECHOSLOVAKIA, ONE OF THE MOST EXPENSIVE AND BEAUTIFUL IN THE WORLD.
I REMEMBER WHEN WE WERE ALMOST ARRIVED, WE PASSED A SMALL TOWN.
OI!
EVERYBODY- EVERY JEW FROM THE TRAIN- GOT VERY EXCITED AND FRIGHTENED.
LOOK!
IT WAS THE BEGINNING OF 1938-BEFORE THE WAR- HANGING HIGH IN THE CENTER OF TOWN, IT WAS A NAZI FLAG..
HERE WAS THE FIRST TIME I SAW, WITH MY OWN EYES, THE SWASTIKA.

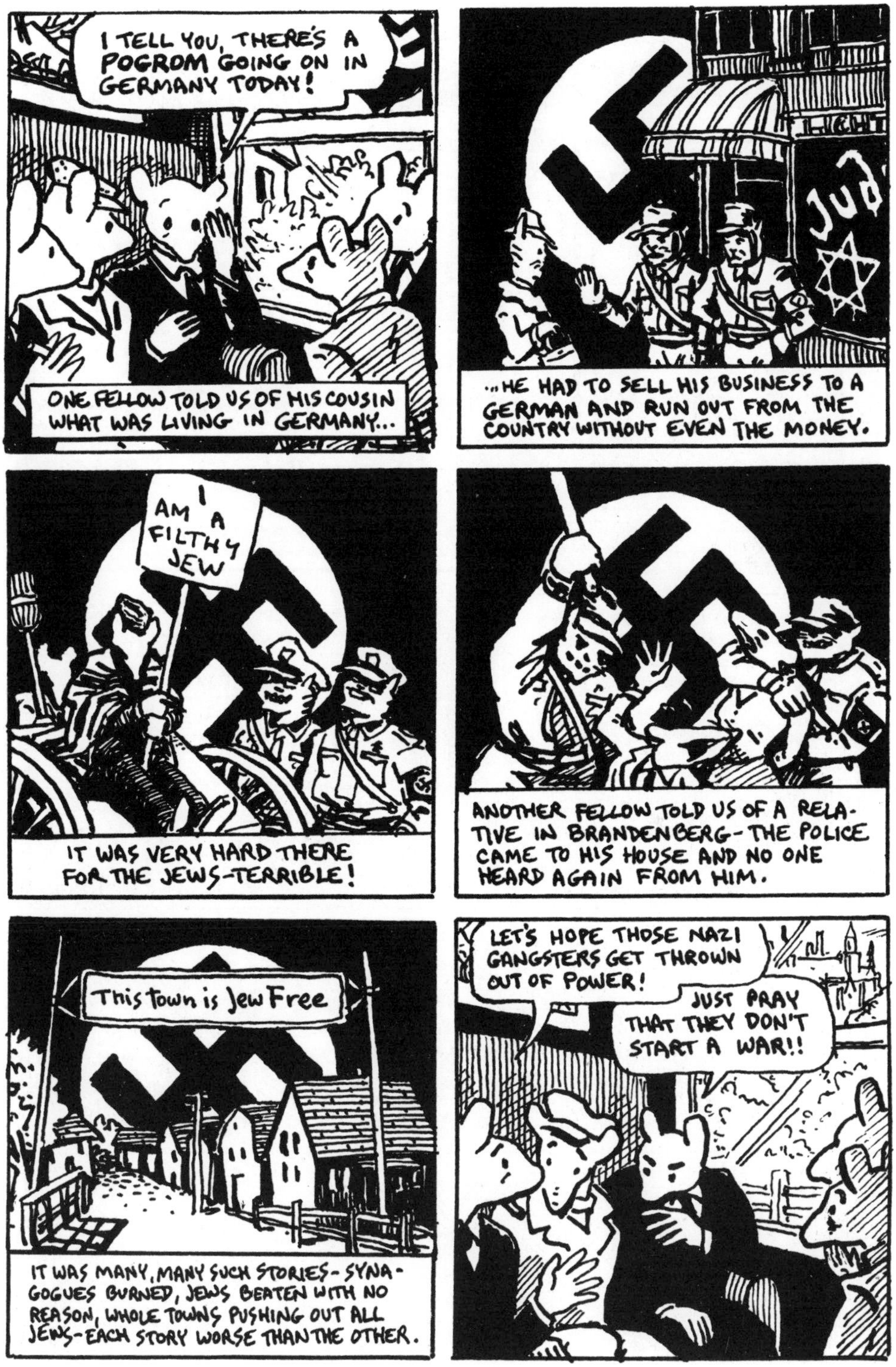
I TELL YOU, THERE'S A POGROM GOING ON IN GERMANY TODAY!
ONE FELLOW TOLD US OF HIS COUSIN WHAT WAS LIVING IN GERMANY...
...HE HAD TO SELL HIS BUSINESS TO A GERMAN AND RUN OUT FROM THE COUNTRY WITHOUT EVEN THE MONEY.
I AM A FILTHY JEW
IT WAS VERY HARD THERE FOR THE JEWS-TERRIBLE!
ANOTHER FELLOW TOLD US OF A RELATIVE IN BRANDENBERG- THE POLICE CAME TO HIS HOUSE AND NO ONE HEARD AGAIN FROM HIM.
This town is Jew Free
IT WAS MANY, MANY SUCH STORIES- SYNAGOGUES BURNED, JEWS BEATEN WITH NO REASON, WHOLE TOWNS PUSHING OUT ALL JEWS- EACH STORY WORSE THAN THE OTHER.
LET'S HOPE THOSE NAZI GANGSTERS GET THROWN OUT OF POWER!
JUST PRAY THAT THEY DON'T START A WAR!!

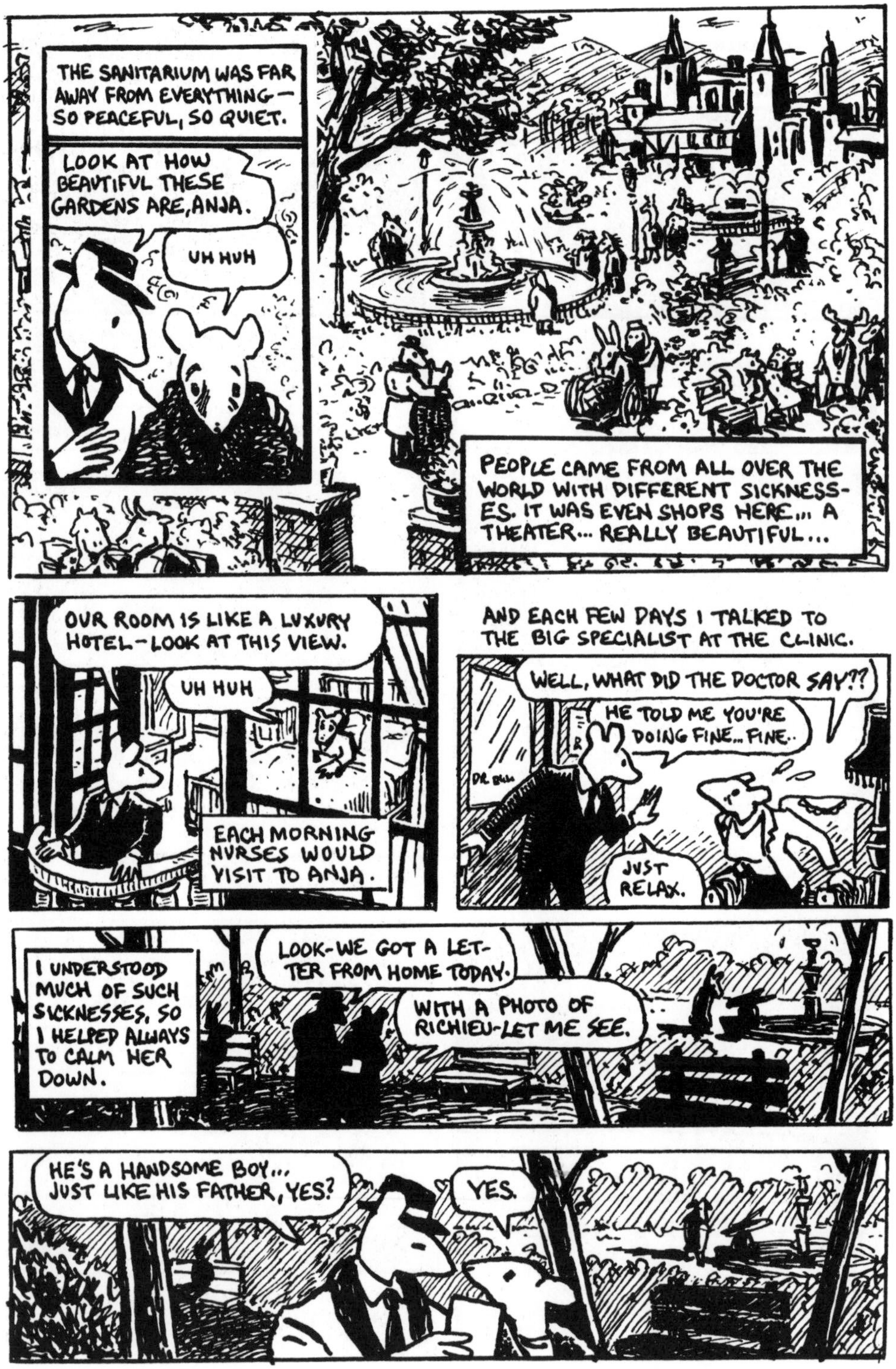
THE SANITARIUM WAS FAR AWAY FROM EVERYTHING— SO PEACEFUL, SO QUIET.
LOOK AT HOW BEAUTIFUL THESE GARDENS ARE, ANJA.
UH HUH
PEOPLE CAME FROM ALL OVER THE WORLD WITH DIFFERENT SICKNESSES. IT WAS EVEN SHOPS HERE... A THEATER... REALLY BEAUTIFUL...
OUR ROOM IS LIKE A LUXURY HOTEL—LOOK AT THIS VIEW.
UH HUH
EACH MORNING NURSES WOULD VISIT TO ANJA.
AND EACH FEW DAYS I TALKED TO THE BIG SPECIALIST AT THE CLINIC.
WELL, WHAT DID THE DOCTOR SAY??
HE TOLD ME YOU'RE DOING FINE... FINE.
JUST RELAX.
I UNDERSTOOD MUCH OF SUCH SICKNESSES, SO I HELPED ALWAYS TO CALM HER DOWN.
LOOK—WE GOT A LETTER FROM HOME TODAY.
WITH A PHOTO OF RICHIEU—LET ME SEE.
HE'S A HANDSOME BOY... JUST LIKE HIS FATHER, YES?
YES.

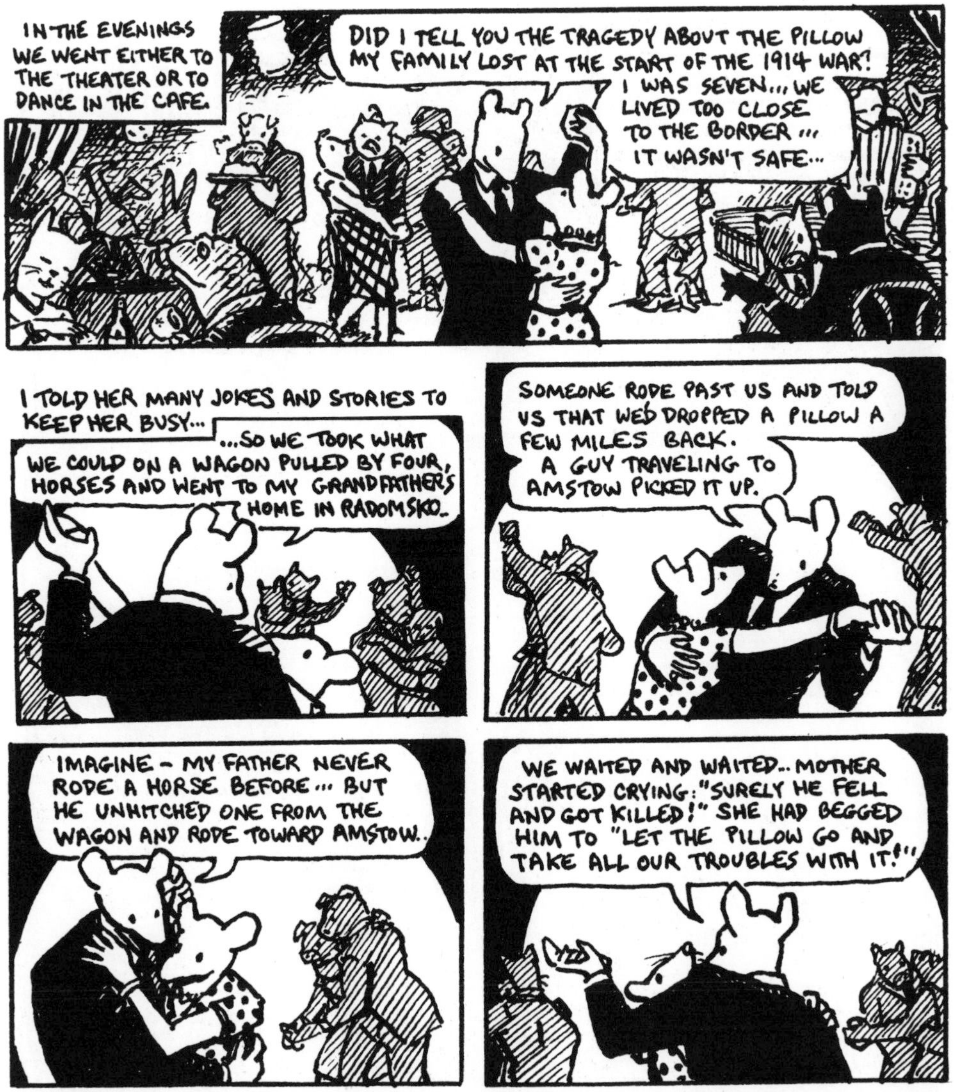
IN THE EVENINGS WE WENT EITHER TO THE THEATER OR TO DANCE IN THE CAFE.
DID I TELL YOU THE TRAGEDY ABOUT THE PILLOW MY FAMILY LOST AT THE START OF THE 1914 WAR?
I WAS SEVEN... WE LIVED TOO CLOSE TO THE BORDER... IT WASN'T SAFE...
I TOLD HER MANY JOKES AND STORIES TO KEEP HER BUSY...
...SO WE TOOK WHAT WE COULD ON A WAGON PULLED BY FOUR HORSES AND WENT TO MY GRANDFATHER'S HOME IN RADOMSKO.
SOMEONE RODE PAST US AND TOLD US THAT WE'D DROPPED A PILLOW A FEW MILES BACK.
A GUY TRAVELING TO AMSTOW PICKED IT UP.
IMAGINE – MY FATHER NEVER RODE A HORSE BEFORE... BUT HE UNHITCHED ONE FROM THE WAGON AND RODE TOWARD AMSTOW.
WE WAITED AND WAITED... MOTHER STARTED CRYING: "SURELY HE FELL AND GOT KILLED!" SHE HAD BEGGED HIM TO "LET THE PILLOW GO AND TAKE ALL OUR TROUBLES WITH IT!"
THE HORSE WAS BONY AND DIDN'T HAVE A SADDLE... FINALLY, LATE THAT NIGHT, FATHER RODE BACK WITH THE PILLOW ...UNDER HIS BLOODY "TUCHUS"...
SO, FATHER GOT HIS PILLOW BACK ...BUT HE COULDN'T SIT DOWN FOR THE REST OF THE WAR!
I LOVE YOU, VLADEK.
AND SHE WAS SO LAUGHING AND SO HAPPY, SO HAPPY, THAT SHE APPROACHED EACH TIME AND KISSED ME, SO HAPPY SHE WAS.

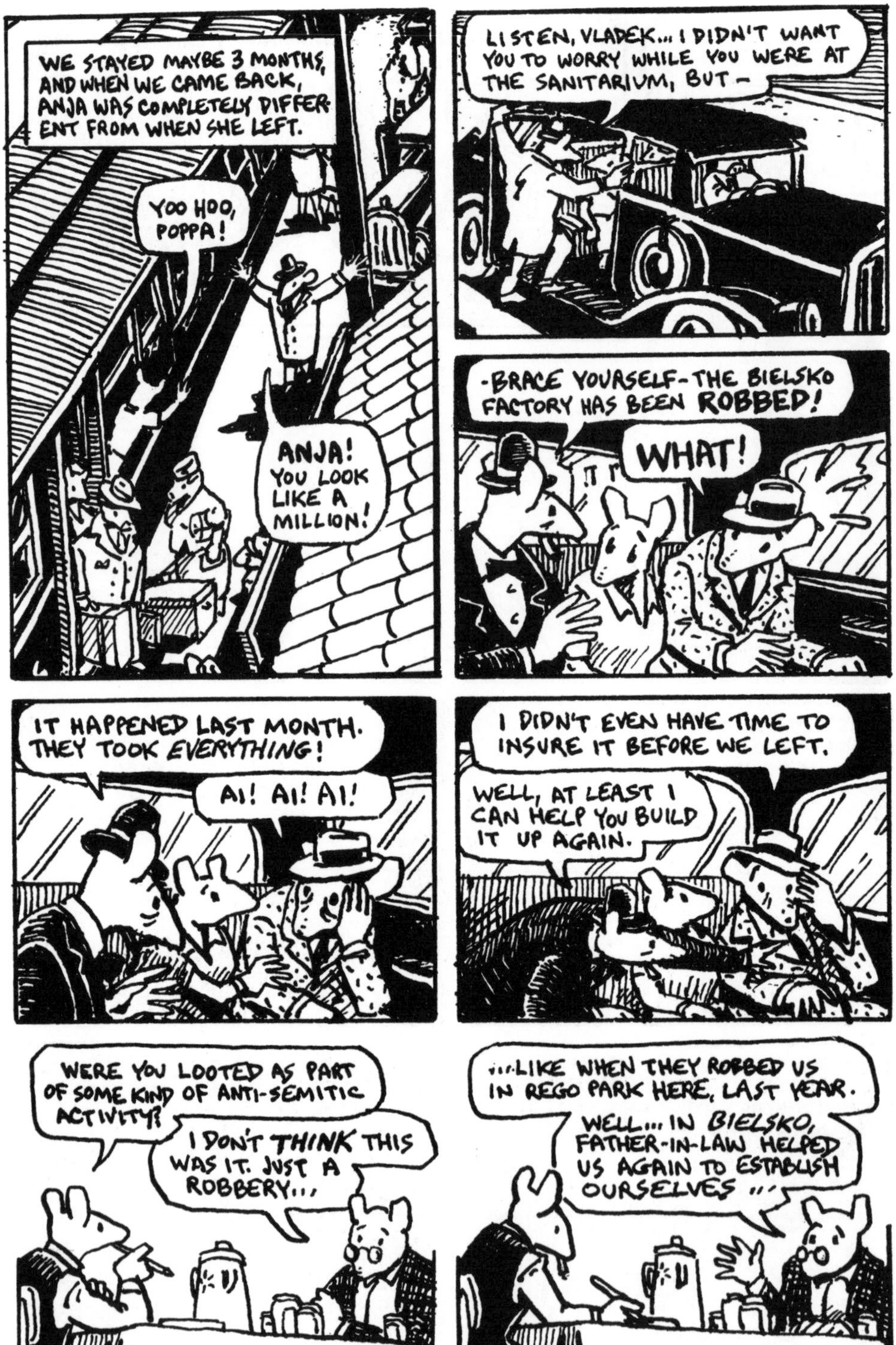

WE STAYED MAYBE 3 MONTHS, AND WHEN WE CAME BACK, ANJA WAS COMPLETELY DIFFERENT FROM WHEN SHE LEFT.
YOO HOO, POPPA!
ANJA! YOU LOOK LIKE A MILLION!
LISTEN, VLADEK... I DIDN'T WANT YOU TO WORRY WHILE YOU WERE AT THE SANITARIUM, BUT—
-BRACE YOURSELF-THE BIELSKO FACTORY HAS BEEN ROBBED!
WHAT!
IT HAPPENED LAST MONTH. THEY TOOK EVERYTHING!
AI! AI! AI!
I DIDN'T EVEN HAVE TIME TO INSURE IT BEFORE WE LEFT.
WELL, AT LEAST I CAN HELP YOU BUILD IT UP AGAIN.
WERE YOU LOOTED AS PART OF SOME KIND OF ANTI-SEMITIC ACTIVITY?
I DON'T THINK THIS WAS IT. JUST A ROBBERY...
...LIKE WHEN THEY ROBBED US IN REGO PARK HERE, LAST YEAR.
WELL... IN BIELSKO, FATHER-IN-LAW HELPED US AGAIN TO ESTABLISH OURSELVES...

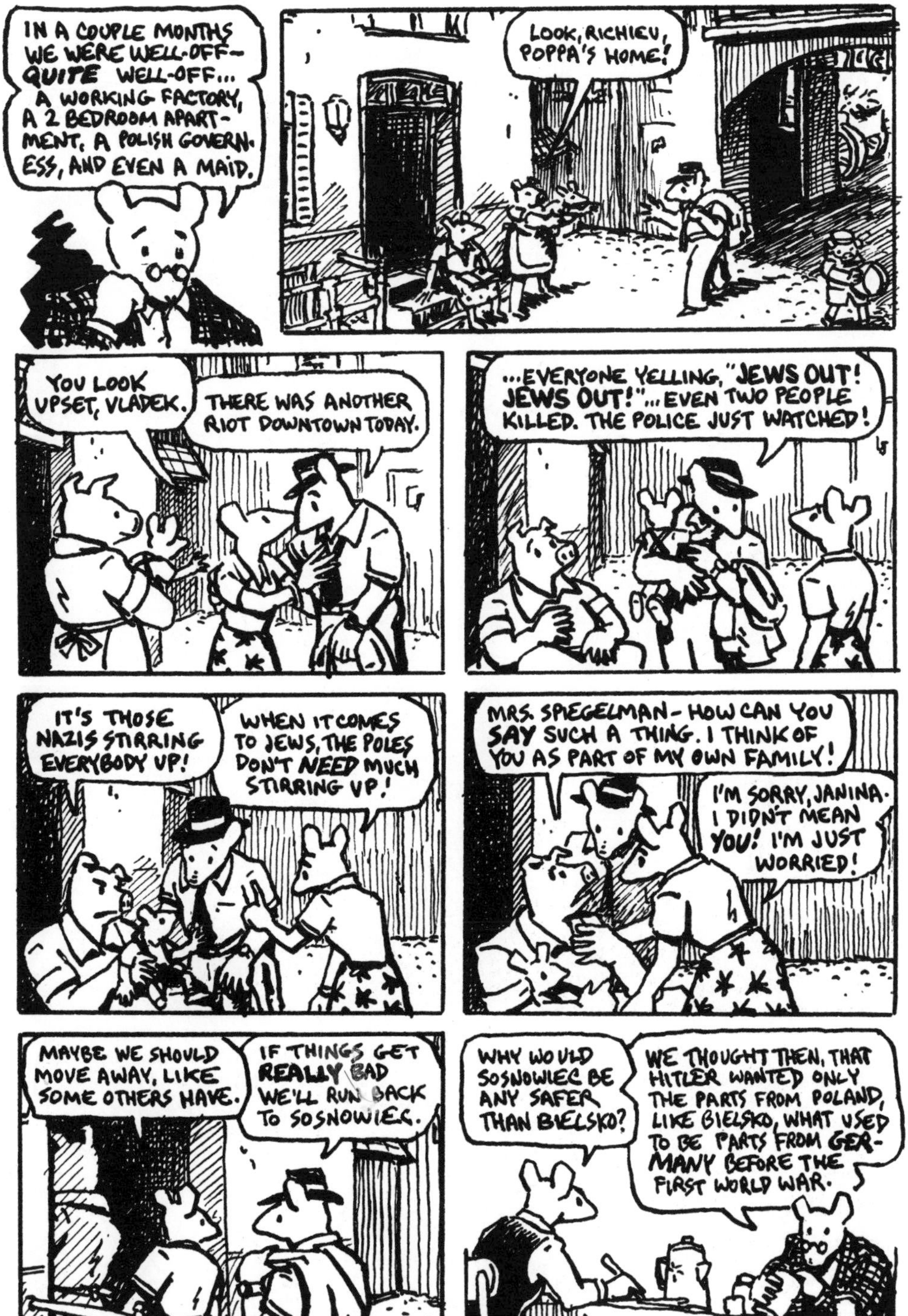
IN A COUPLE MONTHS WE WERE WELL-OFF– QUITE WELL-OFF... A WORKING FACTORY, A 2 BEDROOM APARTMENT, A POLISH GOVERNESS, AND EVEN A MAID.
LOOK, RICHIEU, POPPA'S HOME!
YOU LOOK UPSET, VLADEK.
THERE WAS ANOTHER RIOT DOWNTOWN TODAY.
...EVERYONE YELLING, "JEWS OUT! JEWS OUT!"...EVEN TWO PEOPLE KILLED. THE POLICE JUST WATCHED!
IT'S THOSE NAZIS STIRRING EVERYBODY UP!
WHEN IT COMES TO JEWS, THE POLES DON'T NEED MUCH STIRRING UP!
MRS. SPIEGELMAN– HOW CAN YOU SAY SUCH A THING. I THINK OF YOU AS PART OF MY OWN FAMILY!
I'M SORRY, JANINA. I DIDN'T MEAN YOU! I'M JUST WORRIED!
MAYBE WE SHOULD MOVE AWAY, LIKE SOME OTHERS HAVE.
IF THINGS GET REALLY BAD WE'LL RUN BACK TO SOSNOWIEC.
WHY WOULD SOSNOWIEC BE ANY SAFER THAN BIELSKO?
WE THOUGHT THEN, THAT HITLER WANTED ONLY THE PARTS FROM POLAND, LIKE BIELSKO, WHAT USED TO BE PARTS FROM GERMANY BEFORE THE FIRST WORLD WAR.

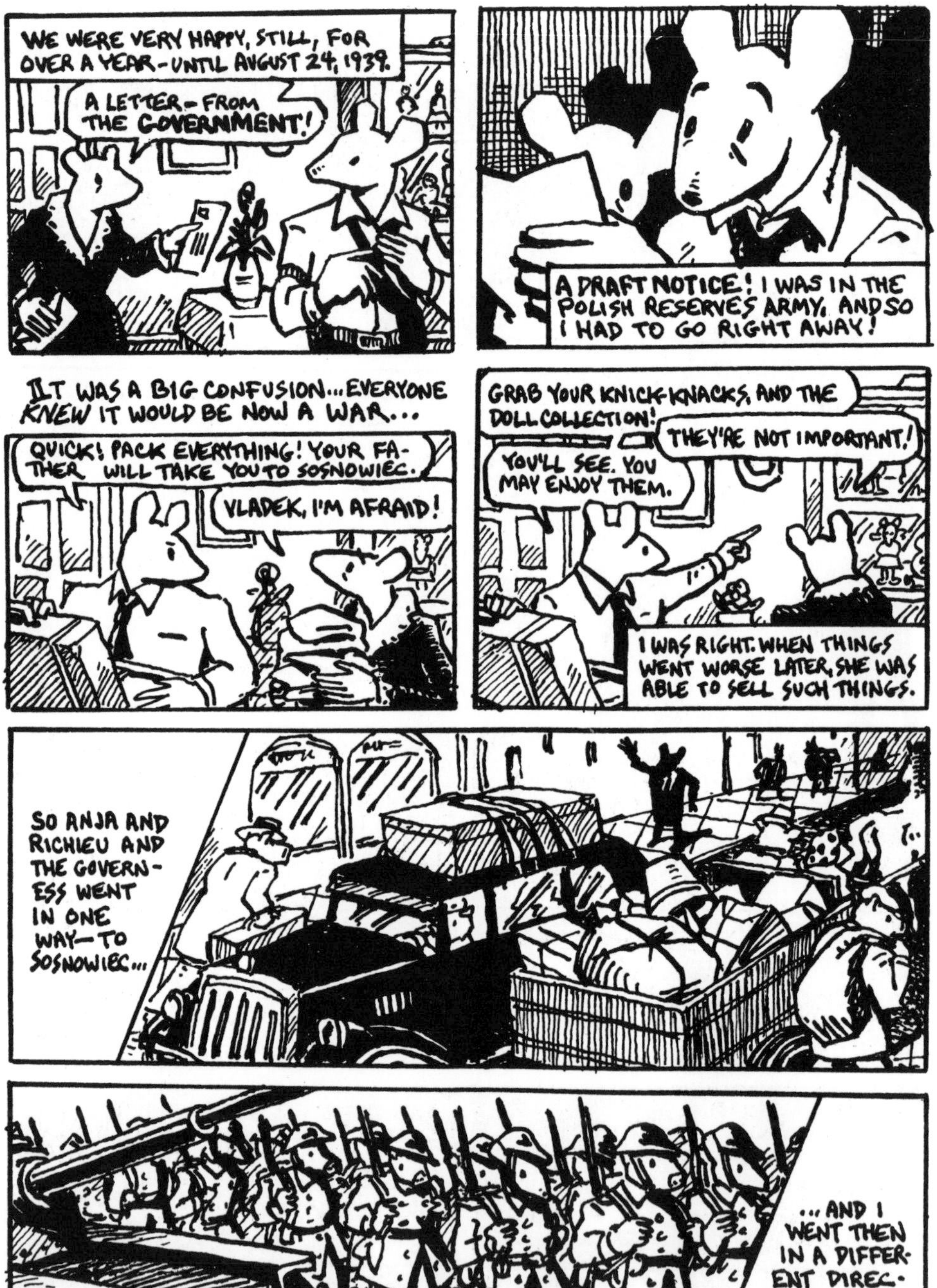
WE WERE VERY HAPPY, STILL, FOR OVER A YEAR – UNTIL AUGUST 24, 1939.
A LETTER – FROM THE GOVERNMENT!
A DRAFT NOTICE! I WAS IN THE POLISH RESERVES ARMY, AND SO I HAD TO GO RIGHT AWAY!
IT WAS A BIG CONFUSION... EVERYONE KNEW IT WOULD BE NOW A WAR...
QUICK! PACK EVERYTHING! YOUR FATHER WILL TAKE YOU TO SOSNOWIEC.
VLADEK, I'M AFRAID!
GRAB YOUR KNICK-KNACKS, AND THE DOLL COLLECTION!
THEY'RE NOT IMPORTANT!
YOU'LL SEE. YOU MAY ENJOY THEM.
I WAS RIGHT. WHEN THINGS WENT WORSE LATER, SHE WAS ABLE TO SELL SUCH THINGS.
SO ANJA AND RICHIEU AND THE GOVERNESS WENT IN ONE WAY—TO SOSNOWIEC...
...AND I WENT THEN IN A DIFFERENT DIRECTION... TO THE FRONTIER AGAINST GERMANY.

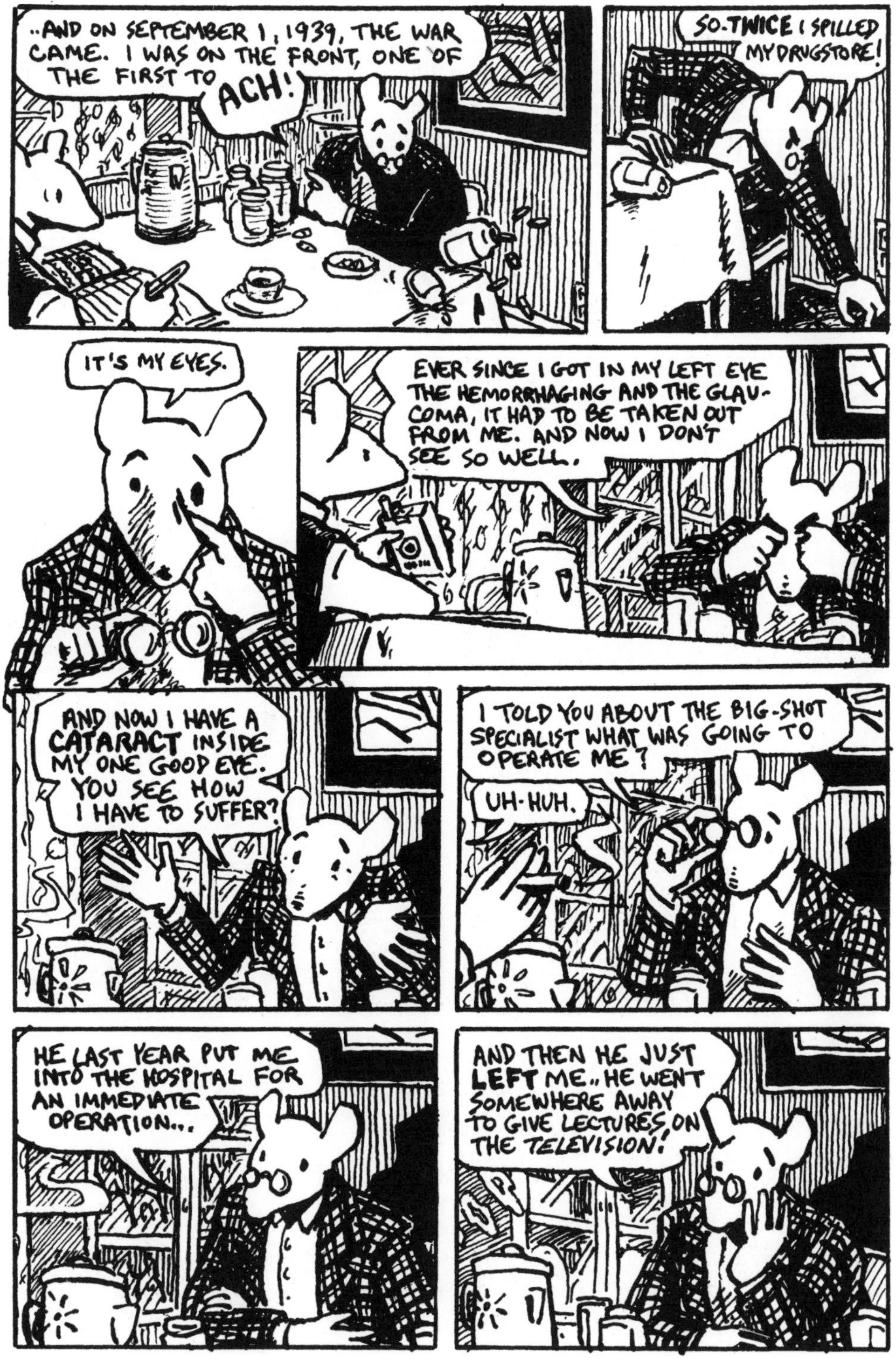
..AND ON SEPTEMBER 1, 1939, THE WAR CAME. I WAS ON THE FRONT, ONE OF THE FIRST TO
ACH!
SO-TWICE I SPILLED MY DRUGSTORE!
IT'S MY EYES.
EVER SINCE I GOT IN MY LEFT EYE THE HEMORRHAGING AND THE GLAU-COMA, IT HAD TO BE TAKEN OUT FROM ME. AND NOW I DON'T SEE SO WELL.
AND NOW I HAVE A CATARACT INSIDE MY ONE GOOD EYE. YOU SEE HOW I HAVE TO SUFFER?
I TOLD YOU ABOUT THE BIG-SHOT SPECIALIST WHAT WAS GOING TO OPERATE ME?
UH-HUH.
HE LAST YEAR PUT ME INTO THE HOSPITAL FOR AN IMMEDIATE OPERATION...
AND THEN HE JUST LEFT ME.. HE WENT SOMEWHERE AWAY TO GIVE LECTURES ON THE TELEVISION!

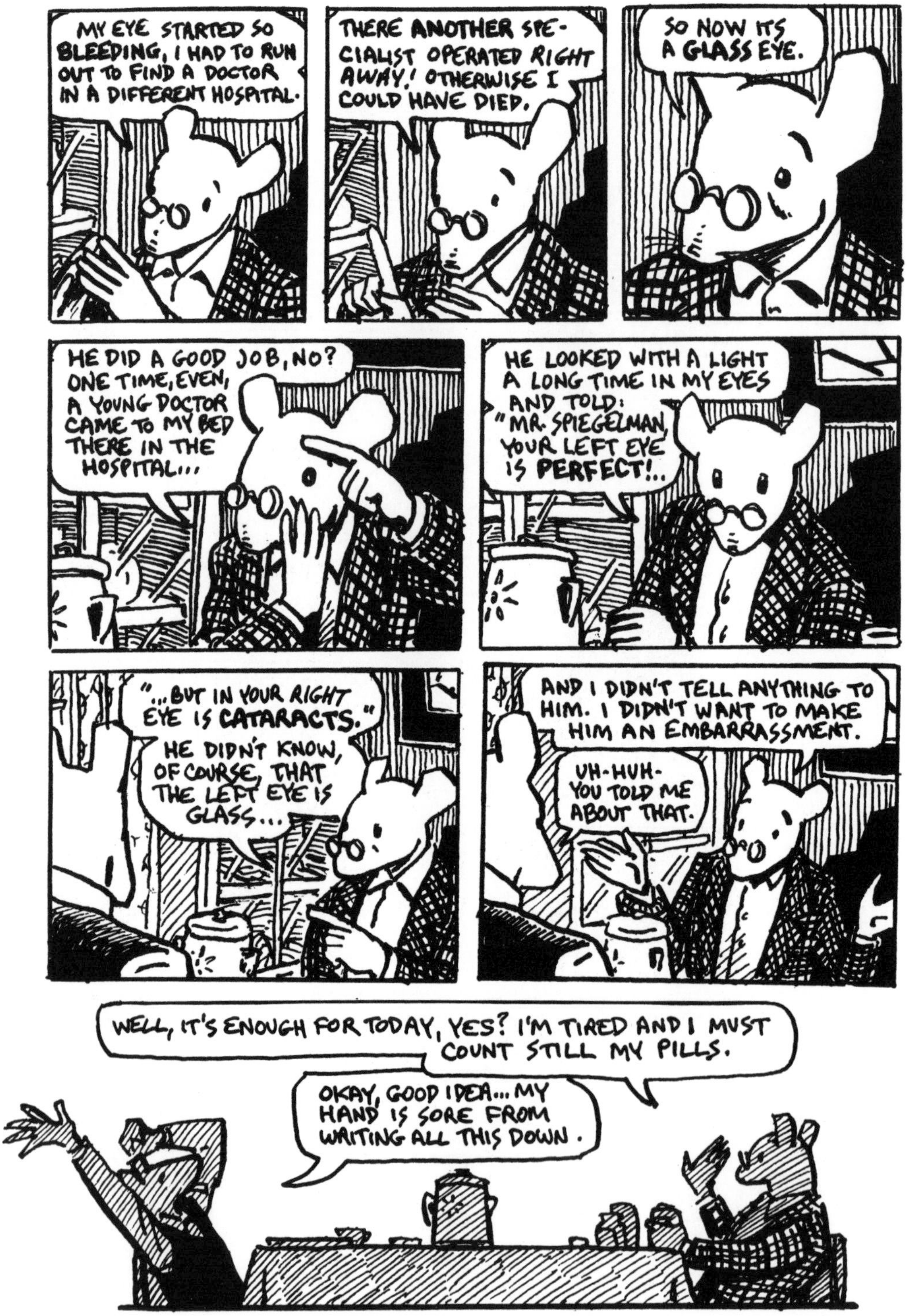
MY EYE STARTED SO BLEEDING, I HAD TO RUN OUT TO FIND A DOCTOR IN A DIFFERENT HOSPITAL.
THERE ANOTHER SPECIALIST OPERATED RIGHT AWAY! OTHERWISE I COULD HAVE DIED.
SO NOW ITS A GLASS EYE.
HE DID A GOOD JOB, NO? ONE TIME, EVEN, A YOUNG DOCTOR CAME TO MY BED THERE IN THE HOSPITAL...
HE LOOKED WITH A LIGHT A LONG TIME IN MY EYES AND TOLD: "MR. SPIEGELMAN, YOUR LEFT EYE IS PERFECT!...
"...BUT IN YOUR RIGHT EYE IS CATARACTS."
HE DIDN'T KNOW, OF COURSE, THAT THE LEFT EYE IS GLASS...
AND I DIDN'T TELL ANYTHING TO HIM. I DIDN'T WANT TO MAKE HIM AN EMBARRASSMENT.
UH-HUH- YOU TOLD ME ABOUT THAT.
WELL, IT'S ENOUGH FOR TODAY, YES? I'M TIRED AND I MUST COUNT STILL MY PILLS.
OKAY, GOOD IDEA... MY HAND IS SORE FROM WRITING ALL THIS DOWN.

CHAPTER THREE

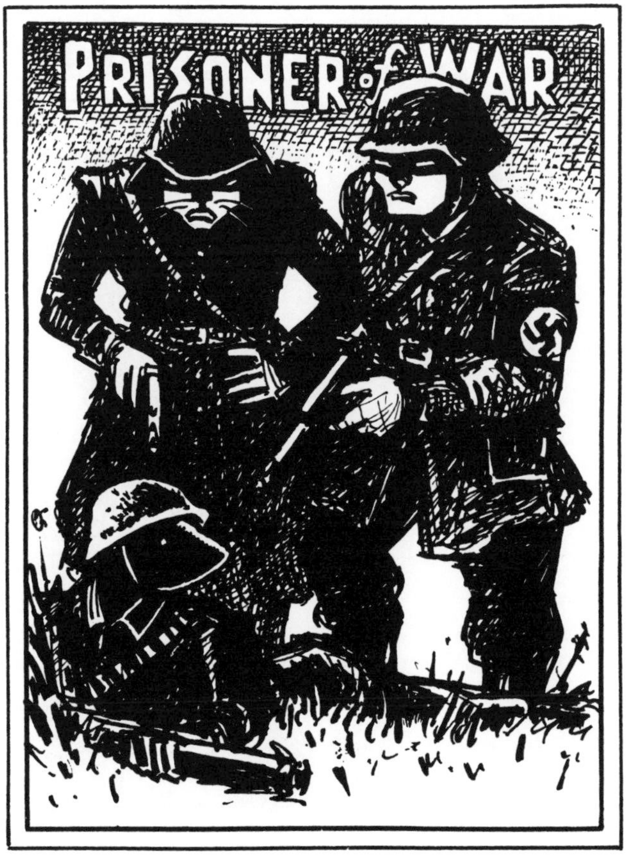

PRISONER of WAR

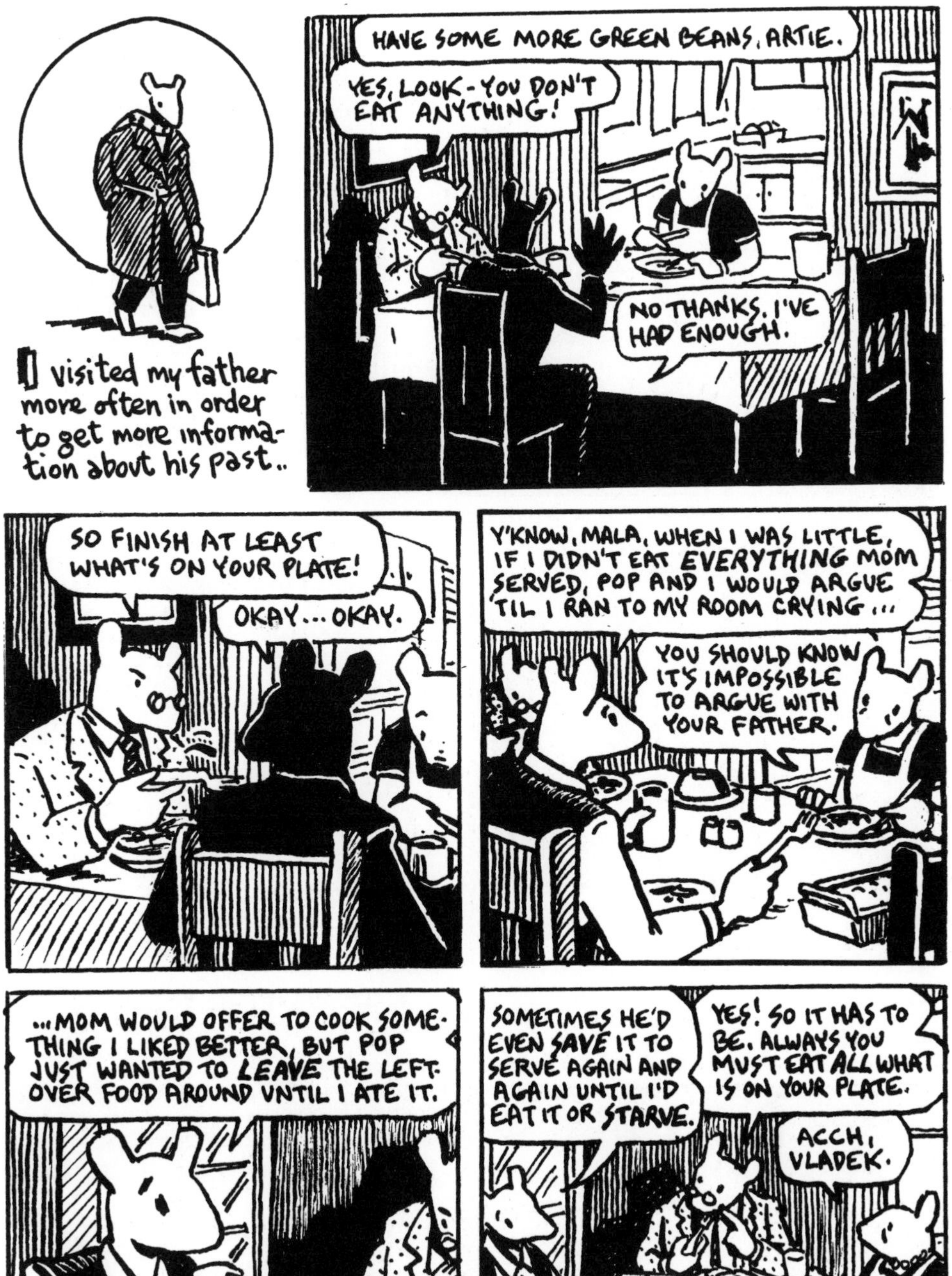
I visited my father more often in order to get more information about his past..
HAVE SOME MORE GREEN BEANS, ARTIE.
YES, LOOK - YOU DON'T EAT ANYTHING!
NO THANKS, I'VE HAD ENOUGH.
SO FINISH AT LEAST WHAT'S ON YOUR PLATE!
OKAY... OKAY.
Y'KNOW, MALA, WHEN I WAS LITTLE, IF I DIDN'T EAT EVERYTHING MOM SERVED, POP AND I WOULD ARGUE 'TIL I RAN TO MY ROOM CRYING...
YOU SHOULD KNOW IT'S IMPOSSIBLE TO ARGUE WITH YOUR FATHER.
...MOM WOULD OFFER TO COOK SOMETHING I LIKED BETTER, BUT POP JUST WANTED TO LEAVE THE LEFTOVER FOOD AROUND UNTIL I ATE IT.
SOMETIMES HE'D EVEN SAVE IT TO SERVE AGAIN AND AGAIN UNTIL I'D EAT IT OR STARVE.
YES! SO IT HAS TO BE. ALWAYS YOU MUST EAT ALL WHAT IS ON YOUR PLATE.
ACCH, VLADEK.

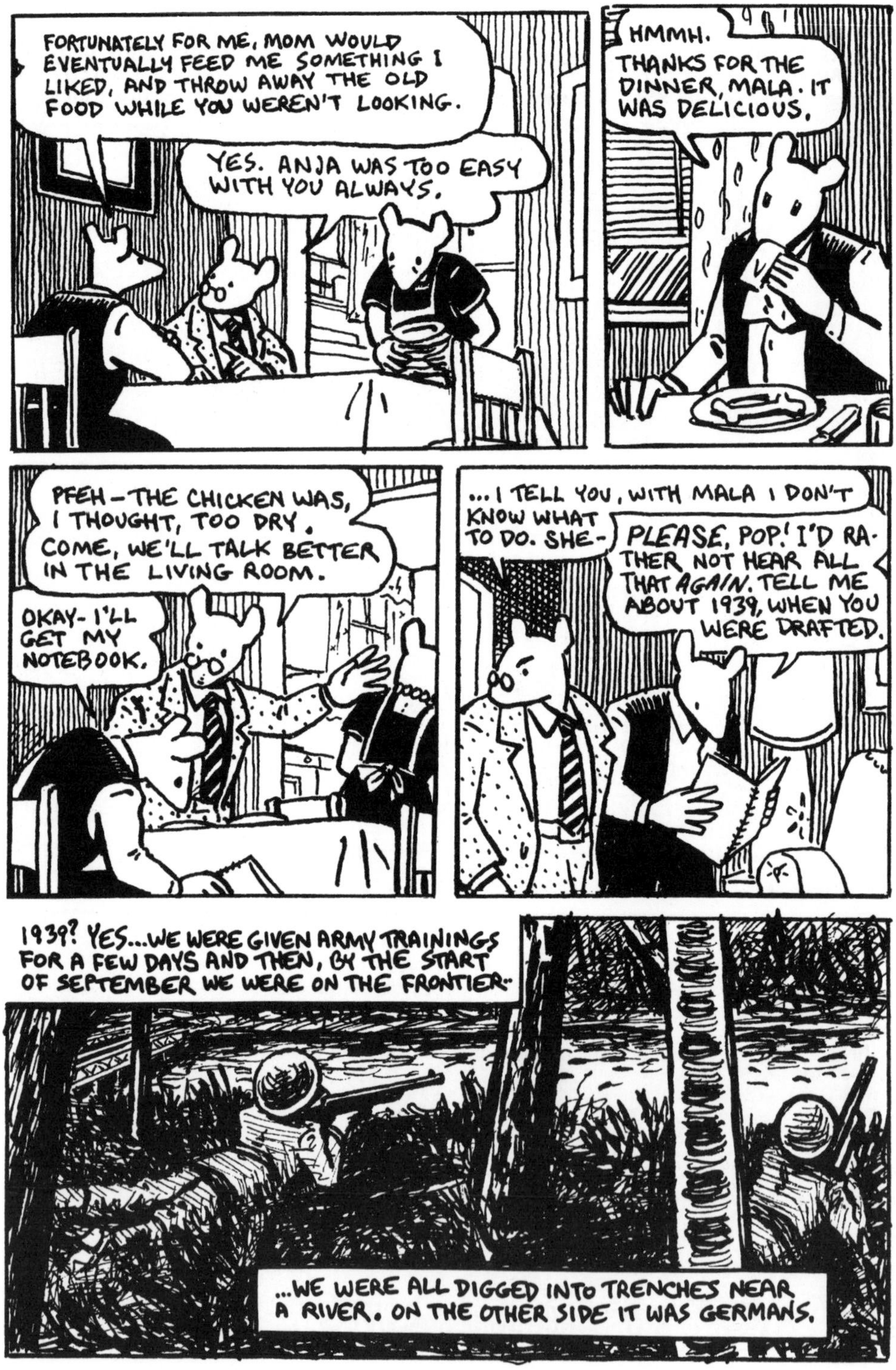
FORTUNATELY FOR ME, MOM WOULD EVENTUALLY FEED ME SOMETHING I LIKED, AND THROW AWAY THE OLD FOOD WHILE YOU WEREN'T LOOKING.
YES. ANJA WAS TOO EASY WITH YOU ALWAYS.
HMMH.
THANKS FOR THE DINNER, MALA. IT WAS DELICIOUS.
PFEH – THE CHICKEN WAS, I THOUGHT, TOO DRY. COME, WE'LL TALK BETTER IN THE LIVING ROOM.
OKAY- I'LL GET MY NOTEBOOK.
...I TELL YOU, WITH MALA I DON'T KNOW WHAT TO DO. SHE-
PLEASE, POP! I'D RATHER NOT HEAR ALL THAT AGAIN. TELL ME ABOUT 1939, WHEN YOU WERE DRAFTED.
1939? YES...WE WERE GIVEN ARMY TRAININGS FOR A FEW DAYS AND THEN, BY THE START OF SEPTEMBER WE WERE ON THE FRONTIER-
...WE WERE ALL DIGGED INTO TRENCHES NEAR A RIVER. ON THE OTHER SIDE IT WAS GERMANS.

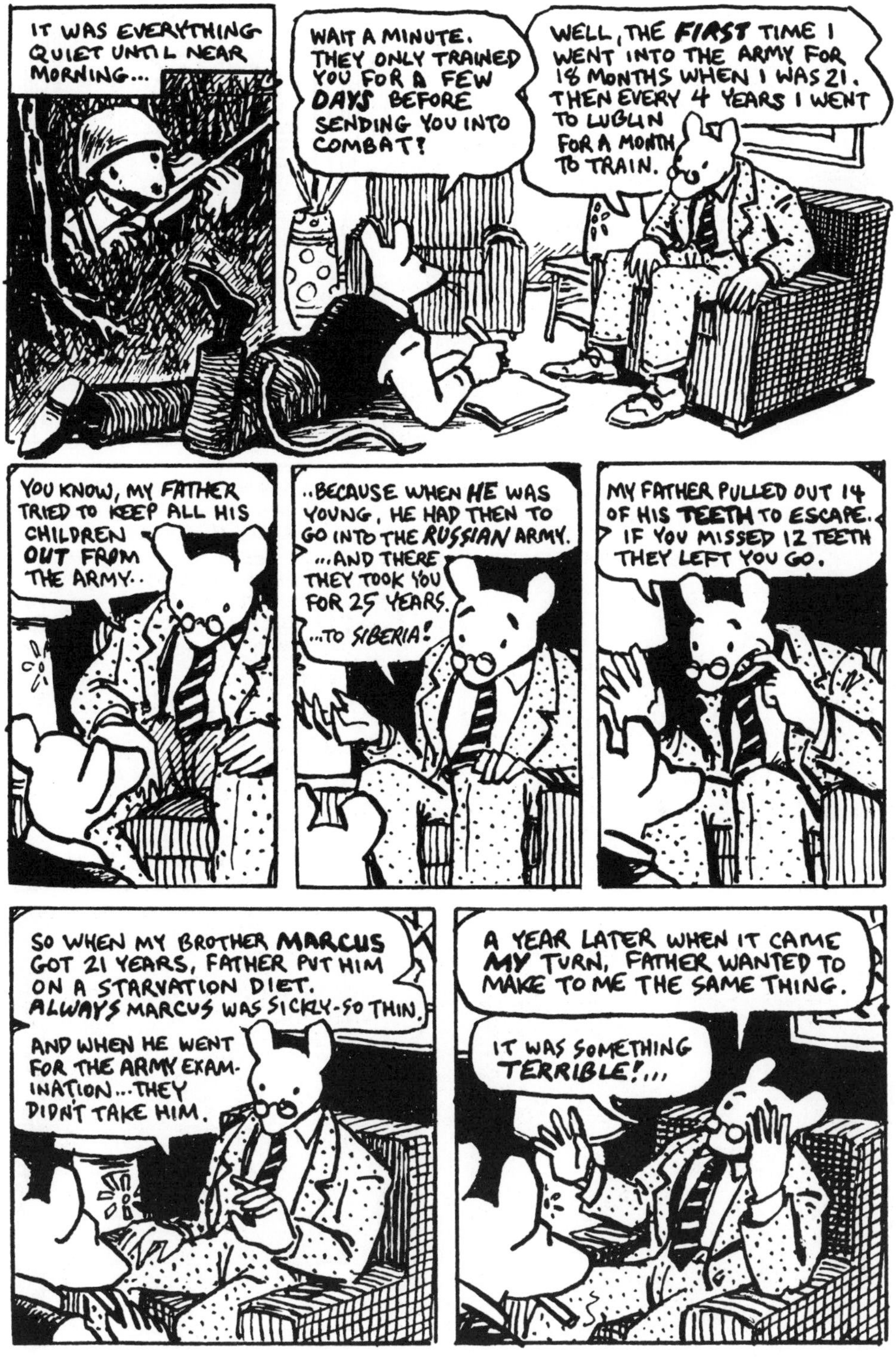
IT WAS EVERYTHING QUIET UNTIL NEAR MORNING...
WAIT A MINUTE. THEY ONLY TRAINED YOU FOR A FEW DAYS BEFORE SENDING YOU INTO COMBAT!
WELL, THE FIRST TIME I WENT INTO THE ARMY FOR 18 MONTHS WHEN I WAS 21. THEN EVERY 4 YEARS I WENT TO LUBLIN FOR A MONTH TO TRAIN.
YOU KNOW, MY FATHER TRIED TO KEEP ALL HIS CHILDREN OUT FROM THE ARMY..
..BECAUSE WHEN HE WAS YOUNG, HE HAD THEN TO GO INTO THE RUSSIAN ARMY.
...AND THERE THEY TOOK YOU FOR 25 YEARS.
...TO SIBERIA!
MY FATHER PULLED OUT 14 OF HIS TEETH TO ESCAPE. IF YOU MISSED 12 TEETH THEY LEFT YOU GO.
SO WHEN MY BROTHER MARCUS GOT 21 YEARS, FATHER PUT HIM ON A STARVATION DIET. ALWAYS MARCUS WAS SICKLY-SO THIN.
AND WHEN HE WENT FOR THE ARMY EXAMINATION... THEY DIDN'T TAKE HIM.
A YEAR LATER WHEN IT CAME MY TURN, FATHER WANTED TO MAKE TO ME THE SAME THING.
IT WAS SOMETHING TERRIBLE!...

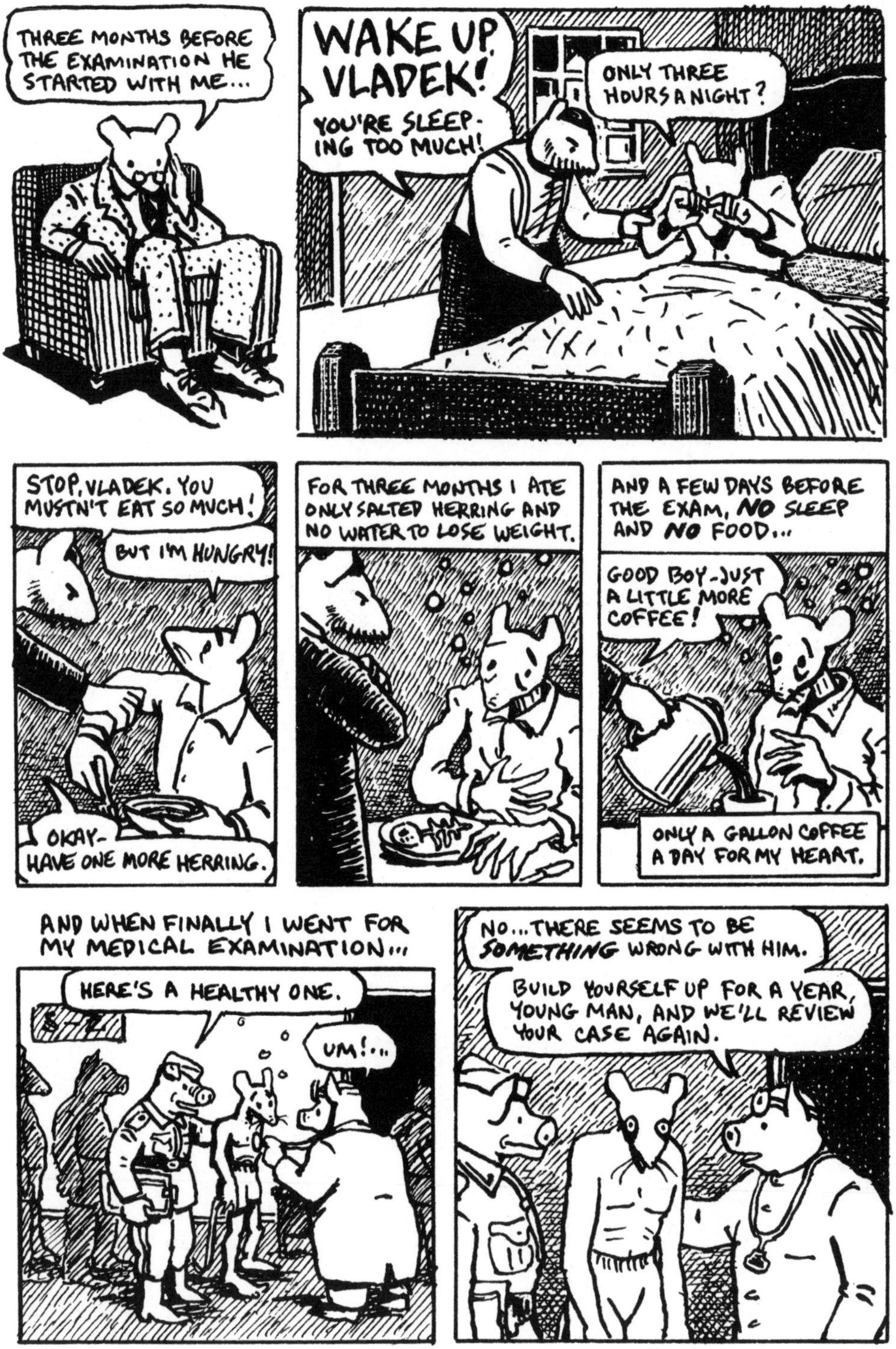
THREE MONTHS BEFORE THE EXAMINATION HE STARTED WITH ME...
WAKE UP, VLADEK!
YOU'RE SLEEPING TOO MUCH!
ONLY THREE HOURS A NIGHT?
STOP, VLADEK. YOU MUSTN'T EAT SO MUCH!
BUT I'M HUNGRY!
OKAY- HAVE ONE MORE HERRING.
FOR THREE MONTHS I ATE ONLY SALTED HERRING AND NO WATER TO LOSE WEIGHT.
AND A FEW DAYS BEFORE THE EXAM, NO SLEEP AND NO FOOD...
GOOD BOY-JUST A LITTLE MORE COFFEE!
ONLY A GALLON COFFEE A DAY FOR MY HEART.
AND WHEN FINALLY I WENT FOR MY MEDICAL EXAMINATION...
HERE'S A HEALTHY ONE.
S-Z
UM!...
NO...THERE SEEMS TO BE SOMETHING WRONG WITH HIM.
BUILD YOURSELF UP FOR A YEAR, YOUNG MAN, AND WE'LL REVIEW YOUR CASE AGAIN.

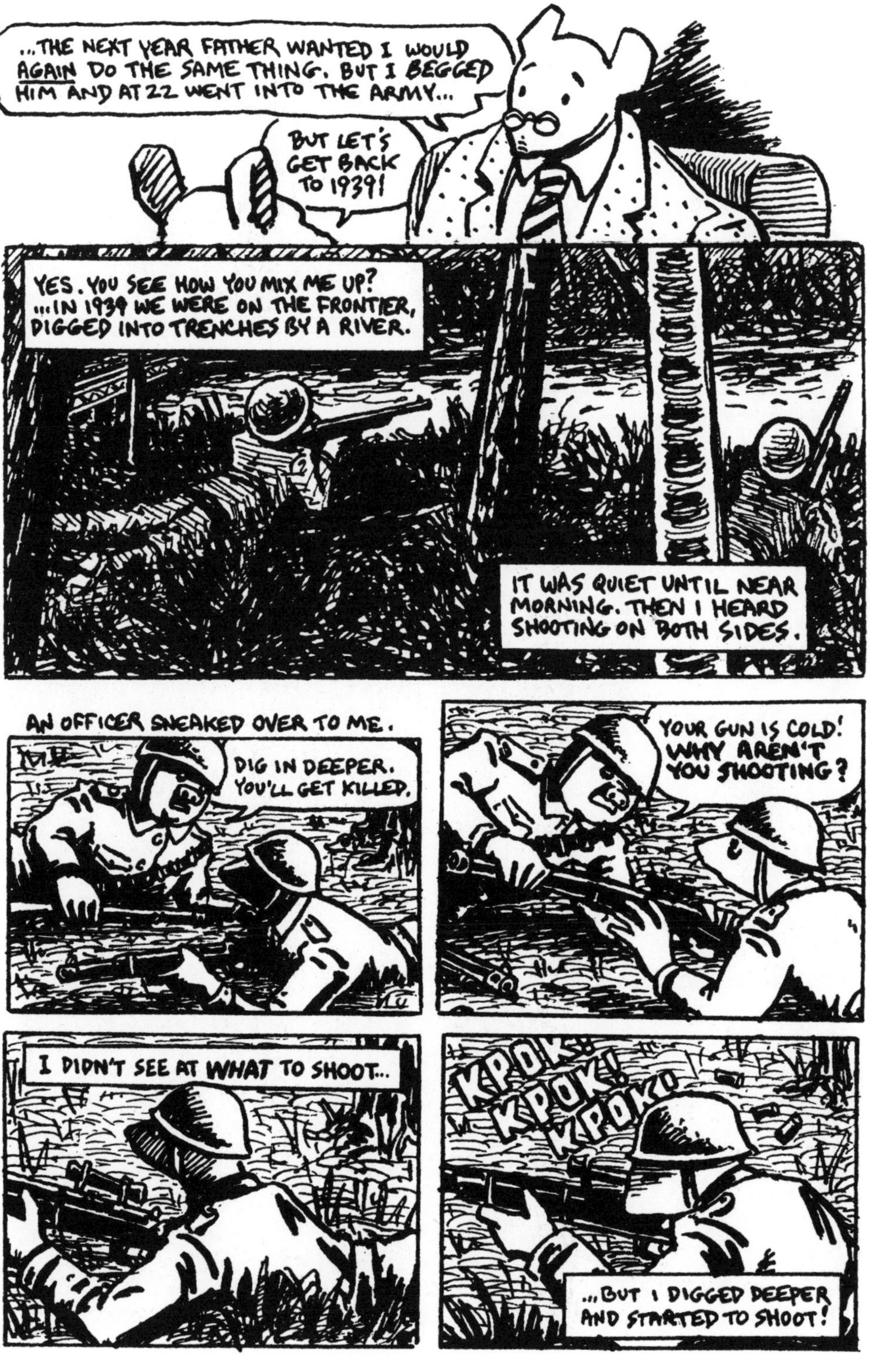
...THE NEXT YEAR FATHER WANTED I WOULD AGAIN DO THE SAME THING. BUT I BEGGED HIM AND AT 22 WENT INTO THE ARMY...
BUT LET'S GET BACK TO 1939!
YES. YOU SEE HOW YOU MIX ME UP? ...IN 1939 WE WERE ON THE FRONTIER, DIGGED INTO TRENCHES BY A RIVER.
IT WAS QUIET UNTIL NEAR MORNING. THEN I HEARD SHOOTING ON BOTH SIDES.
AN OFFICER SNEAKED OVER TO ME.
DIG IN DEEPER. YOU'LL GET KILLED.
YOUR GUN IS COLD! WHY AREN'T YOU SHOOTING?
I DIDN'T SEE AT WHAT TO SHOOT...
KPOK! KPOK! KPOK!
...BUT I DIGGED DEEPER AND STARTED TO SHOOT!

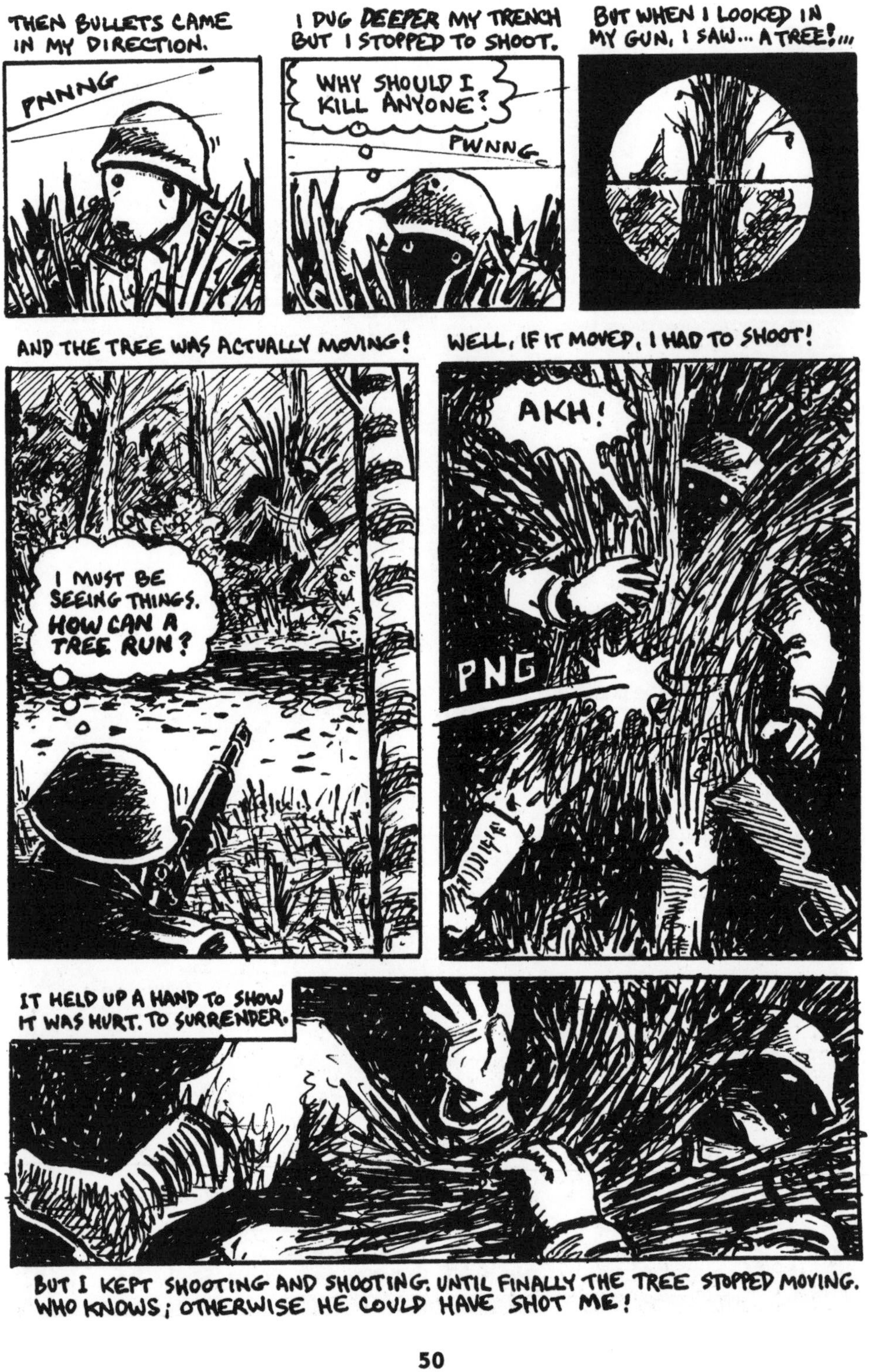
THEN BULLETS CAME IN MY DIRECTION.
PNNNG
I DUG DEEPER MY TRENCH BUT I STOPPED TO SHOOT.
WHY SHOULD I KILL ANYONE?
PWNNG
BUT WHEN I LOOKED IN MY GUN, I SAW... A TREE!...
AND THE TREE WAS ACTUALLY MOVING!
I MUST BE SEEING THINGS. HOW CAN A TREE RUN?
WELL, IF IT MOVED, I HAD TO SHOOT!
AKH!
PNG
IT HELD UP A HAND TO SHOW IT WAS HURT. TO SURRENDER.
BUT I KEPT SHOOTING AND SHOOTING. UNTIL FINALLY THE TREE STOPPED MOVING. WHO KNOWS; OTHERWISE HE COULD HAVE SHOT ME!

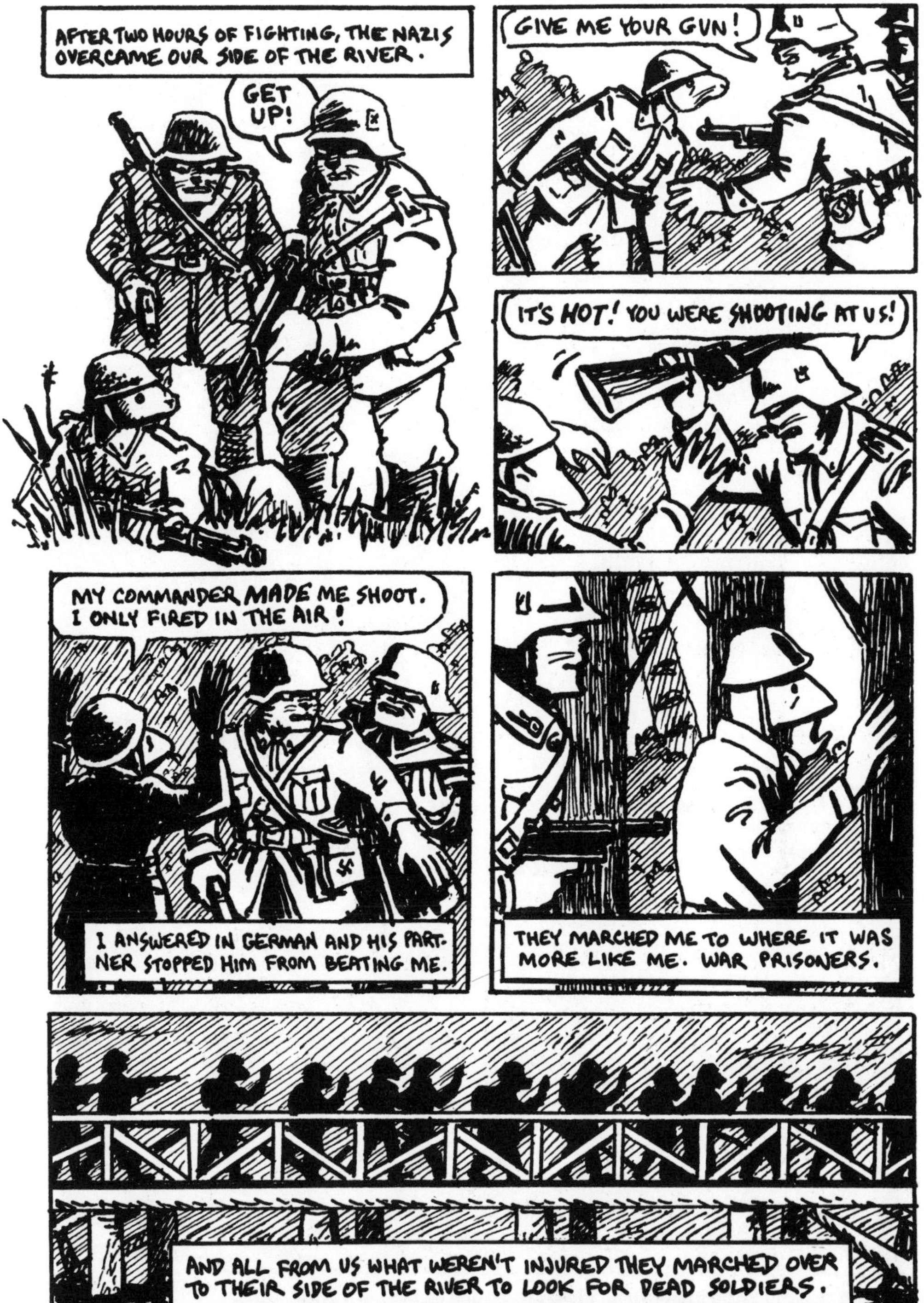
AFTER TWO HOURS OF FIGHTING, THE NAZIS OVERCAME OUR SIDE OF THE RIVER.
GET UP!
GIVE ME YOUR GUN!
IT'S HOT! YOU WERE SHOOTING AT US!
MY COMMANDER MADE ME SHOOT. I ONLY FIRED IN THE AIR!
I ANSWERED IN GERMAN AND HIS PARTNER STOPPED HIM FROM BEATING ME.
THEY MARCHED ME TO WHERE IT WAS MORE LIKE ME. WAR PRISONERS.
AND ALL FROM US WHAT WEREN'T INJURED THEY MARCHED OVER TO THEIR SIDE OF THE RIVER TO LOOK FOR DEAD SOLDIERS.

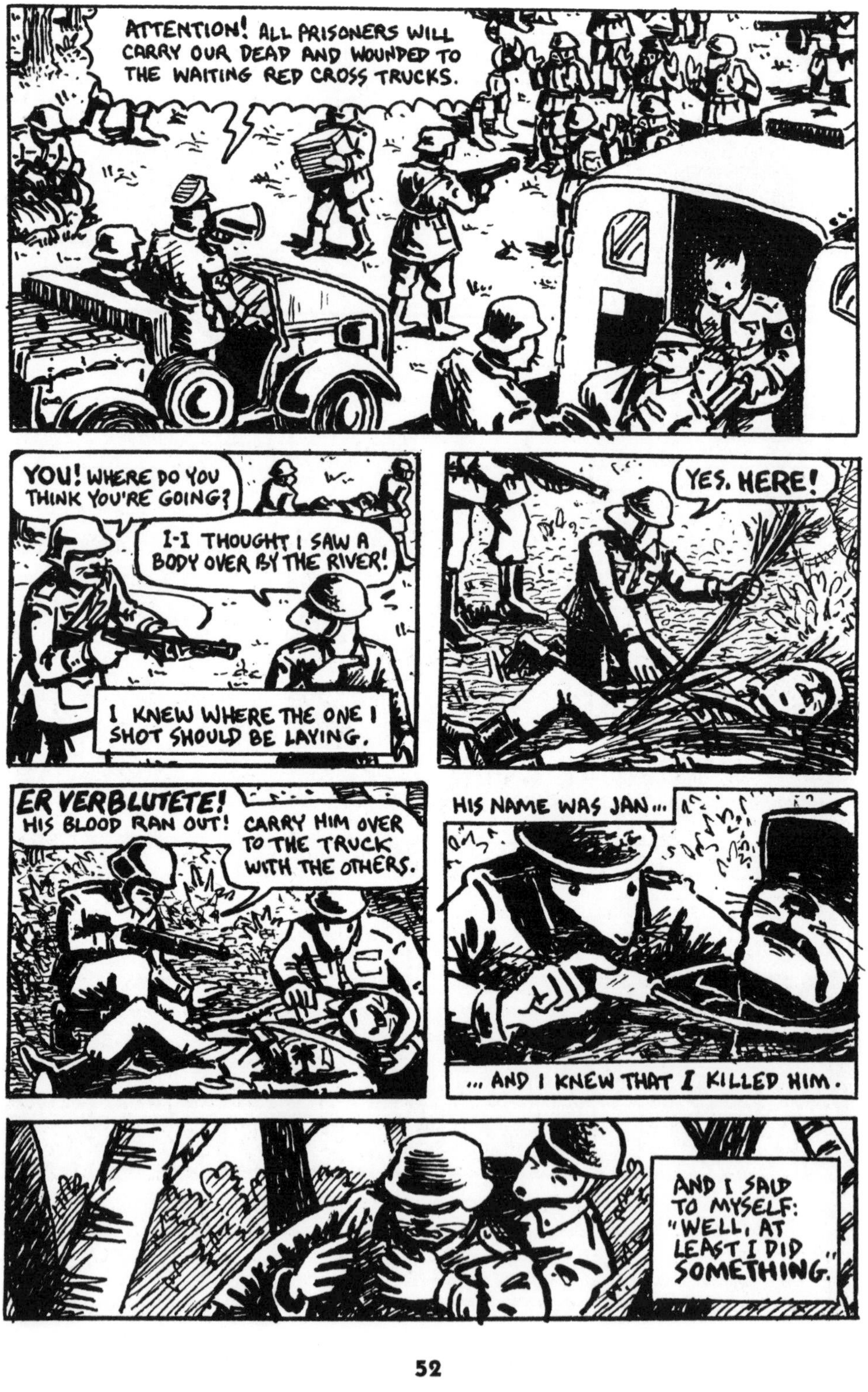
ATTENTION! ALL PRISONERS WILL CARRY OUR DEAD AND WOUNDED TO THE WAITING RED CROSS TRUCKS.
YOU! WHERE DO YOU THINK YOU'RE GOING?
I-I THOUGHT I SAW A BODY OVER BY THE RIVER!
I KNEW WHERE THE ONE I SHOT SHOULD BE LAYING.
YES. HERE!
ER VERBLUTETE! HIS BLOOD RAN OUT!
CARRY HIM OVER TO THE TRUCK WITH THE OTHERS.
HIS NAME WAS JAN...
... AND I KNEW THAT I KILLED HIM.
AND I SAID TO MYSELF: "WELL, AT LEAST I DID SOMETHING."

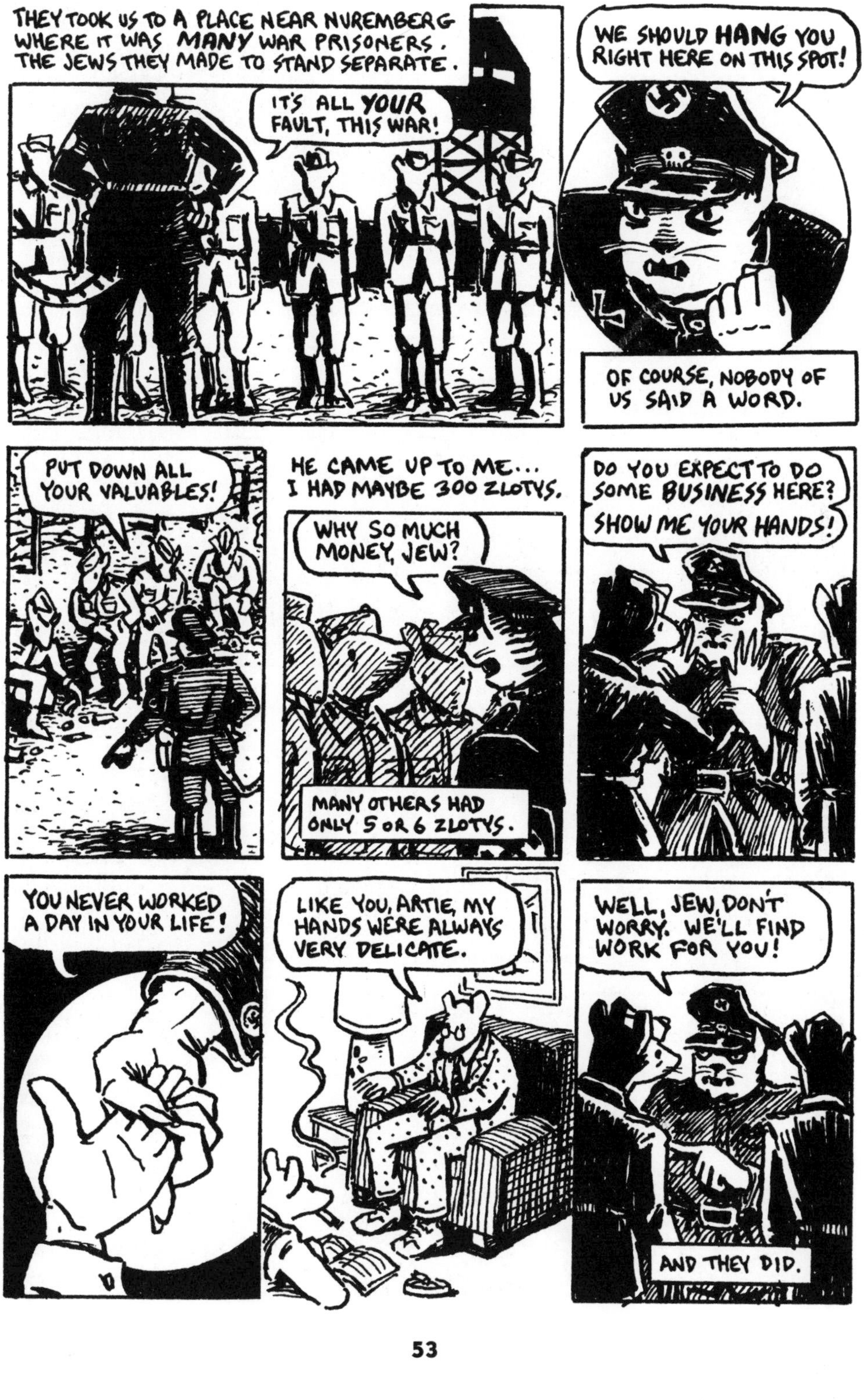
THEY TOOK US TO A PLACE NEAR NUREMBERG WHERE IT WAS MANY WAR PRISONERS. THE JEWS THEY MADE TO STAND SEPARATE.
IT'S ALL YOUR FAULT, THIS WAR!
WE SHOULD HANG YOU RIGHT HERE ON THIS SPOT!
OF COURSE, NOBODY OF US SAID A WORD.
PUT DOWN ALL YOUR VALUABLES!
HE CAME UP TO ME... I HAD MAYBE 300 ZLOTYS.
WHY SO MUCH MONEY, JEW?
MANY OTHERS HAD ONLY 5 OR 6 ZLOTYS.
DO YOU EXPECT TO DO SOME BUSINESS HERE?
SHOW ME YOUR HANDS!
YOU NEVER WORKED A DAY IN YOUR LIFE!
LIKE YOU, ARTIE, MY HANDS WERE ALWAYS VERY DELICATE.
WELL, JEW, DON'T WORRY. WE'LL FIND WORK FOR YOU!
AND THEY DID.

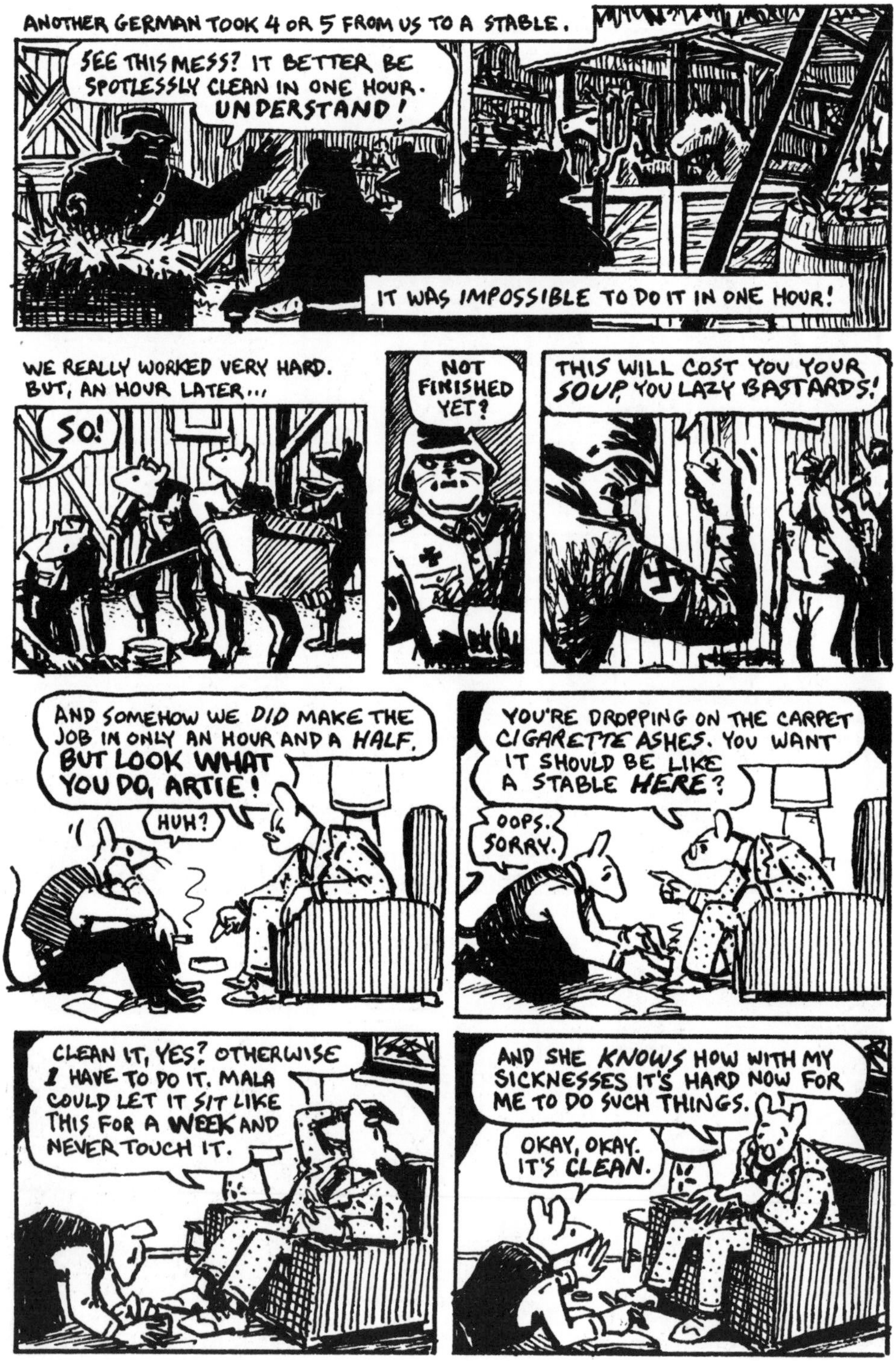
ANOTHER GERMAN TOOK 4 OR 5 FROM US TO A STABLE.
SEE THIS MESS? IT BETTER BE SPOTLESSLY CLEAN IN ONE HOUR. UNDERSTAND!
IT WAS IMPOSSIBLE TO DO IT IN ONE HOUR!
WE REALLY WORKED VERY HARD. BUT, AN HOUR LATER...
SO!
NOT FINISHED YET?
THIS WILL COST YOU YOUR SOUP, YOU LAZY BASTARDS!
AND SOMEHOW WE DID MAKE THE JOB IN ONLY AN HOUR AND A HALF. BUT LOOK WHAT YOU DO, ARTIE!
HUH?
YOU'RE DROPPING ON THE CARPET CIGARETTE ASHES. YOU WANT IT SHOULD BE LIKE A STABLE HERE?
OOPS. SORRY.
CLEAN IT, YES? OTHERWISE I HAVE TO DO IT. MALA COULD LET IT SIT LIKE THIS FOR A WEEK AND NEVER TOUCH IT.
AND SHE KNOWS HOW WITH MY SICKNESSES IT'S HARD NOW FOR ME TO DO SUCH THINGS.
OKAY, OKAY. IT'S CLEAN.

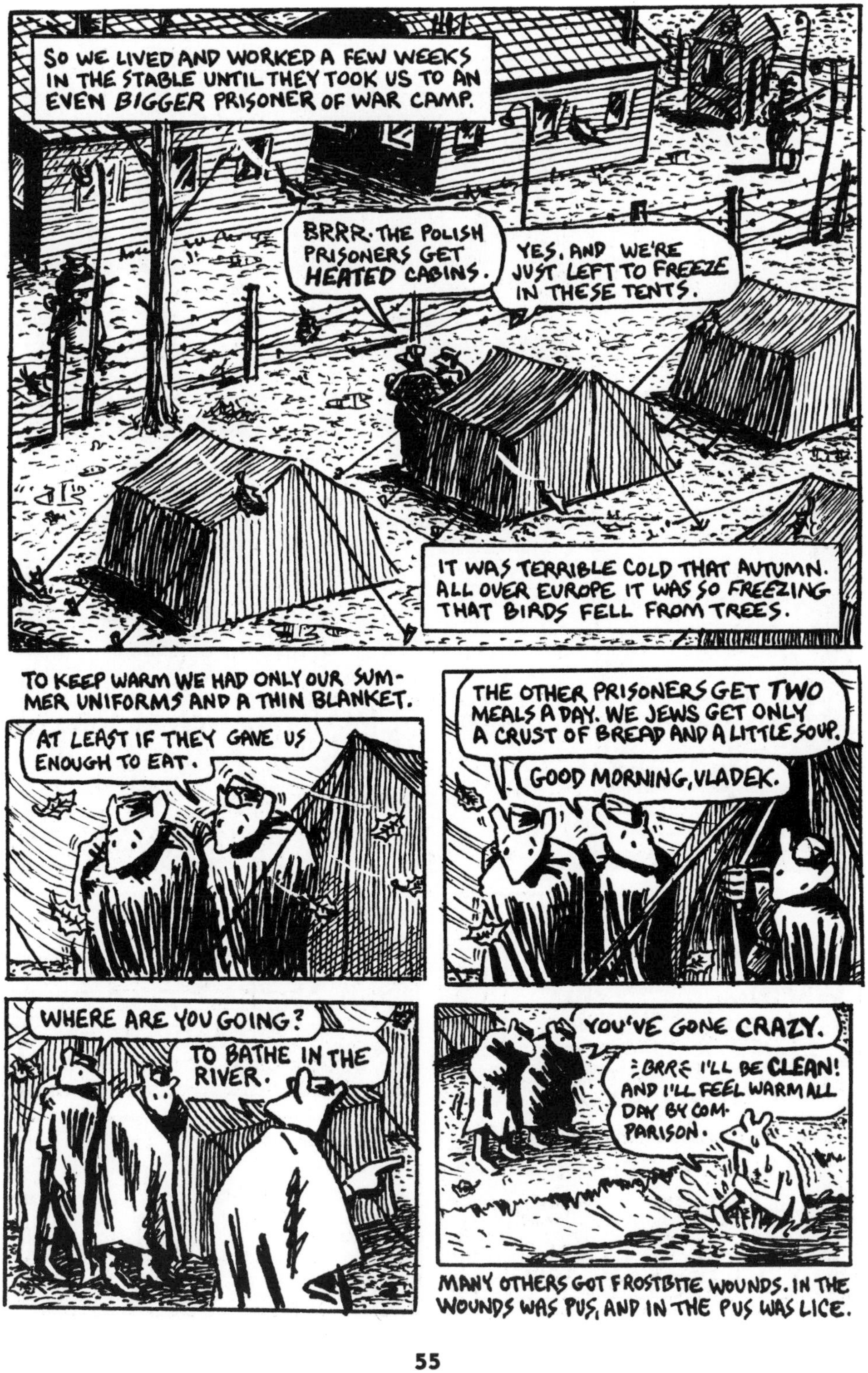
SO WE LIVED AND WORKED A FEW WEEKS IN THE STABLE UNTIL THEY TOOK US TO AN EVEN *BIGGER* PRISONER OF WAR CAMP.
BRRR. THE POLISH PRISONERS GET HEATED CABINS.
YES, AND WE'RE JUST LEFT TO FREEZE IN THESE TENTS.
IT WAS TERRIBLE COLD THAT AUTUMN. ALL OVER EUROPE IT WAS SO FREEZING THAT BIRDS FELL FROM TREES.
TO KEEP WARM WE HAD ONLY OUR SUMMER UNIFORMS AND A THIN BLANKET.
AT LEAST IF THEY GAVE US ENOUGH TO EAT.
THE OTHER PRISONERS GET TWO MEALS A DAY. WE JEWS GET ONLY A CRUST OF BREAD AND A LITTLE SOUP.
GOOD MORNING, VLADEK.
WHERE ARE YOU GOING?
TO BATHE IN THE RIVER.
YOU'VE GONE CRAZY.
BRR! I'LL BE CLEAN! AND I'LL FEEL WARM ALL DAY BY COMPARISON.
MANY OTHERS GOT FROSTBITE WOUNDS. IN THE WOUNDS WAS PUS, AND IN THE PUS WAS LICE.

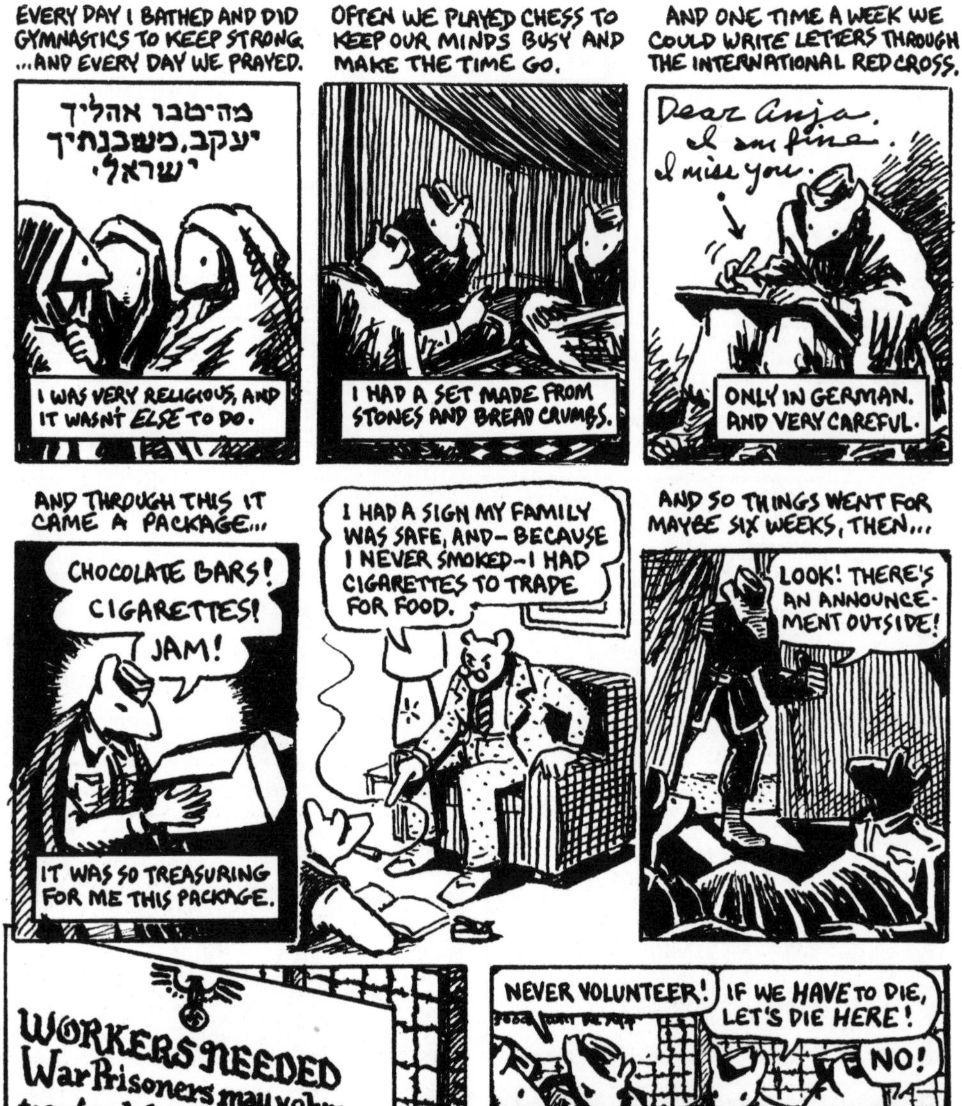

EVERY DAY I BATHED AND DID GYMNASTICS TO KEEP STRONG. ...AND EVERY DAY WE PRAYED.
מה־טבו אהליך
יעקב, משכנתיך
ישראל.
I WAS VERY RELIGIOUS, AND IT WASN'T *ELSE* TO DO.
OFTEN WE PLAYED CHESS TO KEEP OUR MINDS BUSY AND MAKE THE TIME GO.
I HAD A SET MADE FROM STONES AND BREAD CRUMBS.
AND ONE TIME A WEEK WE COULD WRITE LETTERS THROUGH THE INTERNATIONAL RED CROSS.
Dear Anja. I am fine. I miss you.
ONLY IN GERMAN. AND VERY CAREFUL.
AND THROUGH THIS IT CAME A PACKAGE...
CHOCOLATE BARS! CIGARETTES!
JAM!
IT WAS SO TREASURING FOR ME THIS PACKAGE.
I HAD A SIGN MY FAMILY WAS SAFE, AND—BECAUSE I NEVER SMOKED—I HAD CIGARETTES TO TRADE FOR FOOD.
AND SO THINGS WENT FOR MAYBE SIX WEEKS, THEN...
LOOK! THERE'S AN ANNOUNCEMENT OUTSIDE!
WORKERS NEEDED
War Prisoners may volunteer for labor assignments to replace German workers called to the front. Housing and abundant food will be supplied.
IT'S A TRICK!
NEVER VOLUNTEER!
IF WE *HAVE* TO DIE, LET'S DIE HERE!
NO!
I DIDN'T AGREE!
I'M NOT GOING TO DIE, AND I WON'T DIE HERE!
I WANT TO BE TREATED LIKE A HUMAN BEING!

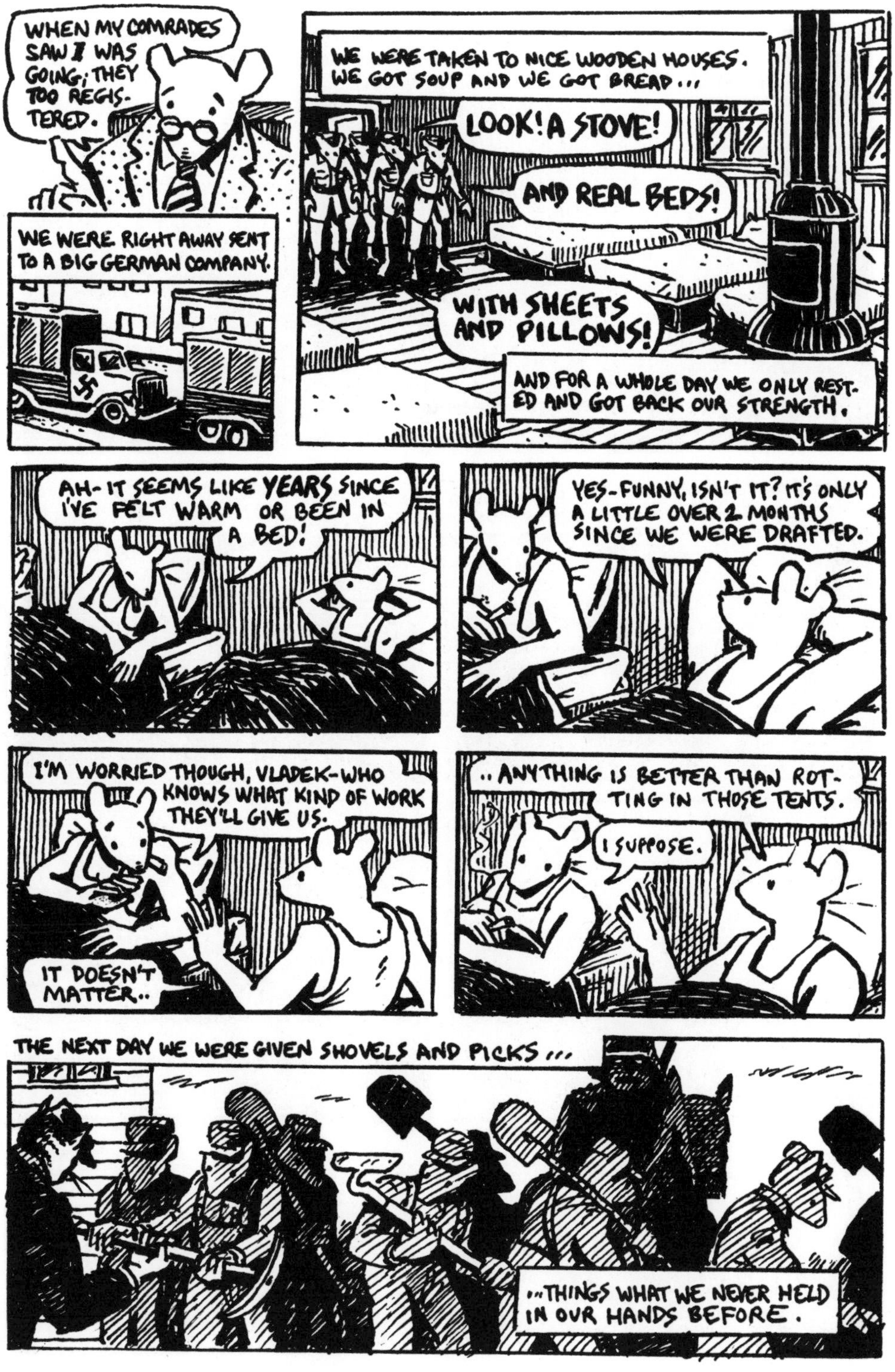
WHEN MY COMRADES SAW I WAS GOING, THEY TOO REGISTERED.
WE WERE RIGHT AWAY SENT TO A BIG GERMAN COMPANY.
WE WERE TAKEN TO NICE WOODEN HOUSES. WE GOT SOUP AND WE GOT BREAD...
LOOK! A STOVE!
AND REAL BEDS!
WITH SHEETS AND PILLOWS!
AND FOR A WHOLE DAY WE ONLY RESTED AND GOT BACK OUR STRENGTH.
AH- IT SEEMS LIKE YEARS SINCE I'VE FELT WARM OR BEEN IN A BED!
YES- FUNNY, ISN'T IT? IT'S ONLY A LITTLE OVER 2 MONTHS SINCE WE WERE DRAFTED.
I'M WORRIED THOUGH, VLADEK- WHO KNOWS WHAT KIND OF WORK THEY'LL GIVE US.
IT DOESN'T MATTER..
..ANYTHING IS BETTER THAN ROTTING IN THOSE TENTS.
I SUPPOSE.
THE NEXT DAY WE WERE GIVEN SHOVELS AND PICKS...
...THINGS WHAT WE NEVER HELD IN OUR HANDS BEFORE.

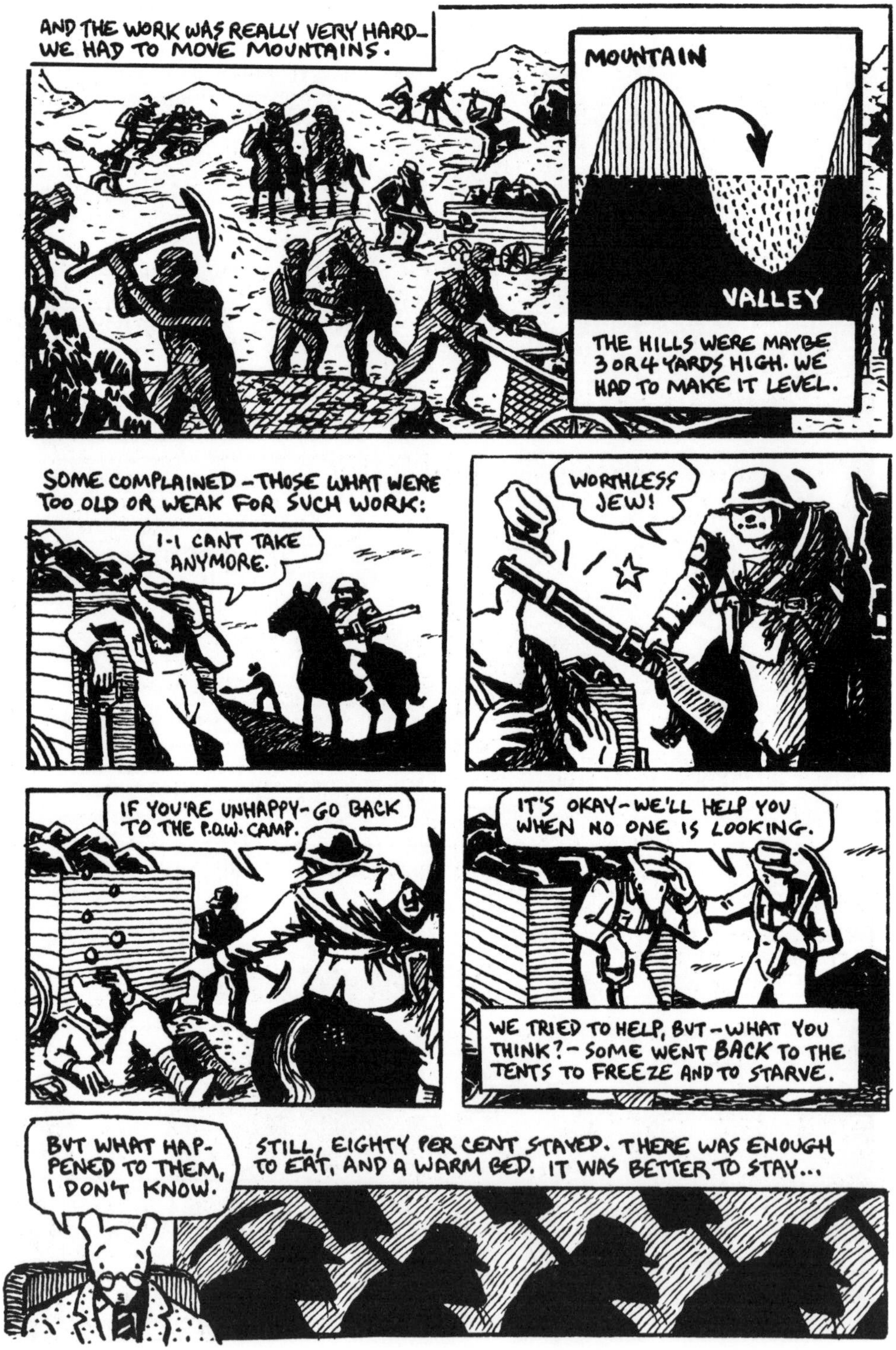
AND THE WORK WAS REALLY VERY HARD- WE HAD TO MOVE MOUNTAINS.
MOUNTAIN
VALLEY
THE HILLS WERE MAYBE 3 OR 4 YARDS HIGH. WE HAD TO MAKE IT LEVEL.
SOME COMPLAINED - THOSE WHAT WERE TOO OLD OR WEAK FOR SUCH WORK:
I-I CANT TAKE ANYMORE.
WORTHLESS JEW!
IF YOU'RE UNHAPPY- GO BACK TO THE P.O.W. CAMP.
IT'S OKAY- WE'LL HELP YOU WHEN NO ONE IS LOOKING.
WE TRIED TO HELP, BUT - WHAT YOU THINK? - SOME WENT BACK TO THE TENTS TO FREEZE AND TO STARVE.
BUT WHAT HAPPENED TO THEM, I DON'T KNOW.
STILL, EIGHTY PER CENT STAYED. THERE WAS ENOUGH TO EAT, AND A WARM BED. IT WAS BETTER TO STAY...

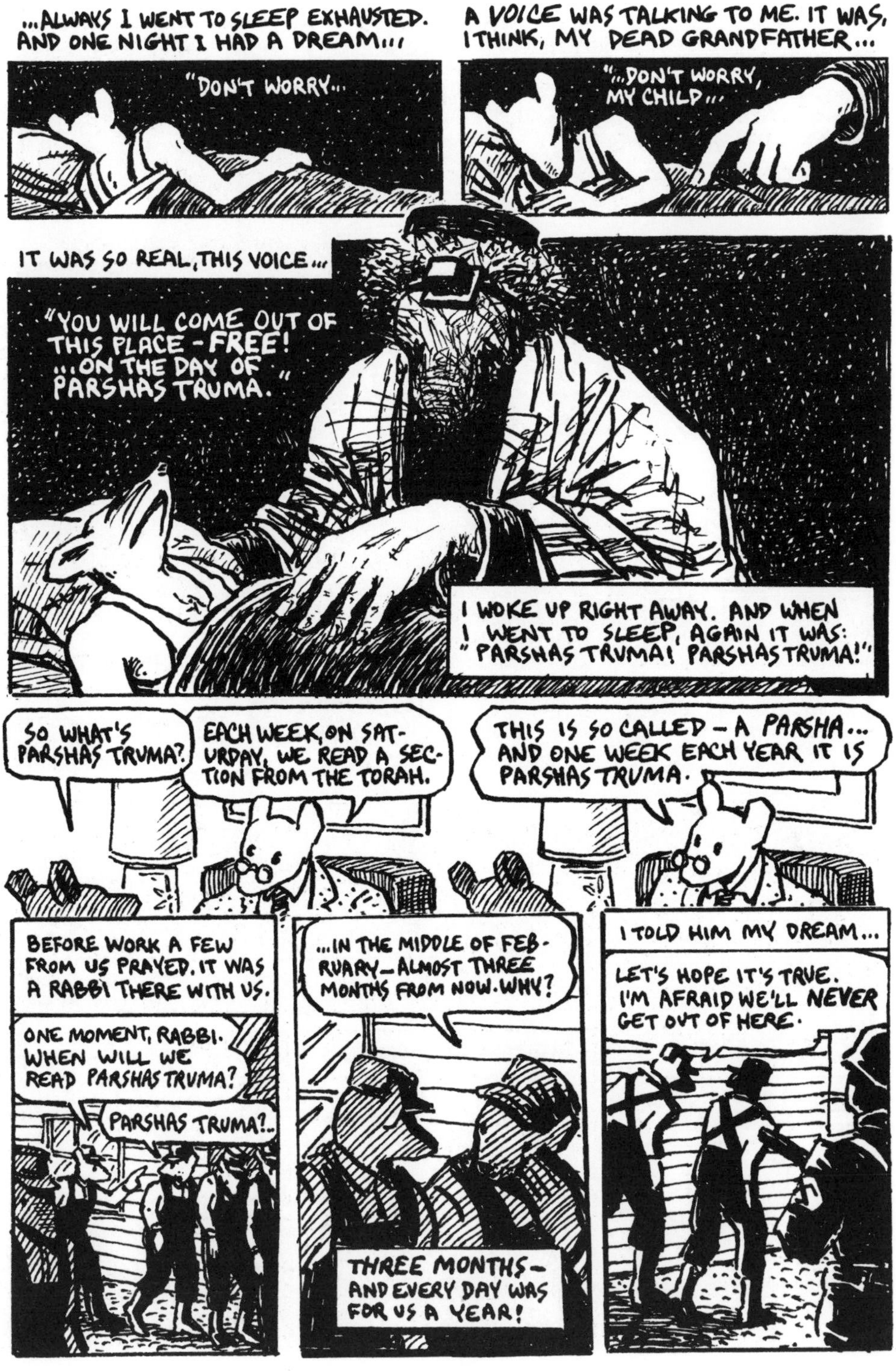
...ALWAYS I WENT TO SLEEP EXHAUSTED. AND ONE NIGHT I HAD A DREAM...
"DON'T WORRY...
A VOICE WAS TALKING TO ME. IT WAS, I THINK, MY DEAD GRANDFATHER...
"...DON'T WORRY, MY CHILD...
IT WAS SO REAL, THIS VOICE...
"YOU WILL COME OUT OF THIS PLACE - FREE! ...ON THE DAY OF PARSHAS TRUMA."
I WOKE UP RIGHT AWAY. AND WHEN I WENT TO SLEEP, AGAIN IT WAS: "PARSHAS TRUMA! PARSHAS TRUMA!"
SO WHAT'S PARSHAS TRUMA?
EACH WEEK, ON SATURDAY, WE READ A SECTION FROM THE TORAH.
THIS IS SO CALLED - A PARSHA... AND ONE WEEK EACH YEAR IT IS PARSHAS TRUMA.
BEFORE WORK A FEW FROM US PRAYED. IT WAS A RABBI THERE WITH US.
ONE MOMENT, RABBI. WHEN WILL WE READ PARSHAS TRUMA?
PARSHAS TRUMA?..
...IN THE MIDDLE OF FEBRUARY— ALMOST THREE MONTHS FROM NOW. WHY?
THREE MONTHS— AND EVERY DAY WAS FOR US A YEAR!
I TOLD HIM MY DREAM...
LET'S HOPE IT'S TRUE. I'M AFRAID WE'LL NEVER GET OUT OF HERE.

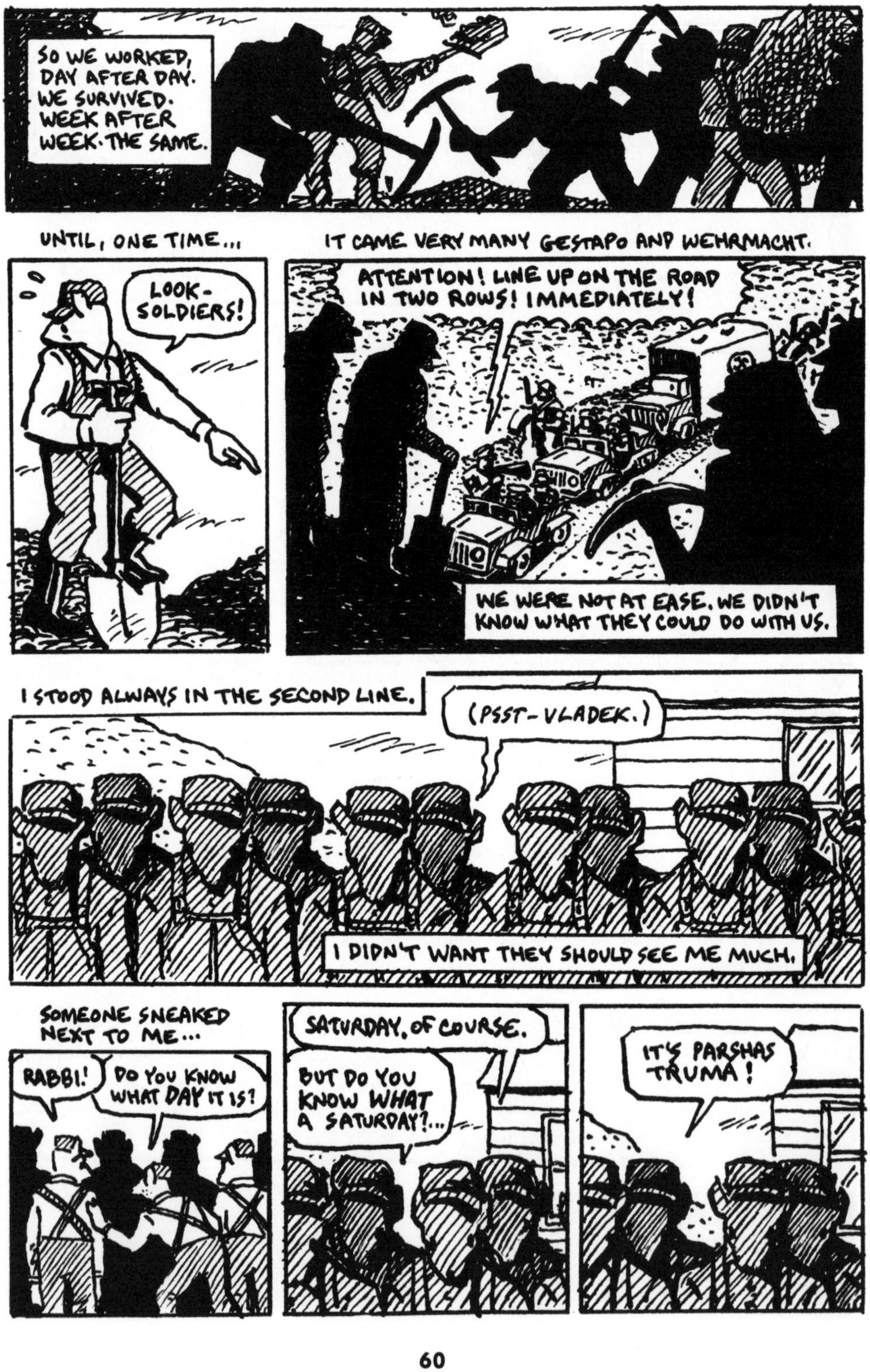

SO WE WORKED, DAY AFTER DAY. WE SURVIVED. WEEK AFTER WEEK THE SAME.
UNTIL, ONE TIME...
LOOK-SOLDIERS!
IT CAME VERY MANY GESTAPO AND WEHRMACHT.
ATTENTION! LINE UP ON THE ROAD IN TWO ROWS! IMMEDIATELY!
WE WERE NOT AT EASE. WE DIDN'T KNOW WHAT THEY COULD DO WITH US.
I STOOD ALWAYS IN THE SECOND LINE.
(PSST-VLADEK.)
I DIDN'T WANT THEY SHOULD SEE ME MUCH.
SOMEONE SNEAKED NEXT TO ME...
RABBI!
DO YOU KNOW WHAT DAY IT IS?
SATURDAY, OF COURSE.
BUT DO YOU KNOW WHAT A SATURDAY?...
IT'S PARSHAS TRUMA!

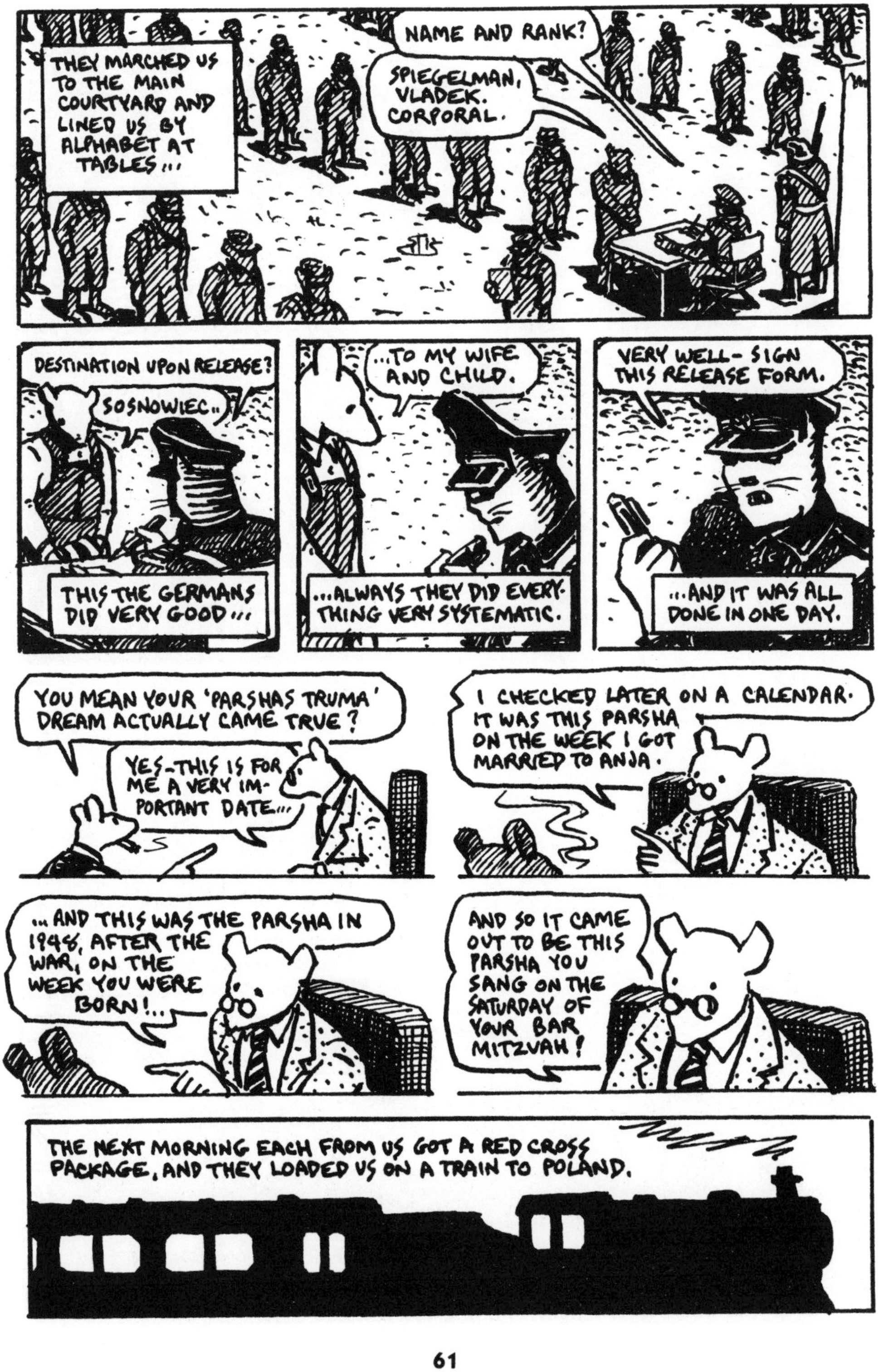
THEY MARCHED US TO THE MAIN COURTYARD AND LINED US BY ALPHABET AT TABLES...
NAME AND RANK?
SPIEGELMAN, VLADEK. CORPORAL.
DESTINATION UPON RELEASE?
SOSNOWIEC..
THIS THE GERMANS DID VERY GOOD...
...TO MY WIFE AND CHILD.
...ALWAYS THEY DID EVERY-THING VERY SYSTEMATIC.
VERY WELL- SIGN THIS RELEASE FORM.
...AND IT WAS ALL DONE IN ONE DAY.
YOU MEAN YOUR 'PARSHAS TRUMA' DREAM ACTUALLY CAME TRUE?
YES-THIS IS FOR ME A VERY IM-PORTANT DATE...
I CHECKED LATER ON A CALENDAR. IT WAS THIS PARSHA ON THE WEEK I GOT MARRIED TO ANJA.
...AND THIS WAS THE PARSHA IN 1948, AFTER THE WAR, ON THE WEEK YOU WERE BORN!...
AND SO IT CAME OUT TO BE THIS PARSHA YOU SANG ON THE SATURDAY OF YOUR BAR MITZVAH!
THE NEXT MORNING EACH FROM US GOT A RED CROSS PACKAGE, AND THEY LOADED US ON A TRAIN TO POLAND.

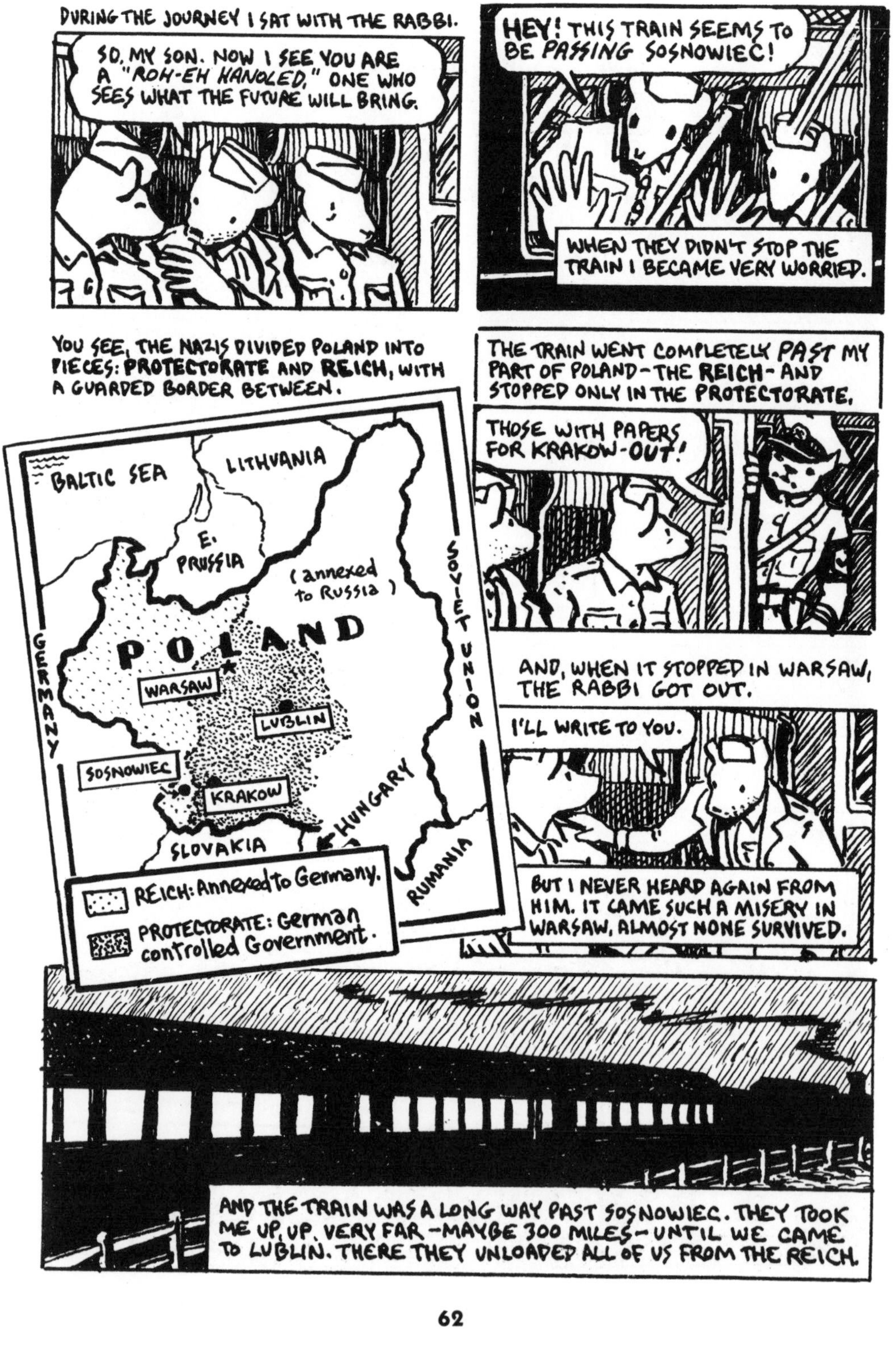

DURING THE JOURNEY I SAT WITH THE RABBI.
SO, MY SON. NOW I SEE YOU ARE A "ROH-EH HANOLED," ONE WHO SEES WHAT THE FUTURE WILL BRING.
HEY! THIS TRAIN SEEMS TO BE PASSING SOSNOWIEC!
WHEN THEY DIDN'T STOP THE TRAIN I BECAME VERY WORRIED.
YOU SEE, THE NAZIS DIVIDED POLAND INTO PIECES: PROTECTORATE AND REICH, WITH A GUARDED BORDER BETWEEN.
BALTIC SEA
LITHUANIA
E. PRUSSIA
(annexed to Russia)
SOVIET UNION
GERMANY
POLAND
WARSAW
LUBLIN
SOSNOWIEC
KRAKOW
HUNGARY
SLOVAKIA
RUMANIA
REICH: Annexed to Germany.
PROTECTORATE: German controlled Government.
THE TRAIN WENT COMPLETELY PAST MY PART OF POLAND - THE REICH - AND STOPPED ONLY IN THE PROTECTORATE.
THOSE WITH PAPERS FOR KRAKOW-OUT!
AND, WHEN IT STOPPED IN WARSAW, THE RABBI GOT OUT.
I'LL WRITE TO YOU.
BUT I NEVER HEARD AGAIN FROM HIM. IT CAME SUCH A MISERY IN WARSAW, ALMOST NONE SURVIVED.
AND THE TRAIN WAS A LONG WAY PAST SOSNOWIEC. THEY TOOK ME UP, UP, VERY FAR - MAYBE 300 MILES - UNTIL WE CAME TO LUBLIN. THERE THEY UNLOADED ALL OF US FROM THE REICH.

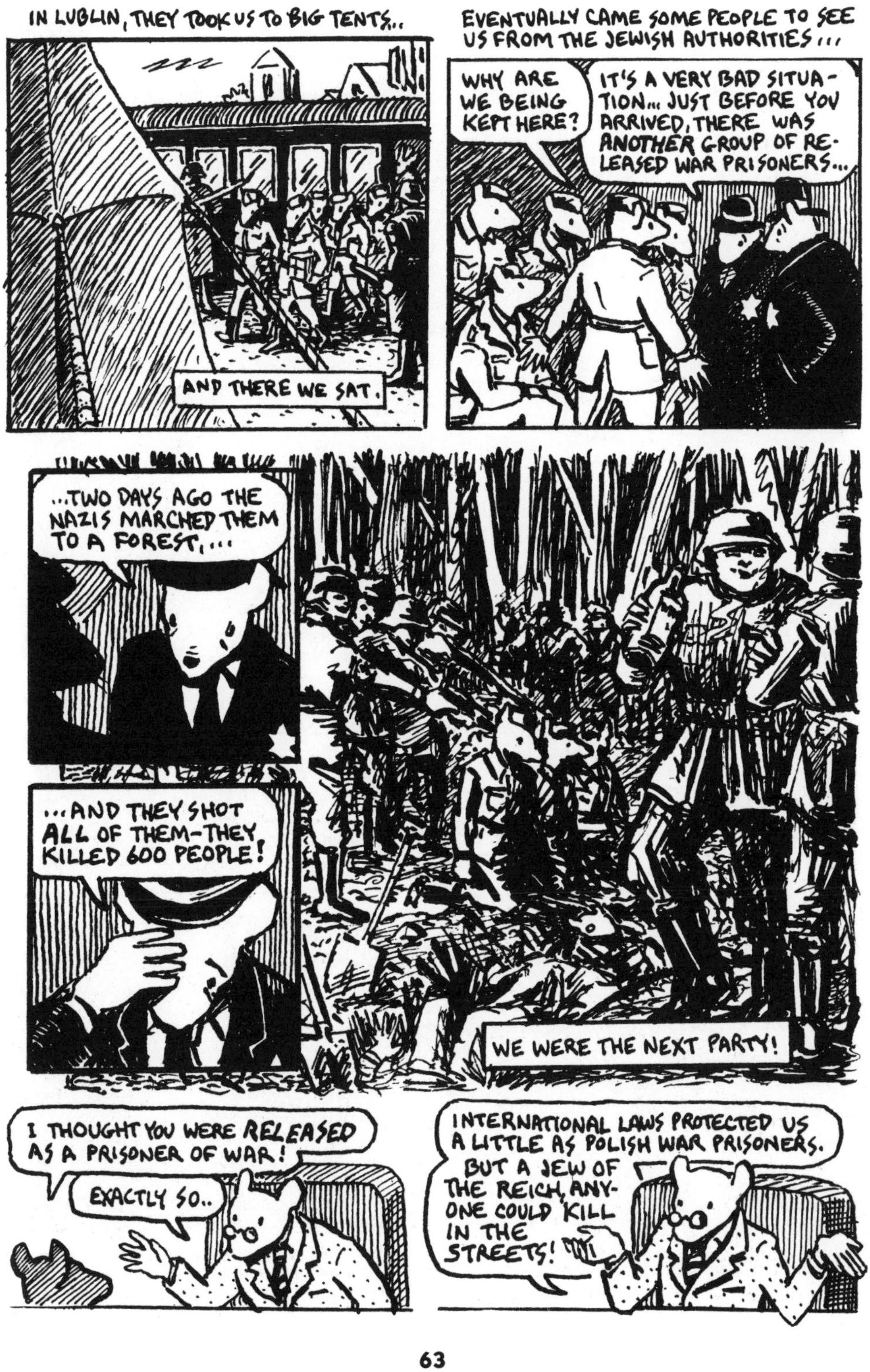
IN LUBLIN, THEY TOOK US TO BIG TENTS..
AND THERE WE SAT.
EVENTUALLY CAME SOME PEOPLE TO SEE US FROM THE JEWISH AUTHORITIES...
WHY ARE WE BEING KEPT HERE?
IT'S A VERY BAD SITUATION... JUST BEFORE YOU ARRIVED, THERE WAS ANOTHER GROUP OF RELEASED WAR PRISONERS...
...TWO DAYS AGO THE NAZIS MARCHED THEM TO A FOREST,...
...AND THEY SHOT ALL OF THEM-THEY KILLED 600 PEOPLE!
WE WERE THE NEXT PARTY!
I THOUGHT YOU WERE RELEASED AS A PRISONER OF WAR!
EXACTLY SO..
INTERNATIONAL LAWS PROTECTED US A LITTLE AS POLISH WAR PRISONERS.
BUT A JEW OF THE REICH, ANYONE COULD KILL IN THE STREETS!

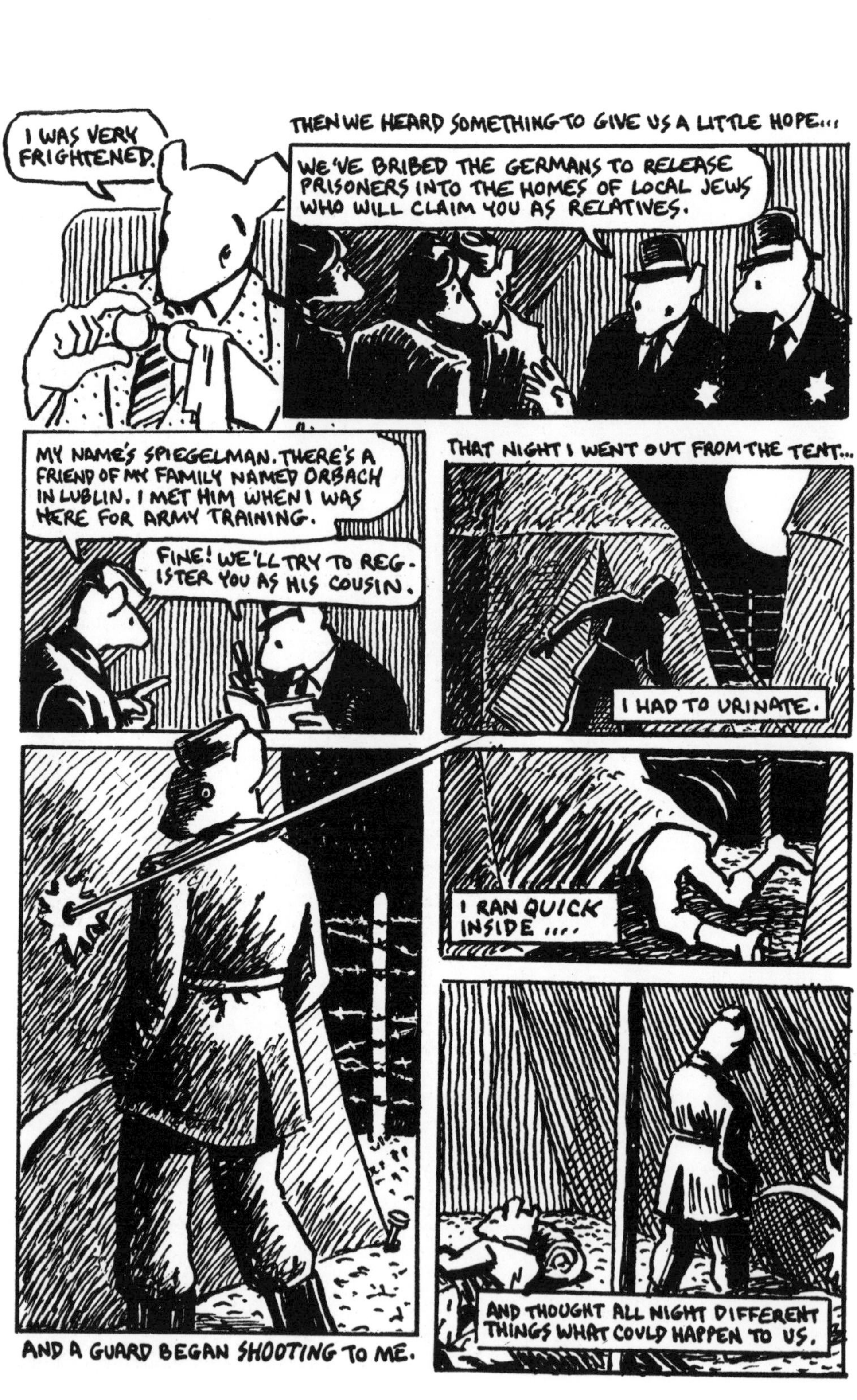
I WAS VERY FRIGHTENED.
THEN WE HEARD SOMETHING TO GIVE US A LITTLE HOPE...
WE'VE BRIBED THE GERMANS TO RELEASE PRISONERS INTO THE HOMES OF LOCAL JEWS WHO WILL CLAIM YOU AS RELATIVES.
MY NAME'S SPIEGELMAN. THERE'S A FRIEND OF MY FAMILY NAMED ORBACH IN LUBLIN. I MET HIM WHEN I WAS HERE FOR ARMY TRAINING.
FINE! WE'LL TRY TO REGISTER YOU AS HIS COUSIN.
THAT NIGHT I WENT OUT FROM THE TENT...
I HAD TO URINATE.
AND A GUARD BEGAN SHOOTING TO ME.
I RAN QUICK INSIDE....
AND THOUGHT ALL NIGHT DIFFERENT THINGS WHAT COULD HAPPEN TO US.

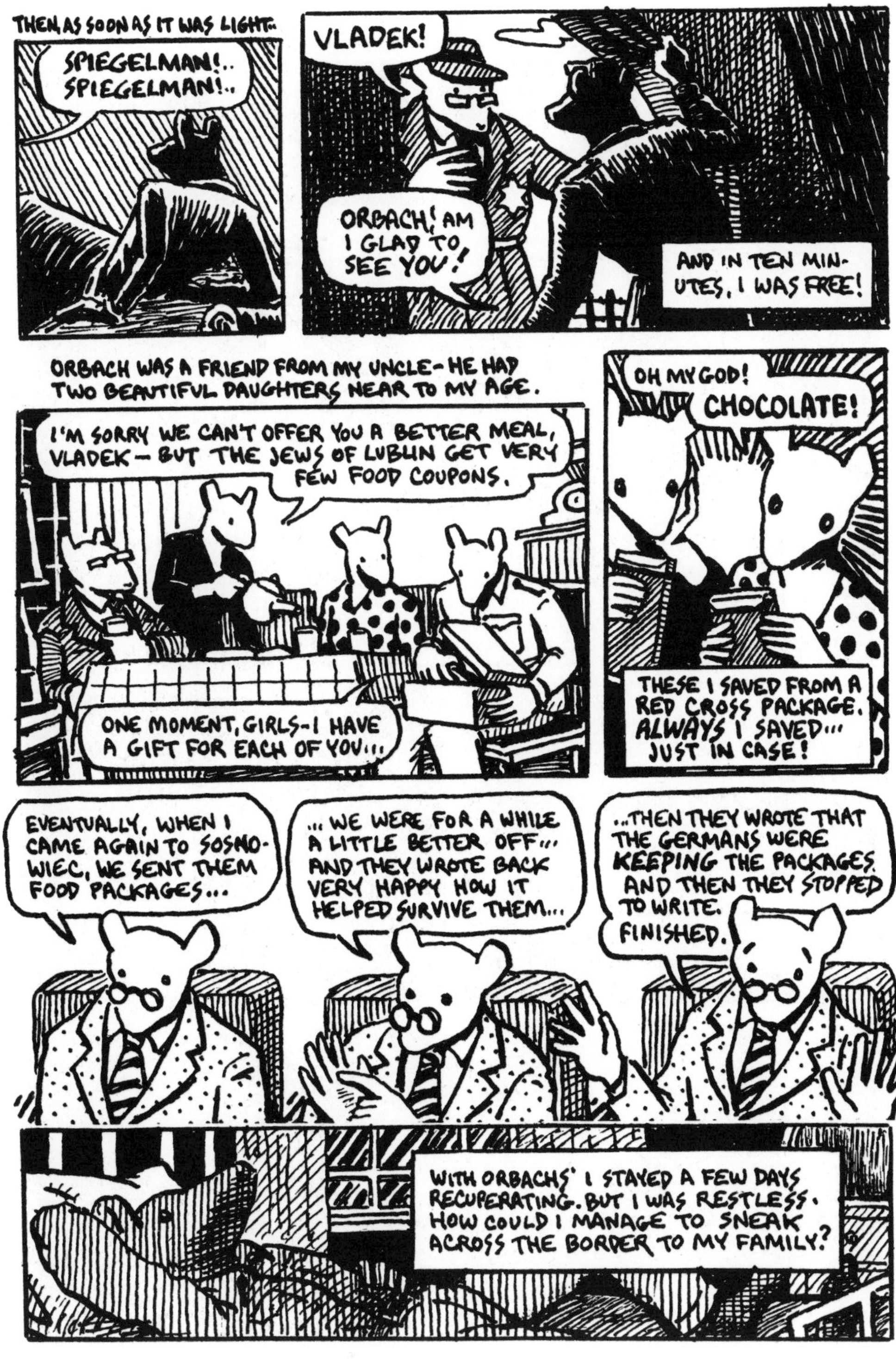
THEN, AS SOON AS IT WAS LIGHT...
SPIEGELMAN!.. SPIEGELMAN!..
VLADEK!
ORBACH! AM I GLAD TO SEE YOU!
AND IN TEN MINUTES, I WAS FREE!
ORBACH WAS A FRIEND FROM MY UNCLE- HE HAD TWO BEAUTIFUL DAUGHTERS NEAR TO MY AGE.
I'M SORRY WE CAN'T OFFER YOU A BETTER MEAL, VLADEK- BUT THE JEWS OF LUBLIN GET VERY FEW FOOD COUPONS.
ONE MOMENT, GIRLS- I HAVE A GIFT FOR EACH OF YOU...
OH MY GOD!
CHOCOLATE!
THESE I SAVED FROM A RED CROSS PACKAGE. ALWAYS I SAVED... JUST IN CASE!
EVENTUALLY, WHEN I CAME AGAIN TO SOSNOWIEC, WE SENT THEM FOOD PACKAGES...
... WE WERE FOR A WHILE A LITTLE BETTER OFF... AND THEY WROTE BACK VERY HAPPY HOW IT HELPED SURVIVE THEM...
...THEN THEY WROTE THAT THE GERMANS WERE KEEPING THE PACKAGES. AND THEN THEY STOPPED TO WRITE. FINISHED.
WITH ORBACHS' I STAYED A FEW DAYS RECUPERATING. BUT I WAS RESTLESS. HOW COULD I MANAGE TO SNEAK ACROSS THE BORDER TO MY FAMILY?

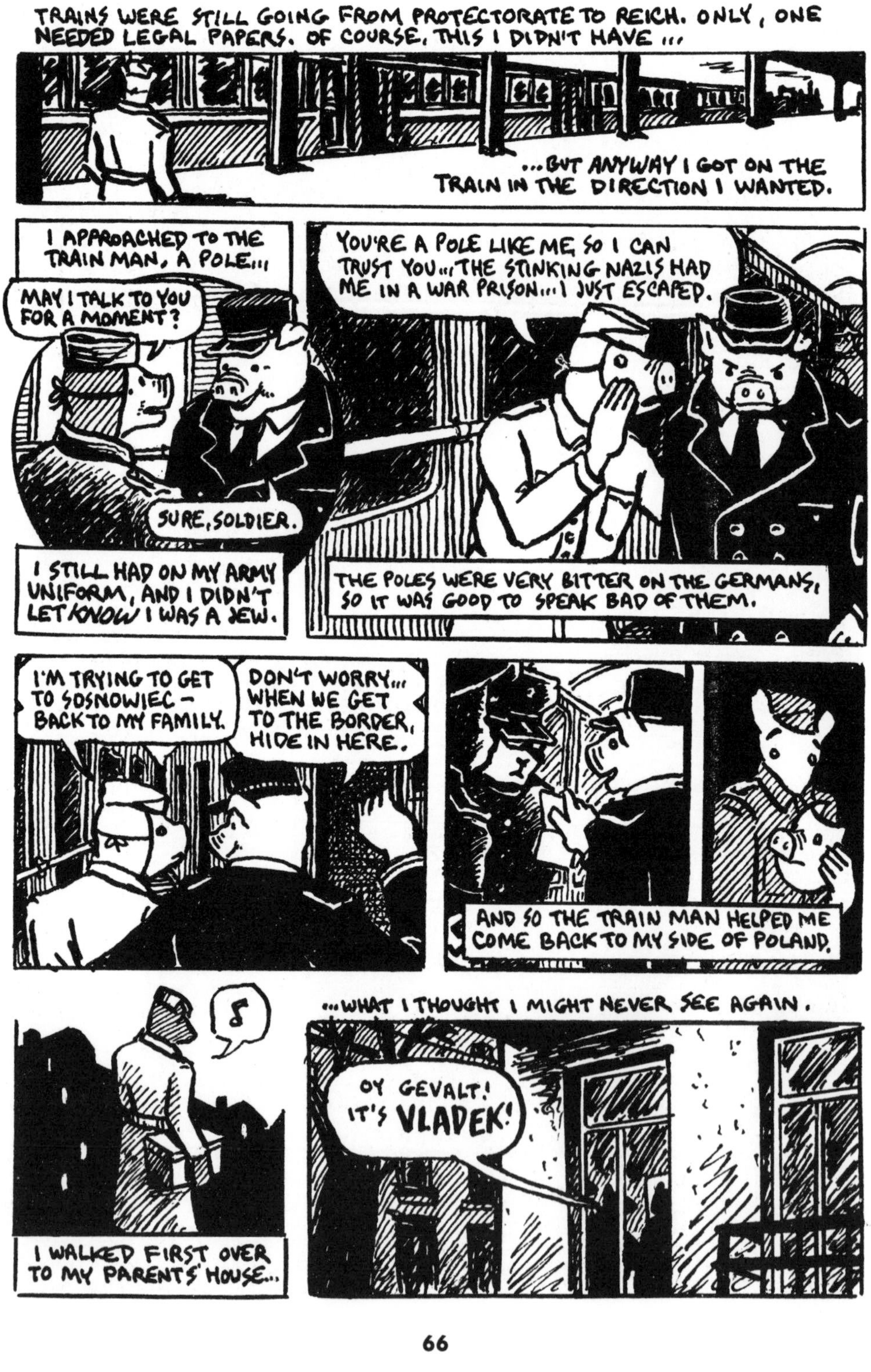
TRAINS WERE STILL GOING FROM PROTECTORATE TO REICH. ONLY, ONE NEEDED LEGAL PAPERS. OF COURSE, THIS I DIDN'T HAVE ...
...BUT ANYWAY I GOT ON THE TRAIN IN THE DIRECTION I WANTED.
I APPROACHED TO THE TRAIN MAN, A POLE...
MAY I TALK TO YOU FOR A MOMENT?
SURE, SOLDIER.
I STILL HAD ON MY ARMY UNIFORM, AND I DIDN'T LET KNOW I WAS A JEW.
YOU'RE A POLE LIKE ME, SO I CAN TRUST YOU... THE STINKING NAZIS HAD ME IN A WAR PRISON... I JUST ESCAPED.
THE POLES WERE VERY BITTER ON THE GERMANS, SO IT WAS GOOD TO SPEAK BAD OF THEM.
I'M TRYING TO GET TO SOSNOWIEC – BACK TO MY FAMILY.
DON'T WORRY... WHEN WE GET TO THE BORDER, HIDE IN HERE.
AND SO THE TRAIN MAN HELPED ME COME BACK TO MY SIDE OF POLAND.
I WALKED FIRST OVER TO MY PARENTS' HOUSE...
...WHAT I THOUGHT I MIGHT NEVER SEE AGAIN.
OY GEVALT! IT'S VLADEK!

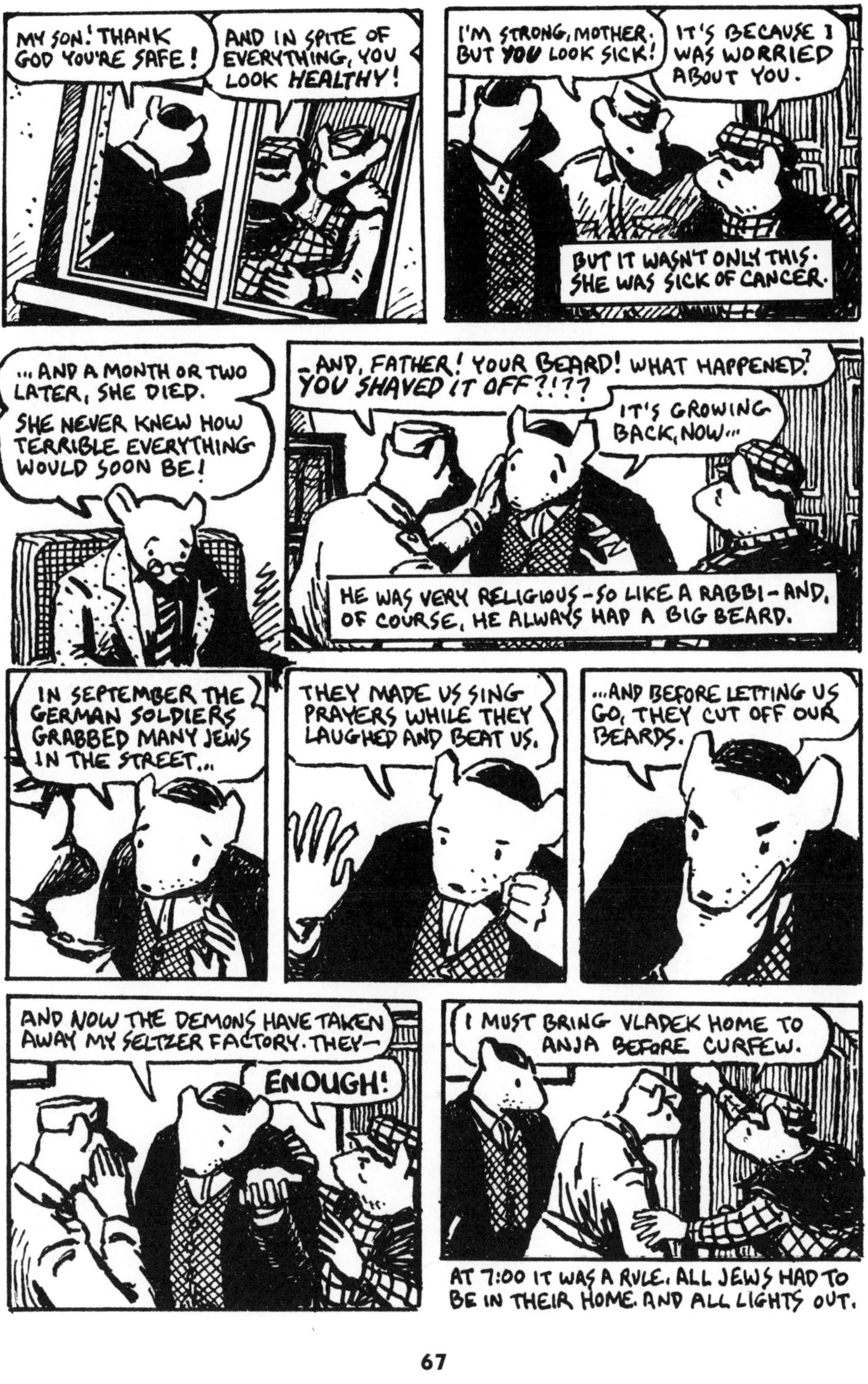
MY SON! THANK GOD YOU'RE SAFE!
AND IN SPITE OF EVERYTHING, YOU LOOK HEALTHY!
I'M STRONG, MOTHER. BUT YOU LOOK SICK!
IT'S BECAUSE I WAS WORRIED ABOUT YOU.
BUT IT WASN'T ONLY THIS. SHE WAS SICK OF CANCER.
...AND A MONTH OR TWO LATER, SHE DIED.
SHE NEVER KNEW HOW TERRIBLE EVERYTHING WOULD SOON BE!
-AND, FATHER! YOUR BEARD! WHAT HAPPENED? YOU SHAVED IT OFF?!??
IT'S GROWING BACK, NOW...
HE WAS VERY RELIGIOUS-SO LIKE A RABBI-AND, OF COURSE, HE ALWAYS HAD A BIG BEARD.
IN SEPTEMBER THE GERMAN SOLDIERS GRABBED MANY JEWS IN THE STREET...
THEY MADE US SING PRAYERS WHILE THEY LAUGHED AND BEAT US.
...AND BEFORE LETTING US GO, THEY CUT OFF OUR BEARDS.
AND NOW THE DEMONS HAVE TAKEN AWAY MY SELTZER FACTORY. THEY-
ENOUGH!
I MUST BRING VLADEK HOME TO ANJA BEFORE CURFEW.
AT 7:00 IT WAS A RULE. ALL JEWS HAD TO BE IN THEIR HOME. AND ALL LIGHTS OUT.

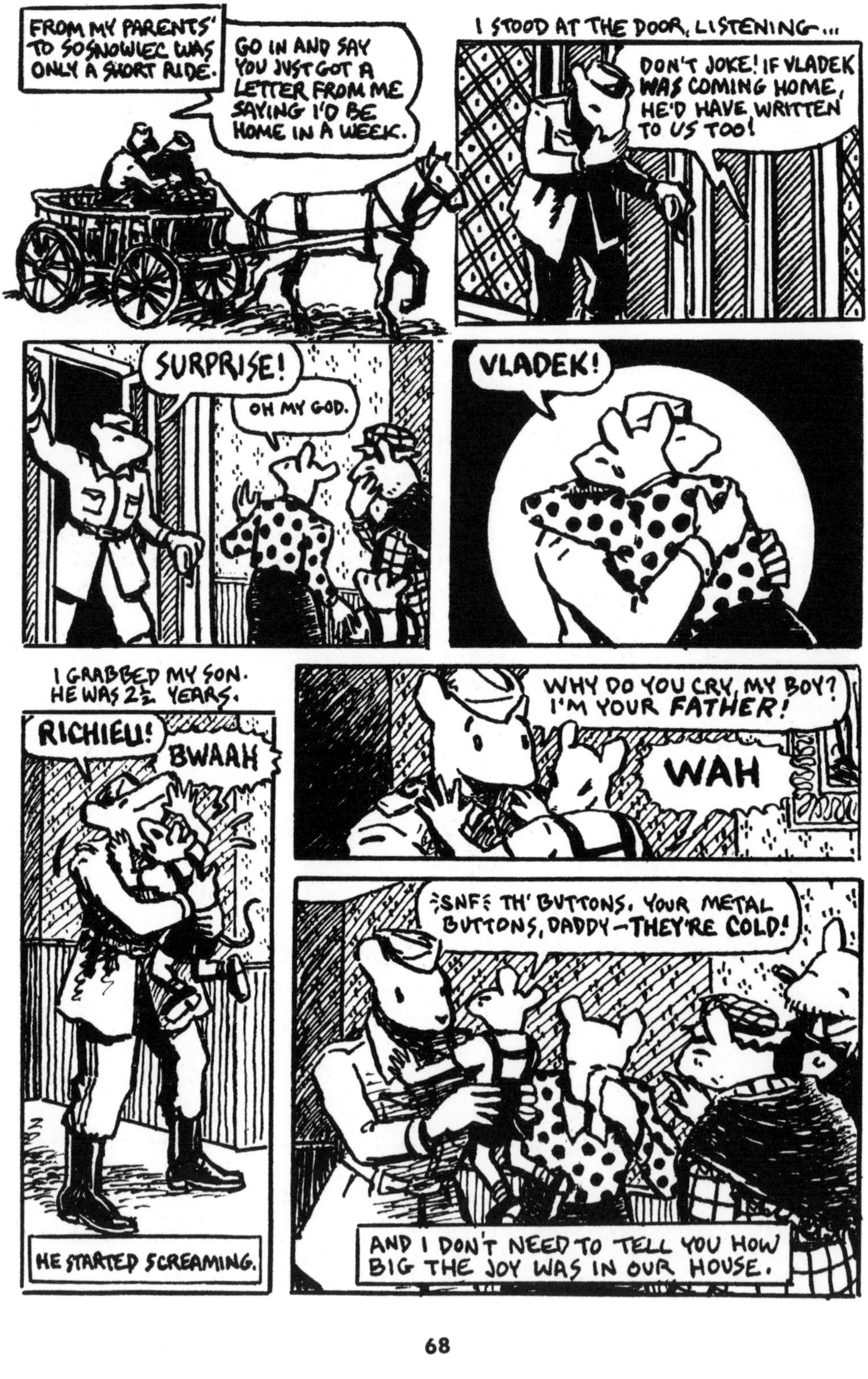

FROM MY PARENTS' TO SOSNOWIEC WAS ONLY A SHORT RIDE.
GO IN AND SAY YOU JUST GOT A LETTER FROM ME SAYING I'D BE HOME IN A WEEK.
I STOOD AT THE DOOR, LISTENING...
DON'T JOKE! IF VLADEK WAS COMING HOME, HE'D HAVE WRITTEN TO US TOO!
SURPRISE!
OH MY GOD.
VLADEK!
I GRABBED MY SON. HE WAS 2½ YEARS.
RICHIEU!
BWAAH
HE STARTED SCREAMING.
WHY DO YOU CRY, MY BOY? I'M YOUR FATHER!
WAH
SNF TH' BUTTONS. YOUR METAL BUTTONS, DADDY—THEY'RE COLD!
AND I DON'T NEED TO TELL YOU HOW BIG THE JOY WAS IN OUR HOUSE.

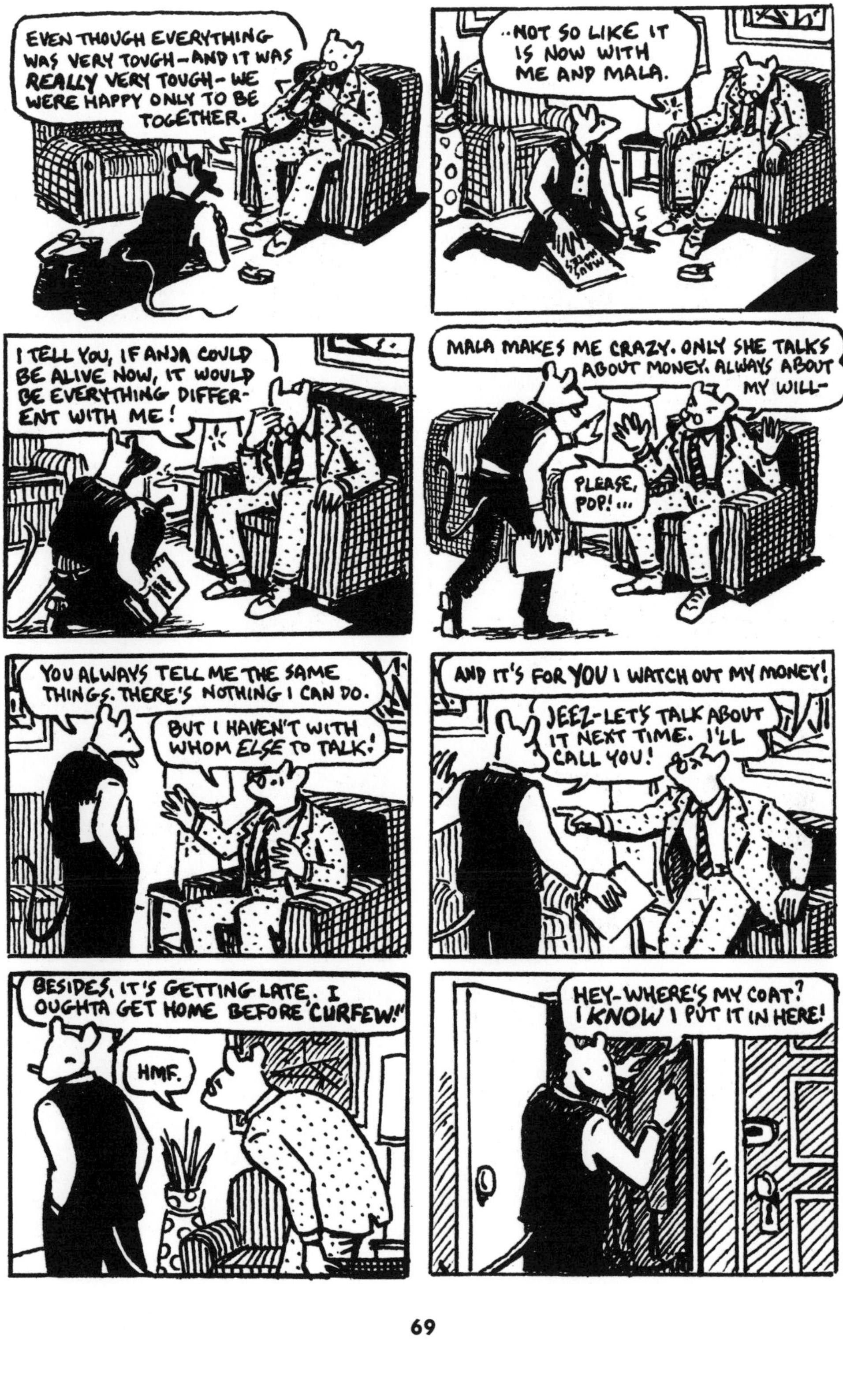
EVEN THOUGH EVERYTHING WAS VERY TOUGH—AND IT WAS REALLY VERY TOUGH—WE WERE HAPPY ONLY TO BE TOGETHER.
..NOT SO LIKE IT IS NOW WITH ME AND MALA.
I TELL YOU, IF ANJA COULD BE ALIVE NOW, IT WOULD BE EVERYTHING DIFFERENT WITH ME!
MALA MAKES ME CRAZY. ONLY SHE TALKS ABOUT MONEY. ALWAYS ABOUT MY WILL-
PLEASE, POP!...
YOU ALWAYS TELL ME THE SAME THINGS. THERE'S NOTHING I CAN DO.
BUT I HAVEN'T WITH WHOM ELSE TO TALK!
AND IT'S FOR YOU I WATCH OUT MY MONEY!
JEEZ-LET'S TALK ABOUT IT NEXT TIME. I'LL CALL YOU!
BESIDES, IT'S GETTING LATE. I OUGHTA GET HOME BEFORE "CURFEW!"
HMF.
HEY-WHERE'S MY COAT? I KNOW I PUT IT IN HERE!

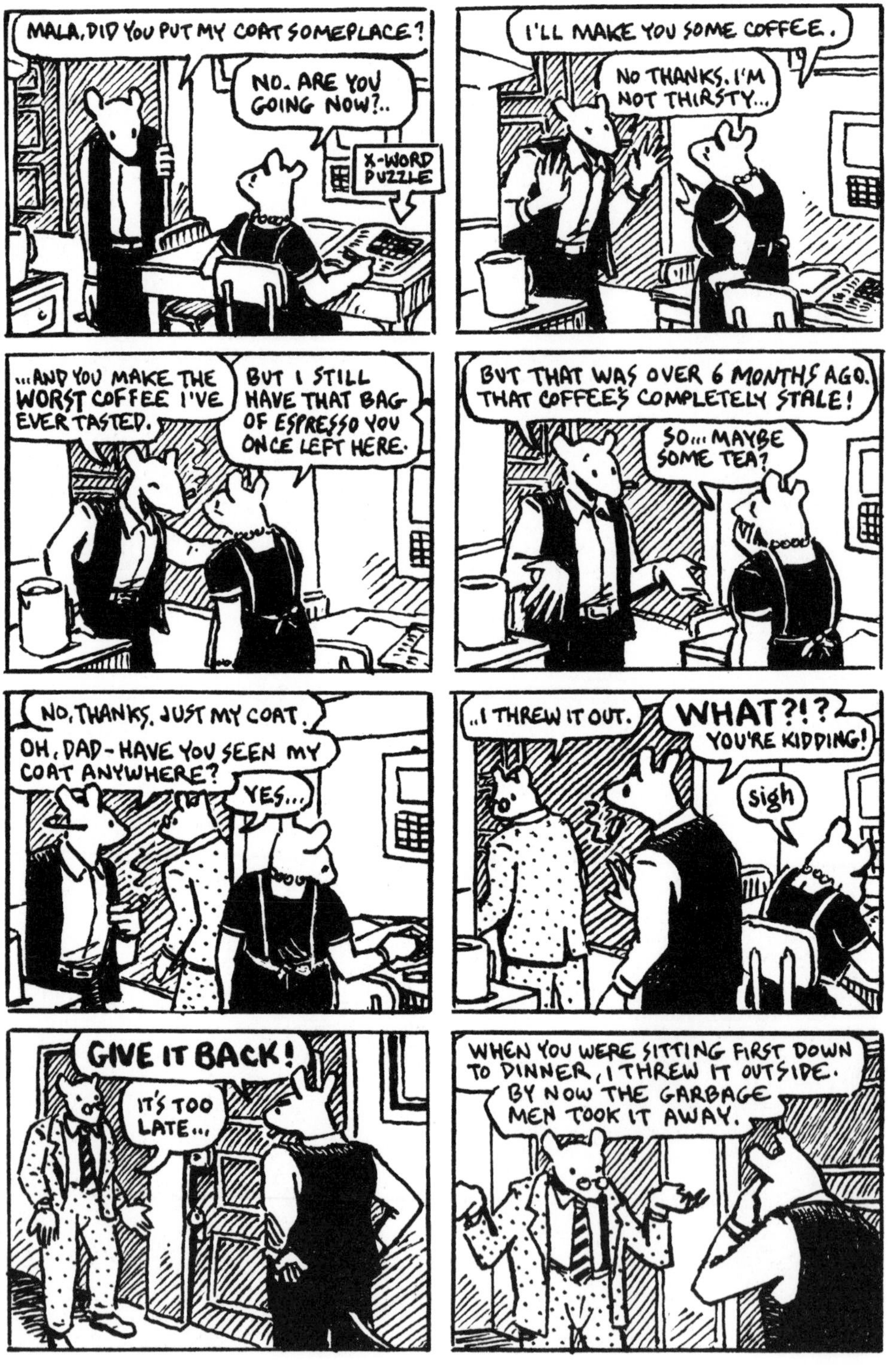
MALA, DID YOU PUT MY COAT SOMEPLACE?
NO. ARE YOU GOING NOW?..
X-WORD PUZZLE
I'LL MAKE YOU SOME COFFEE.
NO THANKS. I'M NOT THIRSTY...
...AND YOU MAKE THE WORST COFFEE I'VE EVER TASTED.
BUT I STILL HAVE THAT BAG OF ESPRESSO YOU ONCE LEFT HERE.
BUT THAT WAS OVER 6 MONTHS AGO. THAT COFFEE'S COMPLETELY STALE!
SO... MAYBE SOME TEA?
NO, THANKS. JUST MY COAT.
OH, DAD-HAVE YOU SEEN MY COAT ANYWHERE?
YES...
..I THREW IT OUT.
WHAT?!?
YOU'RE KIDDING!
sigh
GIVE IT BACK!
IT'S TOO LATE...
WHEN YOU WERE SITTING FIRST DOWN TO DINNER, I THREW IT OUTSIDE. BY NOW THE GARBAGE MEN TOOK IT AWAY.

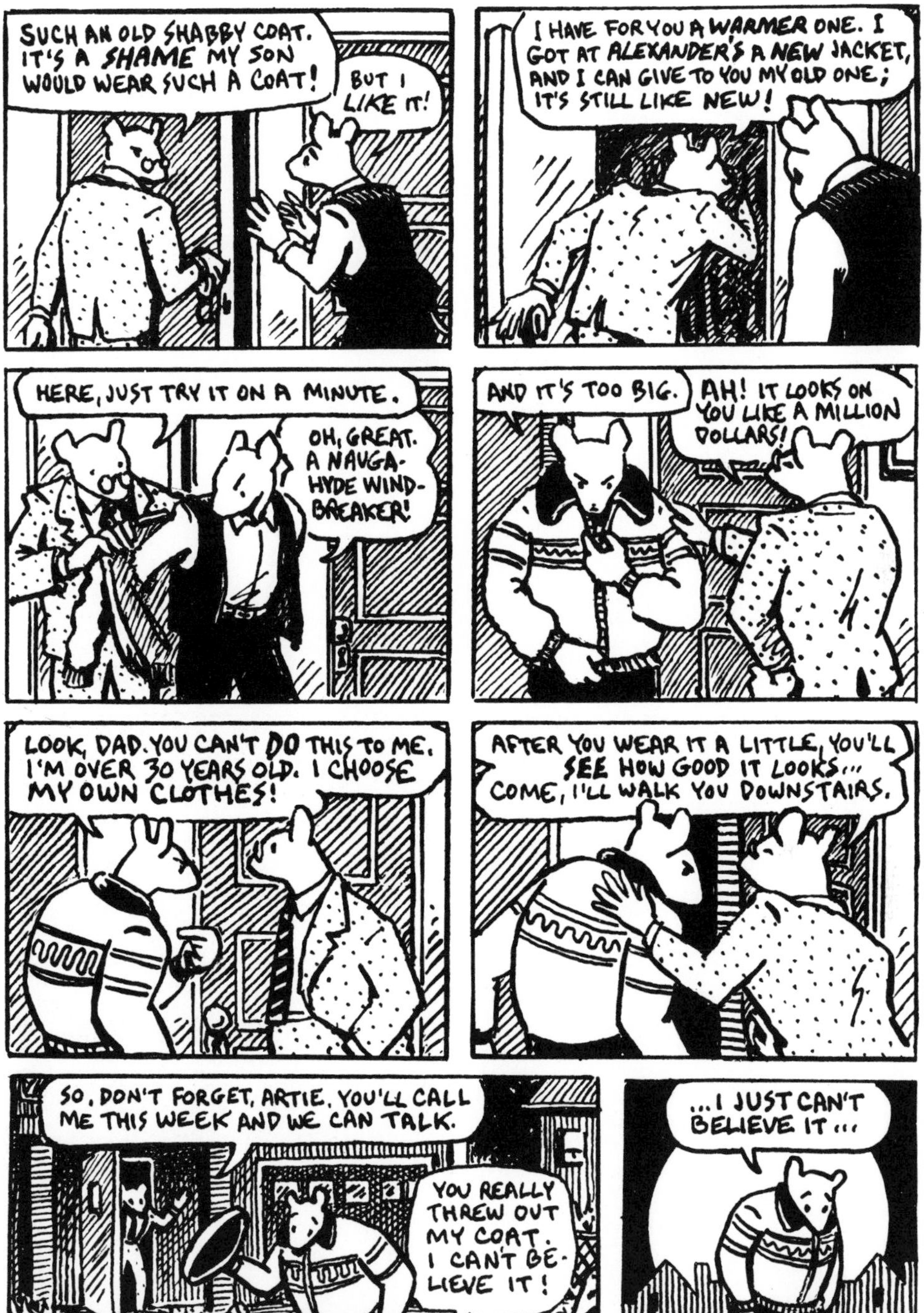
SUCH AN OLD SHABBY COAT. IT'S A SHAME MY SON WOULD WEAR SUCH A COAT!
BUT I LIKE IT!
I HAVE FOR YOU A WARMER ONE. I GOT AT ALEXANDER'S A NEW JACKET, AND I CAN GIVE TO YOU MY OLD ONE; IT'S STILL LIKE NEW!
HERE, JUST TRY IT ON A MINUTE.
OH, GREAT. A NAUGA-HYDE WIND-BREAKER!
AND IT'S TOO BIG.
AH! IT LOOKS ON YOU LIKE A MILLION DOLLARS!
LOOK, DAD. YOU CAN'T DO THIS TO ME. I'M OVER 30 YEARS OLD. I CHOOSE MY OWN CLOTHES!
AFTER YOU WEAR IT A LITTLE, YOU'LL SEE HOW GOOD IT LOOKS... COME, I'LL WALK YOU DOWNSTAIRS.
SO, DON'T FORGET, ARTIE, YOU'LL CALL ME THIS WEEK AND WE CAN TALK.
YOU REALLY THREW OUT MY COAT. I CAN'T BE-LIEVE IT!
...I JUST CAN'T BELIEVE IT...

CHAPTER FOUR

THE NOOSE TIGHTENS

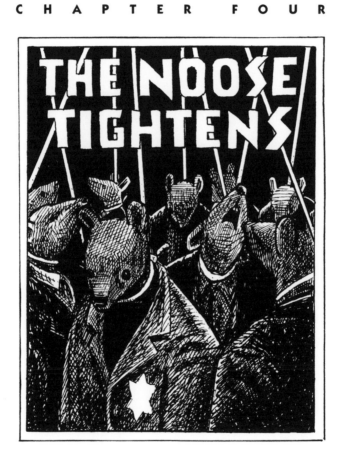

75

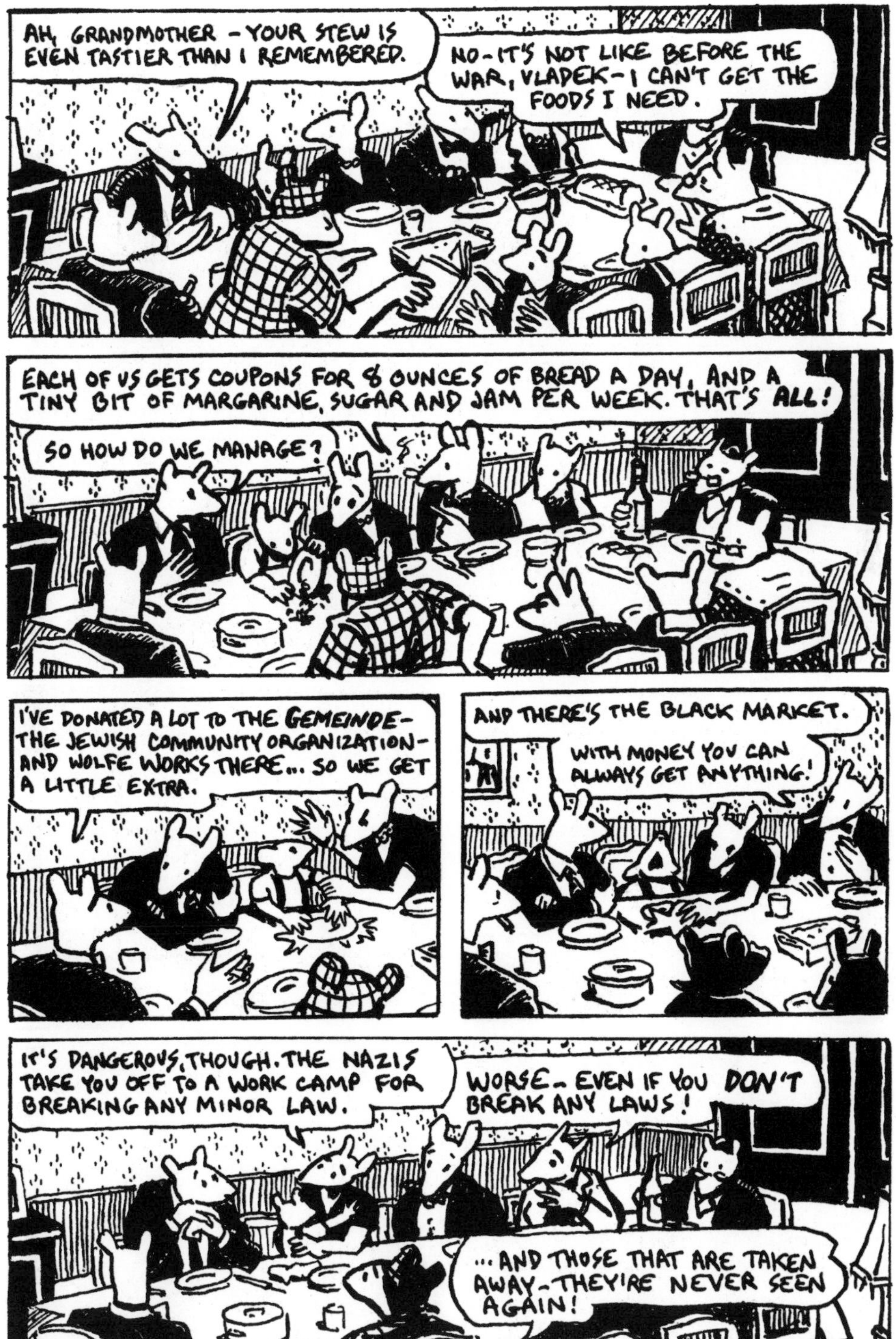
AH, GRANDMOTHER - YOUR STEW IS EVEN TASTIER THAN I REMEMBERED.
NO - IT'S NOT LIKE BEFORE THE WAR, VLADEK - I CAN'T GET THE FOODS I NEED.
EACH OF US GETS COUPONS FOR 8 OUNCES OF BREAD A DAY, AND A TINY BIT OF MARGARINE, SUGAR AND JAM PER WEEK. THAT'S ALL!
SO HOW DO WE MANAGE?
I'VE DONATED A LOT TO THE GEMEINDE - THE JEWISH COMMUNITY ORGANIZATION - AND WOLFE WORKS THERE... SO WE GET A LITTLE EXTRA.
AND THERE'S THE BLACK MARKET.
WITH MONEY YOU CAN ALWAYS GET ANYTHING!
IT'S DANGEROUS, THOUGH. THE NAZIS TAKE YOU OFF TO A WORK CAMP FOR BREAKING ANY MINOR LAW.
WORSE - EVEN IF YOU DON'T BREAK ANY LAWS!
...AND THOSE THAT ARE TAKEN AWAY - THEY'RE NEVER SEEN AGAIN!

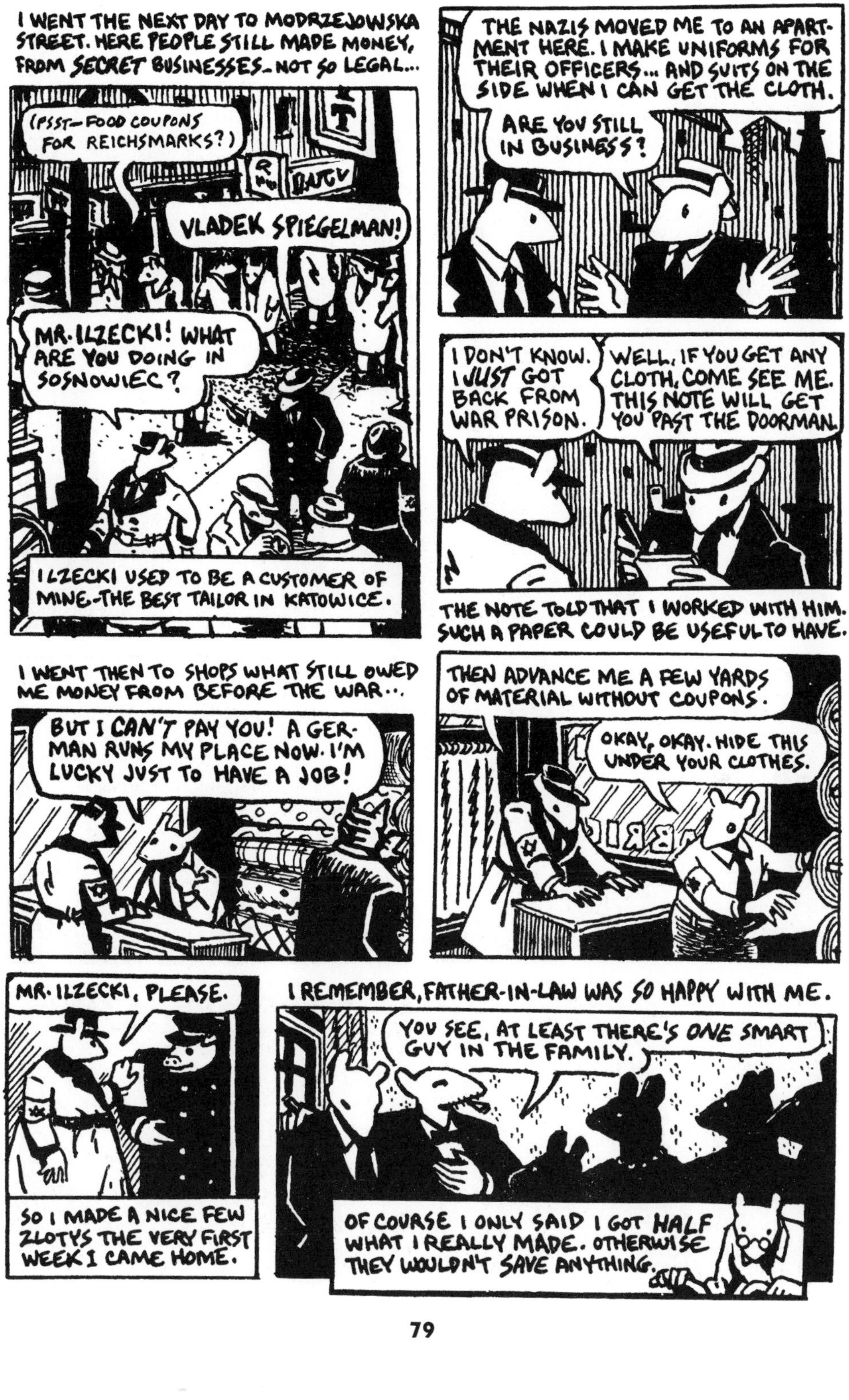
I WENT THE NEXT DAY TO MODRZEJOWSKA STREET. HERE PEOPLE STILL MADE MONEY, FROM SECRET BUSINESSES - NOT SO LEGAL...
(PSST-FOOD COUPONS FOR REICHSMARKS?)
VLADEK SPIEGELMAN!
MR. ILZECKI! WHAT ARE YOU DOING IN SOSNOWIEC?
ILZECKI USED TO BE A CUSTOMER OF MINE-THE BEST TAILOR IN KATOWICE.
THE NAZIS MOVED ME TO AN APARTMENT HERE. I MAKE UNIFORMS FOR THEIR OFFICERS... AND SUITS ON THE SIDE WHEN I CAN GET THE CLOTH.
ARE YOU STILL IN BUSINESS?
I DON'T KNOW. I JUST GOT BACK FROM WAR PRISON.
WELL, IF YOU GET ANY CLOTH, COME SEE ME. THIS NOTE WILL GET YOU PAST THE DOORMAN.
THE NOTE TOLD THAT I WORKED WITH HIM. SUCH A PAPER COULD BE USEFUL TO HAVE.
I WENT THEN TO SHOPS WHAT STILL OWED ME MONEY FROM BEFORE THE WAR..
BUT I CAN'T PAY YOU! A GERMAN RUNS MY PLACE NOW. I'M LUCKY JUST TO HAVE A JOB!
THEN ADVANCE ME A FEW YARDS OF MATERIAL WITHOUT COUPONS.
OKAY, OKAY. HIDE THIS UNDER YOUR CLOTHES.
MR. ILZECKI, PLEASE.
SO I MADE A NICE FEW ZLOTYS THE VERY FIRST WEEK I CAME HOME.
I REMEMBER, FATHER-IN-LAW WAS SO HAPPY WITH ME.
YOU SEE, AT LEAST THERE'S ONE SMART GUY IN THE FAMILY.
OF COURSE I ONLY SAID I GOT HALF WHAT I REALLY MADE. OTHERWISE THEY WOULDN'T SAVE ANYTHING.

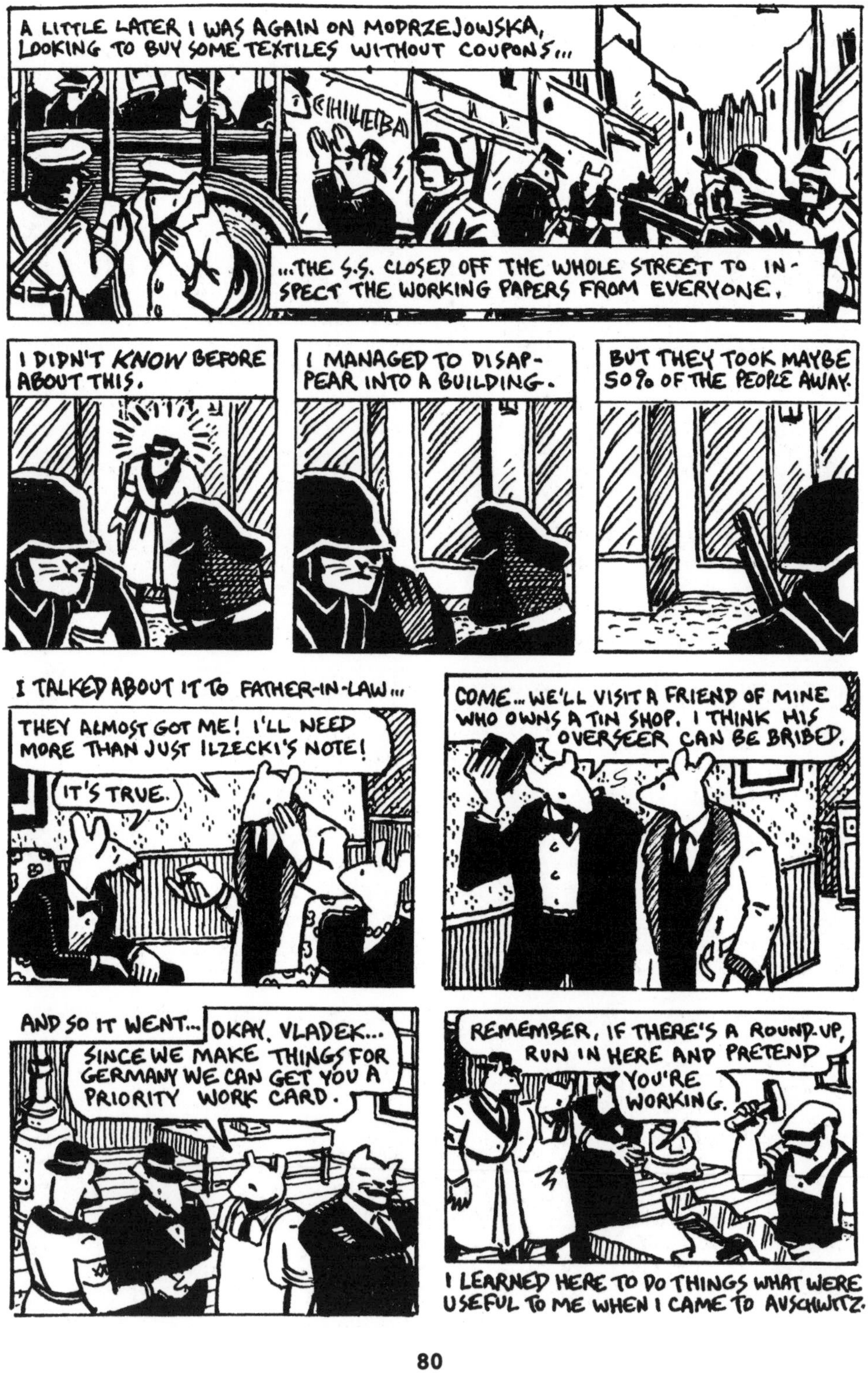

A LITTLE LATER I WAS AGAIN ON MODRZEJOWSKA, LOOKING TO BUY SOME TEXTILES WITHOUT COUPONS...
SCHILLERBA
...THE S.S. CLOSED OFF THE WHOLE STREET TO IN-SPECT THE WORKING PAPERS FROM EVERYONE.
I DIDN'T KNOW BEFORE ABOUT THIS.
I MANAGED TO DISAP-PEAR INTO A BUILDING.
BUT THEY TOOK MAYBE 50% OF THE PEOPLE AWAY.
I TALKED ABOUT IT TO FATHER-IN-LAW...
THEY ALMOST GOT ME! I'LL NEED MORE THAN JUST ILZECKI'S NOTE!
IT'S TRUE.
COME... WE'LL VISIT A FRIEND OF MINE WHO OWNS A TIN SHOP. I THINK HIS OVERSEER CAN BE BRIBED.
AND SO IT WENT...
OKAY, VLADEK... SINCE WE MAKE THINGS FOR GERMANY WE CAN GET YOU A PRIORITY WORK CARD.
REMEMBER, IF THERE'S A ROUND-UP, RUN IN HERE AND PRETEND YOU'RE WORKING.
I LEARNED HERE TO DO THINGS WHAT WERE USEFUL TO ME WHEN I CAME TO AUSCHWITZ.

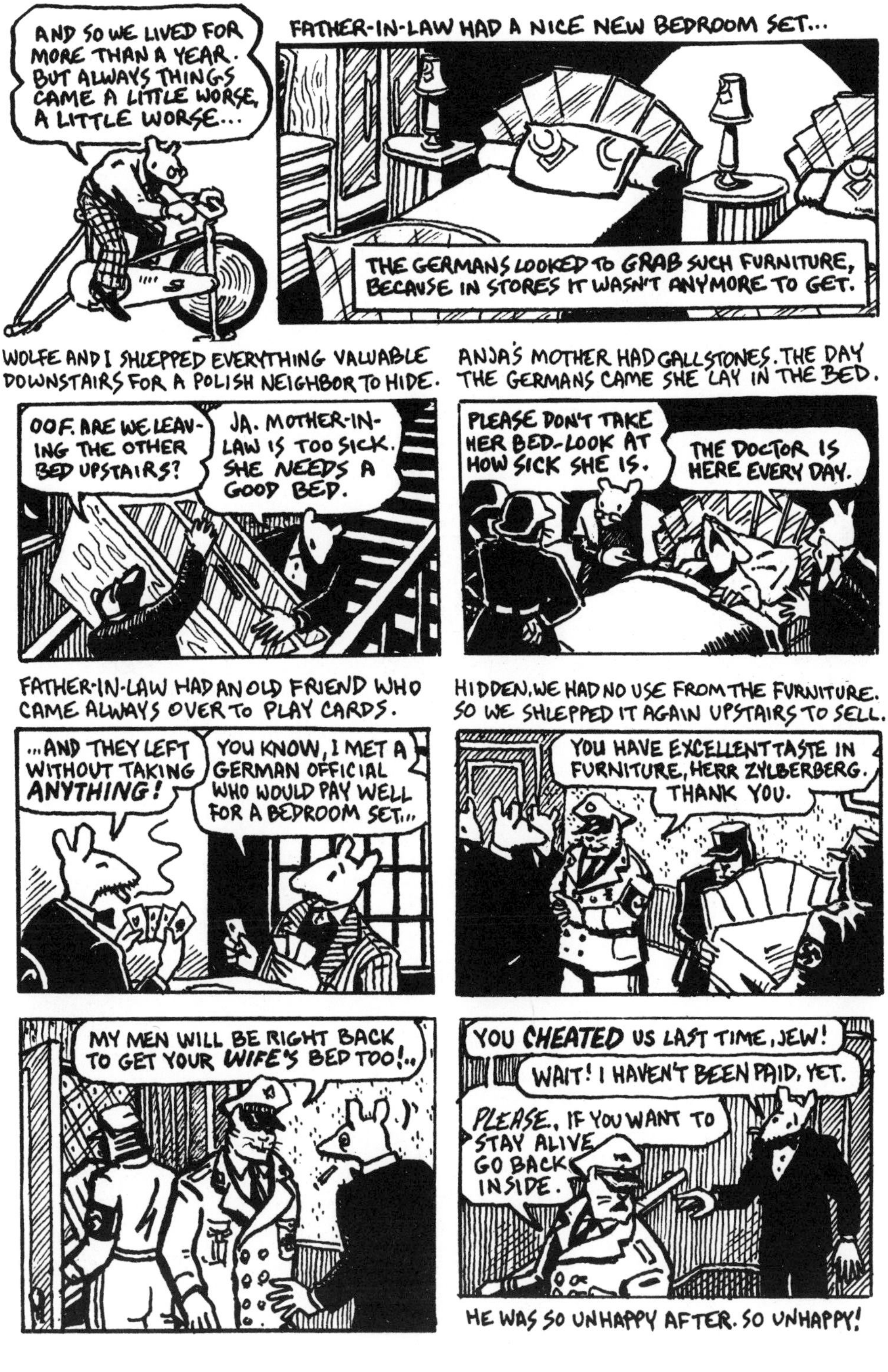
AND SO WE LIVED FOR MORE THAN A YEAR. BUT ALWAYS THINGS CAME A LITTLE WORSE, A LITTLE WORSE...
FATHER-IN-LAW HAD A NICE NEW BEDROOM SET...
THE GERMANS LOOKED TO GRAB SUCH FURNITURE, BECAUSE IN STORES IT WASN'T ANYMORE TO GET.
WOLFE AND I SHLEPPED EVERYTHING VALUABLE DOWNSTAIRS FOR A POLISH NEIGHBOR TO HIDE.
OOF. ARE WE LEAVING THE OTHER BED UPSTAIRS?
JA. MOTHER-IN-LAW IS TOO SICK. SHE NEEDS A GOOD BED.
ANJA'S MOTHER HAD GALLSTONES. THE DAY THE GERMANS CAME SHE LAY IN THE BED.
PLEASE DON'T TAKE HER BED-LOOK AT HOW SICK SHE IS.
THE DOCTOR IS HERE EVERY DAY.
FATHER-IN-LAW HAD AN OLD FRIEND WHO CAME ALWAYS OVER TO PLAY CARDS.
...AND THEY LEFT WITHOUT TAKING ANYTHING!
YOU KNOW, I MET A GERMAN OFFICIAL WHO WOULD PAY WELL FOR A BEDROOM SET...
HIDDEN, WE HAD NO USE FROM THE FURNITURE. SO WE SHLEPPED IT AGAIN UPSTAIRS TO SELL.
YOU HAVE EXCELLENT TASTE IN FURNITURE, HERR ZYLBERBERG.
THANK YOU.
MY MEN WILL BE RIGHT BACK TO GET YOUR WIFE'S BED TOO!..
YOU CHEATED US LAST TIME, JEW!
WAIT! I HAVEN'T BEEN PAID, YET.
PLEASE, IF YOU WANT TO STAY ALIVE GO BACK INSIDE.
HE WAS SO UNHAPPY AFTER. SO UNHAPPY!

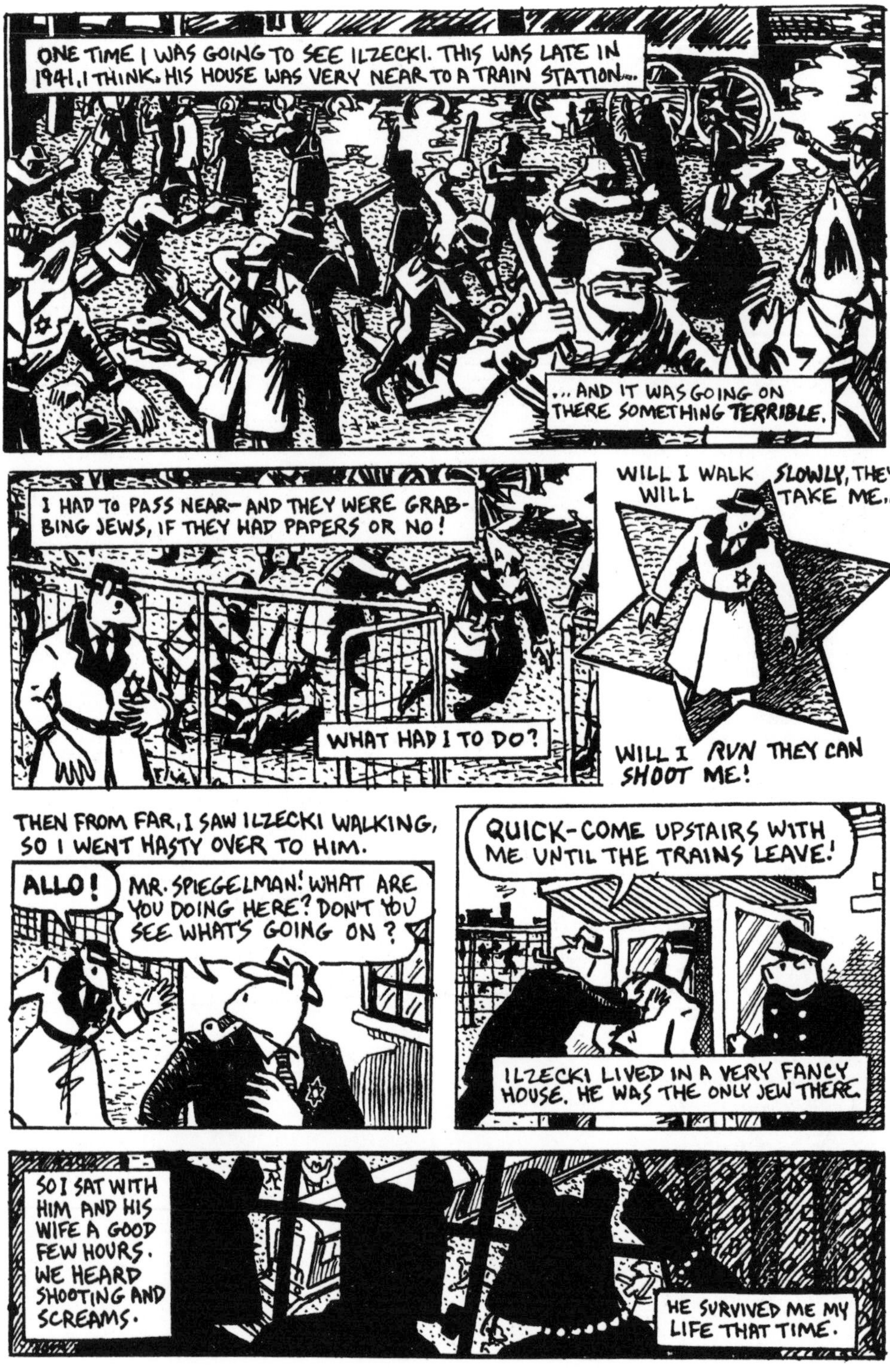
ONE TIME I WAS GOING TO SEE ILZECKI. THIS WAS LATE IN 1941, I THINK. HIS HOUSE WAS VERY NEAR TO A TRAIN STATION...
...AND IT WAS GOING ON THERE SOMETHING TERRIBLE.
I HAD TO PASS NEAR– AND THEY WERE GRABBING JEWS, IF THEY HAD PAPERS OR NO!
WHAT HAD I TO DO?
WILL I WALK SLOWLY, THEY WILL TAKE ME...
WILL I RUN THEY CAN SHOOT ME!
THEN FROM FAR, I SAW ILZECKI WALKING, SO I WENT HASTY OVER TO HIM.
ALLO!
MR. SPIEGELMAN! WHAT ARE YOU DOING HERE? DON'T YOU SEE WHAT'S GOING ON?
QUICK– COME UPSTAIRS WITH ME UNTIL THE TRAINS LEAVE!
ILZECKI LIVED IN A VERY FANCY HOUSE. HE WAS THE ONLY JEW THERE.
SO I SAT WITH HIM AND HIS WIFE A GOOD FEW HOURS. WE HEARD SHOOTING AND SCREAMS.
HE SURVIVED ME MY LIFE THAT TIME.

83

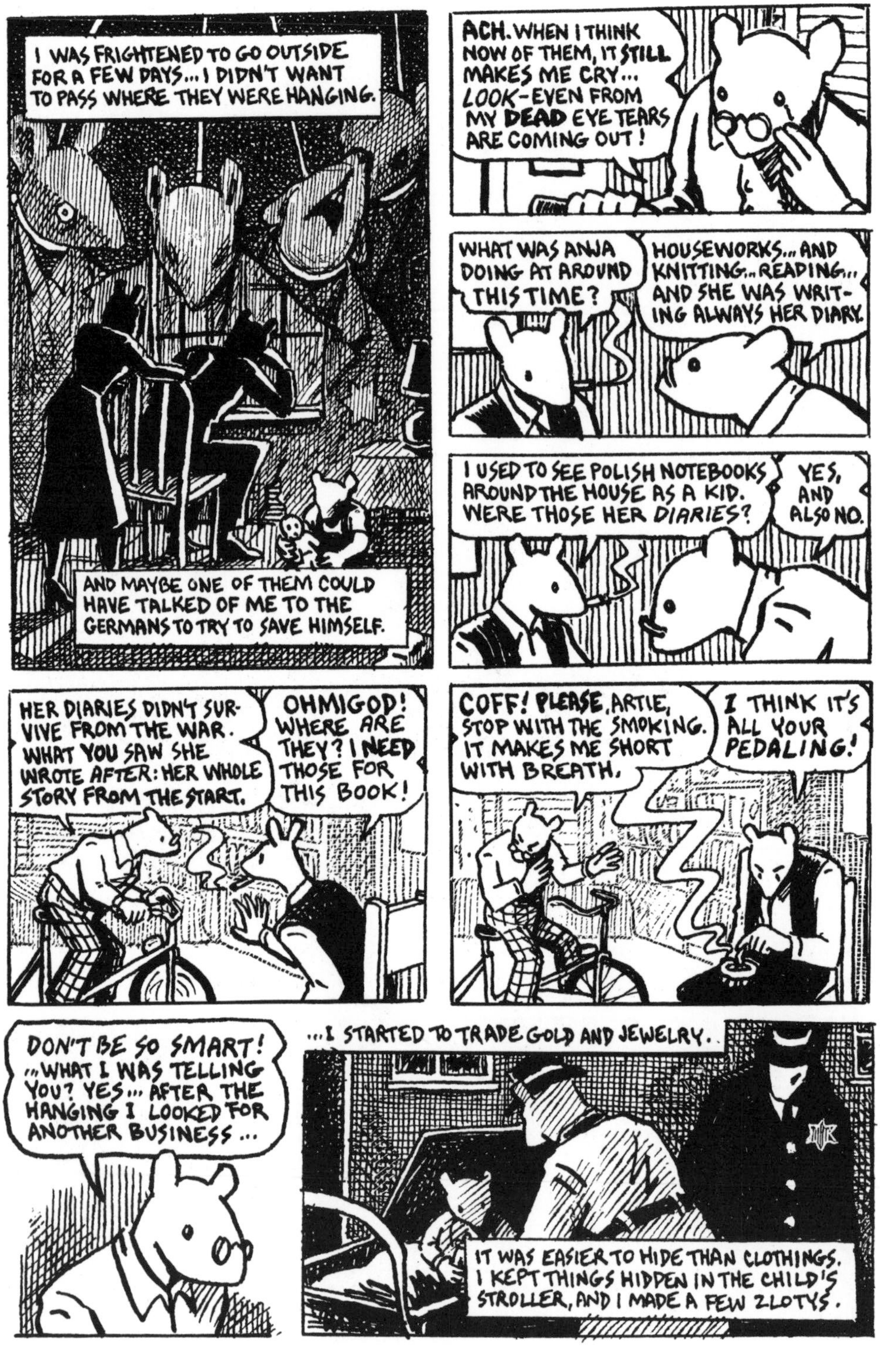
I WAS FRIGHTENED TO GO OUTSIDE FOR A FEW DAYS... I DIDN'T WANT TO PASS WHERE THEY WERE HANGING.
AND MAYBE ONE OF THEM COULD HAVE TALKED OF ME TO THE GERMANS TO TRY TO SAVE HIMSELF.
ACH. WHEN I THINK NOW OF THEM, IT STILL MAKES ME CRY... LOOK- EVEN FROM MY DEAD EYE TEARS ARE COMING OUT!
WHAT WAS ANJA DOING AT AROUND THIS TIME?
HOUSEWORKS... AND KNITTING.. READING... AND SHE WAS WRITING ALWAYS HER DIARY.
I USED TO SEE POLISH NOTEBOOKS AROUND THE HOUSE AS A KID. WERE THOSE HER DIARIES?
YES, AND ALSO NO.
HER DIARIES DIDN'T SURVIVE FROM THE WAR. WHAT YOU SAW SHE WROTE AFTER: HER WHOLE STORY FROM THE START.
OHMIGOD! WHERE ARE THEY? I NEED THOSE FOR THIS BOOK!
COFF! PLEASE, ARTIE, STOP WITH THE SMOKING. IT MAKES ME SHORT WITH BREATH.
I THINK IT'S ALL YOUR PEDALING!
DON'T BE SO SMART! ...WHAT I WAS TELLING YOU? YES... AFTER THE HANGING I LOOKED FOR ANOTHER BUSINESS...
...I STARTED TO TRADE GOLD AND JEWELRY.
IT WAS EASIER TO HIDE THAN CLOTHINGS. I KEPT THINGS HIDDEN IN THE CHILD'S STROLLER, AND I MADE A FEW ZLOTYS.

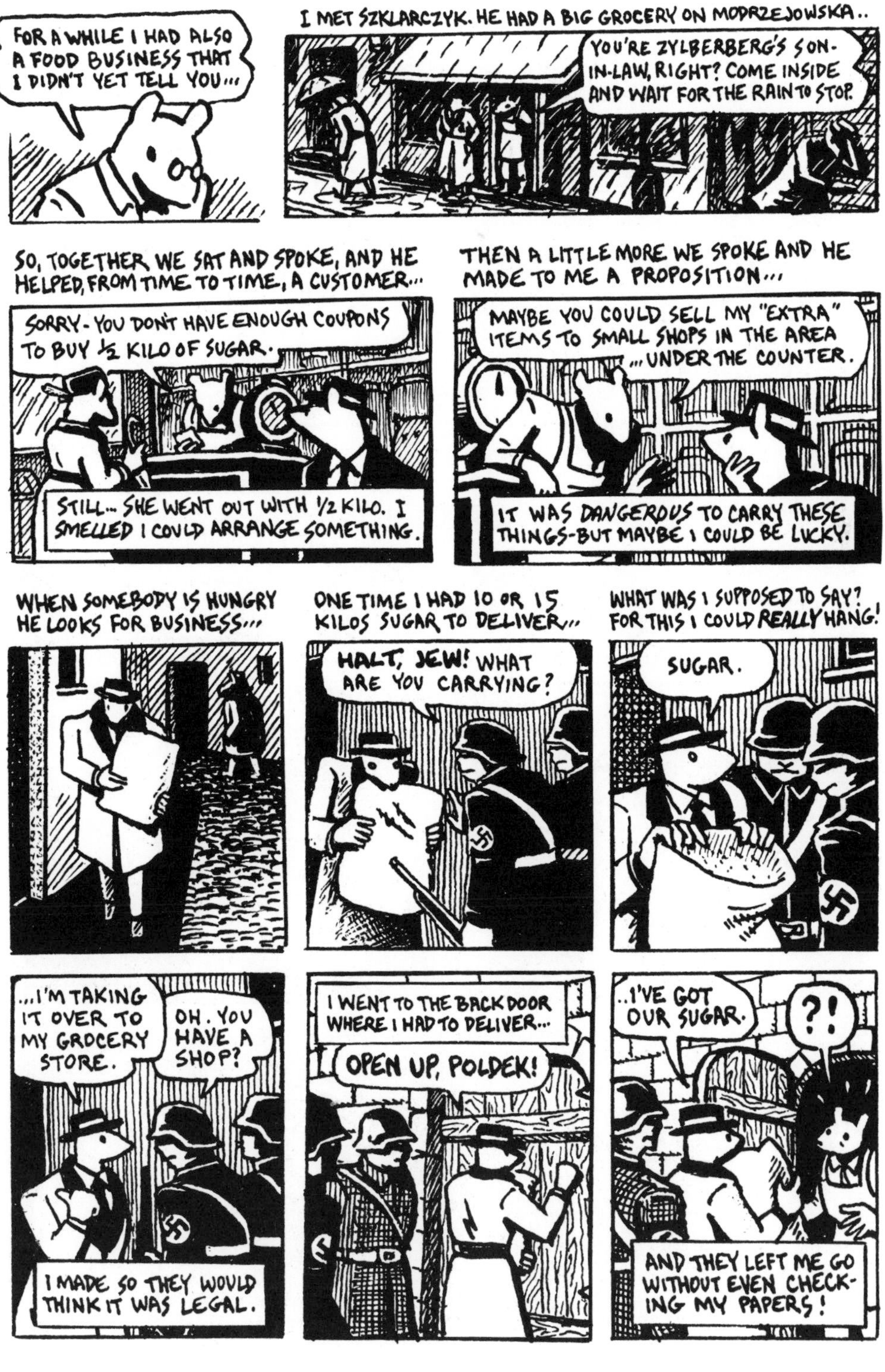
FOR A WHILE I HAD ALSO A FOOD BUSINESS THAT I DIDN'T YET TELL YOU...
I MET SZKLARCZYK. HE HAD A BIG GROCERY ON MODRZEJOWSKA..
YOU'RE ZYLBERBERG'S SON-IN-LAW, RIGHT? COME INSIDE AND WAIT FOR THE RAIN TO STOP.
SO, TOGETHER WE SAT AND SPOKE, AND HE HELPED, FROM TIME TO TIME, A CUSTOMER...
SORRY - YOU DON'T HAVE ENOUGH COUPONS TO BUY 1/2 KILO OF SUGAR.
STILL... SHE WENT OUT WITH 1/2 KILO. I SMELLED I COULD ARRANGE SOMETHING.
THEN A LITTLE MORE WE SPOKE AND HE MADE TO ME A PROPOSITION...
MAYBE YOU COULD SELL MY "EXTRA" ITEMS TO SMALL SHOPS IN THE AREA ...UNDER THE COUNTER.
IT WAS DANGEROUS TO CARRY THESE THINGS - BUT MAYBE I COULD BE LUCKY.
WHEN SOMEBODY IS HUNGRY HE LOOKS FOR BUSINESS...
ONE TIME I HAD 10 OR 15 KILOS SUGAR TO DELIVER...
HALT, JEW! WHAT ARE YOU CARRYING?
WHAT WAS I SUPPOSED TO SAY? FOR THIS I COULD REALLY HANG!
SUGAR.
...I'M TAKING IT OVER TO MY GROCERY STORE.
OH. YOU HAVE A SHOP?
I MADE SO THEY WOULD THINK IT WAS LEGAL.
I WENT TO THE BACK DOOR WHERE I HAD TO DELIVER...
OPEN UP, POLDEK!
..I'VE GOT OUR SUGAR.
?!
AND THEY LEFT ME GO WITHOUT EVEN CHECKING MY PAPERS!

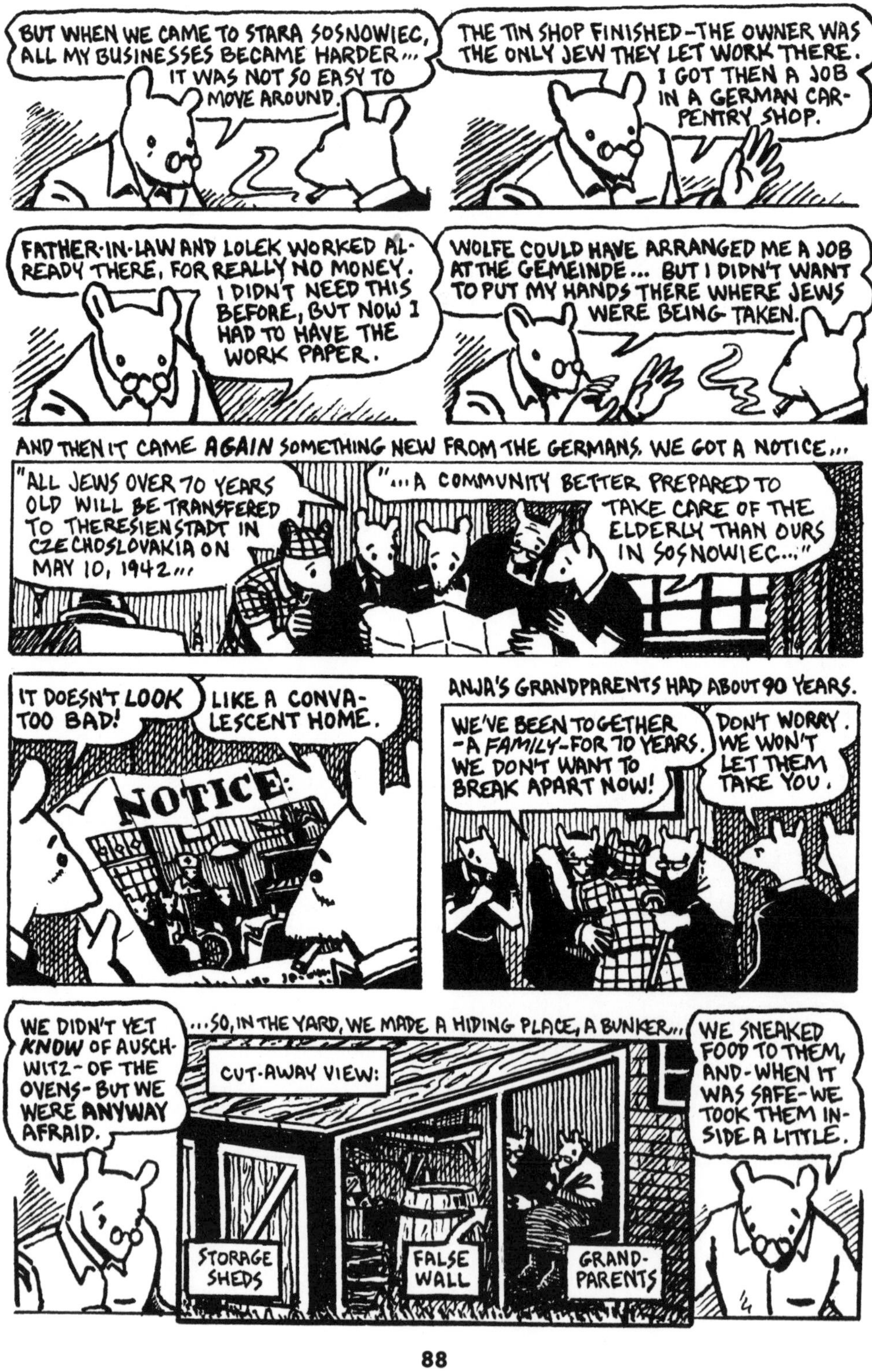

BUT WHEN WE CAME TO STARA SOSNOWIEC, ALL MY BUSINESSES BECAME HARDER... IT WAS NOT SO EASY TO MOVE AROUND.
THE TIN SHOP FINISHED—THE OWNER WAS THE ONLY JEW THEY LET WORK THERE. I GOT THEN A JOB IN A GERMAN CARPENTRY SHOP.
FATHER-IN-LAW AND LOLEK WORKED ALREADY THERE, FOR REALLY NO MONEY. I DIDN'T NEED THIS BEFORE, BUT NOW I HAD TO HAVE THE WORK PAPER.
WOLFE COULD HAVE ARRANGED ME A JOB AT THE GEMEINDE... BUT I DIDN'T WANT TO PUT MY HANDS THERE WHERE JEWS WERE BEING TAKEN.
AND THEN IT CAME **AGAIN** SOMETHING NEW FROM THE GERMANS. WE GOT A NOTICE...
"ALL JEWS OVER 70 YEARS OLD WILL BE TRANSFERED TO THERESIENSTADT IN CZECHOSLOVAKIA ON MAY 10, 1942...
"...A COMMUNITY BETTER PREPARED TO TAKE CARE OF THE ELDERLY THAN OURS IN SOSNOWIEC..."
IT DOESN'T **LOOK** TOO BAD!
LIKE A CONVALESCENT HOME.
NOTICE
ANJA'S GRANDPARENTS HAD ABOUT 90 YEARS.
WE'VE BEEN TOGETHER —A *FAMILY*—FOR 70 YEARS. WE DON'T WANT TO BREAK APART NOW!
DON'T WORRY. WE WON'T LET THEM TAKE YOU.
WE DIDN'T YET **KNOW** OF AUSCHWITZ—OF THE OVENS—BUT WE WERE **ANYWAY** AFRAID.
...SO, IN THE YARD, WE MADE A HIDING PLACE, A BUNKER...
CUT-AWAY VIEW:
STORAGE SHEDS
FALSE WALL
GRAND-PARENTS
WE SNEAKED FOOD TO THEM, AND—WHEN IT WAS SAFE—WE TOOK THEM INSIDE A LITTLE.

89

MY FATHER- HE HAD 62 YEARS - CAME BY STREETCAR TO ME FROM DABROWA, THE VILLAGE NEXT DOOR FROM SOSNOWIEC.

AFTER MY MOTHER DIED WITH CANCER, HE LIVED THERE IN THE HOUSE OF MY SISTER FELA, AND HER FOUR SMALL CHILDREN.

HERE'S A COOKIE, RICHIEU. AUNT FELA BAKED IT FOR YOU.

SAY THANK YOU TO GRANDPA.

I NEED YOUR ADVICE, VLADEK. SHOULD I GO TO THE STADIUM ON WEDNESDAY, OR HIDE AT HOME?

I DON'T KNOW. I'M NOT EVEN SURE WHAT WE'RE GOING TO DO. ...ANJA'S MOTHER SAYS SHE ISN'T GOING. SHE'S SICK AND AFRAID.

AT LEAST ANJA'S FATHER, LOLEK AND I ALL WORK AT THE GERMAN WOODSHOP. WE'RE A LITTLE SAFER. BUT YOU DON'T WORK. YOU HAVE NO PAPERS, YOU DON'T HAVE ANYTHING!

WELL, OUR COUSIN MORDECAI SAYS HE'LL BE AT ONE OF THE INSPECTION TABLES. I COULD BRING MY PAPERS TO HIM...

WHAT DOES FELA SAY?

SHE'S NOT SURE...BUT IF FELA DECIDES TO GO, OF COURSE I'LL GO WITH HER.

CAN I HAVE ANOTHER COOKIE?

RICHIEU!

REALLY, I DIDN'T KNOW HOW TO ADVISE HIM.

BUT FINALLY HE DID GO. PEOPLE WERE AFRAID TO NOT SHOW UP.

SO IT CAME TO THE STADIUM ALMOST ALL THE JEWS OF SOSNOWIEC, AND FROM THE OTHER VILLAGES NEAR, MAYBE 25 OR 30,000 PEOPLE.

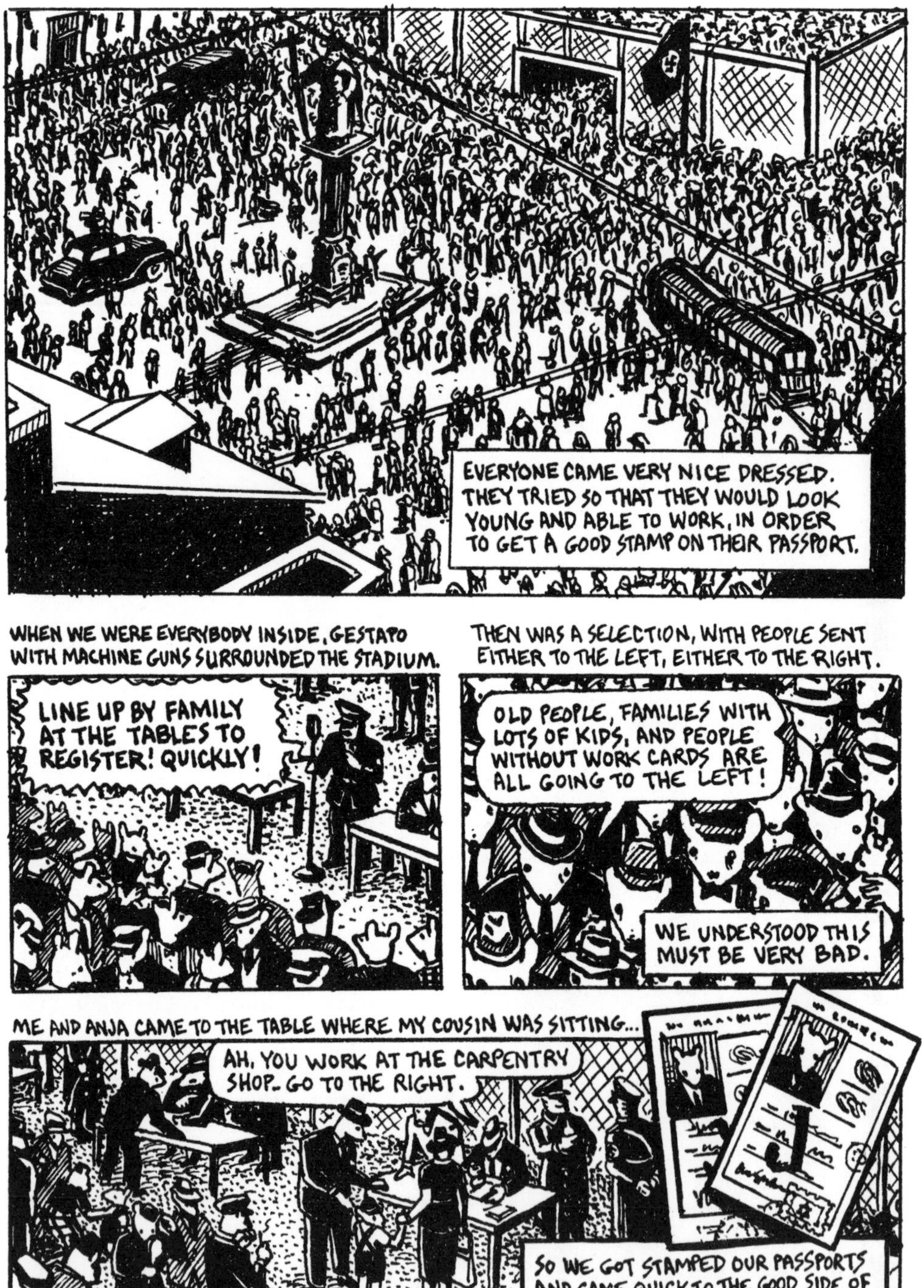
EVERYONE CAME VERY NICE DRESSED. THEY TRIED SO THAT THEY WOULD LOOK YOUNG AND ABLE TO WORK, IN ORDER TO GET A GOOD STAMP ON THEIR PASSPORT.
WHEN WE WERE EVERYBODY INSIDE, GESTAPO WITH MACHINE GUNS SURROUNDED THE STADIUM.
LINE UP BY FAMILY AT THE TABLES TO REGISTER! QUICKLY!
THEN WAS A SELECTION, WITH PEOPLE SENT EITHER TO THE LEFT, EITHER TO THE RIGHT.
OLD PEOPLE, FAMILIES WITH LOTS OF KIDS, AND PEOPLE WITHOUT WORK CARDS ARE ALL GOING TO THE LEFT!
WE UNDERSTOOD THIS MUST BE VERY BAD.
ME AND ANJA CAME TO THE TABLE WHERE MY COUSIN WAS SITTING...
AH, YOU WORK AT THE CARPENTRY SHOP. GO TO THE RIGHT.
SO WE GOT STAMPED OUR PASSPORTS AND CAME QUICK TO THE GOOD SIDE OF THE STADIUM. THOSE THEY SENT LEFT, THEY DIDN'T GET ANY STAMP.

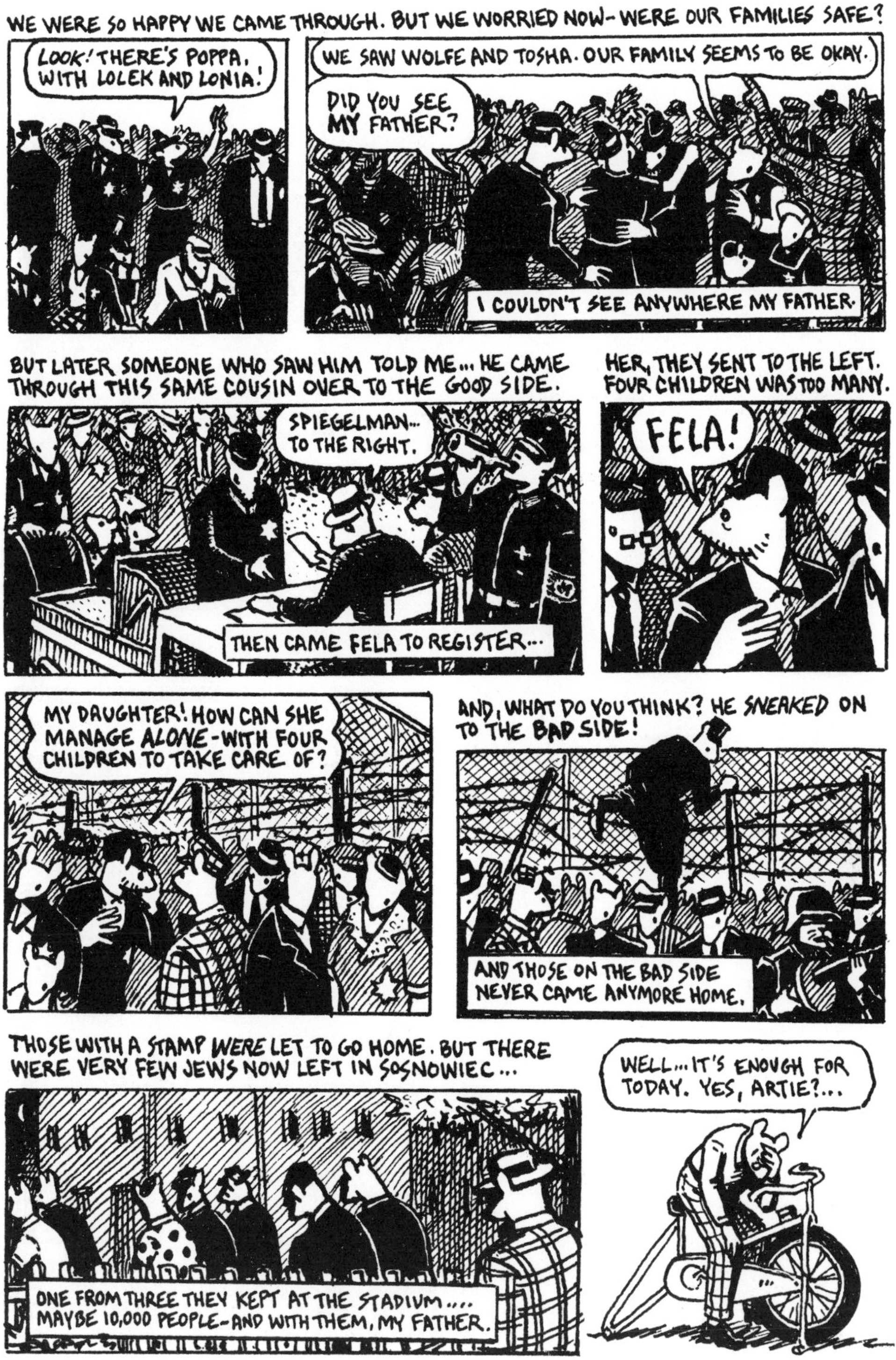
WE WERE SO HAPPY WE CAME THROUGH. BUT WE WORRIED NOW- WERE OUR FAMILIES SAFE?
LOOK! THERE'S POPPA, WITH LOLEK AND LONIA!
WE SAW WOLFE AND TOSHA. OUR FAMILY SEEMS TO BE OKAY.
DID YOU SEE MY FATHER?
I COULDN'T SEE ANYWHERE MY FATHER.
BUT LATER SOMEONE WHO SAW HIM TOLD ME... HE CAME THROUGH THIS SAME COUSIN OVER TO THE GOOD SIDE.
SPIEGELMAN... TO THE RIGHT.
THEN CAME FELA TO REGISTER...
HER, THEY SENT TO THE LEFT. FOUR CHILDREN WAS TOO MANY.
FELA!
MY DAUGHTER! HOW CAN SHE MANAGE ALONE-WITH FOUR CHILDREN TO TAKE CARE OF?
AND, WHAT DO YOU THINK? HE SNEAKED ON TO THE BAD SIDE!
AND THOSE ON THE BAD SIDE NEVER CAME ANYMORE HOME.
THOSE WITH A STAMP WERE LET TO GO HOME. BUT THERE WERE VERY FEW JEWS NOW LEFT IN SOSNOWIEC...
ONE FROM THREE THEY KEPT AT THE STADIUM.... MAYBE 10,000 PEOPLE-AND WITH THEM, MY FATHER.
WELL... IT'S ENOUGH FOR TODAY. YES, ARTIE?...

95

CHAPTER FIVE

MOUSE
HOLES

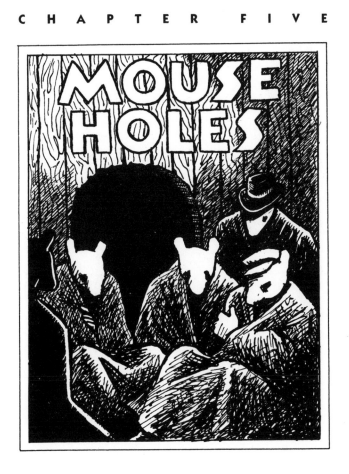

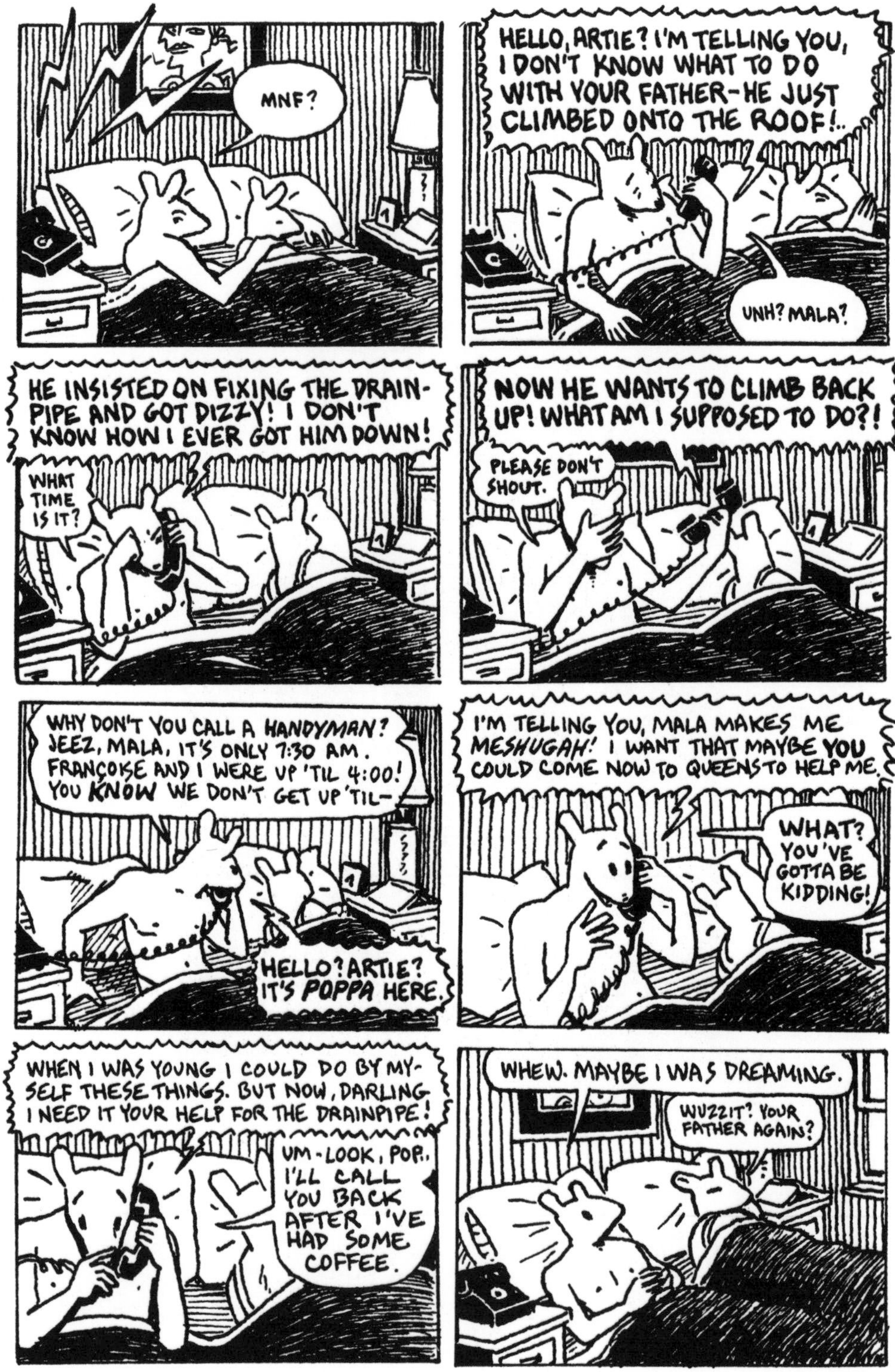
MNF?
HELLO, ARTIE? I'M TELLING YOU, I DON'T KNOW WHAT TO DO WITH YOUR FATHER–HE JUST CLIMBED ONTO THE ROOF!..
UNH? MALA?
HE INSISTED ON FIXING THE DRAIN-PIPE AND GOT DIZZY! I DON'T KNOW HOW I EVER GOT HIM DOWN!
WHAT TIME IS IT?
NOW HE WANTS TO CLIMB BACK UP! WHAT AM I SUPPOSED TO DO?!
PLEASE DON'T SHOUT.
WHY DON'T YOU CALL A HANDYMAN? JEEZ, MALA, IT'S ONLY 7:30 AM. FRANÇOISE AND I WERE UP 'TIL 4:00! YOU KNOW WE DON'T GET UP 'TIL–
HELLO? ARTIE? IT'S POPPA HERE.
I'M TELLING YOU, MALA MAKES ME MESHUGAH! I WANT THAT MAYBE YOU COULD COME NOW TO QUEENS TO HELP ME.
WHAT? YOU'VE GOTTA BE KIDDING!
WHEN I WAS YOUNG I COULD DO BY MYSELF THESE THINGS. BUT NOW, DARLING I NEED IT YOUR HELP FOR THE DRAINPIPE!
UM-LOOK, POP. I'LL CALL YOU BACK AFTER I'VE HAD SOME COFFEE.
WHEW. MAYBE I WAS DREAMING.
WUZZIT? YOUR FATHER AGAIN?

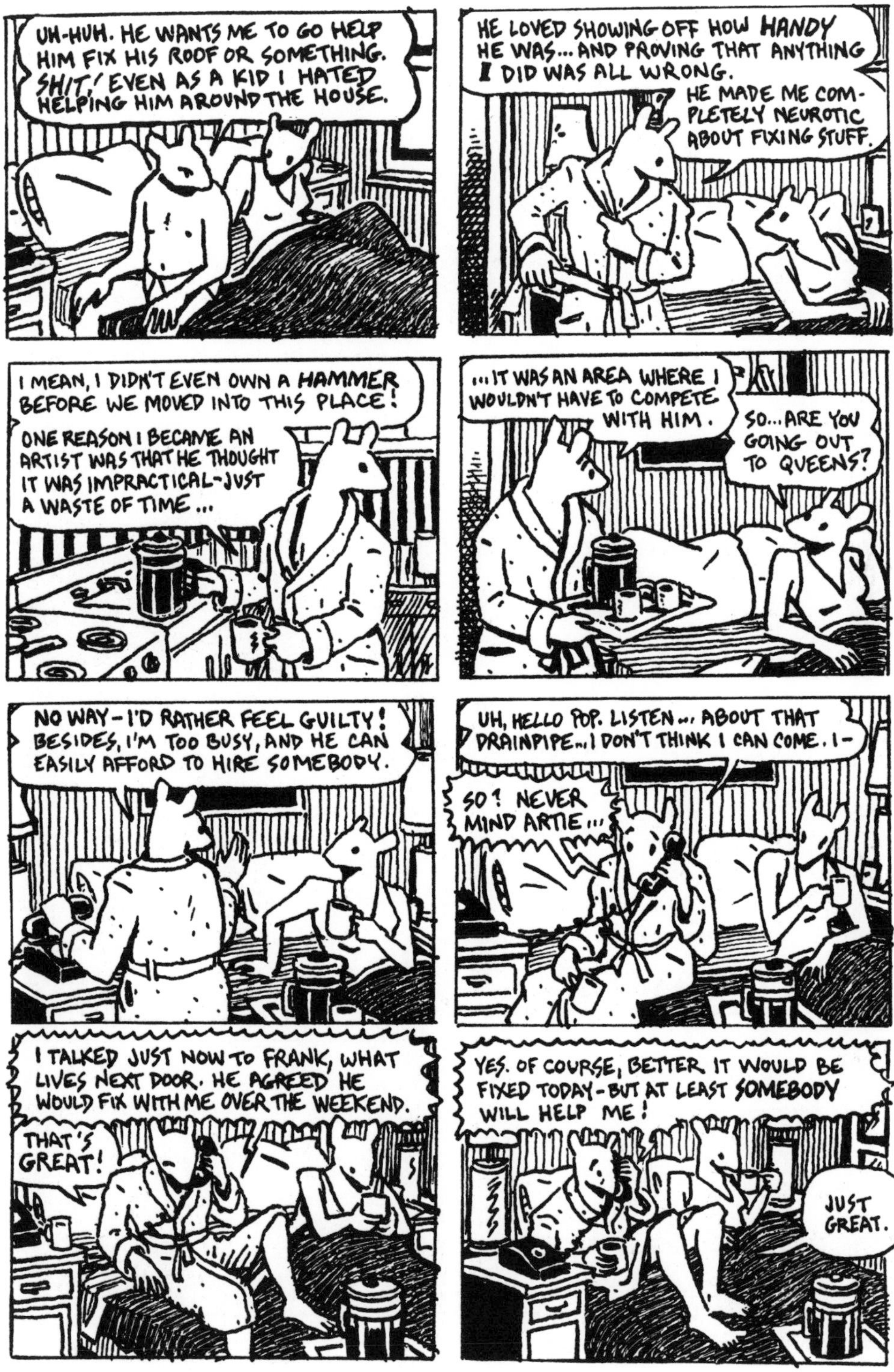

UH-HUH. HE WANTS ME TO GO HELP HIM FIX HIS ROOF OR SOMETHING. SHIT! EVEN AS A KID I HATED HELPING HIM AROUND THE HOUSE.
HE LOVED SHOWING OFF HOW HANDY HE WAS... AND PROVING THAT ANYTHING I DID WAS ALL WRONG.
HE MADE ME COMPLETELY NEUROTIC ABOUT FIXING STUFF.
I MEAN, I DIDN'T EVEN OWN A HAMMER BEFORE WE MOVED INTO THIS PLACE!
ONE REASON I BECAME AN ARTIST WAS THAT HE THOUGHT IT WAS IMPRACTICAL-JUST A WASTE OF TIME...
...IT WAS AN AREA WHERE I WOULDN'T HAVE TO COMPETE WITH HIM.
SO... ARE YOU GOING OUT TO QUEENS?
NO WAY - I'D RATHER FEEL GUILTY! BESIDES, I'M TOO BUSY, AND HE CAN EASILY AFFORD TO HIRE SOMEBODY.
UH, HELLO POP. LISTEN... ABOUT THAT DRAINPIPE... I DON'T THINK I CAN COME. I-
SO? NEVER MIND ARTIE...
I TALKED JUST NOW TO FRANK, WHAT LIVES NEXT DOOR. HE AGREED HE WOULD FIX WITH ME OVER THE WEEKEND.
THAT'S GREAT!
YES. OF COURSE, BETTER IT WOULD BE FIXED TODAY - BUT AT LEAST SOMEBODY WILL HELP ME!
JUST GREAT.

100

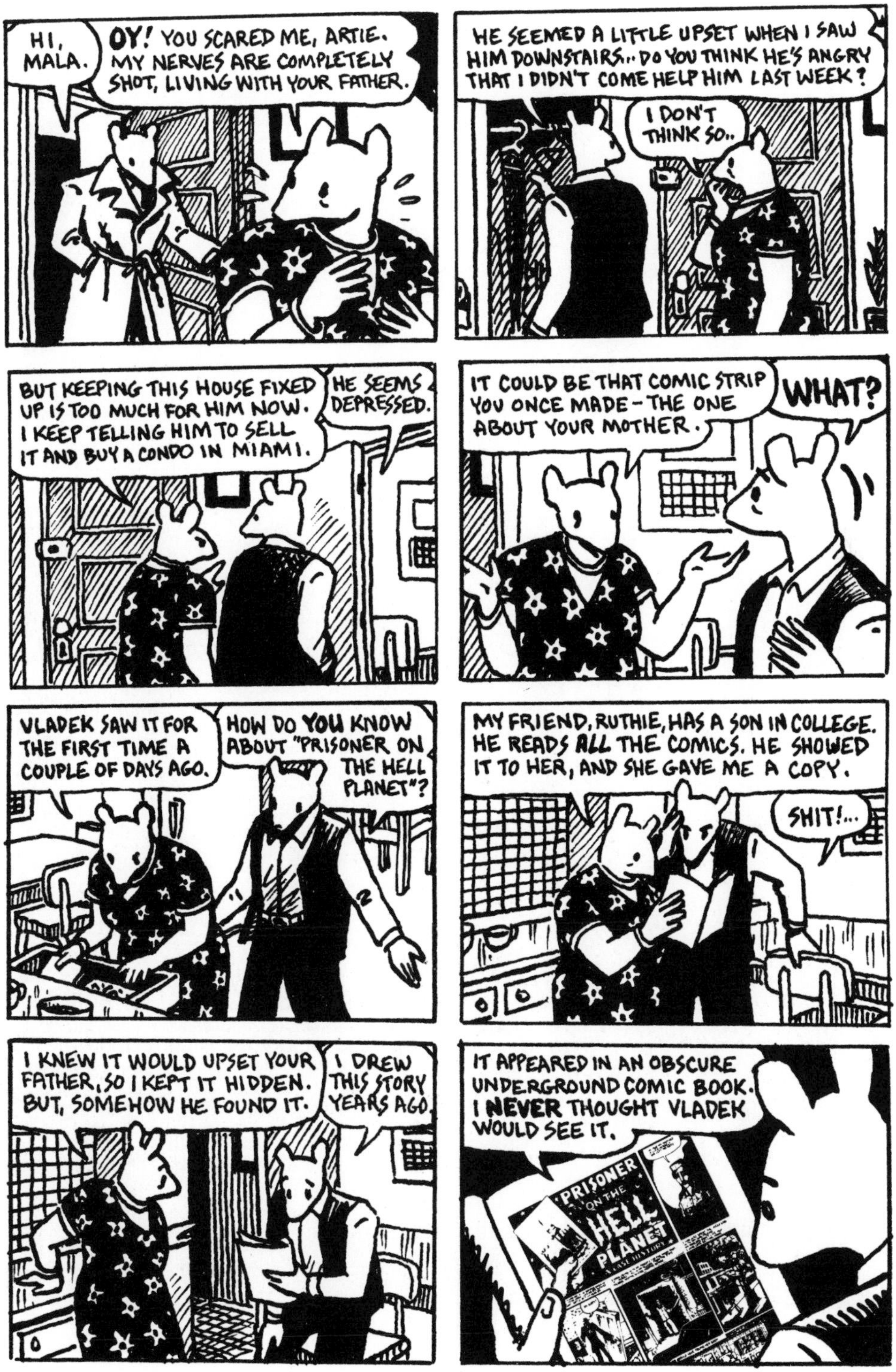
HI, MALA.
OY! YOU SCARED ME, ARTIE. MY NERVES ARE COMPLETELY SHOT, LIVING WITH YOUR FATHER.
HE SEEMED A LITTLE UPSET WHEN I SAW HIM DOWNSTAIRS.. DO YOU THINK HE'S ANGRY THAT I DIDN'T COME HELP HIM LAST WEEK?
I DON'T THINK SO..
BUT KEEPING THIS HOUSE FIXED UP IS TOO MUCH FOR HIM NOW. I KEEP TELLING HIM TO SELL IT AND BUY A CONDO IN MIAMI.
HE SEEMS DEPRESSED.
IT COULD BE THAT COMIC STRIP YOU ONCE MADE - THE ONE ABOUT YOUR MOTHER.
WHAT?
VLADEK SAW IT FOR THE FIRST TIME A COUPLE OF DAYS AGO.
HOW DO YOU KNOW ABOUT "PRISONER ON THE HELL PLANET"?
MY FRIEND, RUTHIE, HAS A SON IN COLLEGE. HE READS ALL THE COMICS. HE SHOWED IT TO HER, AND SHE GAVE ME A COPY.
SHIT!...
I KNEW IT WOULD UPSET YOUR FATHER, SO I KEPT IT HIDDEN. BUT, SOMEHOW HE FOUND IT.
I DREW THIS STORY YEARS AGO.
IT APPEARED IN AN OBSCURE UNDERGROUND COMIC BOOK. I NEVER THOUGHT VLADEK WOULD SEE IT.
PRISONER ON THE HELL PLANET

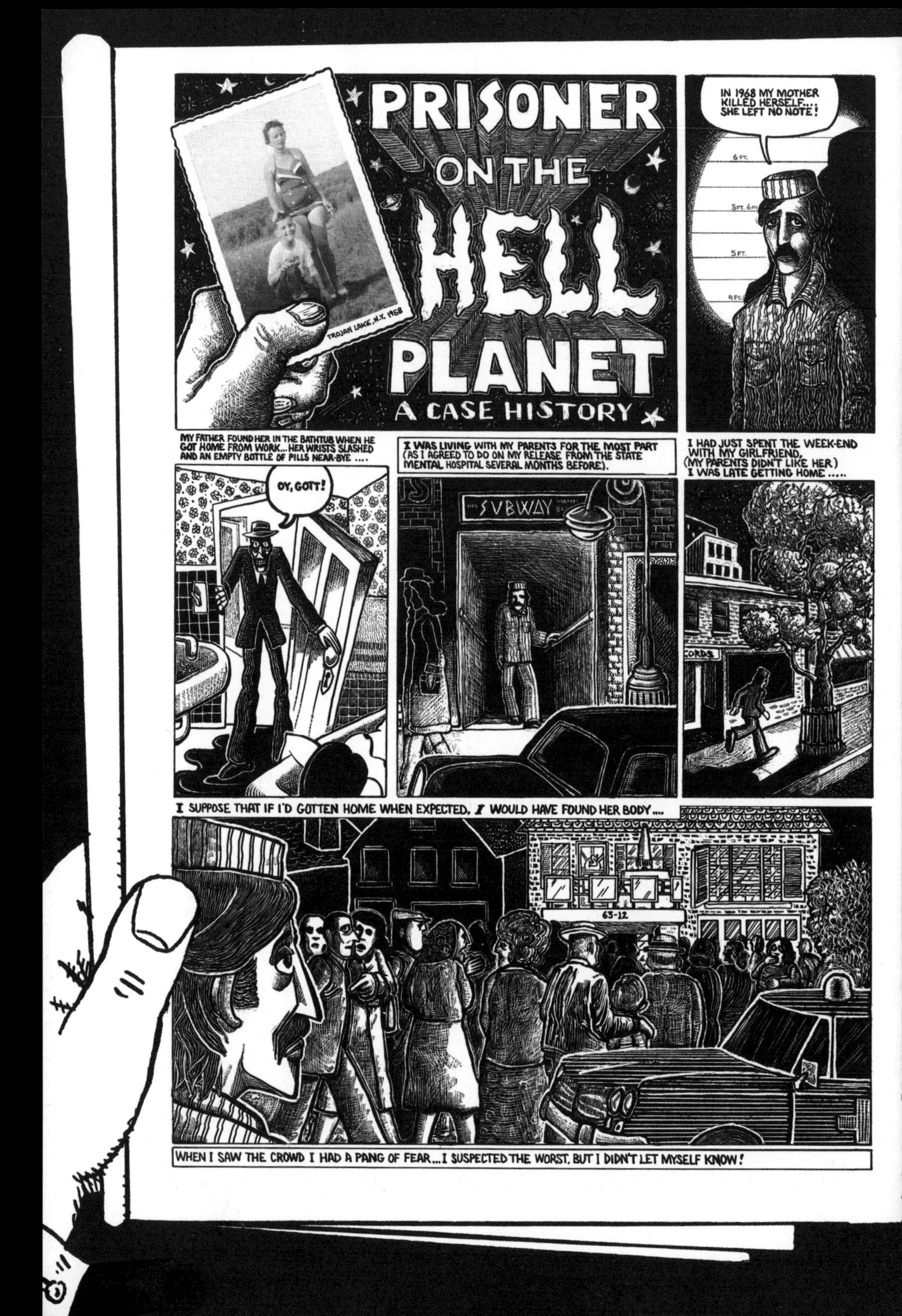
PRISONER ON THE HELL PLANET
A CASE HISTORY
TROJAN LAKE, N.Y. 1968
IN 1968 MY MOTHER KILLED HERSELF... SHE LEFT NO NOTE!
6 FT.
5 FT. 6 IN.
5 FT.
4 FT.
MY FATHER FOUND HER IN THE BATHTUB WHEN HE GOT HOME FROM WORK... HER WRISTS SLASHED AND AN EMPTY BOTTLE OF PILLS NEAR-BYE ....
OY, GOTT!
I WAS LIVING WITH MY PARENTS FOR THE MOST PART (AS I AGREED TO DO ON MY RELEASE FROM THE STATE MENTAL HOSPITAL SEVERAL MONTHS BEFORE).
SUBWAY
I HAD JUST SPENT THE WEEK-END WITH MY GIRLFRIEND, (MY PARENTS DIDN'T LIKE HER) I WAS LATE GETTING HOME .....
CORDS
I SUPPOSE THAT IF I'D GOTTEN HOME WHEN EXPECTED, I WOULD HAVE FOUND HER BODY....
63-12
WHEN I SAW THE CROWD I HAD A PANG OF FEAR... I SUSPECTED THE WORST, BUT I DIDN'T LET MYSELF KNOW!

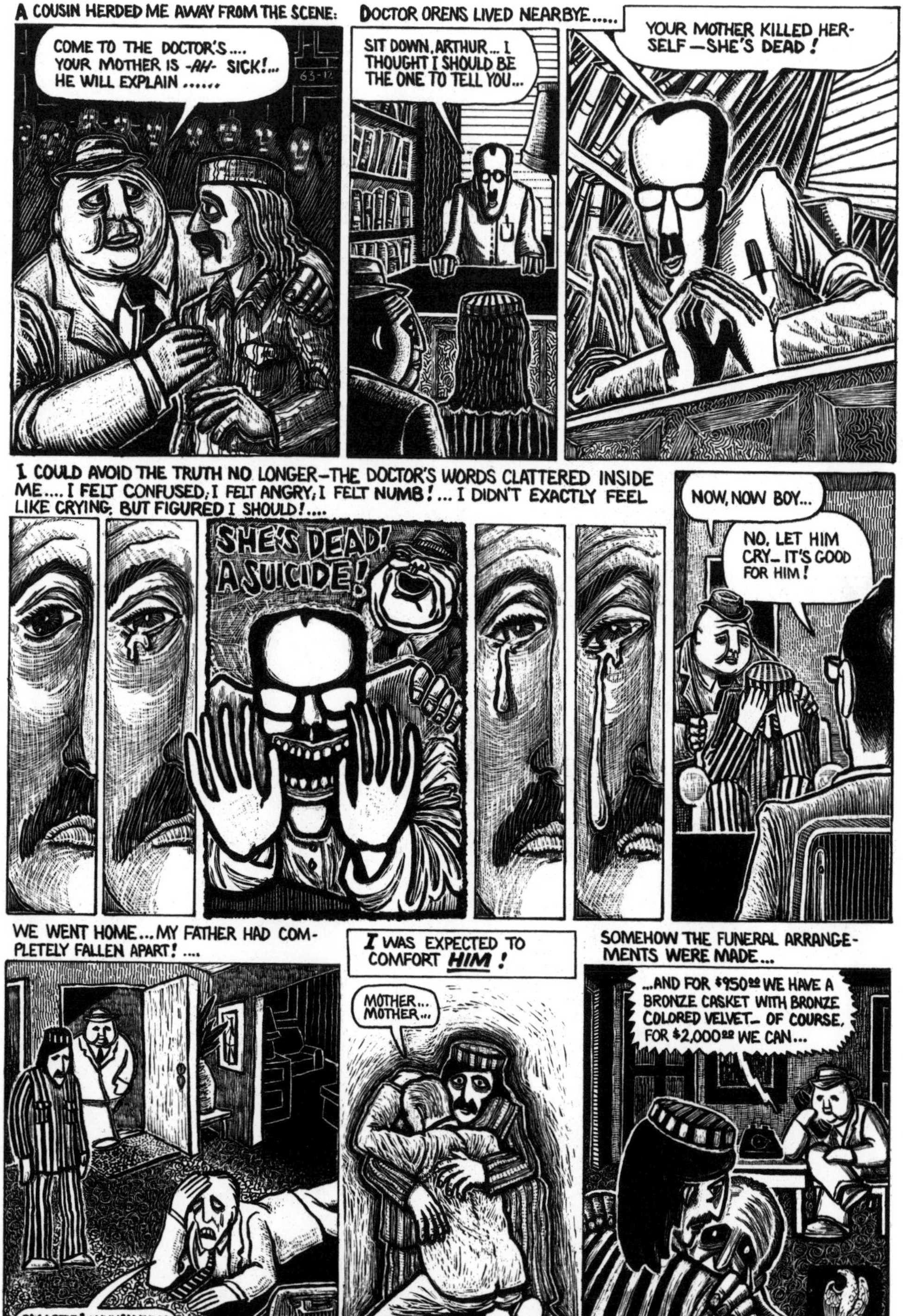
A COUSIN HERDED ME AWAY FROM THE SCENE:
COME TO THE DOCTOR'S.... YOUR MOTHER IS -AH- SICK!... HE WILL EXPLAIN ......
DOCTOR ORENS LIVED NEARBYE.....
SIT DOWN, ARTHUR... I THOUGHT I SHOULD BE THE ONE TO TELL YOU...
YOUR MOTHER KILLED HER-SELF—SHE'S DEAD!
I COULD AVOID THE TRUTH NO LONGER—THE DOCTOR'S WORDS CLATTERED INSIDE ME.... I FELT CONFUSED, I FELT ANGRY, I FELT NUMB!... I DIDN'T EXACTLY FEEL LIKE CRYING, BUT FIGURED I SHOULD!....
SHE'S DEAD! A SUICIDE!
NOW, NOW BOY...
NO, LET HIM CRY— IT'S GOOD FOR HIM!
WE WENT HOME... MY FATHER HAD COMPLETELY FALLEN APART! ....
OY, ARTIE! WHY? WHY! SUCH A TRAGEDY! AND NOT EVEN A NOTE!!!
I WAS EXPECTED TO COMFORT HIM!
MOTHER... MOTHER...
SOMEHOW THE FUNERAL ARRANGEMENTS WERE MADE...
...AND FOR $950.00 WE HAVE A BRONZE CASKET WITH BRONZE COLORED VELVET— OF COURSE, FOR $2,000.00 WE CAN...
PROTECT WHAT YOU HAVE

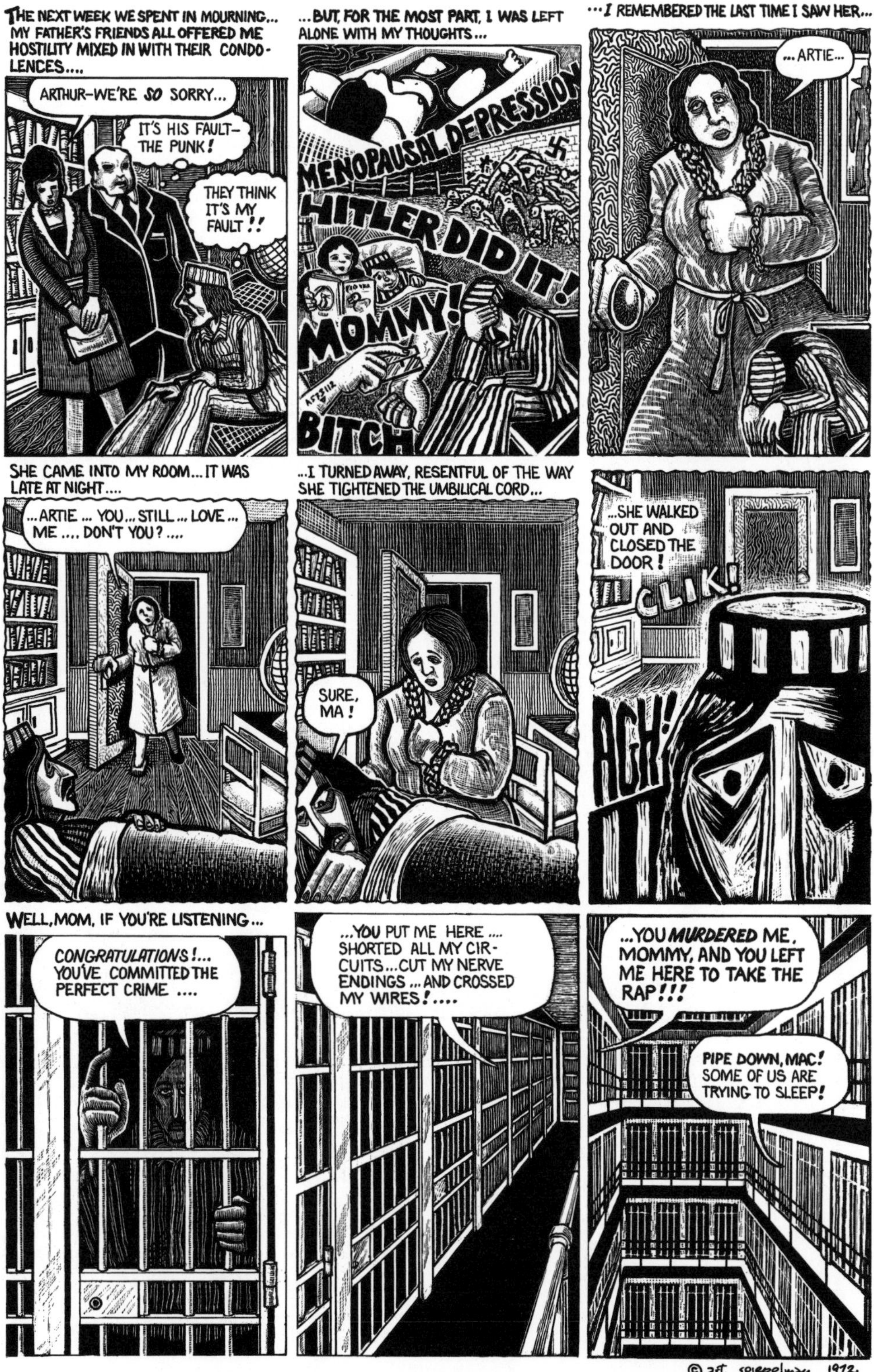
THE NEXT WEEK WE SPENT IN MOURNING... MY FATHER'S FRIENDS ALL OFFERED ME HOSTILITY MIXED IN WITH THEIR CONDO-LENCES....
ARTHUR-WE'RE SO SORRY...
IT'S HIS FAULT-THE PUNK!
THEY THINK IT'S MY FAULT!!
...BUT, FOR THE MOST PART, I WAS LEFT ALONE WITH MY THOUGHTS...
MENOPAUSAL DEPRESSION
HITLER DID IT!
MOMMY!
BITCH
...I REMEMBERED THE LAST TIME I SAW HER...
...ARTIE...
SHE CAME INTO MY ROOM... IT WAS LATE AT NIGHT....
...ARTIE ... YOU... STILL... LOVE... ME .... DON'T YOU? ....
...I TURNED AWAY, RESENTFUL OF THE WAY SHE TIGHTENED THE UMBILICAL CORD...
SURE, MA!
...SHE WALKED OUT AND CLOSED THE DOOR!
CLIK!
AGH!
WELL, MOM, IF YOU'RE LISTENING...
CONGRATULATIONS!... YOU'VE COMMITTED THE PERFECT CRIME ....
...YOU PUT ME HERE .... SHORTED ALL MY CIR-CUITS...CUT MY NERVE ENDINGS ... AND CROSSED MY WIRES!....
...YOU MURDERED ME, MOMMY, AND YOU LEFT ME HERE TO TAKE THE RAP!!!
PIPE DOWN, MAC! SOME OF US ARE TRYING TO SLEEP!

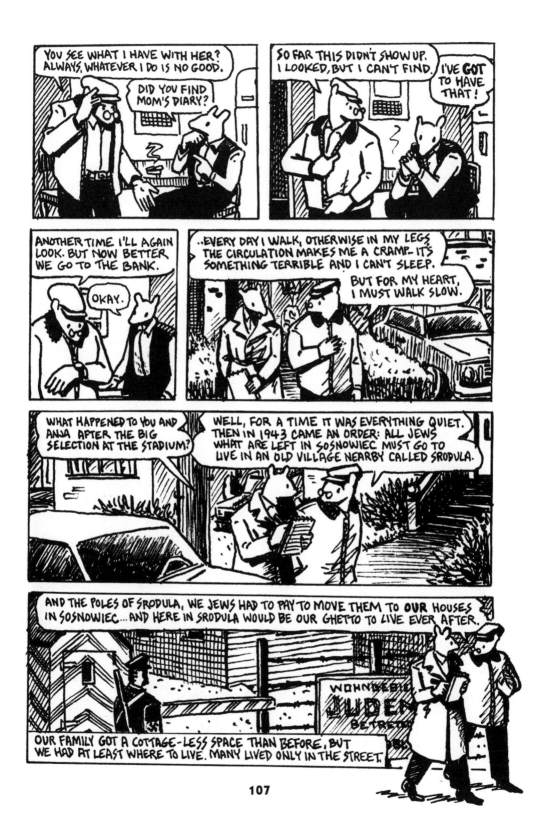

YOU SEE WHAT I HAVE WITH HER? ALWAYS, WHATEVER I DO IS NO GOOD.

DID YOU FIND MOM'S DIARY?

SO FAR THIS DIDN'T SHOW UP. I LOOKED, BUT I CAN'T FIND.

I'VE **GOT** TO HAVE THAT!

ANOTHER TIME I'LL AGAIN LOOK. BUT NOW BETTER WE GO TO THE BANK.

OKAY.

..EVERY DAY I WALK, OTHERWISE IN MY LEGS THE CIRCULATION MAKES ME A CRAMP. IT'S SOMETHING TERRIBLE AND I CAN'T SLEEP.

BUT FOR MY HEART, I MUST WALK SLOW.

WHAT HAPPENED TO YOU AND ANJA AFTER THE BIG SELECTION AT THE STADIUM?

WELL, FOR A TIME IT WAS EVERYTHING QUIET. THEN IN 1943 CAME AN ORDER: ALL JEWS WHAT ARE LEFT IN SOSNOWIEC MUST GO TO LIVE IN AN OLD VILLAGE NEARBY CALLED SRODULA.

AND THE POLES OF SRODULA, WE JEWS HAD TO PAY TO MOVE THEM TO OUR HOUSES IN SOSNOWIEC.... AND HERE IN SRODULA WOULD BE OUR GHETTO TO LIVE EVER AFTER.

WOHNGEBIET JUDEN BETRETEN

OUR FAMILY GOT A COTTAGE-LESS SPACE THAN BEFORE, BUT WE HAD AT LEAST WHERE TO LIVE. MANY LIVED ONLY IN THE STREET.

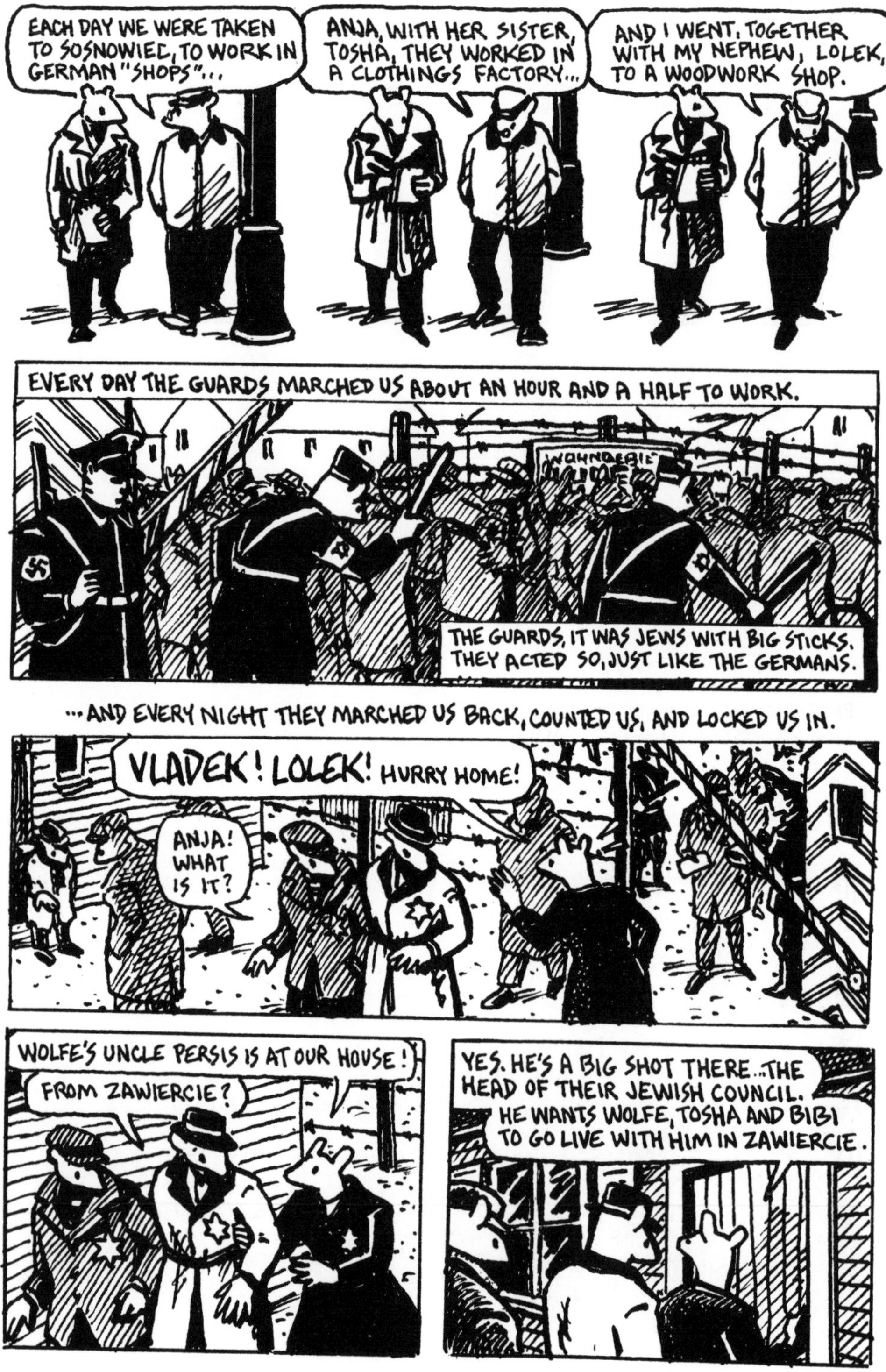
EACH DAY WE WERE TAKEN TO SOSNOWIEC, TO WORK IN GERMAN "SHOPS"...
ANJA, WITH HER SISTER, TOSHA, THEY WORKED IN A CLOTHINGS FACTORY...
AND I WENT, TOGETHER WITH MY NEPHEW, LOLEK, TO A WOODWORK SHOP.
EVERY DAY THE GUARDS MARCHED US ABOUT AN HOUR AND A HALF TO WORK.
THE GUARDS, IT WAS JEWS WITH BIG STICKS. THEY ACTED SO, JUST LIKE THE GERMANS.
...AND EVERY NIGHT THEY MARCHED US BACK, COUNTED US, AND LOCKED US IN.
VLADEK! LOLEK! HURRY HOME!
ANJA! WHAT IS IT?
WOLFE'S UNCLE PERSIS IS AT OUR HOUSE!
FROM ZAWIERCIE?
YES. HE'S A BIG SHOT THERE...THE HEAD OF THEIR JEWISH COUNCIL.
HE WANTS WOLFE, TOSHA AND BIBI TO GO LIVE WITH HIM IN ZAWIERCIE.

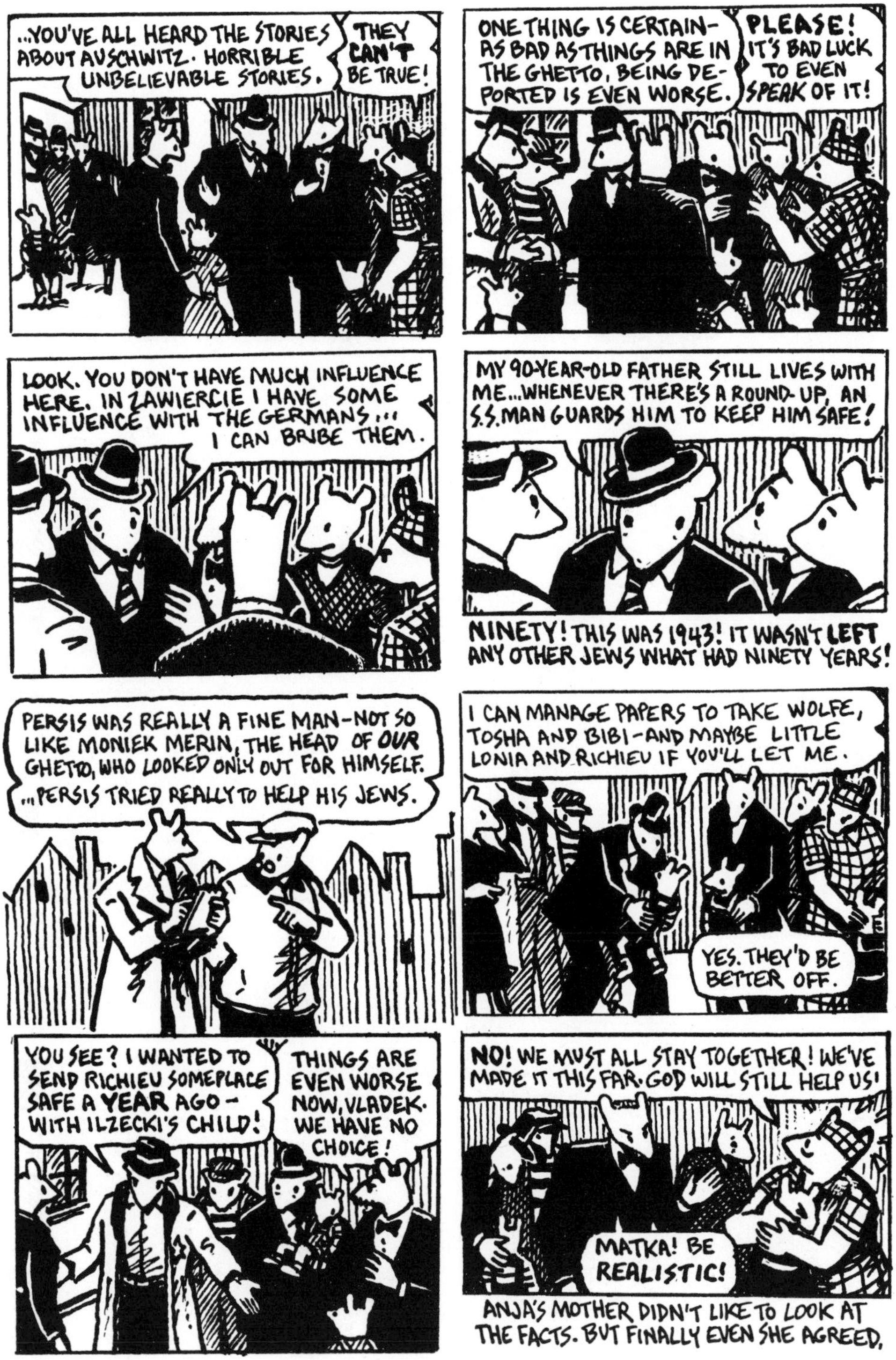
...YOU'VE ALL HEARD THE STORIES ABOUT AUSCHWITZ. HORRIBLE UNBELIEVABLE STORIES.
THEY CAN'T BE TRUE!
ONE THING IS CERTAIN- AS BAD AS THINGS ARE IN THE GHETTO, BEING DEPORTED IS EVEN WORSE.
PLEASE! IT'S BAD LUCK TO EVEN SPEAK OF IT!
LOOK. YOU DON'T HAVE MUCH INFLUENCE HERE. IN ZAWIERCIE I HAVE SOME INFLUENCE WITH THE GERMANS... I CAN BRIBE THEM.
MY 90-YEAR-OLD FATHER STILL LIVES WITH ME...WHENEVER THERE'S A ROUND-UP, AN S.S. MAN GUARDS HIM TO KEEP HIM SAFE!
NINETY! THIS WAS 1943! IT WASN'T LEFT ANY OTHER JEWS WHAT HAD NINETY YEARS!
PERSIS WAS REALLY A FINE MAN-NOT SO LIKE MONIEK MERIN, THE HEAD OF OUR GHETTO, WHO LOOKED ONLY OUT FOR HIMSELF.
...PERSIS TRIED REALLY TO HELP HIS JEWS.
I CAN MANAGE PAPERS TO TAKE WOLFE, TOSHA AND BIBI-AND MAYBE LITTLE LONIA AND RICHIEU IF YOU'LL LET ME.
YES. THEY'D BE BETTER OFF.
YOU SEE? I WANTED TO SEND RICHIEU SOMEPLACE SAFE A YEAR AGO- WITH ILZECKI'S CHILD!
THINGS ARE EVEN WORSE NOW, VLADEK. WE HAVE NO CHOICE!
NO! WE MUST ALL STAY TOGETHER! WE'VE MADE IT THIS FAR. GOD WILL STILL HELP US!
MATKA! BE REALISTIC!
ANJA'S MOTHER DIDN'T LIKE TO LOOK AT THE FACTS. BUT FINALLY EVEN SHE AGREED.

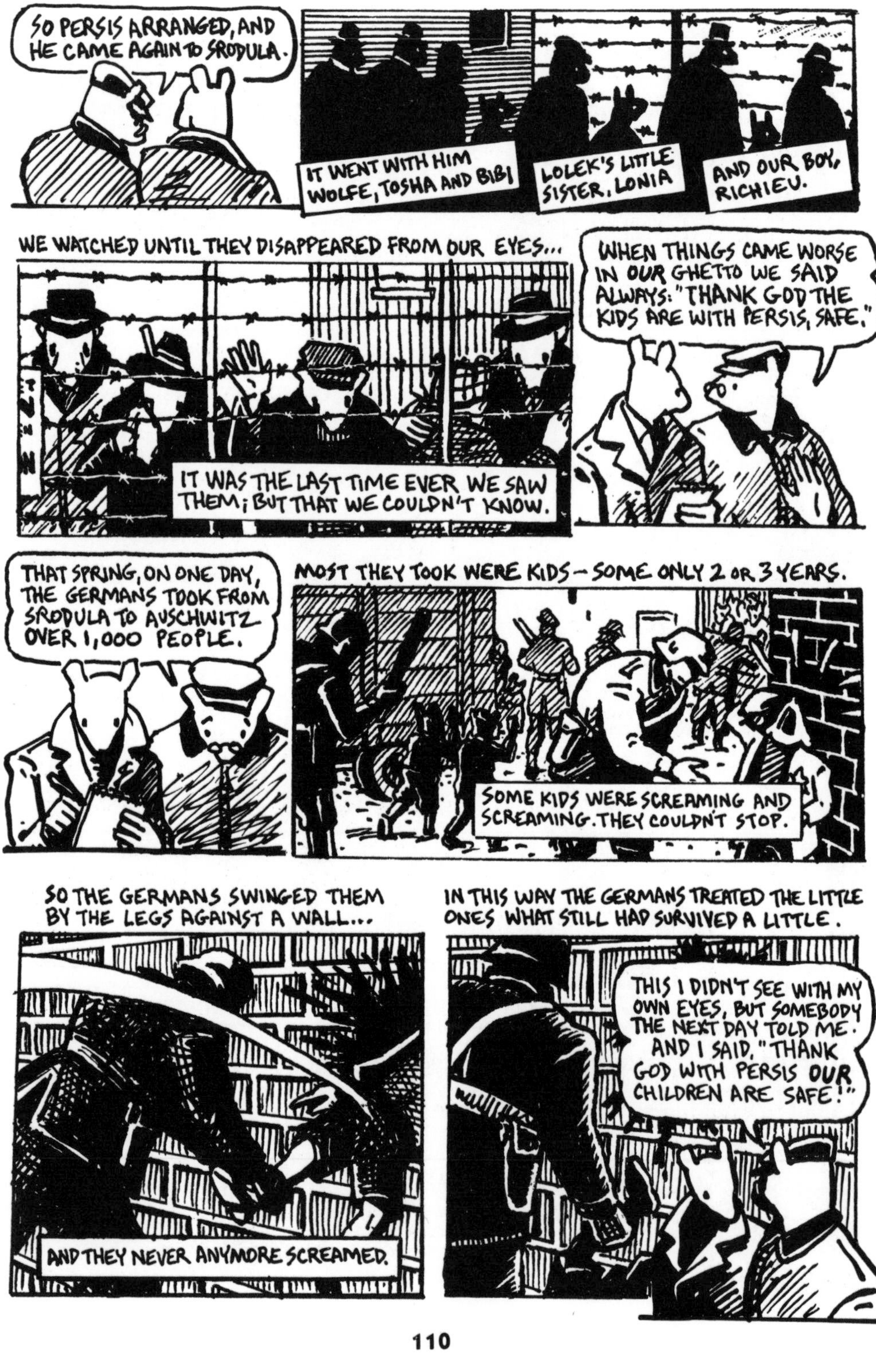
SO PERSIS ARRANGED, AND HE CAME AGAIN TO SRODULA.
IT WENT WITH HIM WOLFE, TOSHA AND BIBI
LOLEK'S LITTLE SISTER, LONIA
AND OUR BOY, RICHIEU.
WE WATCHED UNTIL THEY DISAPPEARED FROM OUR EYES...
IT WAS THE LAST TIME EVER WE SAW THEM; BUT THAT WE COULDN'T KNOW.
WHEN THINGS CAME WORSE IN OUR GHETTO WE SAID ALWAYS: "THANK GOD THE KIDS ARE WITH PERSIS, SAFE."
THAT SPRING, ON ONE DAY, THE GERMANS TOOK FROM SRODULA TO AUSCHWITZ OVER 1,000 PEOPLE.
MOST THEY TOOK WERE KIDS — SOME ONLY 2 OR 3 YEARS.
SOME KIDS WERE SCREAMING AND SCREAMING. THEY COULDN'T STOP.
SO THE GERMANS SWINGED THEM BY THE LEGS AGAINST A WALL...
AND THEY NEVER ANYMORE SCREAMED.
IN THIS WAY THE GERMANS TREATED THE LITTLE ONES WHAT STILL HAD SURVIVED A LITTLE.
THIS I DIDN'T SEE WITH MY OWN EYES, BUT SOMEBODY THE NEXT DAY TOLD ME. AND I SAID, "THANK GOD WITH PERSIS OUR CHILDREN ARE SAFE!"

111

113

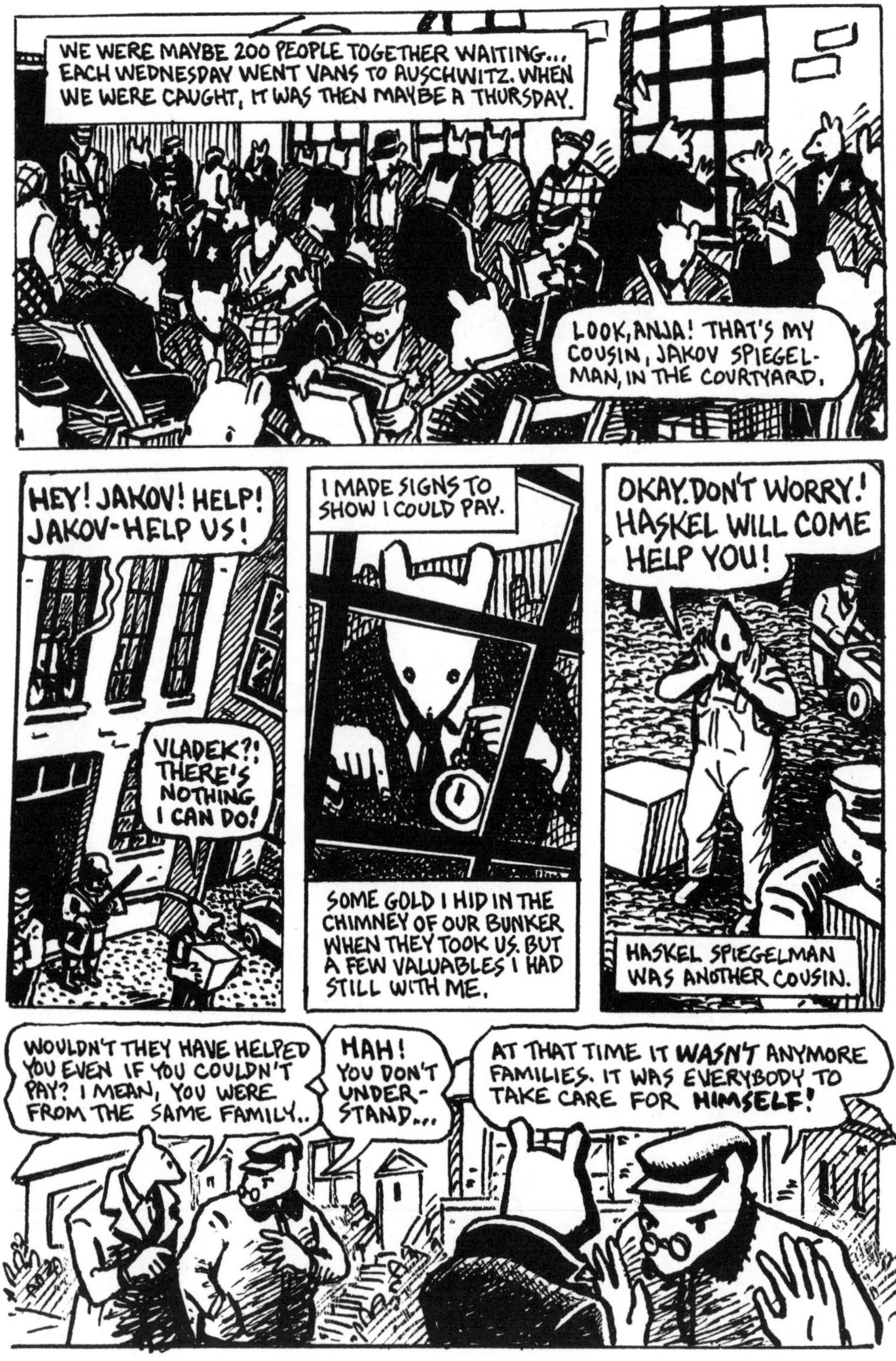
WE WERE MAYBE 200 PEOPLE TOGETHER WAITING... EACH WEDNESDAY WENT VANS TO AUSCHWITZ. WHEN WE WERE CAUGHT, IT WAS THEN MAYBE A THURSDAY.
LOOK, ANJA! THAT'S MY COUSIN, JAKOV SPIEGELMAN, IN THE COURTYARD.
HEY! JAKOV! HELP! JAKOV-HELP US!
VLADEK?! THERE'S NOTHING I CAN DO!
I MADE SIGNS TO SHOW I COULD PAY.
SOME GOLD I HID IN THE CHIMNEY OF OUR BUNKER WHEN THEY TOOK US. BUT A FEW VALUABLES I HAD STILL WITH ME.
OKAY. DON'T WORRY! HASKEL WILL COME HELP YOU!
HASKEL SPIEGELMAN WAS ANOTHER COUSIN.
WOULDN'T THEY HAVE HELPED YOU EVEN IF YOU COULDN'T PAY? I MEAN, YOU WERE FROM THE SAME FAMILY..
HAH! YOU DON'T UNDERSTAND...
AT THAT TIME IT **WASN'T** ANYMORE FAMILIES. IT WAS EVERYBODY TO TAKE CARE FOR **HIMSELF**!

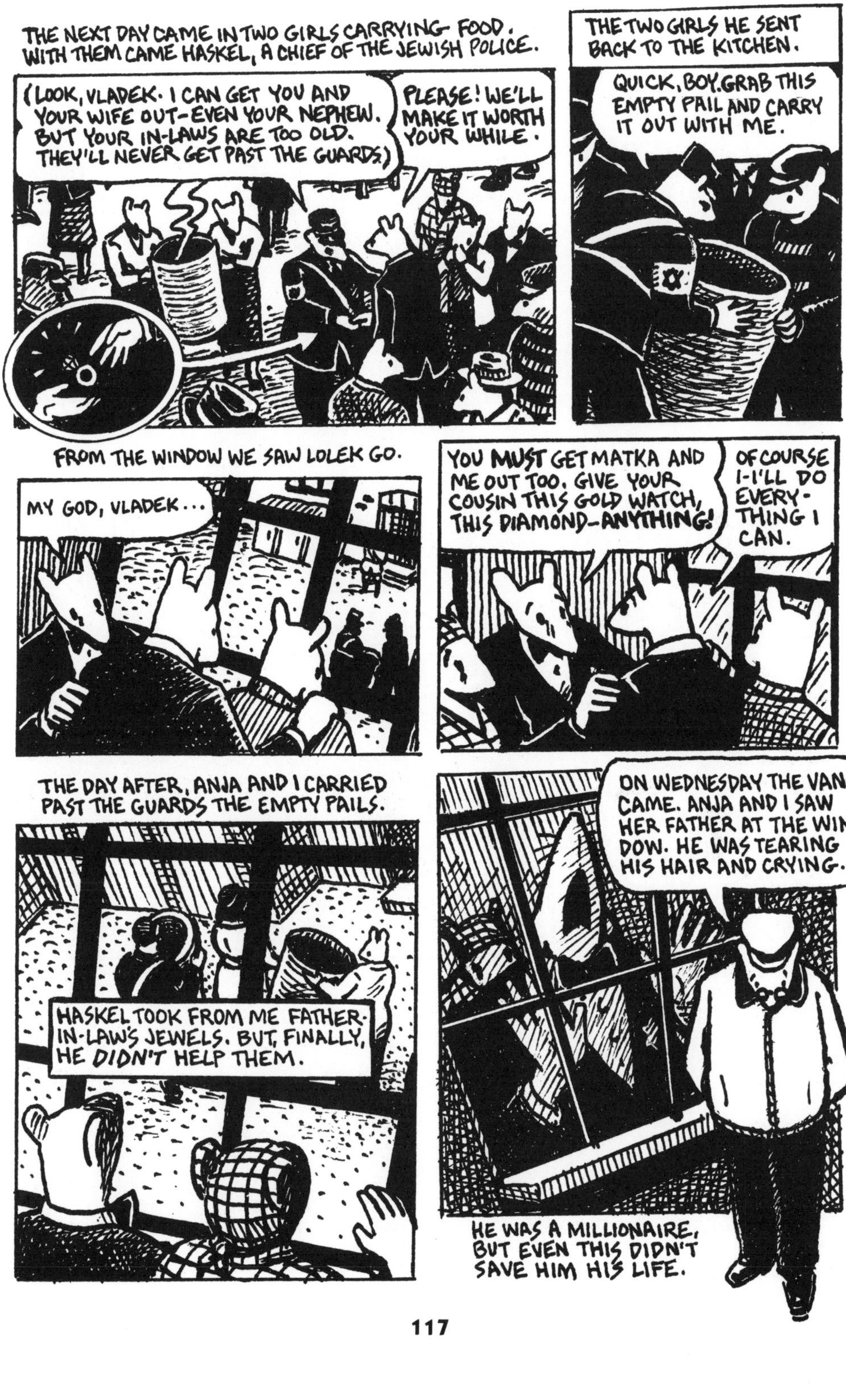
THE NEXT DAY CAME IN TWO GIRLS CARRYING FOOD. WITH THEM CAME HASKEL, A CHIEF OF THE JEWISH POLICE.
(LOOK, VLADEK. I CAN GET YOU AND YOUR WIFE OUT-EVEN YOUR NEPHEW. BUT YOUR IN-LAWS ARE TOO OLD. THEY'LL NEVER GET PAST THE GUARDS.)
PLEASE! WE'LL MAKE IT WORTH YOUR WHILE.
THE TWO GIRLS HE SENT BACK TO THE KITCHEN.
QUICK, BOY. GRAB THIS EMPTY PAIL AND CARRY IT OUT WITH ME.
FROM THE WINDOW WE SAW LOLEK GO.
MY GOD, VLADEK...
YOU MUST GET MATKA AND ME OUT TOO. GIVE YOUR COUSIN THIS GOLD WATCH, THIS DIAMOND-ANYTHING!
OF COURSE I-I'LL DO EVERYTHING I CAN.
THE DAY AFTER, ANJA AND I CARRIED PAST THE GUARDS THE EMPTY PAILS.
HASKEL TOOK FROM ME FATHER-IN-LAW'S JEWELS. BUT, FINALLY, HE DIDN'T HELP THEM.
ON WEDNESDAY THE VANS CAME. ANJA AND I SAW HER FATHER AT THE WINDOW. HE WAS TEARING HIS HAIR AND CRYING.
HE WAS A MILLIONAIRE, BUT EVEN THIS DIDN'T SAVE HIM HIS LIFE.

118

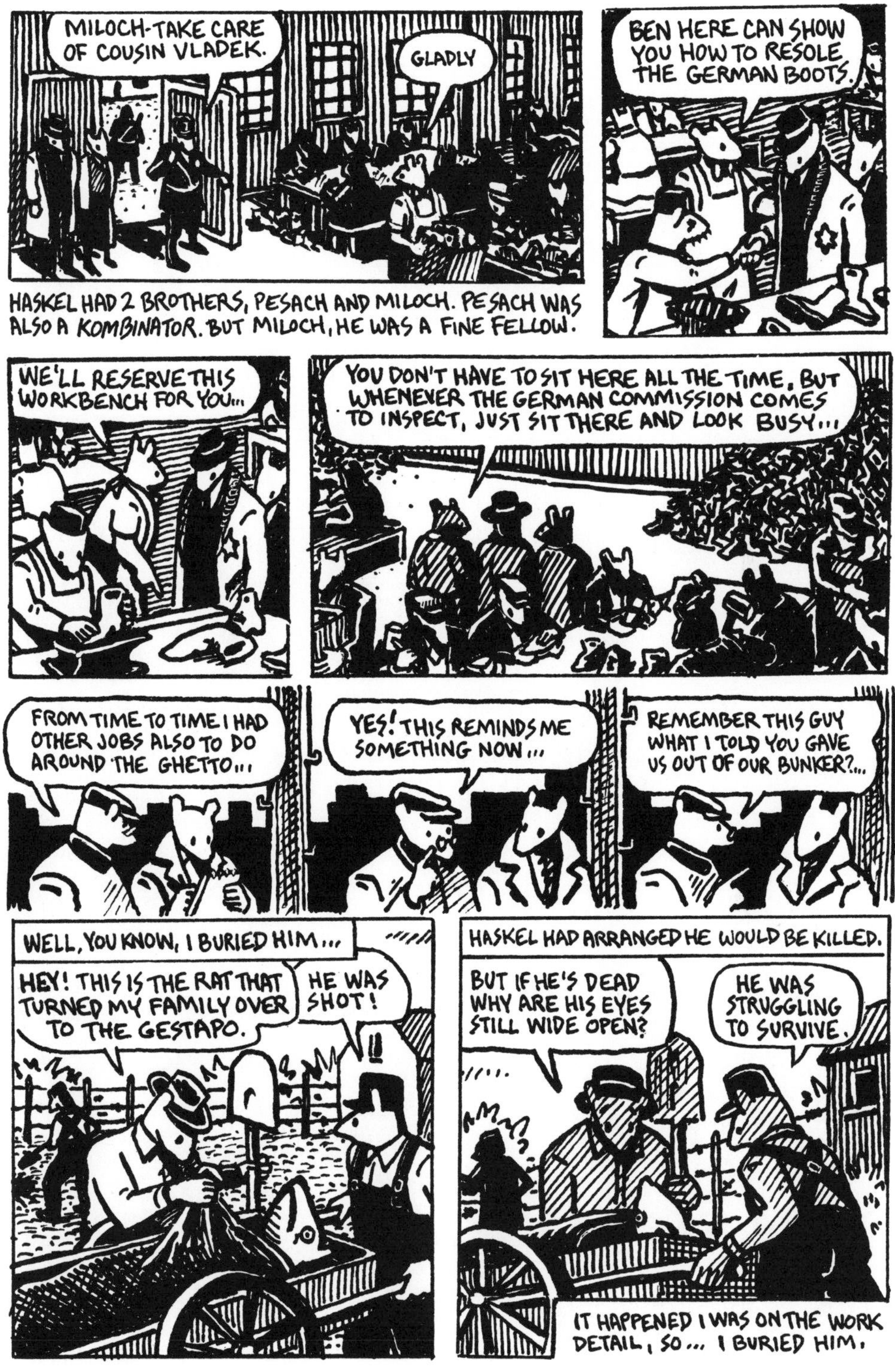
MILOCH-TAKE CARE OF COUSIN VLADEK.
GLADLY
HASKEL HAD 2 BROTHERS, PESACH AND MILOCH. PESACH WAS ALSO A *KOMBINATOR*. BUT MILOCH, HE WAS A FINE FELLOW.
BEN HERE CAN SHOW YOU HOW TO RESOLE THE GERMAN BOOTS.
WE'LL RESERVE THIS WORKBENCH FOR YOU...
YOU DON'T HAVE TO SIT HERE ALL THE TIME, BUT WHENEVER THE GERMAN COMMISSION COMES TO INSPECT, JUST SIT THERE AND LOOK BUSY...
FROM TIME TO TIME I HAD OTHER JOBS ALSO TO DO AROUND THE GHETTO...
YES! THIS REMINDS ME SOMETHING NOW...
REMEMBER THIS GUY WHAT I TOLD YOU GAVE US OUT OF OUR BUNKER?...
WELL, YOU KNOW, I BURIED HIM...
HEY! THIS IS THE RAT THAT TURNED MY FAMILY OVER TO THE GESTAPO.
HE WAS SHOT!
!!
HASKEL HAD ARRANGED HE WOULD BE KILLED.
BUT IF HE'S DEAD WHY ARE HIS EYES STILL WIDE OPEN?
HE WAS STRUGGLING TO SURVIVE.
IT HAPPENED I WAS ON THE WORK DETAIL, SO... I BURIED HIM.

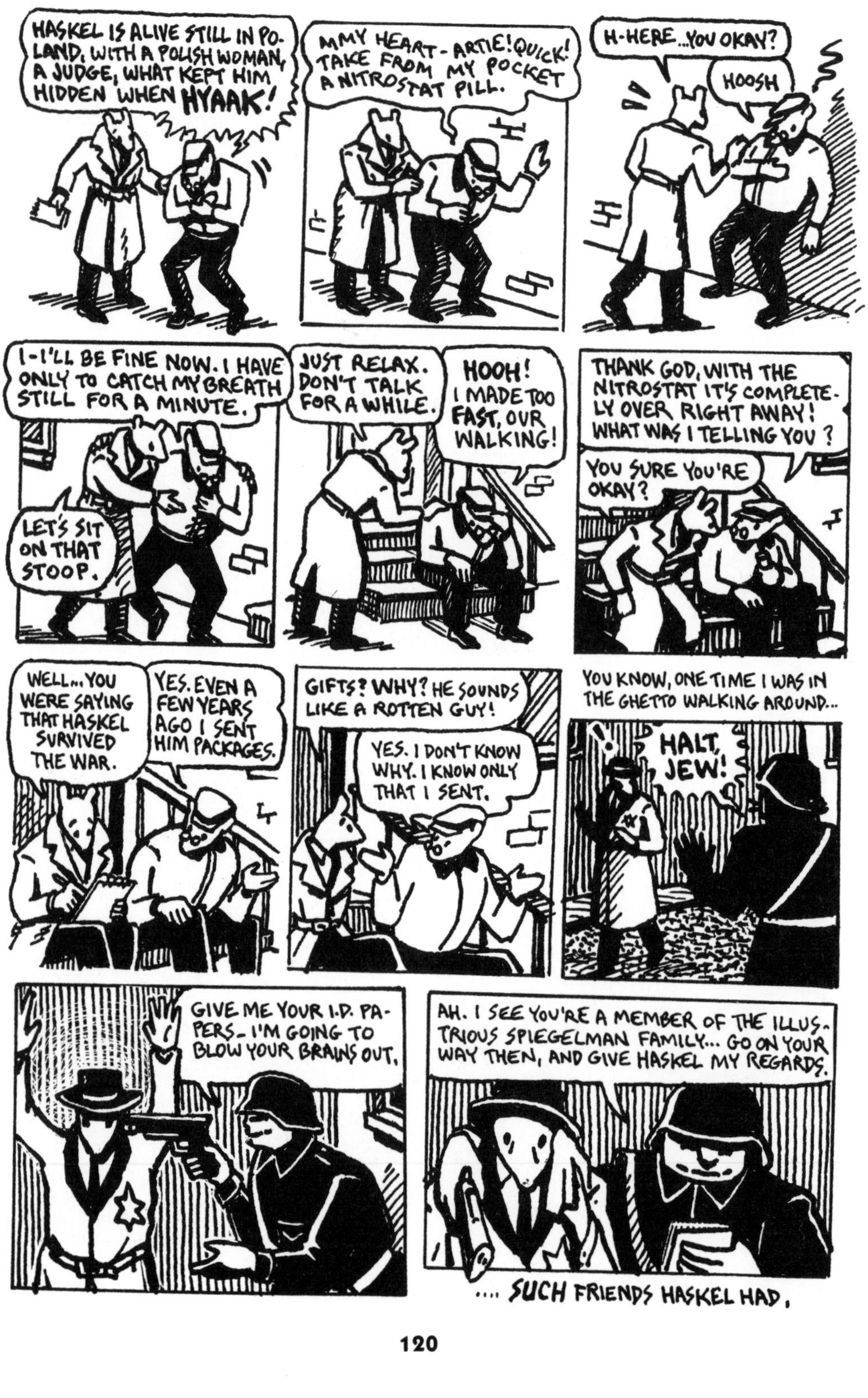
HASKEL IS ALIVE STILL IN POLAND, WITH A POLISH WOMAN, A JUDGE, WHAT KEPT HIM HIDDEN WHEN HYAAK!
MMY HEART - ARTIE! QUICK! TAKE FROM MY POCKET A NITROSTAT PILL.
H-HERE...YOU OKAY?
HOOSH
I-I'LL BE FINE NOW. I HAVE ONLY TO CATCH MY BREATH STILL FOR A MINUTE.
LET'S SIT ON THAT STOOP.
JUST RELAX. DON'T TALK FOR A WHILE.
HOOH! I MADE TOO FAST, OUR WALKING!
THANK GOD, WITH THE NITROSTAT IT'S COMPLETELY OVER RIGHT AWAY! WHAT WAS I TELLING YOU ?
YOU SURE YOU'RE OKAY?
WELL... YOU WERE SAYING THAT HASKEL SURVIVED THE WAR.
YES. EVEN A FEW YEARS AGO I SENT HIM PACKAGES.
GIFTS? WHY? HE SOUNDS LIKE A ROTTEN GUY!
YES. I DON'T KNOW WHY. I KNOW ONLY THAT I SENT.
YOU KNOW, ONE TIME I WAS IN THE GHETTO WALKING AROUND...
HALT, JEW!
GIVE ME YOUR I.D. PAPERS- I'M GOING TO BLOW YOUR BRAINS OUT.
AH. I SEE YOU'RE A MEMBER OF THE ILLUSTRIOUS SPIEGELMAN FAMILY... GO ON YOUR WAY THEN, AND GIVE HASKEL MY REGARDS.
.... SUCH FRIENDS HASKEL HAD.

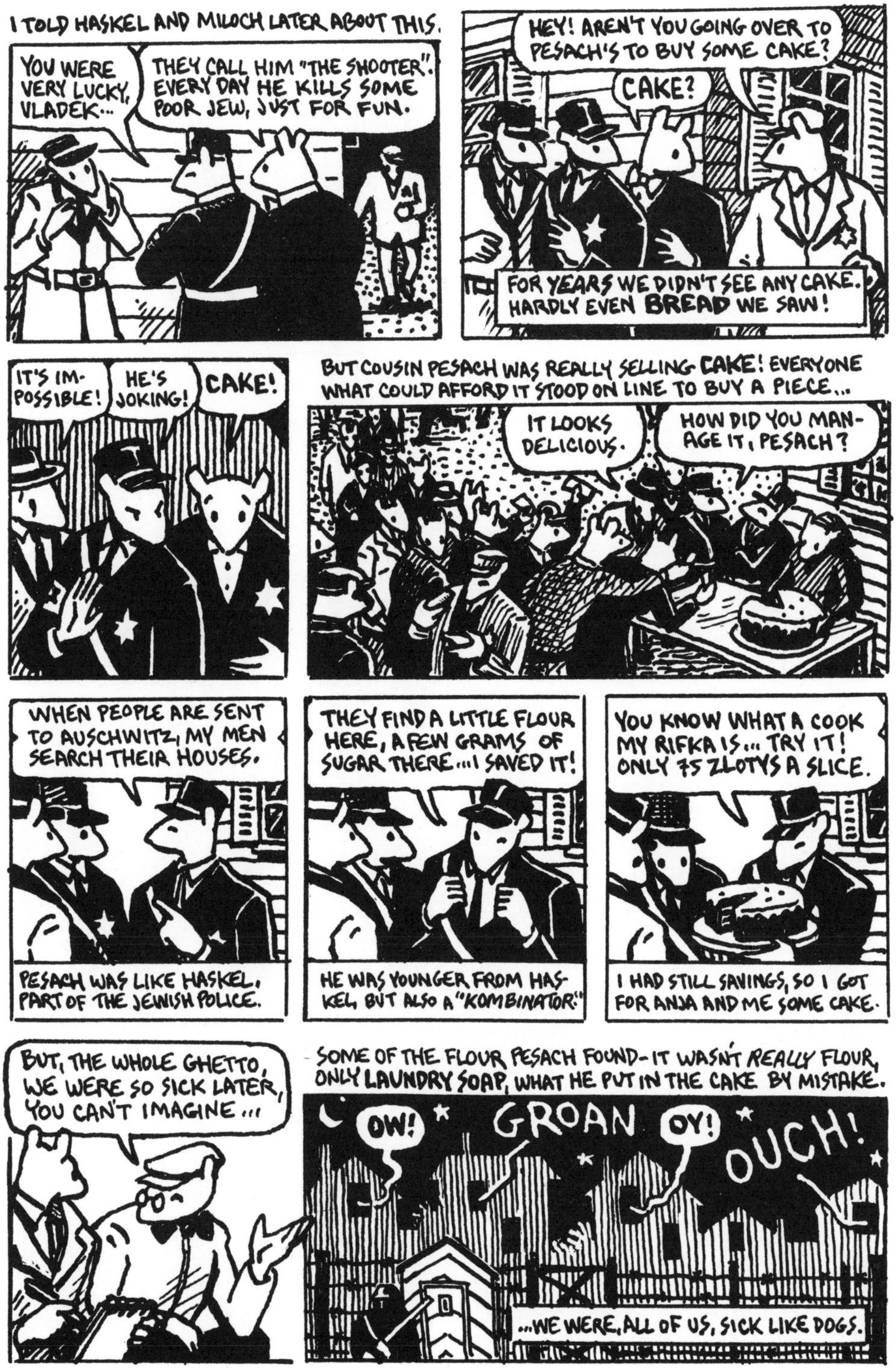
I TOLD HASKEL AND MILOCH LATER ABOUT THIS.
YOU WERE VERY LUCKY, VLADEK...
THEY CALL HIM "THE SHOOTER". EVERY DAY HE KILLS SOME POOR JEW, JUST FOR FUN.
HEY! AREN'T YOU GOING OVER TO PESACH'S TO BUY SOME CAKE?
CAKE?
FOR YEARS WE DIDN'T SEE ANY CAKE. HARDLY EVEN BREAD WE SAW!
IT'S IMPOSSIBLE!
HE'S JOKING!
CAKE!
BUT COUSIN PESACH WAS REALLY SELLING CAKE! EVERYONE WHAT COULD AFFORD IT STOOD ON LINE TO BUY A PIECE...
IT LOOKS DELICIOUS.
HOW DID YOU MANAGE IT, PESACH?
WHEN PEOPLE ARE SENT TO AUSCHWITZ, MY MEN SEARCH THEIR HOUSES.
PESACH WAS LIKE HASKEL, PART OF THE JEWISH POLICE.
THEY FIND A LITTLE FLOUR HERE, A FEW GRAMS OF SUGAR THERE... I SAVED IT!
HE WAS YOUNGER FROM HASKEL, BUT ALSO A "KOMBINATOR."
YOU KNOW WHAT A COOK MY RIFKA IS... TRY IT! ONLY 75 ZLOTYS A SLICE.
I HAD STILL SAVINGS, SO I GOT FOR ANJA AND ME SOME CAKE.
BUT, THE WHOLE GHETTO, WE WERE SO SICK LATER, YOU CAN'T IMAGINE...
- SOME OF THE FLOUR PESACH FOUND - IT WASN'T REALLY FLOUR, ONLY LAUNDRY SOAP, WHAT HE PUT IN THE CAKE BY MISTAKE.
OW!
GROAN
OY!
OUCH!
...WE WERE, ALL OF US, SICK LIKE DOGS.

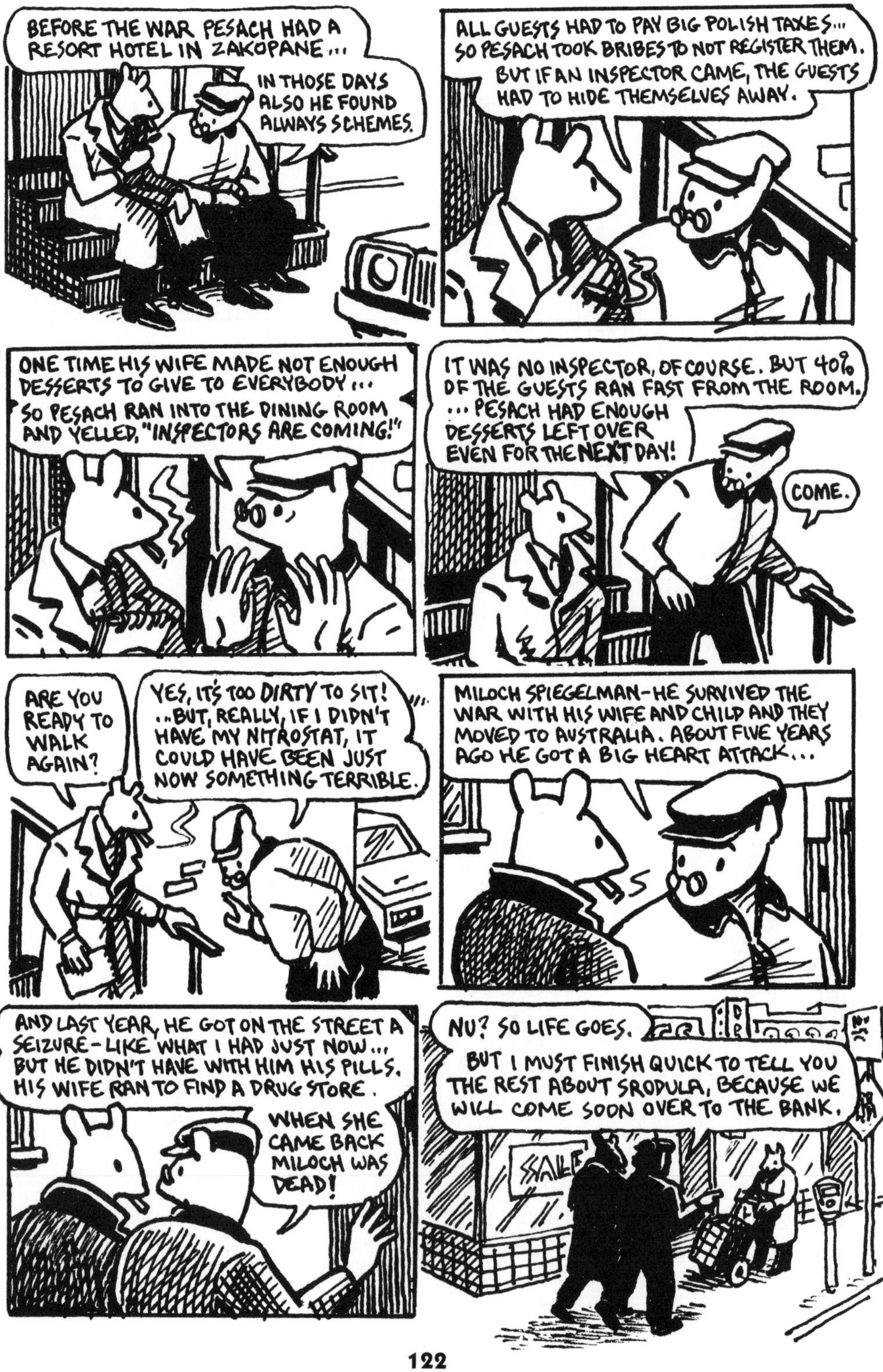
BEFORE THE WAR PESACH HAD A RESORT HOTEL IN ZAKOPANE...
IN THOSE DAYS ALSO HE FOUND ALWAYS SCHEMES.
ALL GUESTS HAD TO PAY BIG POLISH TAXES... SO PESACH TOOK BRIBES TO NOT REGISTER THEM.
BUT IF AN INSPECTOR CAME, THE GUESTS HAD TO HIDE THEMSELVES AWAY.
ONE TIME HIS WIFE MADE NOT ENOUGH DESSERTS TO GIVE TO EVERYBODY...
SO PESACH RAN INTO THE DINING ROOM AND YELLED, "INSPECTORS ARE COMING!"
IT WAS NO INSPECTOR, OF COURSE. BUT 40% OF THE GUESTS RAN FAST FROM THE ROOM.
...PESACH HAD ENOUGH DESSERTS LEFT OVER EVEN FOR THE NEXT DAY!
COME.
ARE YOU READY TO WALK AGAIN?
YES, IT'S TOO DIRTY TO SIT! ..BUT, REALLY, IF I DIDN'T HAVE MY NITROSTAT, IT COULD HAVE BEEN JUST NOW SOMETHING TERRIBLE.
MILOCH SPIEGELMAN-HE SURVIVED THE WAR WITH HIS WIFE AND CHILD AND THEY MOVED TO AUSTRALIA. ABOUT FIVE YEARS AGO HE GOT A BIG HEART ATTACK...
AND LAST YEAR, HE GOT ON THE STREET A SEIZURE-LIKE WHAT I HAD JUST NOW... BUT HE DIDN'T HAVE WITH HIM HIS PILLS. HIS WIFE RAN TO FIND A DRUG STORE.
WHEN SHE CAME BACK MILOCH WAS DEAD!
NU? SO LIFE GOES.
BUT I MUST FINISH QUICK TO TELL YOU THE REST ABOUT SRODULA, BECAUSE WE WILL COME SOON OVER TO THE BANK.
SALE

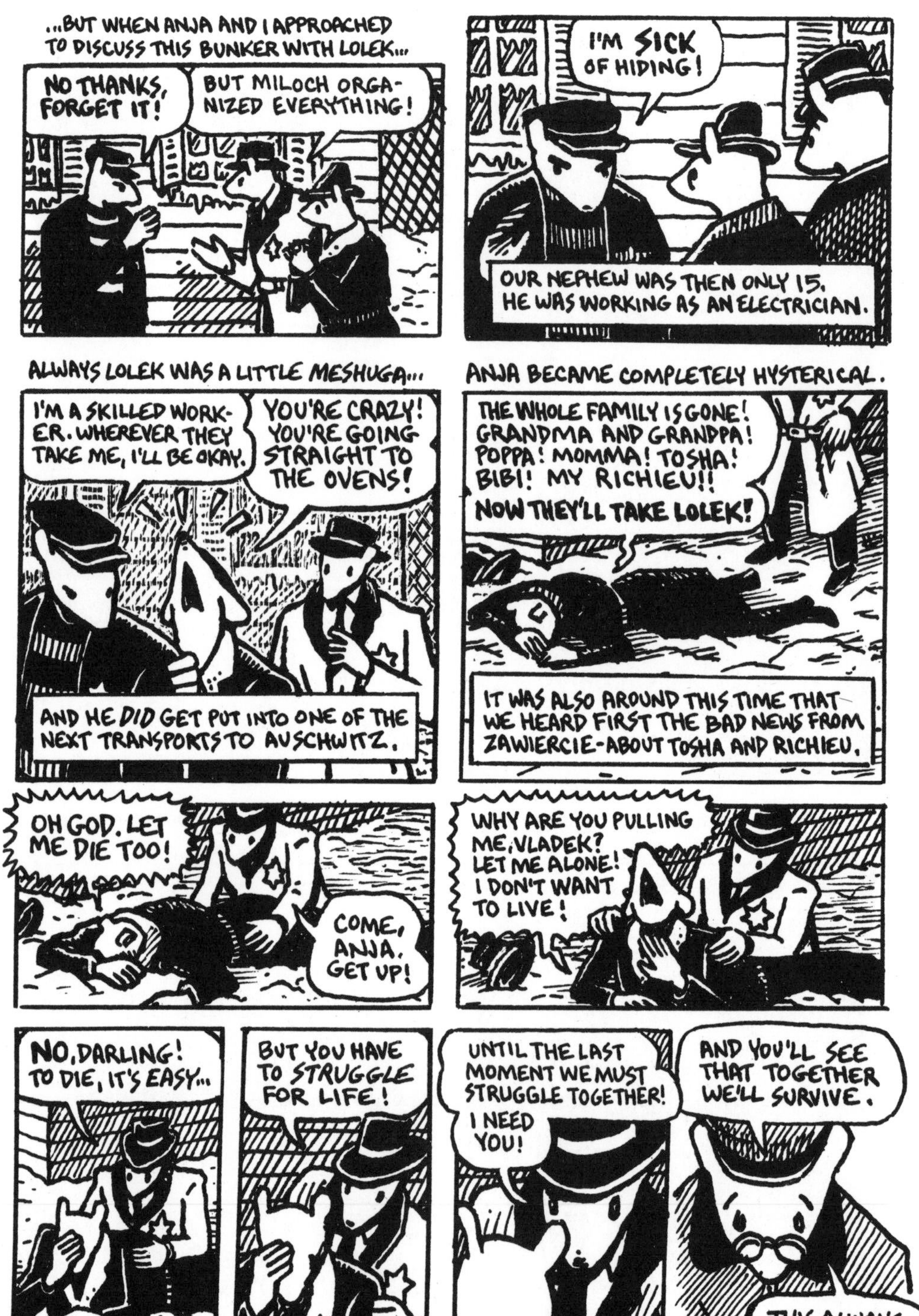
...BUT WHEN ANJA AND I APPROACHED TO DISCUSS THIS BUNKER WITH LOLEK...
NO THANKS, FORGET IT!
BUT MILOCH ORGANIZED EVERYTHING!
I'M SICK OF HIDING!
OUR NEPHEW WAS THEN ONLY 15. HE WAS WORKING AS AN ELECTRICIAN.
ALWAYS LOLEK WAS A LITTLE MESHUGA...
I'M A SKILLED WORKER. WHEREVER THEY TAKE ME, I'LL BE OKAY.
YOU'RE CRAZY! YOU'RE GOING STRAIGHT TO THE OVENS!
AND HE DID GET PUT INTO ONE OF THE NEXT TRANSPORTS TO AUSCHWITZ.
ANJA BECAME COMPLETELY HYSTERICAL.
THE WHOLE FAMILY IS GONE! GRANDMA AND GRANDPA! POPPA! MOMMA! TOSHA! BIBI! MY RICHIEU!!
NOW THEY'LL TAKE LOLEK!
IT WAS ALSO AROUND THIS TIME THAT WE HEARD FIRST THE BAD NEWS FROM ZAWIERCIE-ABOUT TOSHA AND RICHIEU.
OH GOD. LET ME DIE TOO!
COME, ANJA. GET UP!
WHY ARE YOU PULLING ME, VLADEK? LET ME ALONE! I DON'T WANT TO LIVE!
NO, DARLING! TO DIE, IT'S EASY...
BUT YOU HAVE TO STRUGGLE FOR LIFE!
UNTIL THE LAST MOMENT WE MUST STRUGGLE TOGETHER!
I NEED YOU!
AND YOU'LL SEE THAT TOGETHER WE'LL SURVIVE.
THIS ALWAYS I TOLD TO HER.

THE GHETTO FINISHED OUT SO LIKE MILOCH SAID. ABOUT TWELVE FROM US RAN INTO HIS BUNKER WITH HIM, HIS WIFE AND HIS THREE-YEARS-OLD BABY BOY.

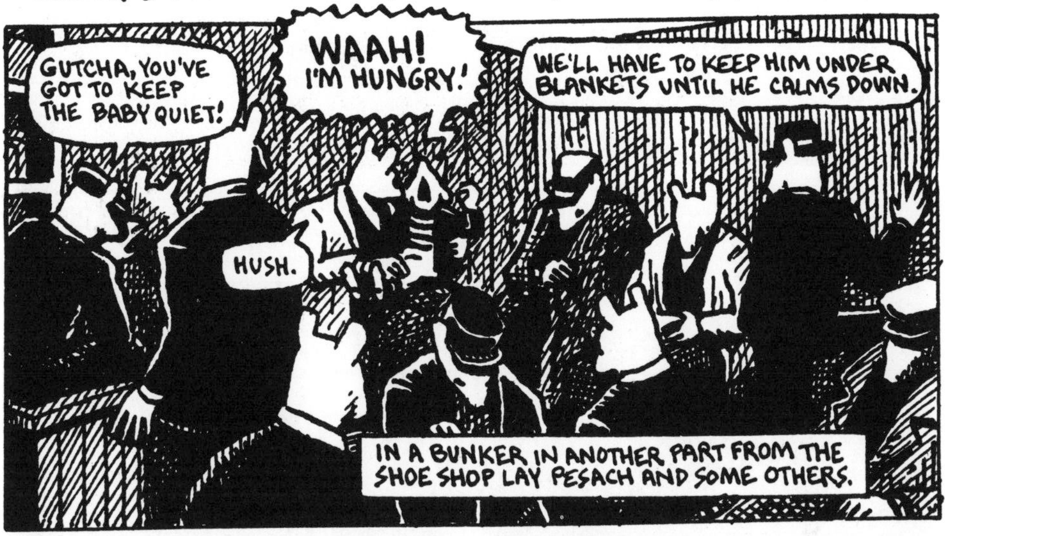
GUTCHA, YOU'VE GOT TO KEEP THE BABY QUIET!
WAAH! I'M HUNGRY!
WE'LL HAVE TO KEEP HIM UNDER BLANKETS UNTIL HE CALMS DOWN.
HUSH.
IN A BUNKER IN ANOTHER PART FROM THE SHOE SHOP LAY PESACH AND SOME OTHERS.

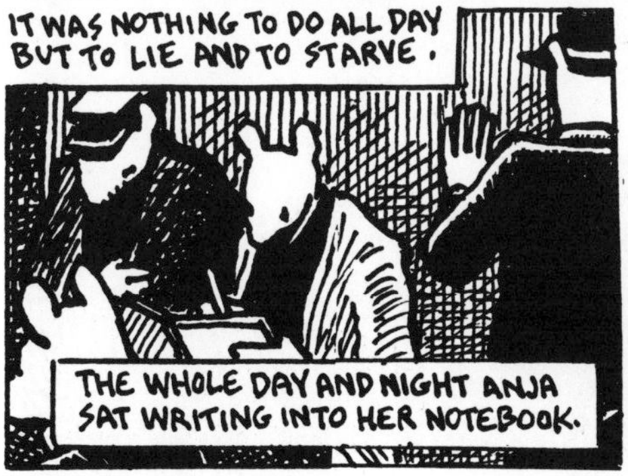
IT WAS NOTHING TO DO ALL DAY BUT TO LIE AND TO STARVE.
THE WHOLE DAY AND NIGHT ANJA SAT WRITING INTO HER NOTEBOOK.

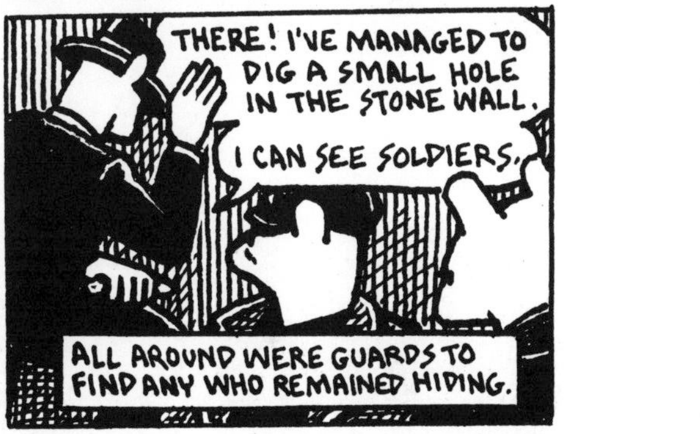
THERE! I'VE MANAGED TO DIG A SMALL HOLE IN THE STONE WALL.
I CAN SEE SOLDIERS.
ALL AROUND WERE GUARDS TO FIND ANY WHO REMAINED HIDING.

WHAT LITTLE FOOD WE HAD, SOON IT WAS GONE.

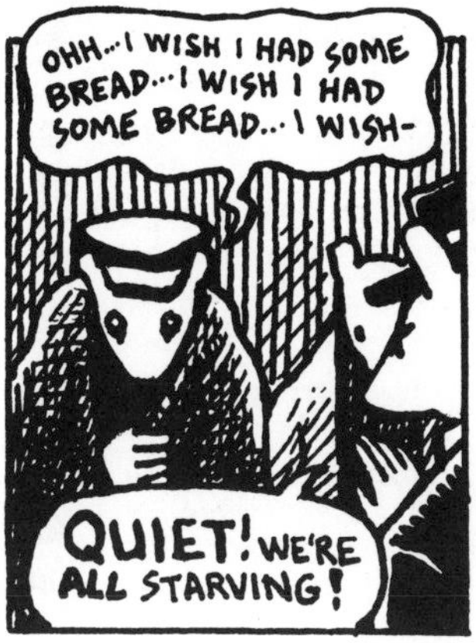
OHH...I WISH I HAD SOME BREAD...I WISH I HAD SOME BREAD...I WISH-
QUIET! WE'RE ALL STARVING!

AT NIGHT WE SNEAKED OUT TO LOOK FOR WHAT TO EAT... BUT IT WAS NOTHING TO FIND.

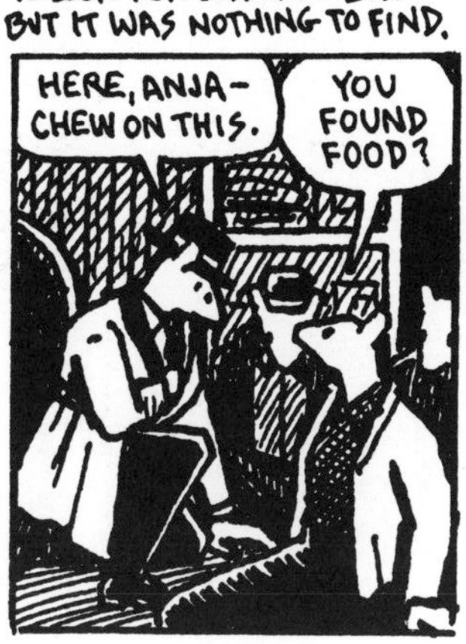
HERE, ANJA- CHEW ON THIS.
YOU FOUND FOOD?

NEVER ANY OF US HAD BEEN SO HUNGRY LIKE THEN.

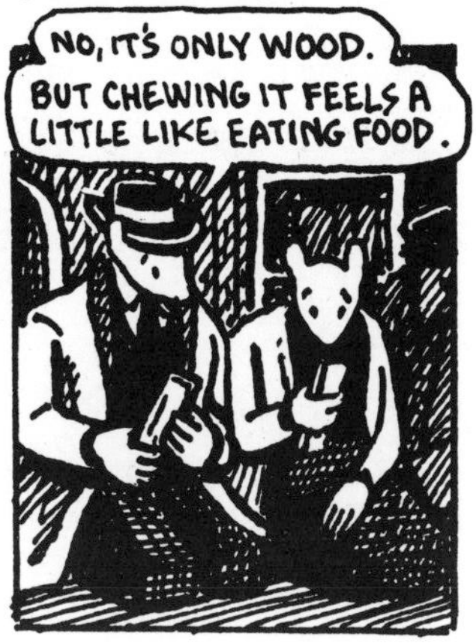
NO, IT'S ONLY WOOD.
BUT CHEWING IT FEELS A LITTLE LIKE EATING FOOD.

ONLY A FEW OF US REMAINED.

THERE HAVEN'T BEEN ANY LIGHTS ON IN THE GUARD-HOUSE FOR TWO NIGHTS... I THINK IT'S SAFE.

A LITTLE BEFORE DAWN WE WENT OUT FROM SRODULA...

THEY'RE ALL GONE!

WHEW

THE GHETTO IS EMPTY!

WOHNG JUDE

AHEAD OF TIME WE ORGANIZED OUR-SELVES GOOD CLOTHES AND I.D. PAPERS.

WE MIXED WITH THE POLES GOING TO WORK.

WE'LL BE HIDING AT THIS AD-DRESS. WHEN YOU FIND A SAFE PLACE, TRY TO CONTACT US, VLADEK.

GOOD LUCK, MILOCH.

WE WENT ALL IN DIF-FERENT DIRECTIONS.

THAT GUY, AVRAM, HIS WOMAN HAD FRIENDS TO KEEP THEM.

AND THE FRIENDS KEPT THEM... UNTIL AVRAM'S MONEY FINISHED. THEN THEY WERE REPORTED.

ANJA AND I DIDN'T HAVE WHERE TO GO.

WE WALKED IN THE DIRECTION OF SOSNOWIEC—BUT WHERE TO GO?!

IT WAS NOWHERE WE HAD TO HIDE.

CAN I HELP YOU, MR. SPIEGELMAN?

YES, I HAVE HERE MY SON, ARTIE. I WANT TO SIGN HIM A KEY, SO HE CAN GO ALSO TO MY SAFETY BOX.

127

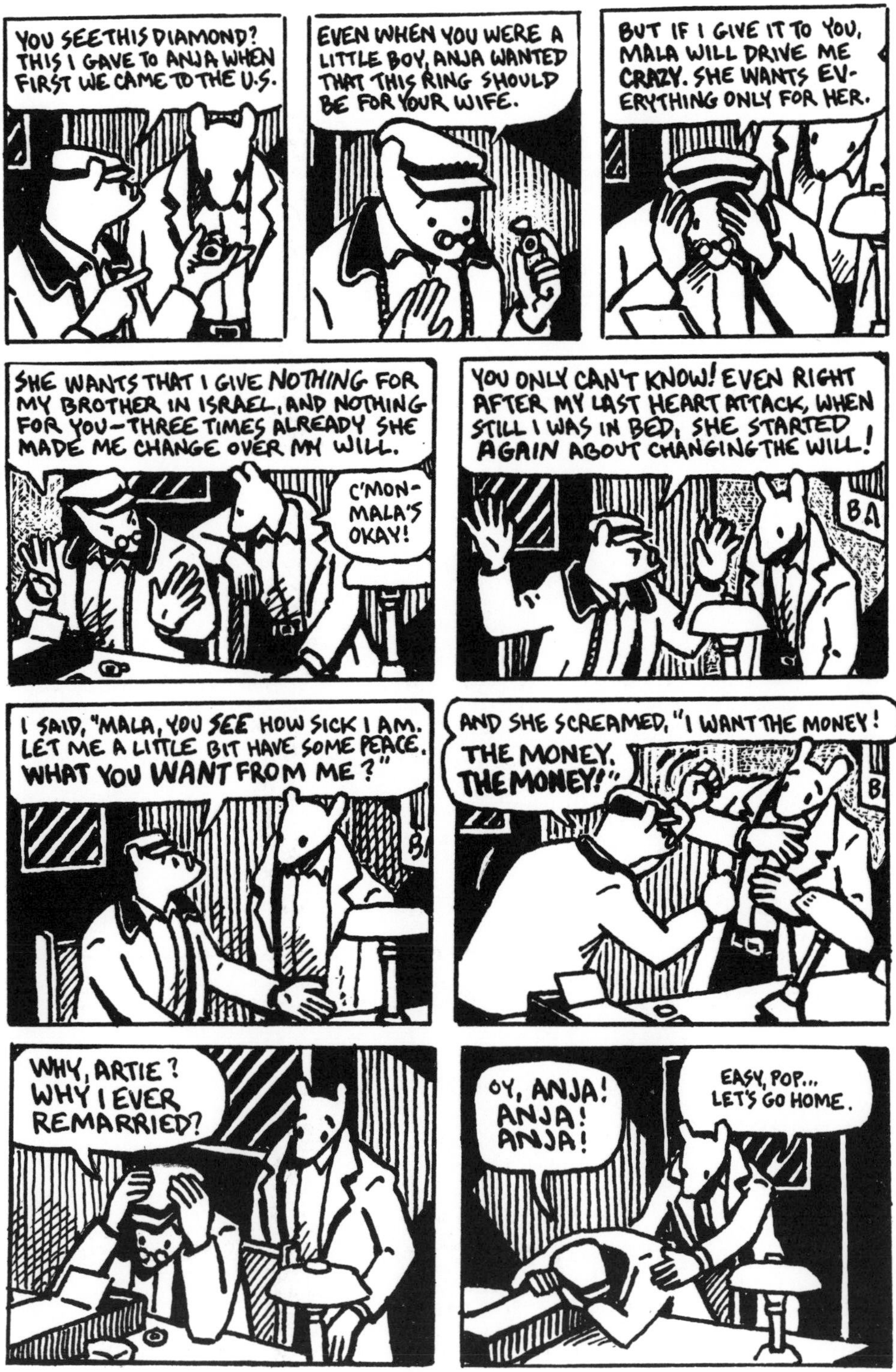
YOU SEE THIS DIAMOND? THIS I GAVE TO ANJA WHEN FIRST WE CAME TO THE U.S.
EVEN WHEN YOU WERE A LITTLE BOY, ANJA WANTED THAT THIS RING SHOULD BE FOR YOUR WIFE.
BUT IF I GIVE IT TO YOU, MALA WILL DRIVE ME CRAZY. SHE WANTS EV-ERYTHING ONLY FOR HER.
SHE WANTS THAT I GIVE NOTHING FOR MY BROTHER IN ISRAEL, AND NOTHING FOR YOU—THREE TIMES ALREADY SHE MADE ME CHANGE OVER MY WILL.
C'MON-MALA'S OKAY!
YOU ONLY CAN'T KNOW! EVEN RIGHT AFTER MY LAST HEART ATTACK, WHEN STILL I WAS IN BED, SHE STARTED AGAIN ABOUT CHANGING THE WILL!
I SAID, "MALA, YOU SEE HOW SICK I AM. LET ME A LITTLE BIT HAVE SOME PEACE. WHAT YOU WANT FROM ME?"
AND SHE SCREAMED, "I WANT THE MONEY! THE MONEY. THE MONEY!"
WHY, ARTIE? WHY I EVER REMARRIED?
OY, ANJA! ANJA! ANJA!
EASY, POP... LET'S GO HOME.

CHAPTER SIX

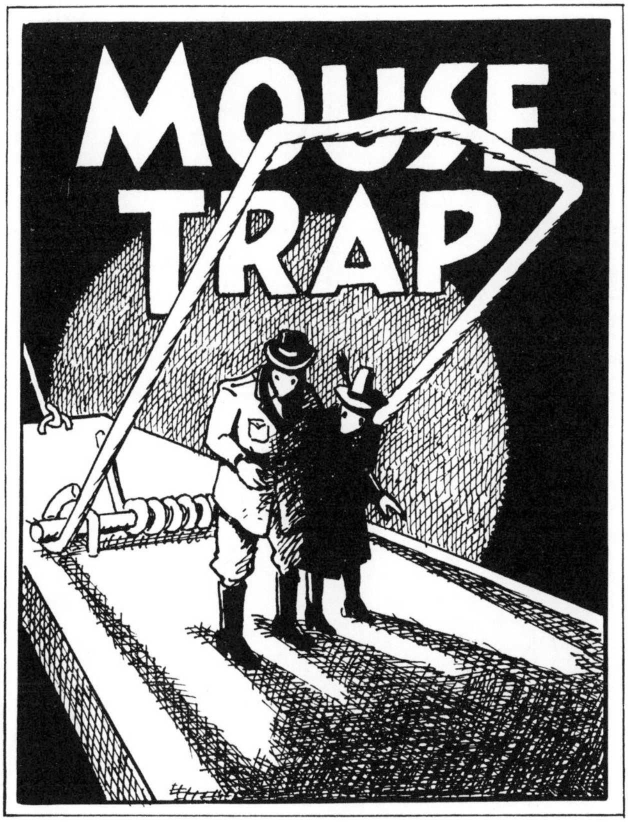
MOUSE
TRAP

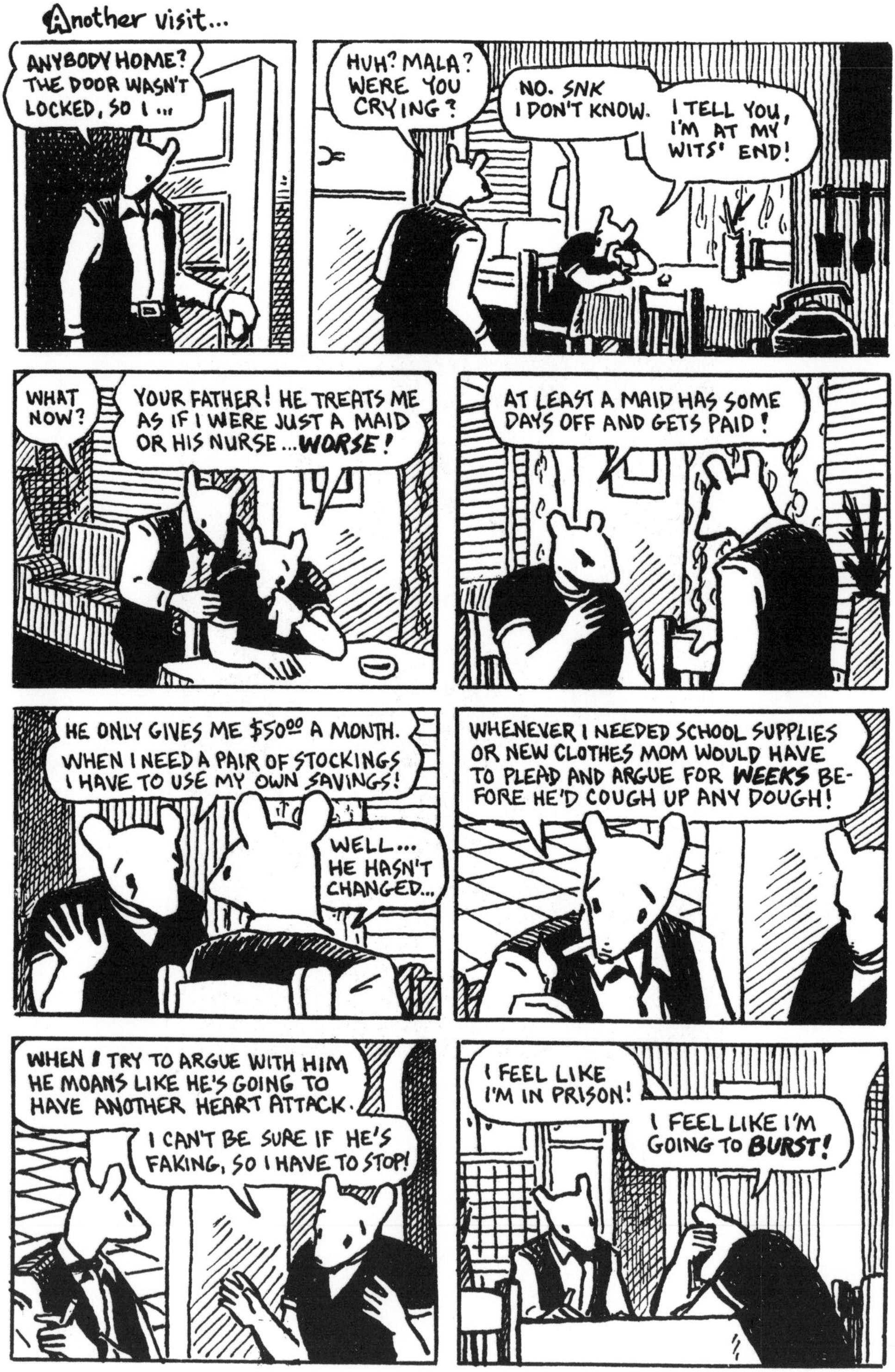
Another visit...
ANYBODY HOME? THE DOOR WASN'T LOCKED, SO I ...
HUH? MALA? WERE YOU CRYING?
NO. SNK I DON'T KNOW.
I TELL YOU, I'M AT MY WITS' END!
WHAT NOW?
YOUR FATHER! HE TREATS ME AS IF I WERE JUST A MAID OR HIS NURSE... WORSE!
AT LEAST A MAID HAS SOME DAYS OFF AND GETS PAID!
HE ONLY GIVES ME $50.00 A MONTH. WHEN I NEED A PAIR OF STOCKINGS I HAVE TO USE MY OWN SAVINGS!
WELL... HE HASN'T CHANGED...
WHENEVER I NEEDED SCHOOL SUPPLIES OR NEW CLOTHES MOM WOULD HAVE TO PLEAD AND ARGUE FOR WEEKS BEFORE HE'D COUGH UP ANY DOUGH!
WHEN I TRY TO ARGUE WITH HIM HE MOANS LIKE HE'S GOING TO HAVE ANOTHER HEART ATTACK.
I CAN'T BE SURE IF HE'S FAKING, SO I HAVE TO STOP!
I FEEL LIKE I'M IN PRISON!
I FEEL LIKE I'M GOING TO BURST!

133

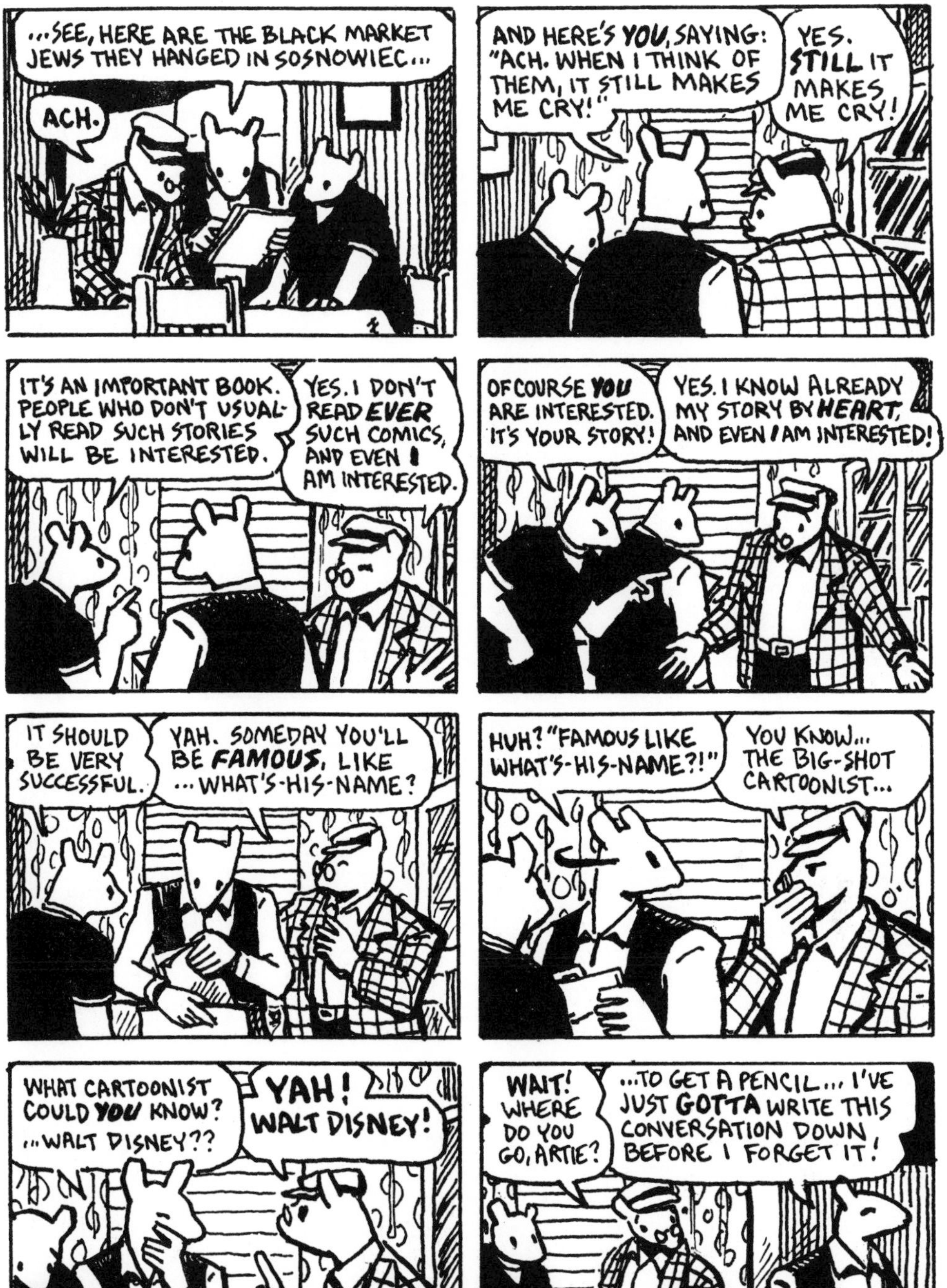
...SEE, HERE ARE THE BLACK MARKET JEWS THEY HANGED IN SOSNOWIEC...
ACH.
AND HERE'S YOU, SAYING: "ACH. WHEN I THINK OF THEM, IT STILL MAKES ME CRY!"
YES. STILL IT MAKES ME CRY!
IT'S AN IMPORTANT BOOK. PEOPLE WHO DON'T USUALLY READ SUCH STORIES WILL BE INTERESTED.
YES. I DON'T READ EVER SUCH COMICS, AND EVEN I AM INTERESTED.
OF COURSE YOU ARE INTERESTED. IT'S YOUR STORY!
YES. I KNOW ALREADY MY STORY BY HEART, AND EVEN I AM INTERESTED!
IT SHOULD BE VERY SUCCESSFUL.
YAH. SOMEDAY YOU'LL BE FAMOUS, LIKE ...WHAT'S-HIS-NAME?
HUH? "FAMOUS LIKE WHAT'S-HIS-NAME?!"
YOU KNOW... THE BIG-SHOT CARTOONIST...
WHAT CARTOONIST COULD YOU KNOW? ...WALT DISNEY??
YAH! WALT DISNEY!
WAIT! WHERE DO YOU GO, ARTIE?
...TO GET A PENCIL... I'VE JUST GOTTA WRITE THIS CONVERSATION DOWN BEFORE I FORGET IT!

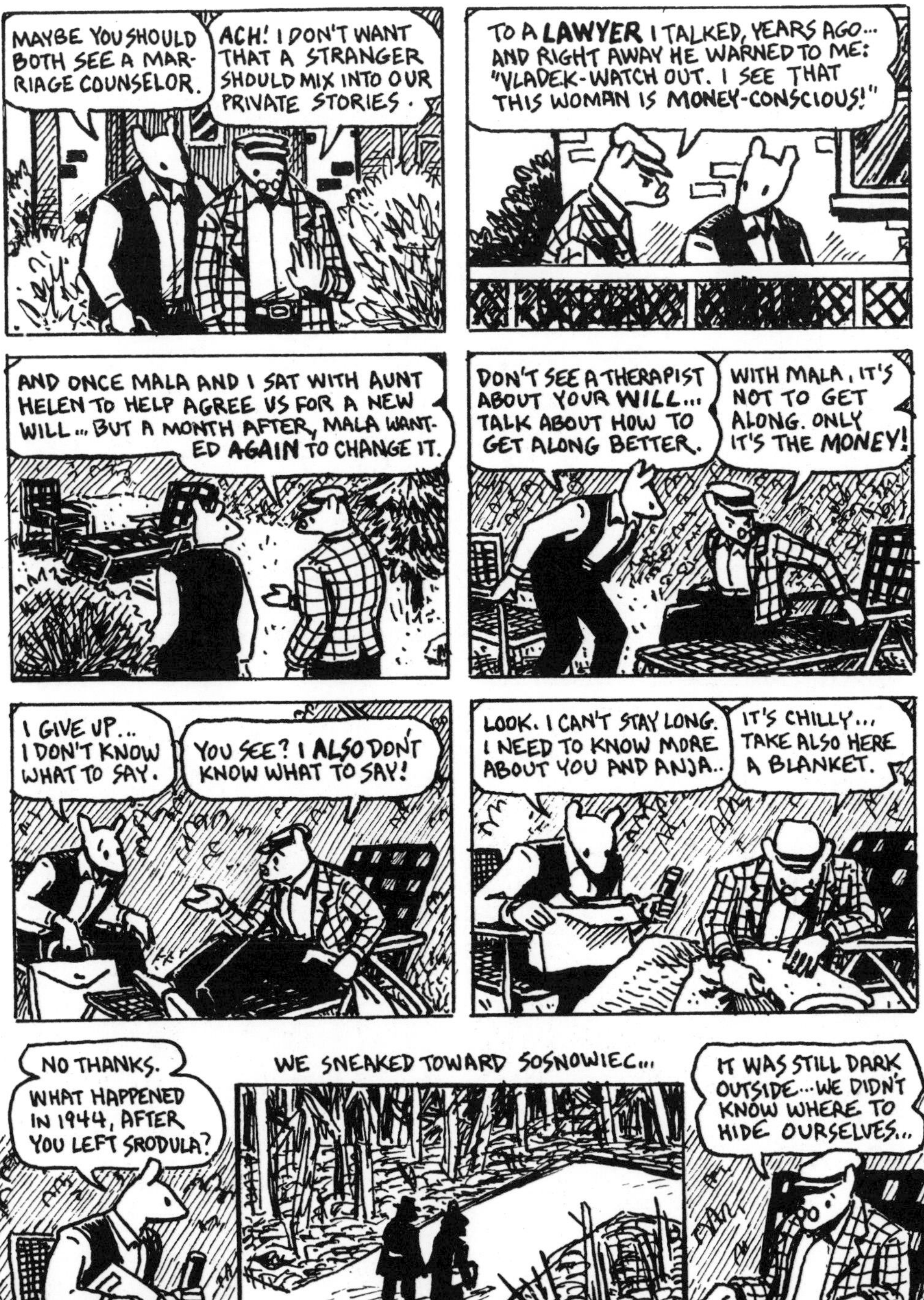

MAYBE YOU SHOULD BOTH SEE A MAR-RIAGE COUNSELOR.
ACH! I DON'T WANT THAT A STRANGER SHOULD MIX INTO OUR PRIVATE STORIES.
TO A LAWYER I TALKED, YEARS AGO... AND RIGHT AWAY HE WARNED TO ME: "VLADEK-WATCH OUT. I SEE THAT THIS WOMAN IS MONEY-CONSCIOUS!"
AND ONCE MALA AND I SAT WITH AUNT HELEN TO HELP AGREE US FOR A NEW WILL... BUT A MONTH AFTER, MALA WANTED AGAIN TO CHANGE IT.
DON'T SEE A THERAPIST ABOUT YOUR WILL... TALK ABOUT HOW TO GET ALONG BETTER.
WITH MALA, IT'S NOT TO GET ALONG. ONLY IT'S THE MONEY!
I GIVE UP... I DON'T KNOW WHAT TO SAY.
YOU SEE? I ALSO DON'T KNOW WHAT TO SAY!
LOOK. I CAN'T STAY LONG. I NEED TO KNOW MORE ABOUT YOU AND ANJA..
IT'S CHILLY... TAKE ALSO HERE A BLANKET.
NO THANKS. WHAT HAPPENED IN 1944, AFTER YOU LEFT SRODULA?
WE SNEAKED TOWARD SOSNOWIEC...
IT WAS STILL DARK OUTSIDE... WE DIDN'T KNOW WHERE TO HIDE OURSELVES...

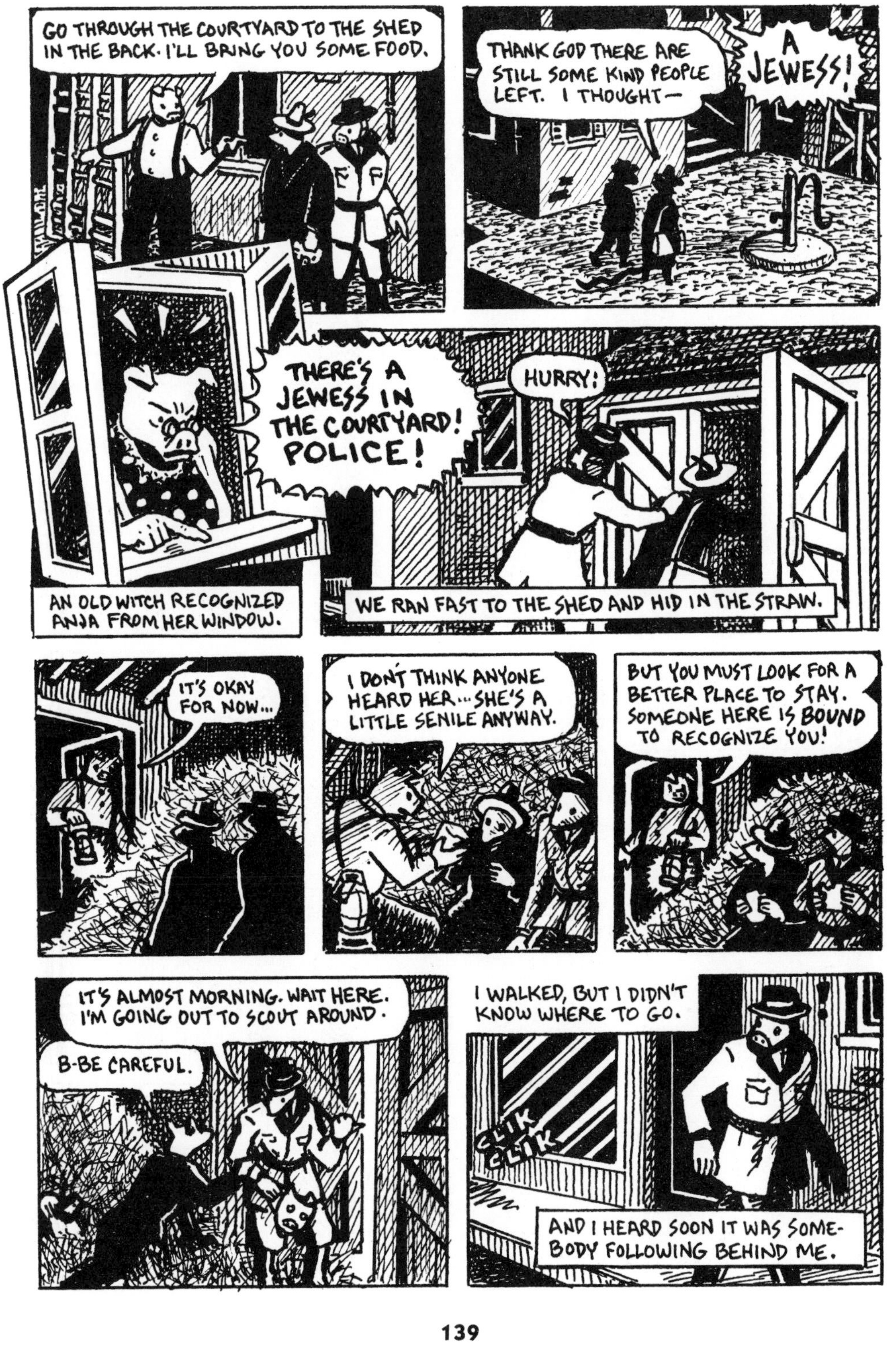
GO THROUGH THE COURTYARD TO THE SHED IN THE BACK. I'LL BRING YOU SOME FOOD.
THANK GOD THERE ARE STILL SOME KIND PEOPLE LEFT. I THOUGHT—
A JEWESS!
THERE'S A JEWESS IN THE COURTYARD! POLICE!
HURRY!
AN OLD WITCH RECOGNIZED ANJA FROM HER WINDOW.
WE RAN FAST TO THE SHED AND HID IN THE STRAW.
IT'S OKAY FOR NOW...
I DON'T THINK ANYONE HEARD HER... SHE'S A LITTLE SENILE ANYWAY.
BUT YOU MUST LOOK FOR A BETTER PLACE TO STAY. SOMEONE HERE IS BOUND TO RECOGNIZE YOU!
IT'S ALMOST MORNING. WAIT HERE. I'M GOING OUT TO SCOUT AROUND.
B-BE CAREFUL.
I WALKED, BUT I DIDN'T KNOW WHERE TO GO.
CLIK CLIK
AND I HEARD SOON IT WAS SOMEBODY FOLLOWING BEHIND ME.

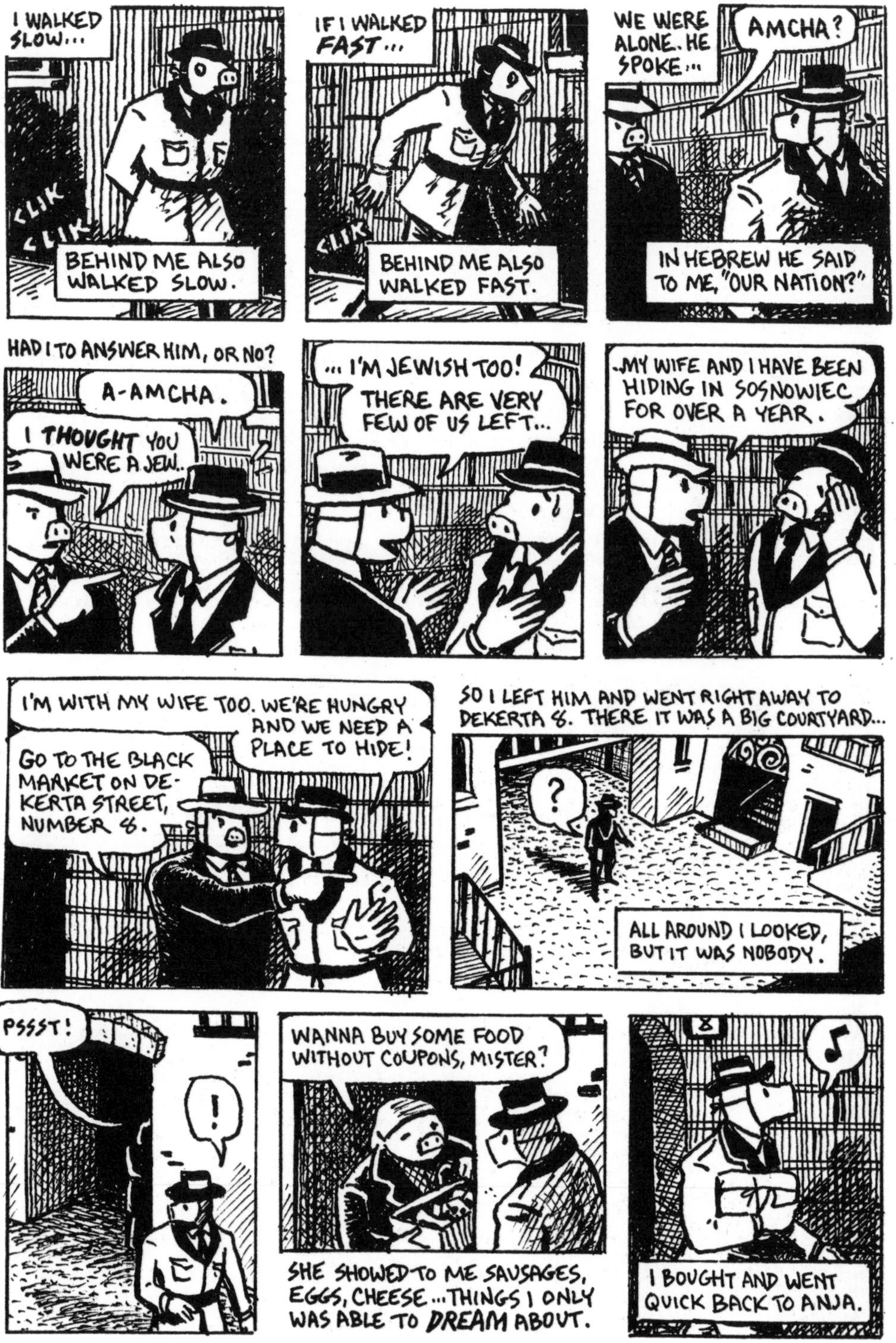
I WALKED SLOW...
CLIK
CLIK
BEHIND ME ALSO WALKED SLOW.
IF I WALKED FAST...
CLIK
BEHIND ME ALSO WALKED FAST.
WE WERE ALONE. HE SPOKE...
AMCHA?
IN HEBREW HE SAID TO ME, "OUR NATION?"
HAD I TO ANSWER HIM, OR NO?
A-AMCHA.
I THOUGHT YOU WERE A JEW..
... I'M JEWISH TOO!
THERE ARE VERY FEW OF US LEFT...
...MY WIFE AND I HAVE BEEN HIDING IN SOSNOWIEC FOR OVER A YEAR.
I'M WITH MY WIFE TOO. WE'RE HUNGRY AND WE NEED A PLACE TO HIDE!
GO TO THE BLACK MARKET ON DEKERTA STREET, NUMBER 8.
SO I LEFT HIM AND WENT RIGHT AWAY TO DEKERTA 8. THERE IT WAS A BIG COURTYARD...
?
ALL AROUND I LOOKED, BUT IT WAS NOBODY.
PSSST!
!
WANNA BUY SOME FOOD WITHOUT COUPONS, MISTER?
SHE SHOWED TO ME SAUSAGES, EGGS, CHEESE... THINGS I ONLY WAS ABLE TO DREAM ABOUT.
8
I BOUGHT AND WENT QUICK BACK TO ANJA.

142

144

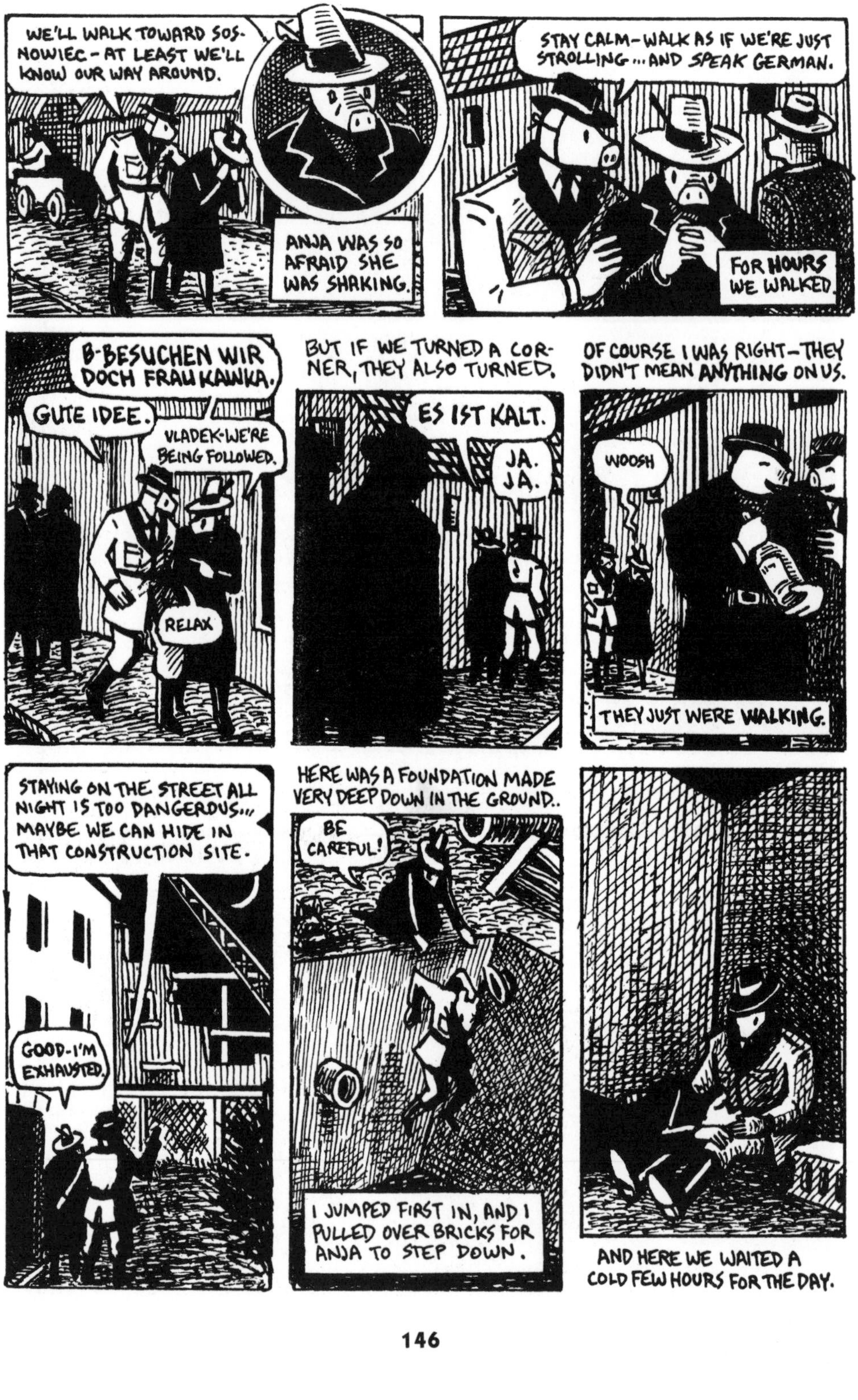
WE'LL WALK TOWARD SOS-NOWIEC - AT LEAST WE'LL KNOW OUR WAY AROUND.
ANJA WAS SO AFRAID SHE WAS SHAKING.
STAY CALM - WALK AS IF WE'RE JUST STROLLING... AND SPEAK GERMAN.
FOR HOURS WE WALKED.
B-BESUCHEN WIR DOCH FRAU KAWKA.
GUTE IDEE.
VLADEK - WE'RE BEING FOLLOWED.
RELAX
BUT IF WE TURNED A CORNER, THEY ALSO TURNED.
ES IST KALT.
JA. JA.
OF COURSE I WAS RIGHT - THEY DIDN'T MEAN ANYTHING ON US.
WOOSH
THEY JUST WERE WALKING.
STAYING ON THE STREET ALL NIGHT IS TOO DANGEROUS... MAYBE WE CAN HIDE IN THAT CONSTRUCTION SITE.
GOOD - I'M EXHAUSTED.
HERE WAS A FOUNDATION MADE VERY DEEP DOWN IN THE GROUND..
BE CAREFUL!
I JUMPED FIRST IN, AND I PULLED OVER BRICKS FOR ANJA TO STEP DOWN.
AND HERE WE WAITED A COLD FEW HOURS FOR THE DAY.

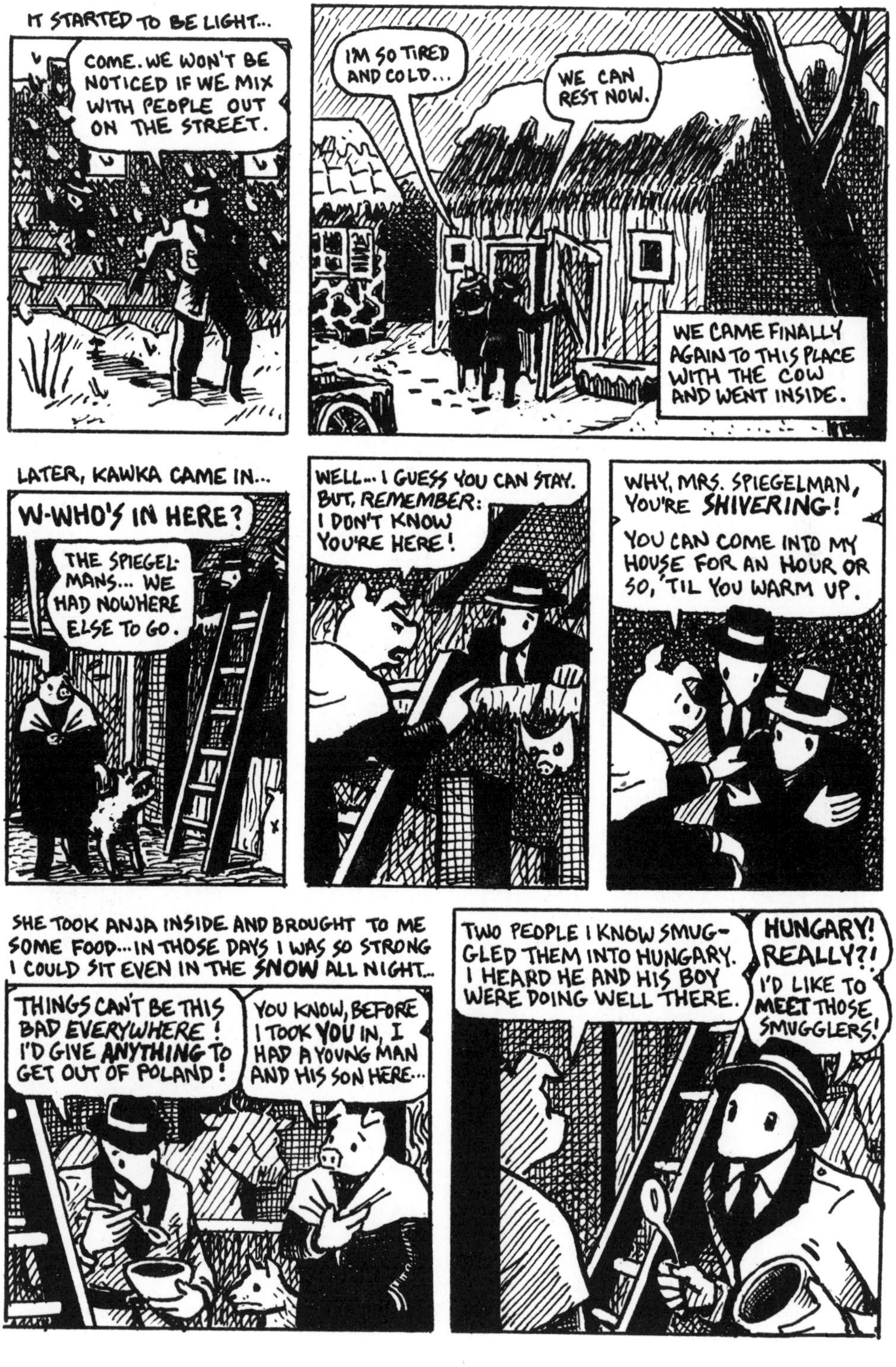
IT STARTED TO BE LIGHT...
COME. WE WON'T BE NOTICED IF WE MIX WITH PEOPLE OUT ON THE STREET.
I'M SO TIRED AND COLD...
WE CAN REST NOW.
WE CAME FINALLY AGAIN TO THIS PLACE WITH THE COW AND WENT INSIDE.
LATER, KAWKA CAME IN...
W-WHO'S IN HERE?
THE SPIEGELMANS... WE HAD NOWHERE ELSE TO GO.
WELL... I GUESS YOU CAN STAY. BUT, REMEMBER: I DON'T KNOW YOU'RE HERE!
WHY, MRS. SPIEGELMAN, YOU'RE SHIVERING!
YOU CAN COME INTO MY HOUSE FOR AN HOUR OR SO, 'TIL YOU WARM UP.
SHE TOOK ANJA INSIDE AND BROUGHT TO ME SOME FOOD... IN THOSE DAYS I WAS SO STRONG I COULD SIT EVEN IN THE SNOW ALL NIGHT...
THINGS CAN'T BE THIS BAD EVERYWHERE! I'D GIVE ANYTHING TO GET OUT OF POLAND!
YOU KNOW, BEFORE I TOOK YOU IN, I HAD A YOUNG MAN AND HIS SON HERE...
TWO PEOPLE I KNOW SMUGGLED THEM INTO HUNGARY. I HEARD HE AND HIS BOY WERE DOING WELL THERE.
HUNGARY! REALLY?!
I'D LIKE TO MEET THOSE SMUGGLERS!

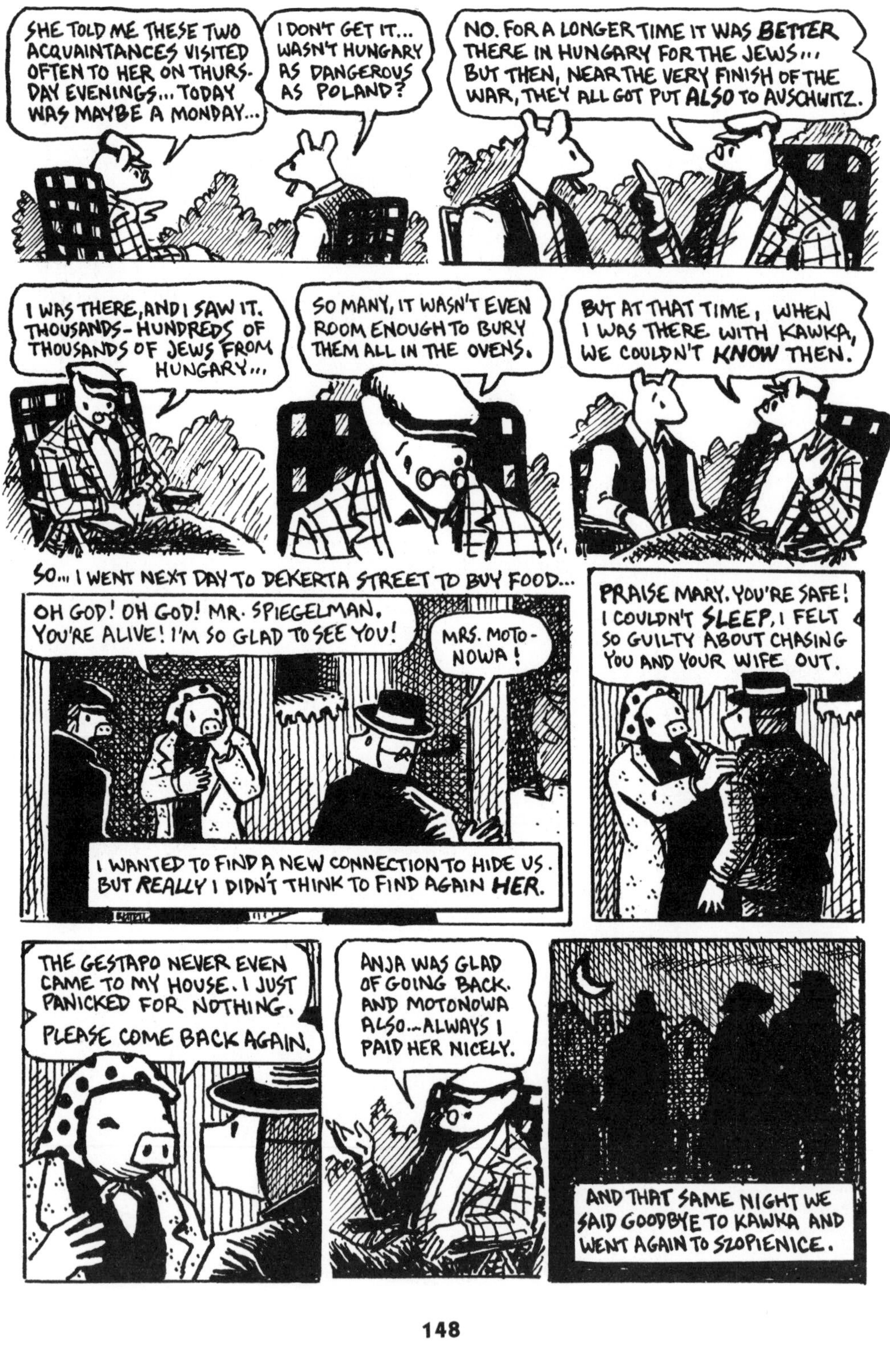
SHE TOLD ME THESE TWO ACQUAINTANCES VISITED OFTEN TO HER ON THURS-DAY EVENINGS... TODAY WAS MAYBE A MONDAY...
I DON'T GET IT... WASN'T HUNGARY AS DANGEROUS AS POLAND?
NO. FOR A LONGER TIME IT WAS BETTER THERE IN HUNGARY FOR THE JEWS... BUT THEN, NEAR THE VERY FINISH OF THE WAR, THEY ALL GOT PUT ALSO TO AUSCHWITZ.
I WAS THERE, AND I SAW IT. THOUSANDS- HUNDREDS OF THOUSANDS OF JEWS FROM HUNGARY...
SO MANY, IT WASN'T EVEN ROOM ENOUGH TO BURY THEM ALL IN THE OVENS.
BUT AT THAT TIME, WHEN I WAS THERE WITH KAWKA, WE COULDN'T KNOW THEN.
SO... I WENT NEXT DAY TO DEKERTA STREET TO BUY FOOD...
OH GOD! OH GOD! MR. SPIEGELMAN. YOU'RE ALIVE! I'M SO GLAD TO SEE YOU!
MRS. MOTO-NOWA!
I WANTED TO FIND A NEW CONNECTION TO HIDE US. BUT REALLY I DIDN'T THINK TO FIND AGAIN HER.
PRAISE MARY. YOU'RE SAFE! I COULDN'T SLEEP, I FELT SO GUILTY ABOUT CHASING YOU AND YOUR WIFE OUT.
THE GESTAPO NEVER EVEN CAME TO MY HOUSE. I JUST PANICKED FOR NOTHING.
PLEASE COME BACK AGAIN.
ANJA WAS GLAD OF GOING BACK. AND MOTONOWA ALSO... ALWAYS I PAID HER NICELY.
AND THAT SAME NIGHT WE SAID GOODBYE TO KAWKA AND WENT AGAIN TO SZOPIENICE.

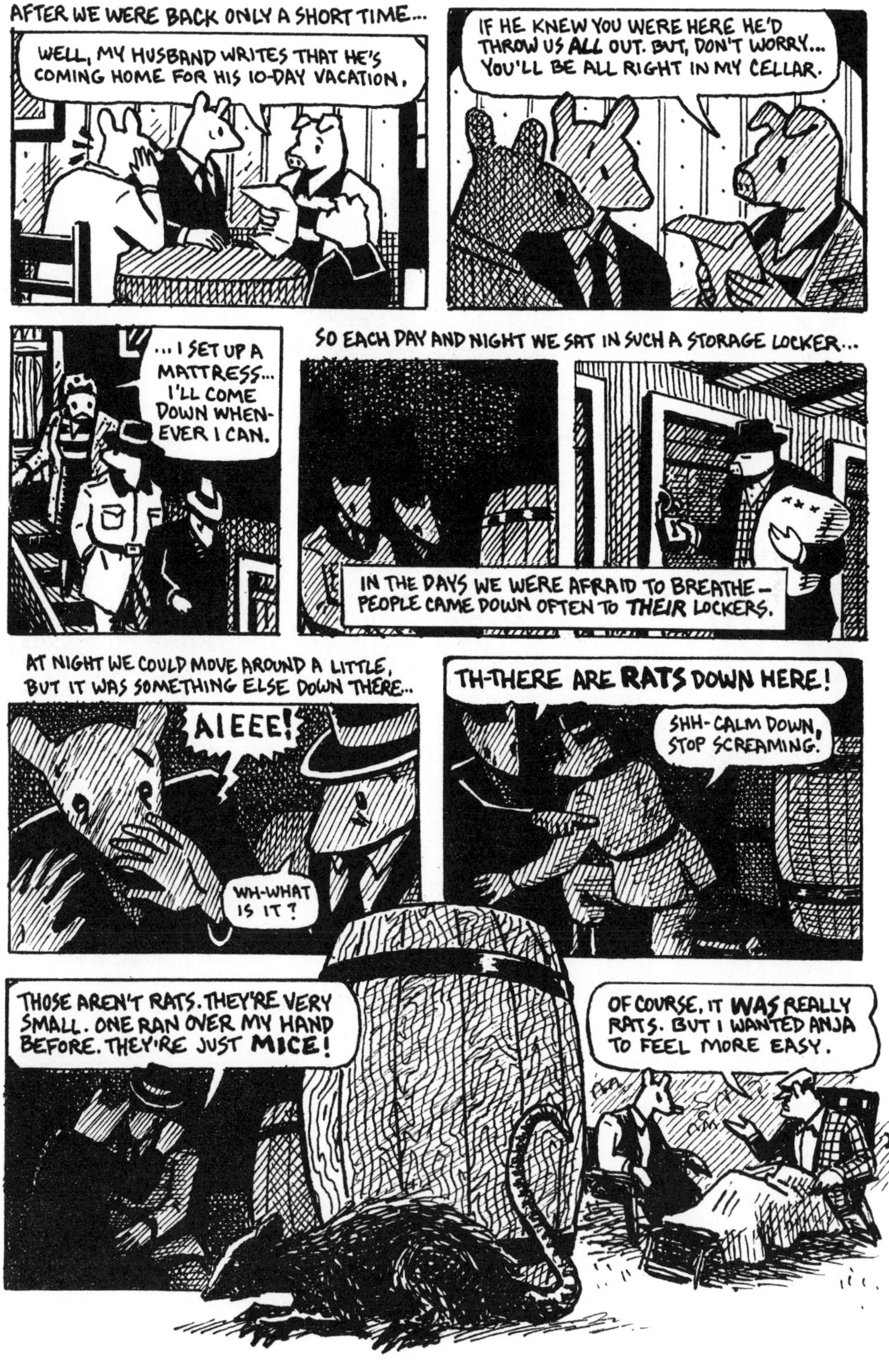
AFTER WE WERE BACK ONLY A SHORT TIME...
WELL, MY HUSBAND WRITES THAT HE'S COMING HOME FOR HIS 10-DAY VACATION.
IF HE KNEW YOU WERE HERE HE'D THROW US ALL OUT. BUT, DON'T WORRY... YOU'LL BE ALL RIGHT IN MY CELLAR.
...I SET UP A MATTRESS... I'LL COME DOWN WHENEVER I CAN.
SO EACH DAY AND NIGHT WE SAT IN SUCH A STORAGE LOCKER...
IN THE DAYS WE WERE AFRAID TO BREATHE — PEOPLE CAME DOWN OFTEN TO THEIR LOCKERS.
AT NIGHT WE COULD MOVE AROUND A LITTLE, BUT IT WAS SOMETHING ELSE DOWN THERE...
AIEEE!
WH-WHAT IS IT?
TH-THERE ARE RATS DOWN HERE!
SHH- CALM DOWN, STOP SCREAMING!
THOSE AREN'T RATS. THEY'RE VERY SMALL. ONE RAN OVER MY HAND BEFORE. THEY'RE JUST MICE!
OF COURSE, IT WAS REALLY RATS. BUT I WANTED ANJA TO FEEL MORE EASY.

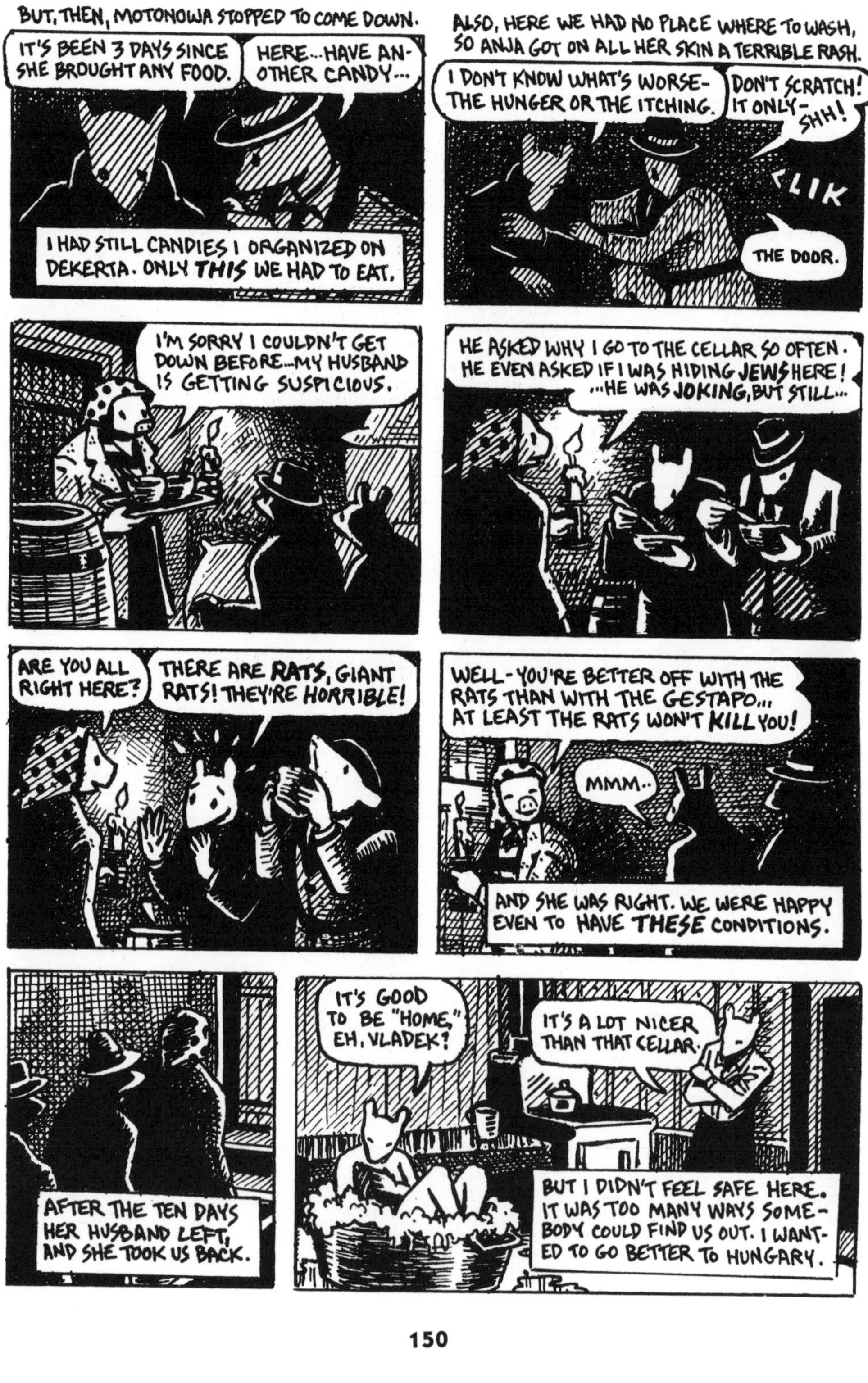
BUT, THEN, MOTONOWA STOPPED TO COME DOWN.
IT'S BEEN 3 DAYS SINCE SHE BROUGHT ANY FOOD.
HERE...HAVE ANOTHER CANDY...
I HAD STILL CANDIES I ORGANIZED ON DEKERTA. ONLY **THIS** WE HAD TO EAT.
ALSO, HERE WE HAD NO PLACE WHERE TO WASH, SO ANJA GOT ON ALL HER SKIN A TERRIBLE RASH.
I DON'T KNOW WHAT'S WORSE- THE HUNGER OR THE ITCHING.
DON'T SCRATCH! IT ONLY-
SHH!
CLIK
THE DOOR.
I'M SORRY I COULDN'T GET DOWN BEFORE...MY HUSBAND IS GETTING SUSPICIOUS.
HE ASKED WHY I GO TO THE CELLAR SO OFTEN. HE EVEN ASKED IF I WAS HIDING **JEWS** HERE! ...HE WAS **JOKING**, BUT STILL...
ARE YOU ALL RIGHT HERE?
THERE ARE **RATS**, GIANT RATS! THEY'RE **HORRIBLE**!
WELL- YOU'RE BETTER OFF WITH THE RATS THAN WITH THE GESTAPO... AT LEAST THE RATS WON'T **KILL** YOU!
MMM..
AND SHE WAS RIGHT. WE WERE HAPPY EVEN TO HAVE **THESE** CONDITIONS.
AFTER THE TEN DAYS HER HUSBAND LEFT, AND SHE TOOK US BACK.
IT'S GOOD TO BE "HOME," EH, VLADEK?
IT'S A LOT NICER THAN THAT CELLAR.
BUT I DIDN'T FEEL SAFE HERE. IT WAS TOO MANY WAYS SOMEBODY COULD FIND US OUT. I WANTED TO GO BETTER TO HUNGARY.

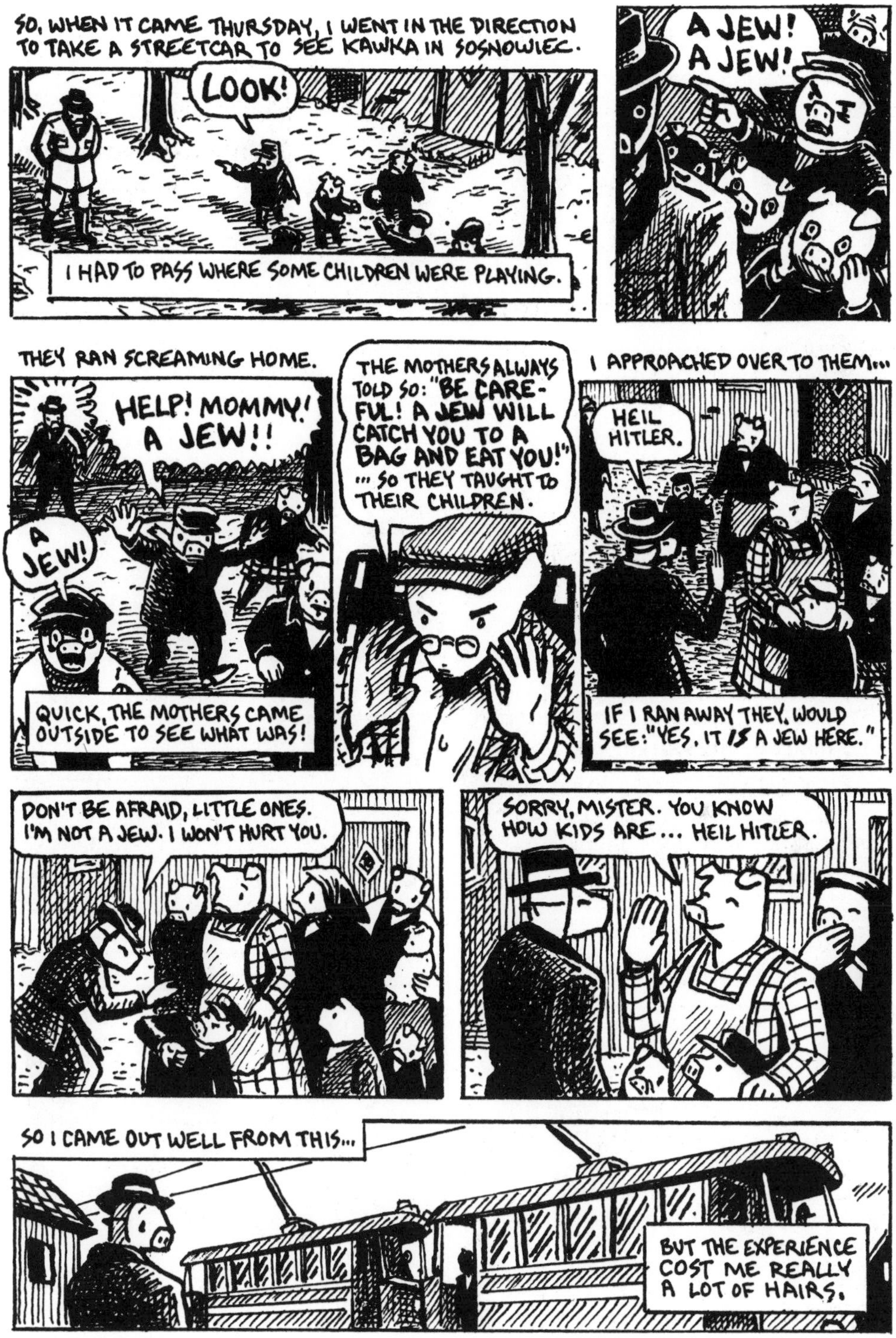
SO, WHEN IT CAME THURSDAY, I WENT IN THE DIRECTION TO TAKE A STREETCAR TO SEE KAWKA IN SOSNOWIEC.
LOOK!
I HAD TO PASS WHERE SOME CHILDREN WERE PLAYING.
A JEW! A JEW!
THEY RAN SCREAMING HOME.
HELP! MOMMY! A JEW!!
A JEW!
QUICK, THE MOTHERS CAME OUTSIDE TO SEE WHAT WAS!
THE MOTHERS ALWAYS TOLD SO: "BE CAREFUL! A JEW WILL CATCH YOU TO A BAG AND EAT YOU!" ...SO THEY TAUGHT TO THEIR CHILDREN.
I APPROACHED OVER TO THEM...
HEIL HITLER.
IF I RAN AWAY THEY WOULD SEE: "YES, IT IS A JEW HERE."
DON'T BE AFRAID, LITTLE ONES. I'M NOT A JEW. I WON'T HURT YOU.
SORRY, MISTER. YOU KNOW HOW KIDS ARE... HEIL HITLER.
SO I CAME OUT WELL FROM THIS...
BUT THE EXPERIENCE COST ME REALLY A LOT OF HAIRS.

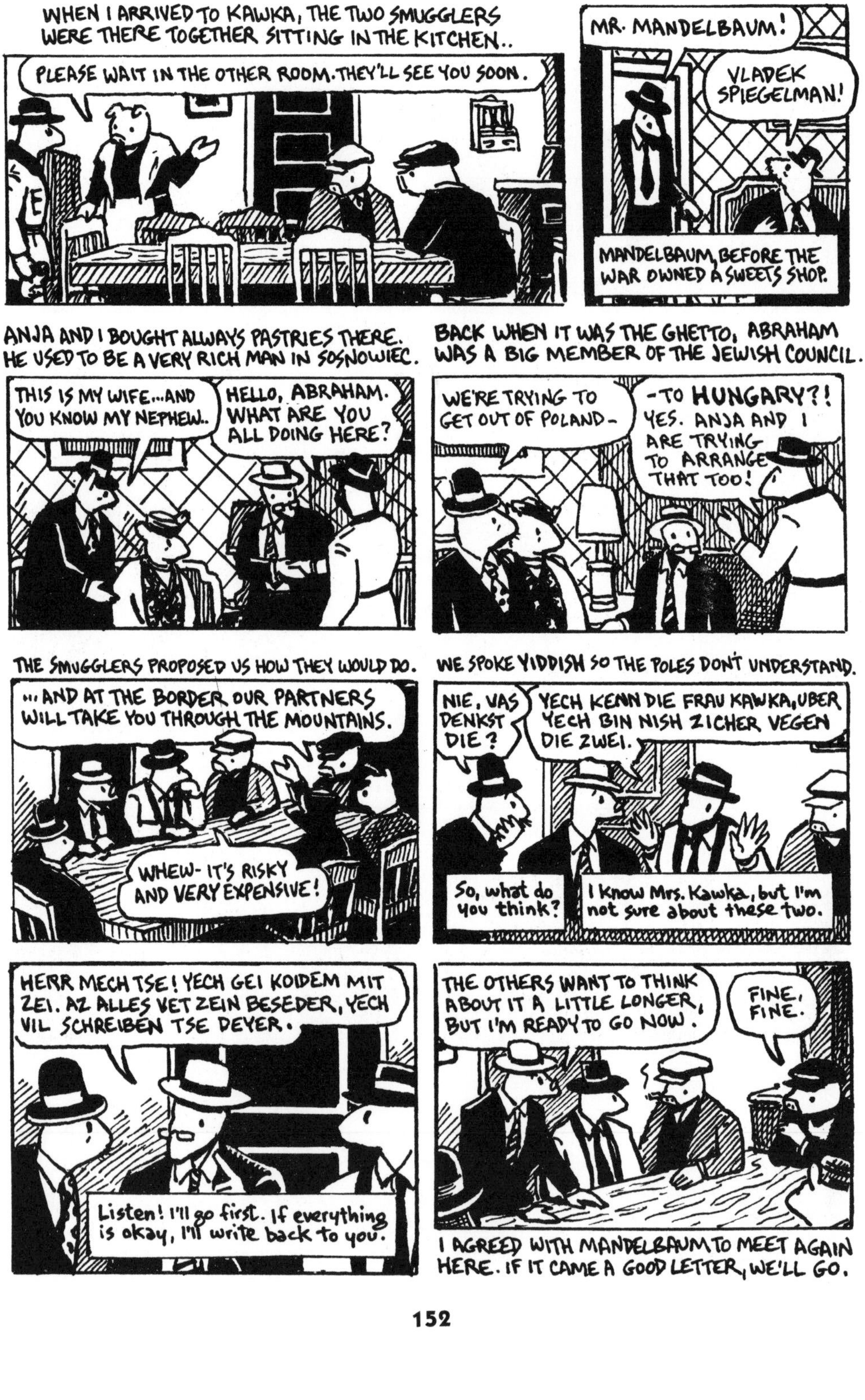
WHEN I ARRIVED TO KAWKA, THE TWO SMUGGLERS WERE THERE TOGETHER SITTING IN THE KITCHEN..
PLEASE WAIT IN THE OTHER ROOM. THEY'LL SEE YOU SOON.
MR. MANDELBAUM!
VLADEK SPIEGELMAN!
MANDELBAUM, BEFORE THE WAR OWNED A SWEETS SHOP.
ANJA AND I BOUGHT ALWAYS PASTRIES THERE. HE USED TO BE A VERY RICH MAN IN SOSNOWIEC.
THIS IS MY WIFE...AND YOU KNOW MY NEPHEW..
HELLO, ABRAHAM. WHAT ARE YOU ALL DOING HERE?
BACK WHEN IT WAS THE GHETTO, ABRAHAM WAS A BIG MEMBER OF THE JEWISH COUNCIL.
WE'RE TRYING TO GET OUT OF POLAND-
-TO HUNGARY?! YES. ANJA AND I ARE TRYING TO ARRANGE THAT TOO!
THE SMUGGLERS PROPOSED US HOW THEY WOULD DO.
...AND AT THE BORDER OUR PARTNERS WILL TAKE YOU THROUGH THE MOUNTAINS.
WHEW- IT'S RISKY AND VERY EXPENSIVE!
WE SPOKE YIDDISH SO THE POLES DON'T UNDERSTAND.
NIE, VAS DENKST DIE?
YECH KENN DIE FRAU KAWKA, UBER YECH BIN NISH ZICHER VEGEN DIE ZWEI.
So, what do you think?
I know Mrs. Kawka, but I'm not sure about these two.
HERR MECH TSE! YECH GEI KOIDEM MIT ZEI. AZ ALLES VET ZEIN BESEDER, YECH VIL SCHREIBEN TSE DEYER.
Listen! I'll go first. If everything is okay, I'll write back to you.
THE OTHERS WANT TO THINK ABOUT IT A LITTLE LONGER, BUT I'M READY TO GO NOW.
FINE, FINE.
I AGREED WITH MANDELBAUM TO MEET AGAIN HERE. IF IT CAME A GOOD LETTER, WE'LL GO.

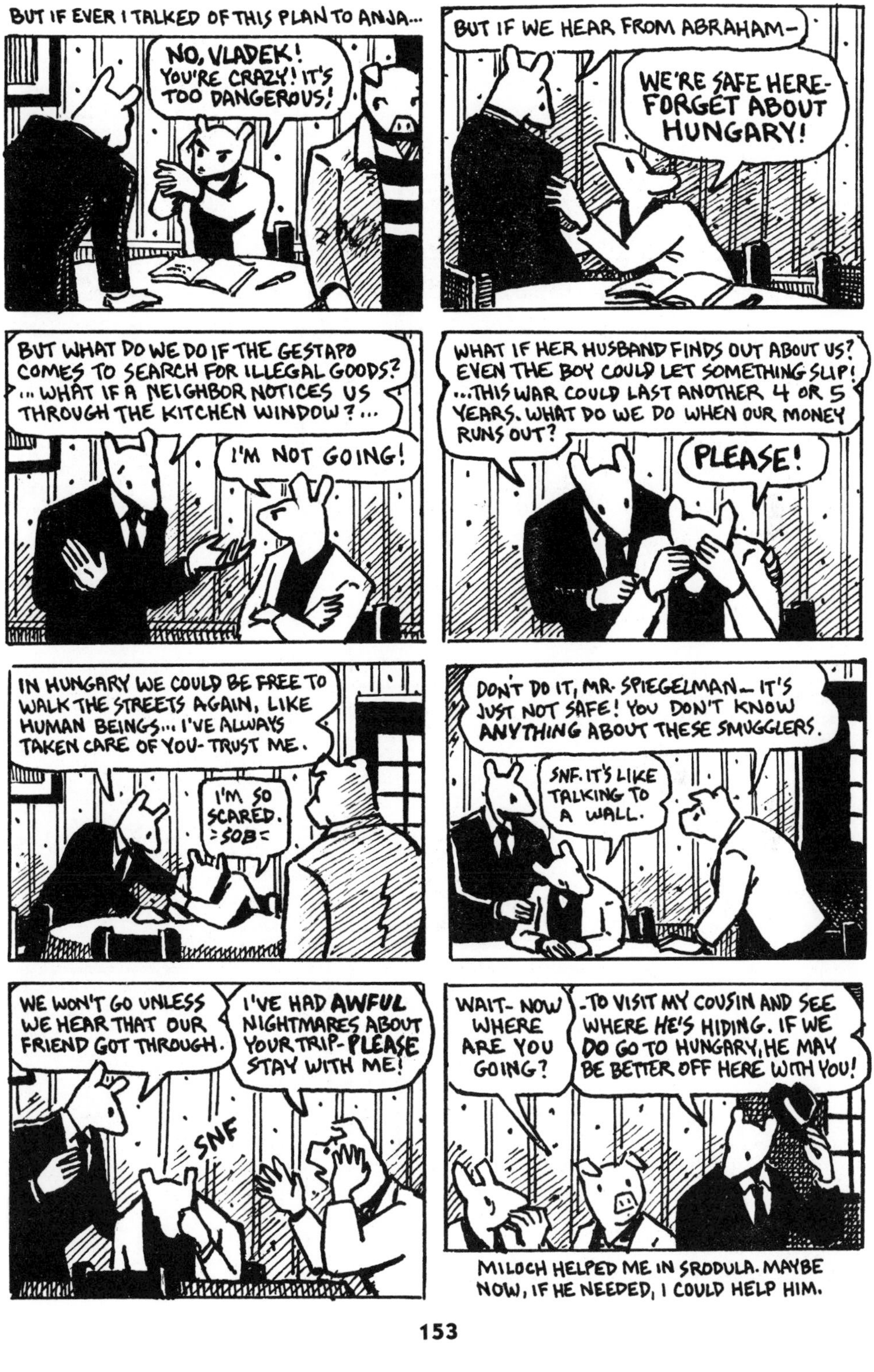

BUT IF EVER I TALKED OF THIS PLAN TO ANJA...
NO, VLADEK! YOU'RE CRAZY! IT'S TOO DANGEROUS!
BUT IF WE HEAR FROM ABRAHAM–
WE'RE SAFE HERE– FORGET ABOUT HUNGARY!
BUT WHAT DO WE DO IF THE GESTAPO COMES TO SEARCH FOR ILLEGAL GOODS? ...WHAT IF A NEIGHBOR NOTICES US THROUGH THE KITCHEN WINDOW?...
I'M NOT GOING!
WHAT IF HER HUSBAND FINDS OUT ABOUT US? EVEN THE BOY COULD LET SOMETHING SLIP! ...THIS WAR COULD LAST ANOTHER 4 OR 5 YEARS. WHAT DO WE DO WHEN OUR MONEY RUNS OUT?
PLEASE!
IN HUNGARY WE COULD BE FREE TO WALK THE STREETS AGAIN, LIKE HUMAN BEINGS... I'VE ALWAYS TAKEN CARE OF YOU– TRUST ME.
I'M SO SCARED. =SOB=
DON'T DO IT, MR. SPIEGELMAN– IT'S JUST NOT SAFE! YOU DON'T KNOW ANYTHING ABOUT THESE SMUGGLERS.
SNF. IT'S LIKE TALKING TO A WALL.
WE WON'T GO UNLESS WE HEAR THAT OUR FRIEND GOT THROUGH.
I'VE HAD AWFUL NIGHTMARES ABOUT YOUR TRIP– PLEASE STAY WITH ME!
SNF
WAIT– NOW WHERE ARE YOU GOING?
–TO VISIT MY COUSIN AND SEE WHERE HE'S HIDING. IF WE DO GO TO HUNGARY, HE MAY BE BETTER OFF HERE WITH YOU!
MILOCH HELPED ME IN SRODULA. MAYBE NOW, IF HE NEEDED, I COULD HELP HIM.

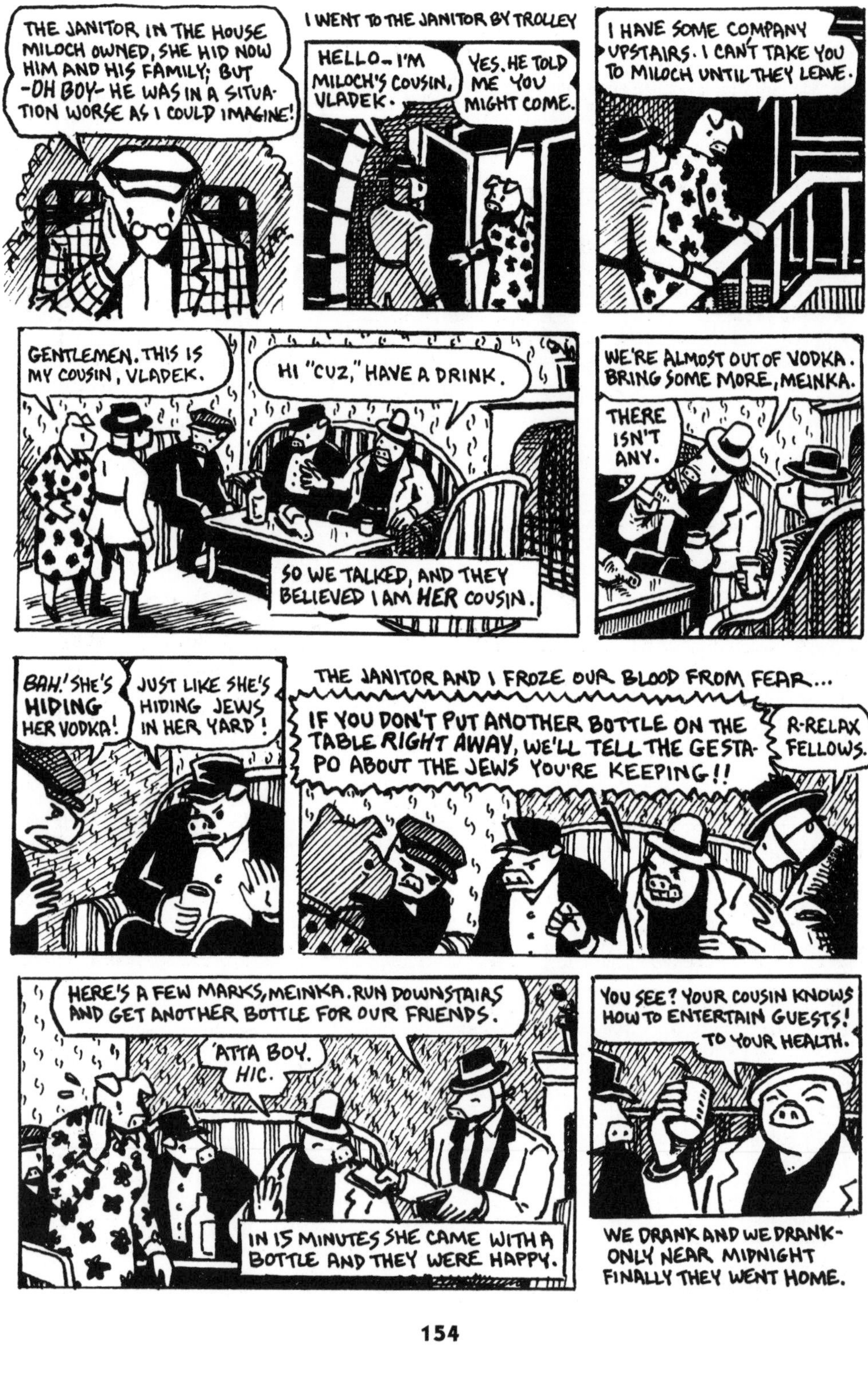

THE JANITOR IN THE HOUSE MILOCH OWNED, SHE HID NOW HIM AND HIS FAMILY; BUT -OH BOY- HE WAS IN A SITUATION WORSE AS I COULD IMAGINE!
I WENT TO THE JANITOR BY TROLLEY
HELLO - I'M MILOCH'S COUSIN, VLADEK.
YES. HE TOLD ME YOU MIGHT COME.
I HAVE SOME COMPANY UPSTAIRS. I CAN'T TAKE YOU TO MILOCH UNTIL THEY LEAVE.
GENTLEMEN. THIS IS MY COUSIN, VLADEK.
HI "CUZ," HAVE A DRINK.
SO WE TALKED, AND THEY BELIEVED I AM HER COUSIN.
WE'RE ALMOST OUT OF VODKA. BRING SOME MORE, MEINKA.
THERE ISN'T ANY.
BAH! SHE'S HIDING HER VODKA!
JUST LIKE SHE'S HIDING JEWS IN HER YARD!
THE JANITOR AND I FROZE OUR BLOOD FROM FEAR...
IF YOU DON'T PUT ANOTHER BOTTLE ON THE TABLE RIGHT AWAY, WE'LL TELL THE GESTAPO ABOUT THE JEWS YOU'RE KEEPING!!
R-RELAX FELLOWS.
HERE'S A FEW MARKS, MEINKA. RUN DOWNSTAIRS AND GET ANOTHER BOTTLE FOR OUR FRIENDS.
'ATTA BOY. HIC.
IN 15 MINUTES SHE CAME WITH A BOTTLE AND THEY WERE HAPPY.
YOU SEE? YOUR COUSIN KNOWS HOW TO ENTERTAIN GUESTS!
TO YOUR HEALTH.
WE DRANK AND WE DRANK - ONLY NEAR MIDNIGHT FINALLY THEY WENT HOME.

155

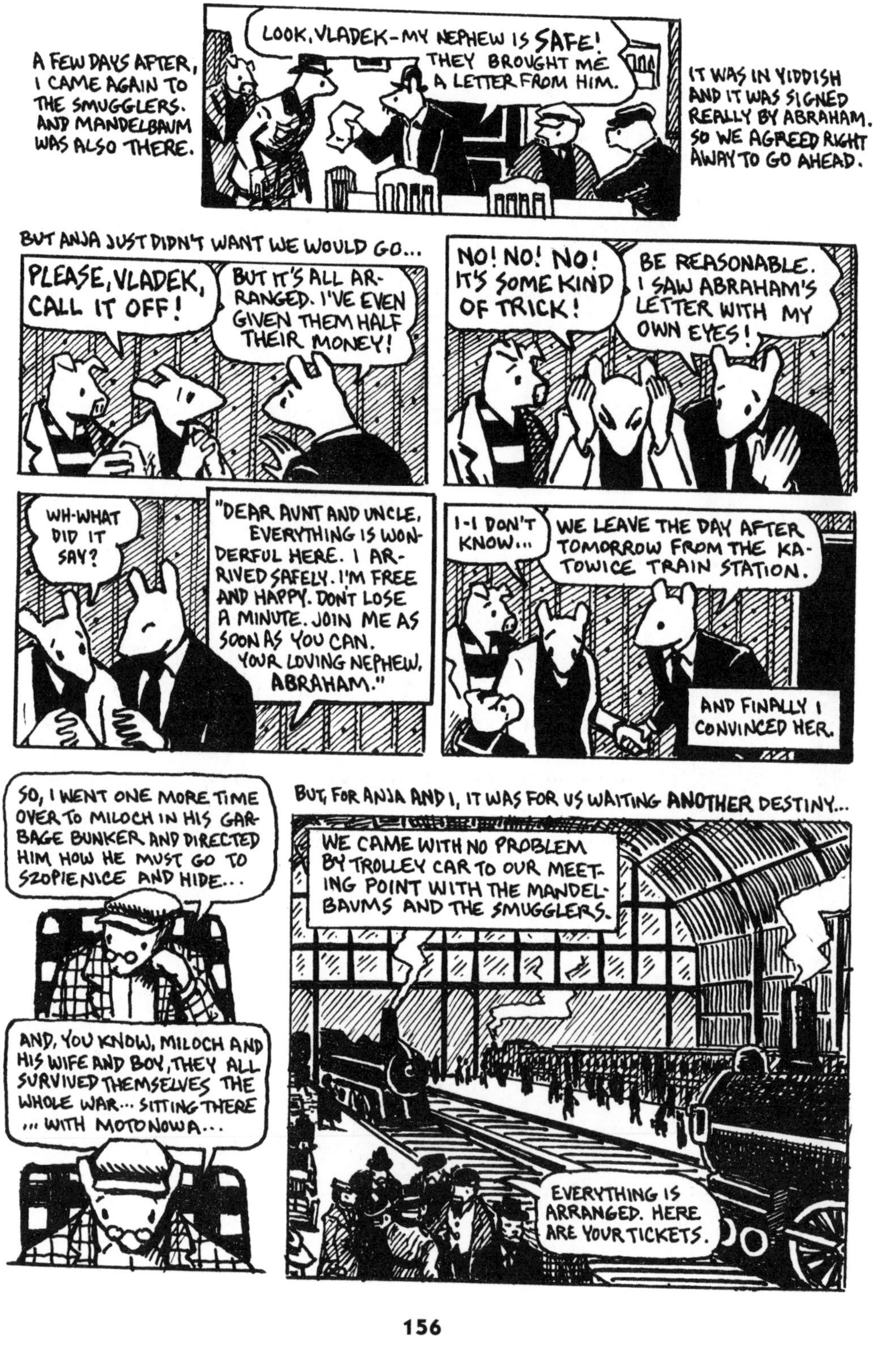

A FEW DAYS AFTER, I CAME AGAIN TO THE SMUGGLERS. AND MANDELBAUM WAS ALSO THERE.
LOOK, VLADEK-MY NEPHEW IS SAFE! THEY BROUGHT ME A LETTER FROM HIM.
IT WAS IN YIDDISH AND IT WAS SIGNED REALLY BY ABRAHAM. SO WE AGREED RIGHT AWAY TO GO AHEAD.
BUT ANJA JUST DIDN'T WANT WE WOULD GO...
PLEASE, VLADEK, CALL IT OFF!
BUT IT'S ALL ARRANGED. I'VE EVEN GIVEN THEM HALF THEIR MONEY!
NO! NO! NO! IT'S SOME KIND OF TRICK!
BE REASONABLE. I SAW ABRAHAM'S LETTER WITH MY OWN EYES!
WH-WHAT DID IT SAY?
"DEAR AUNT AND UNCLE, EVERYTHING IS WONDERFUL HERE. I ARRIVED SAFELY. I'M FREE AND HAPPY. DON'T LOSE A MINUTE. JOIN ME AS SOON AS YOU CAN. YOUR LOVING NEPHEW, ABRAHAM."
I-I DON'T KNOW...
WE LEAVE THE DAY AFTER TOMORROW FROM THE KATOWICE TRAIN STATION.
AND FINALLY I CONVINCED HER.
SO, I WENT ONE MORE TIME OVER TO MILOCH IN HIS GARBAGE BUNKER AND DIRECTED HIM HOW HE MUST GO TO SZOPIENICE AND HIDE...
AND, YOU KNOW, MILOCH AND HIS WIFE AND BOY, THEY ALL SURVIVED THEMSELVES THE WHOLE WAR... SITTING THERE ... WITH MOTONOWA...
BUT, FOR ANJA AND I, IT WAS FOR US WAITING ANOTHER DESTINY...
WE CAME WITH NO PROBLEM BY TROLLEY CAR TO OUR MEETING POINT WITH THE MANDELBAUMS AND THE SMUGGLERS.
EVERYTHING IS ARRANGED. HERE ARE YOUR TICKETS.

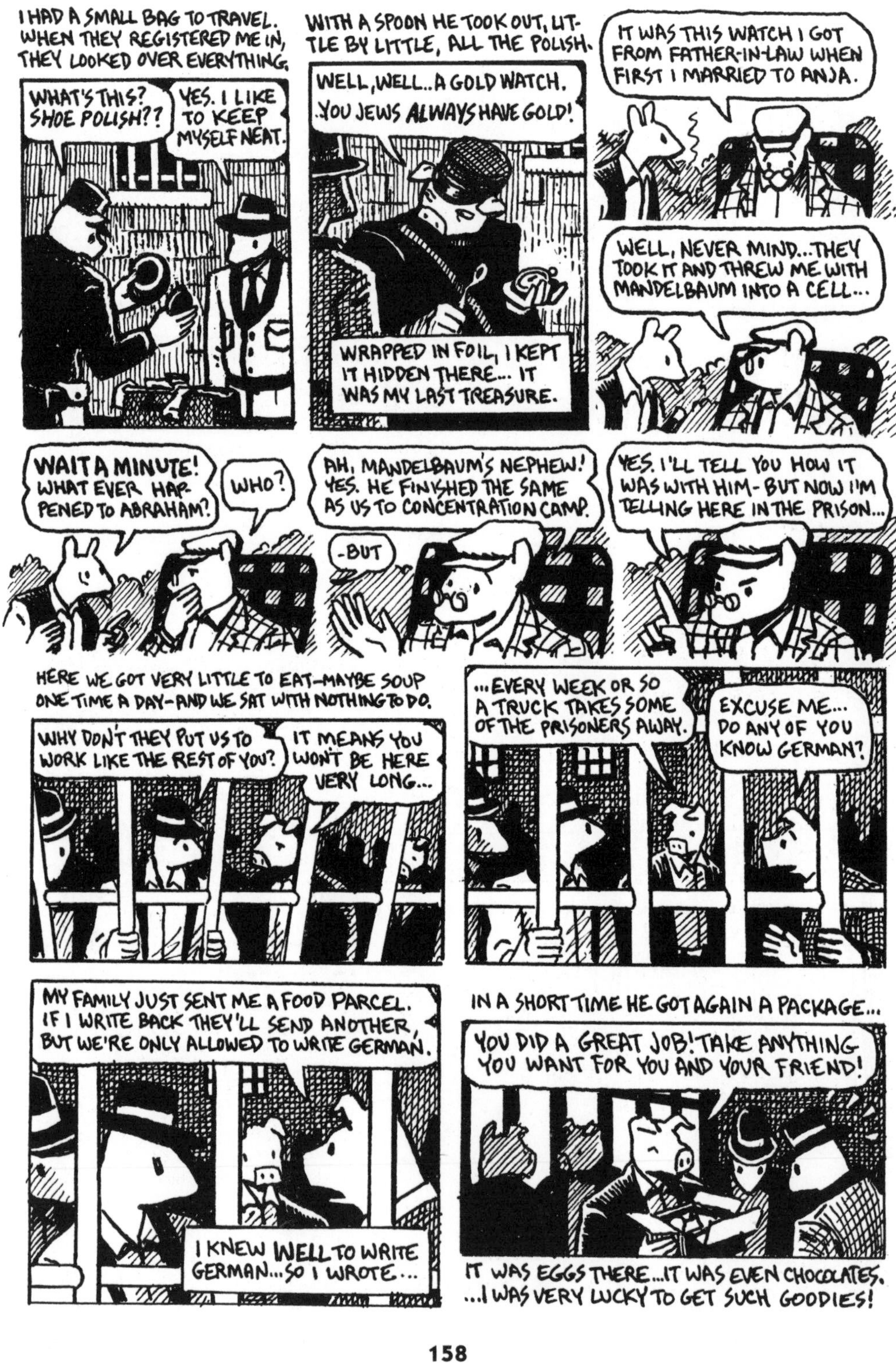

I HAD A SMALL BAG TO TRAVEL. WHEN THEY REGISTERED ME IN, THEY LOOKED OVER EVERYTHING.
WHAT'S THIS? SHOE POLISH??
YES. I LIKE TO KEEP MYSELF NEAT.
WITH A SPOON HE TOOK OUT, LITTLE BY LITTLE, ALL THE POLISH.
WELL, WELL... A GOLD WATCH. YOU JEWS ALWAYS HAVE GOLD!
WRAPPED IN FOIL, I KEPT IT HIDDEN THERE... IT WAS MY LAST TREASURE.
IT WAS THIS WATCH I GOT FROM FATHER-IN-LAW WHEN FIRST I MARRIED TO ANJA.
WELL, NEVER MIND... THEY TOOK IT AND THREW ME WITH MANDELBAUM INTO A CELL...
WAIT A MINUTE! WHAT EVER HAPPENED TO ABRAHAM?
WHO?
AH, MANDELBAUM'S NEPHEW! YES. HE FINISHED THE SAME AS US TO CONCENTRATION CAMP.
-BUT
YES. I'LL TELL YOU HOW IT WAS WITH HIM- BUT NOW I'M TELLING HERE IN THE PRISON...
HERE WE GOT VERY LITTLE TO EAT-MAYBE SOUP ONE TIME A DAY-AND WE SAT WITH NOTHING TO DO.
WHY DON'T THEY PUT US TO WORK LIKE THE REST OF YOU?
IT MEANS YOU WON'T BE HERE VERY LONG...
...EVERY WEEK OR SO A TRUCK TAKES SOME OF THE PRISONERS AWAY.
EXCUSE ME... DO ANY OF YOU KNOW GERMAN?
MY FAMILY JUST SENT ME A FOOD PARCEL. IF I WRITE BACK THEY'LL SEND ANOTHER, BUT WE'RE ONLY ALLOWED TO WRITE GERMAN.
I KNEW WELL TO WRITE GERMAN... SO I WROTE...
IN A SHORT TIME HE GOT AGAIN A PACKAGE...
YOU DID A GREAT JOB! TAKE ANYTHING YOU WANT FOR YOU AND YOUR FRIEND!
IT WAS EGGS THERE... IT WAS EVEN CHOCOLATES. ...I WAS VERY LUCKY TO GET SUCH GOODIES!

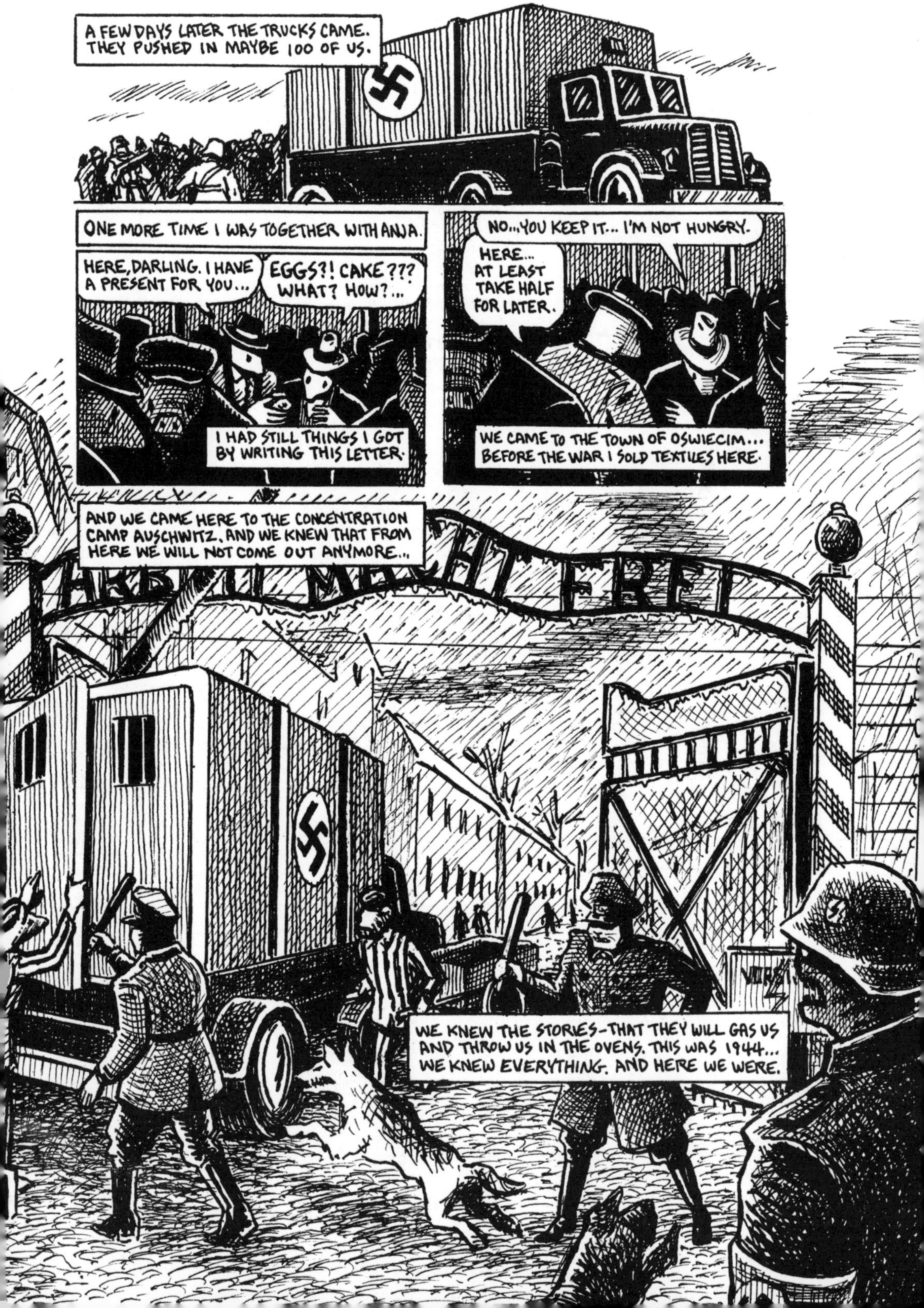
A FEW DAYS LATER THE TRUCKS CAME. THEY PUSHED IN MAYBE 100 OF US.
ONE MORE TIME I WAS TOGETHER WITH ANJA.
HERE, DARLING. I HAVE A PRESENT FOR YOU...
EGGS?! CAKE??? WHAT? HOW?...
I HAD STILL THINGS I GOT BY WRITING THIS LETTER.
NO...YOU KEEP IT... I'M NOT HUNGRY.
HERE... AT LEAST TAKE HALF FOR LATER.
WE CAME TO THE TOWN OF OSWIECIM... BEFORE THE WAR I SOLD TEXTILES HERE.
AND WE CAME HERE TO THE CONCENTRATION CAMP AUSCHWITZ, AND WE KNEW THAT FROM HERE WE WILL NOT COME OUT ANYMORE...
WE KNEW THE STORIES - THAT THEY WILL GAS US AND THROW US IN THE OVENS. THIS WAS 1944... WE KNEW EVERYTHING. AND HERE WE WERE.

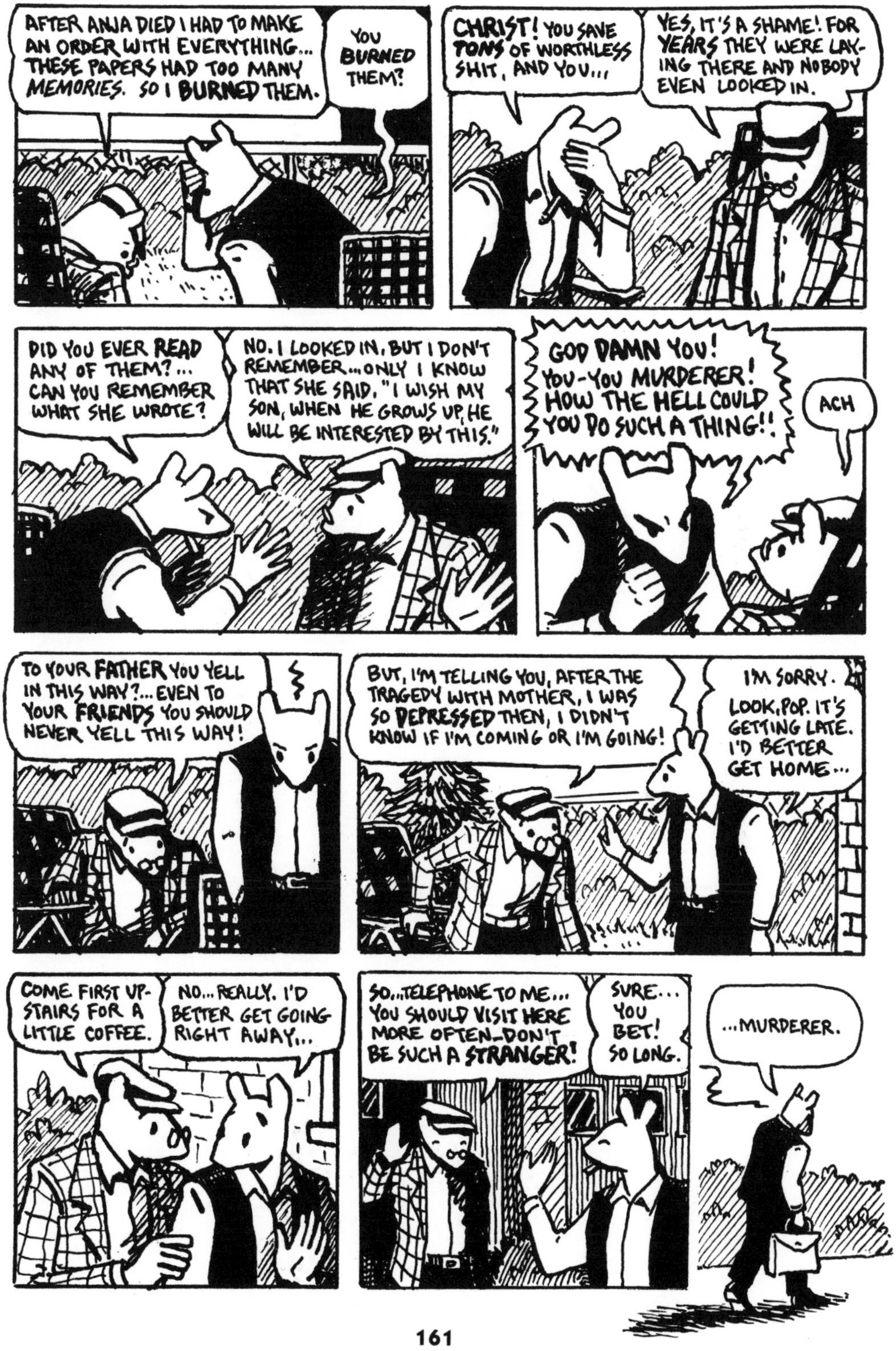

AFTER ANJA DIED I HAD TO MAKE AN ORDER WITH EVERYTHING... THESE PAPERS HAD TOO MANY MEMORIES. SO I BURNED THEM.
YOU BURNED THEM?
CHRIST! YOU SAVE TONS OF WORTHLESS SHIT, AND YOU...
YES, IT'S A SHAME! FOR YEARS THEY WERE LAYING THERE AND NOBODY EVEN LOOKED IN.
DID YOU EVER READ ANY OF THEM?... CAN YOU REMEMBER WHAT SHE WROTE?
NO. I LOOKED IN, BUT I DON'T REMEMBER...ONLY I KNOW THAT SHE SAID, "I WISH MY SON, WHEN HE GROWS UP, HE WILL BE INTERESTED BY THIS."
GOD DAMN YOU! YOU-YOU MURDERER! HOW THE HELL COULD YOU DO SUCH A THING!!
ACH
TO YOUR FATHER YOU YELL IN THIS WAY?... EVEN TO YOUR FRIENDS YOU SHOULD NEVER YELL THIS WAY!
BUT, I'M TELLING YOU, AFTER THE TRAGEDY WITH MOTHER, I WAS SO DEPRESSED THEN, I DIDN'T KNOW IF I'M COMING OR I'M GOING!
I'M SORRY.
LOOK, POP. IT'S GETTING LATE. I'D BETTER GET HOME...
COME FIRST UPSTAIRS FOR A LITTLE COFFEE.
NO... REALLY. I'D BETTER GET GOING RIGHT AWAY...
SO... TELEPHONE TO ME... YOU SHOULD VISIT HERE MORE OFTEN. DON'T BE SUCH A STRANGER!
SURE... YOU BET! SO LONG.
...MURDERER.

MAUS II

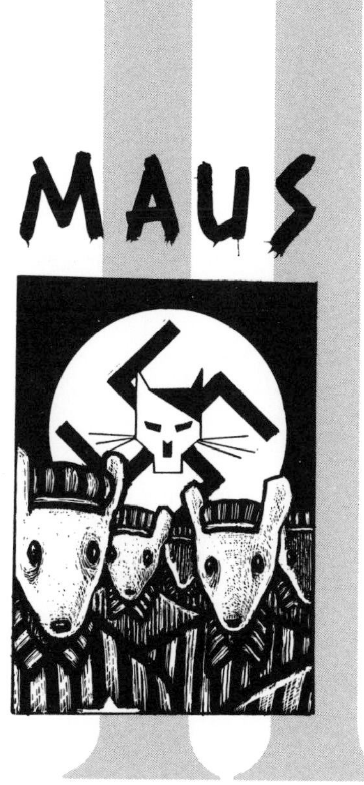

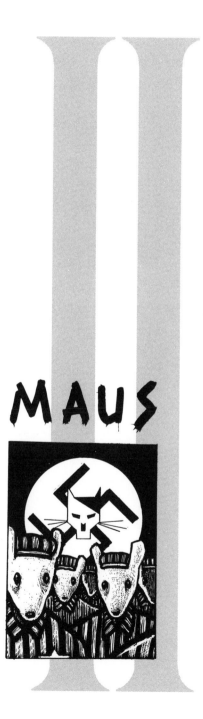

"Mickey Mouse is the most miserable ideal ever revealed.... Healthy emotions tell every independent young man and every honorable youth that the dirty and filth-covered vermin, the greatest bacteria carrier in the animal kingdom, cannot be the ideal type of animal.... Away with Jewish brutalization of the people! Down with Mickey Mouse! Wear the Swastika Cross!"

—newspaper article, Pomerania, Germany, mid-1930s

FOR RICHIEU

AND FOR NADJA
AND DASHIELL

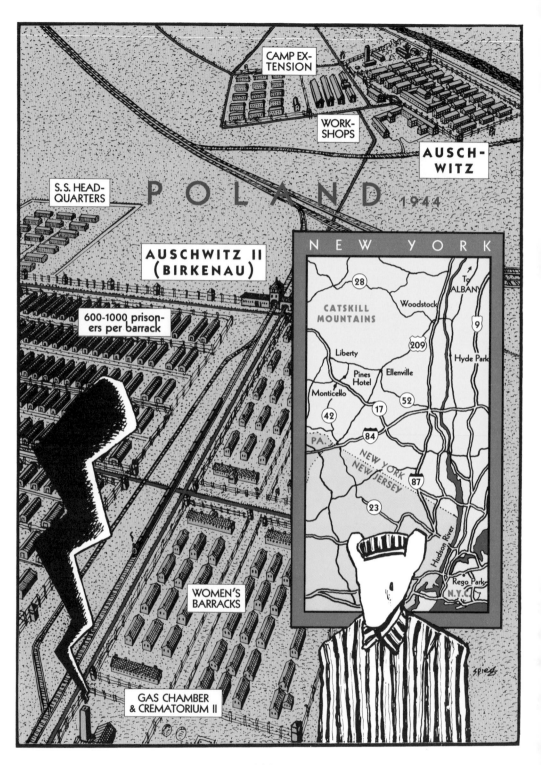

CAMP EX-
TENSION

WORK-
SHOPS

AUSCH-
WITZ

S.S. HEAD-
QUARTERS

P O L A N D 1944

AUSCHWITZ II
(BIRKENAU)

600-1000 prison-
ers per barrack

WOMEN'S
BARRACKS

GAS CHAMBER
& CREMATORIUM II

N E W   Y O R K

28

To
ALBANY

CATSKILL
MOUNTAINS

Woodstock

209

9

Liberty

Ellenville

Hyde Park

Pines
Hotel

Monticello

52

17

42

84

PA.

NEW YORK
NEW JERSEY

87

23

Hudson River

Rego Park

N.Y.C.

spieg

AND HERE MY TROUBLES BEGAN

(FROM MAUSCHWITZ TO THE CATSKILLS AND BEYOND)

CONTENTS

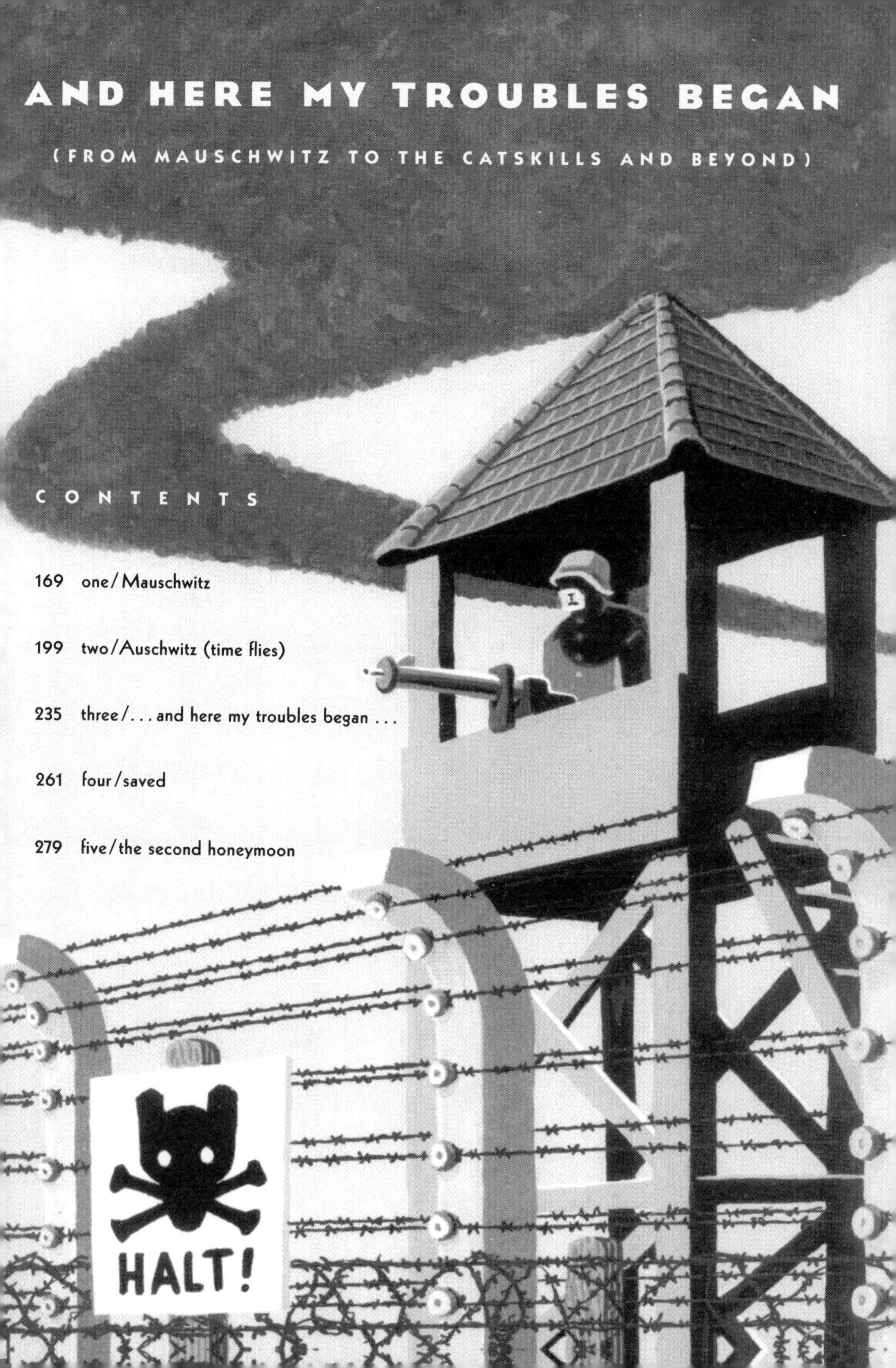

HALT!

CHAPTER ONE

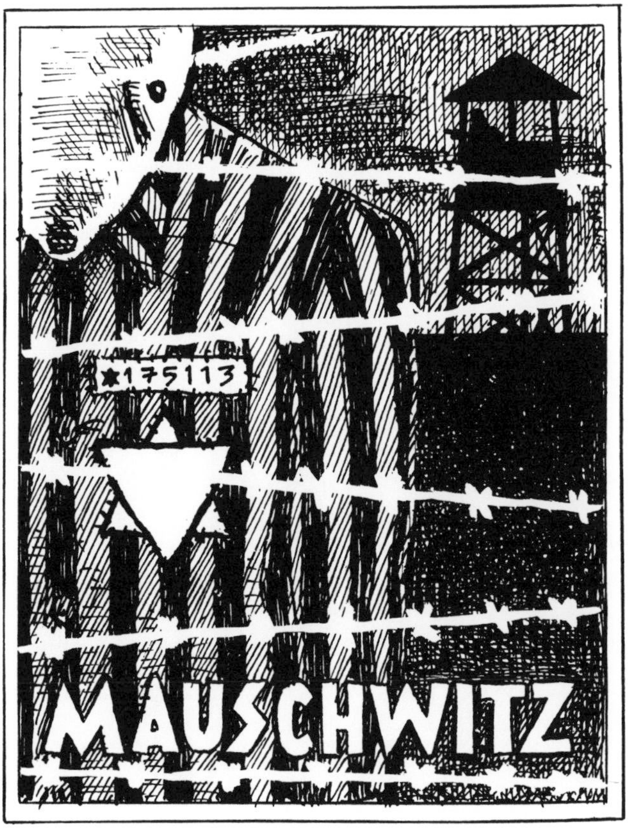

175113
MAUSCHWITZ

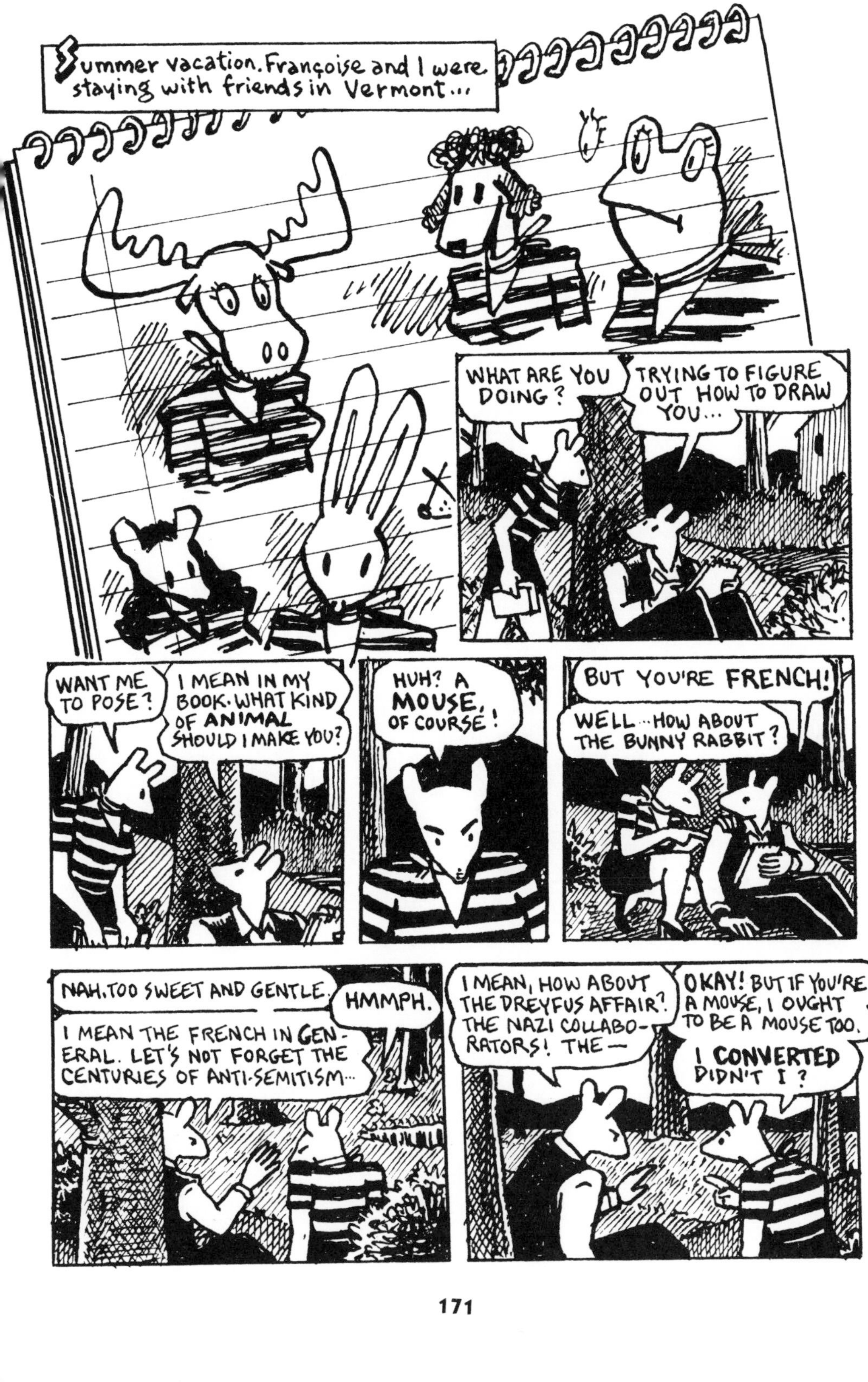
Summer vacation. Françoise and I were staying with friends in Vermont...
WHAT ARE YOU DOING?
TRYING TO FIGURE OUT HOW TO DRAW YOU...
WANT ME TO POSE?
I MEAN IN MY BOOK. WHAT KIND OF ANIMAL SHOULD I MAKE YOU?
HUH? A MOUSE, OF COURSE!
BUT YOU'RE FRENCH!
WELL... HOW ABOUT THE BUNNY RABBIT?
NAH, TOO SWEET AND GENTLE.
HMMPH.
I MEAN THE FRENCH IN GENERAL. LET'S NOT FORGET THE CENTURIES OF ANTI-SEMITISM...
I MEAN, HOW ABOUT THE DREYFUS AFFAIR? THE NAZI COLLABORATORS! THE—
OKAY! BUT IF YOU'RE A MOUSE, I OUGHT TO BE A MOUSE TOO.
I CONVERTED DIDN'T I?

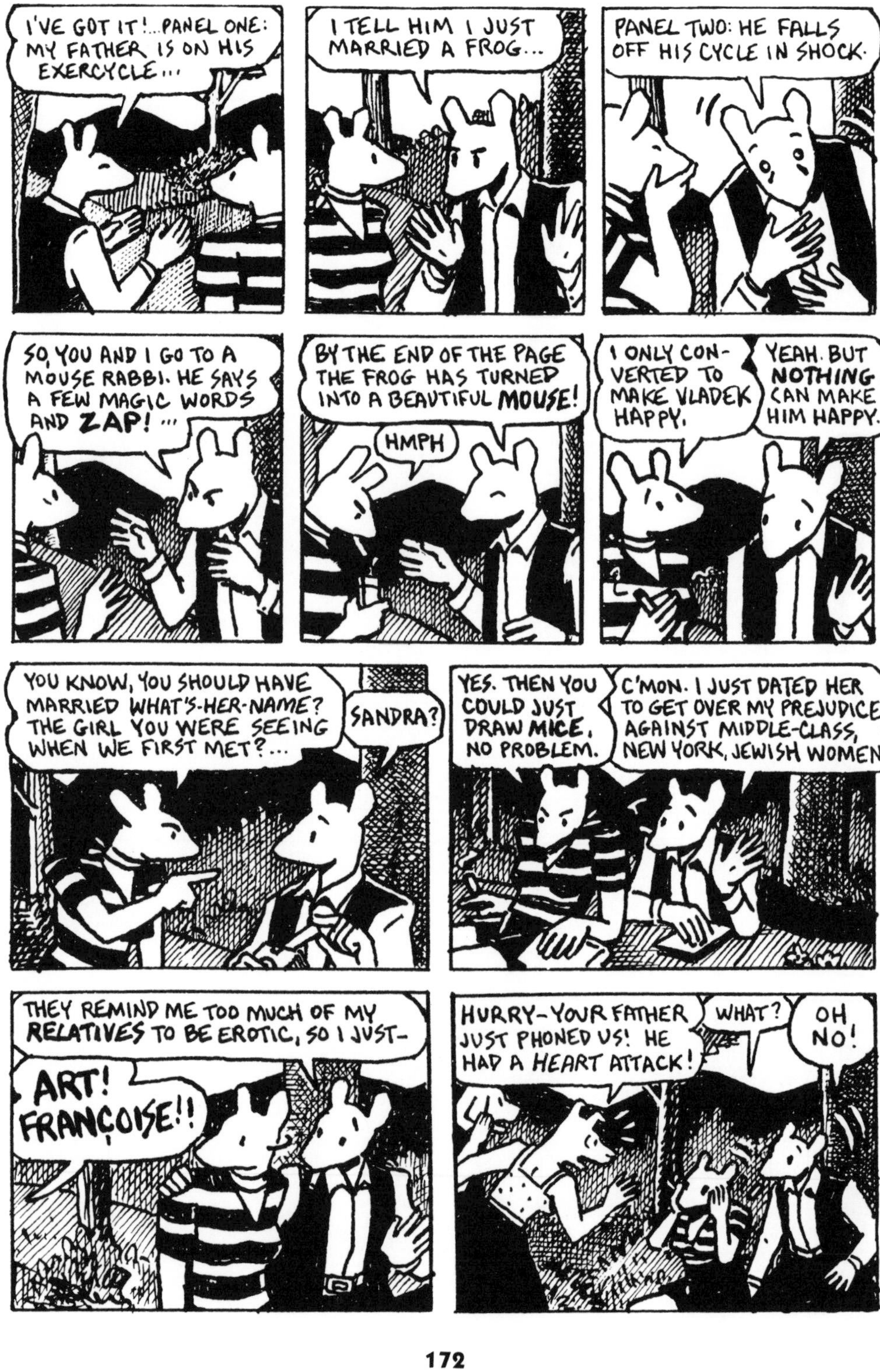
I'VE GOT IT!...PANEL ONE: MY FATHER IS ON HIS EXERCYCLE...
I TELL HIM I JUST MARRIED A FROG...
PANEL TWO: HE FALLS OFF HIS CYCLE IN SHOCK.
SO, YOU AND I GO TO A MOUSE RABBI. HE SAYS A FEW MAGIC WORDS AND ZAP!...
BY THE END OF THE PAGE THE FROG HAS TURNED INTO A BEAUTIFUL MOUSE!
HMPH
I ONLY CONVERTED TO MAKE VLADEK HAPPY.
YEAH. BUT NOTHING CAN MAKE HIM HAPPY.
YOU KNOW, YOU SHOULD HAVE MARRIED WHAT'S-HER-NAME? THE GIRL YOU WERE SEEING WHEN WE FIRST MET?...
SANDRA?
YES. THEN YOU COULD JUST DRAW MICE, NO PROBLEM.
C'MON. I JUST DATED HER TO GET OVER MY PREJUDICE AGAINST MIDDLE-CLASS, NEW YORK, JEWISH WOMEN.
THEY REMIND ME TOO MUCH OF MY RELATIVES TO BE EROTIC, SO I JUST-
ART! FRANÇOISE!!
HURRY-YOUR FATHER JUST PHONED US! HE HAD A HEART ATTACK!
WHAT?
OH NO!

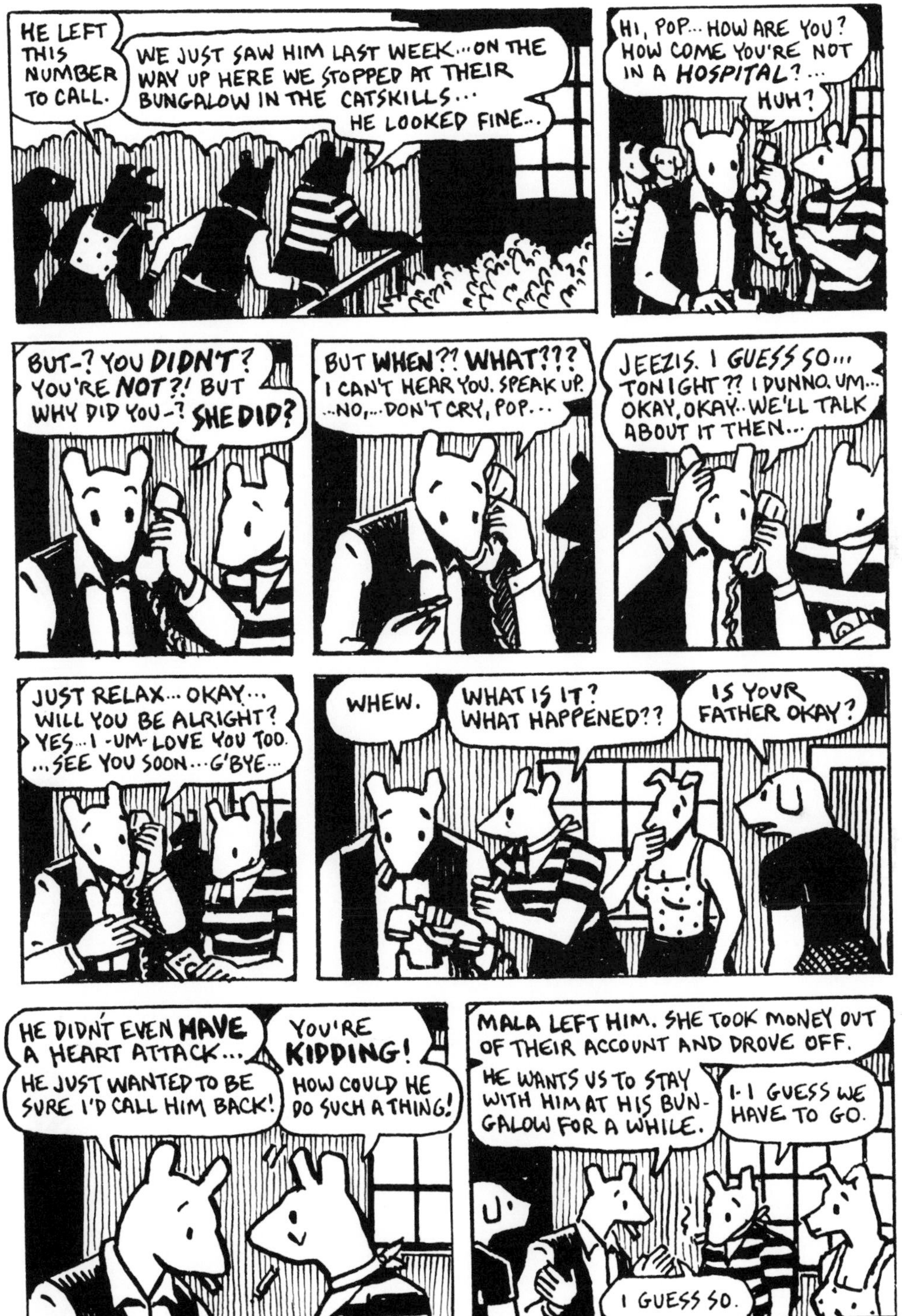
HE LEFT THIS NUMBER TO CALL.
WE JUST SAW HIM LAST WEEK... ON THE WAY UP HERE WE STOPPED AT THEIR BUNGALOW IN THE CATSKILLS... HE LOOKED FINE...
HI, POP... HOW ARE YOU? HOW COME YOU'RE NOT IN A HOSPITAL?... HUH?
BUT-? YOU DIDN'T? YOU'RE NOT?! BUT WHY DID YOU-? SHE DID?
BUT WHEN?? WHAT??? I CAN'T HEAR YOU. SPEAK UP. ...NO,... DON'T CRY, POP...
JEEZIS. I GUESS SO... TONIGHT?? I DUNNO. UM... OKAY, OKAY.. WE'LL TALK ABOUT IT THEN...
JUST RELAX... OKAY... WILL YOU BE ALRIGHT? YES... I -UM- LOVE YOU TOO. ...SEE YOU SOON... G'BYE...
WHEW.
WHAT IS IT? WHAT HAPPENED??
IS YOUR FATHER OKAY?
HE DIDN'T EVEN HAVE A HEART ATTACK...
HE JUST WANTED TO BE SURE I'D CALL HIM BACK!
YOU'RE KIDDING!
HOW COULD HE DO SUCH A THING!
MALA LEFT HIM. SHE TOOK MONEY OUT OF THEIR ACCOUNT AND DROVE OFF.
HE WANTS US TO STAY WITH HIM AT HIS BUN-GALOW FOR A WHILE.
I- I GUESS WE HAVE TO GO.
I GUESS SO.

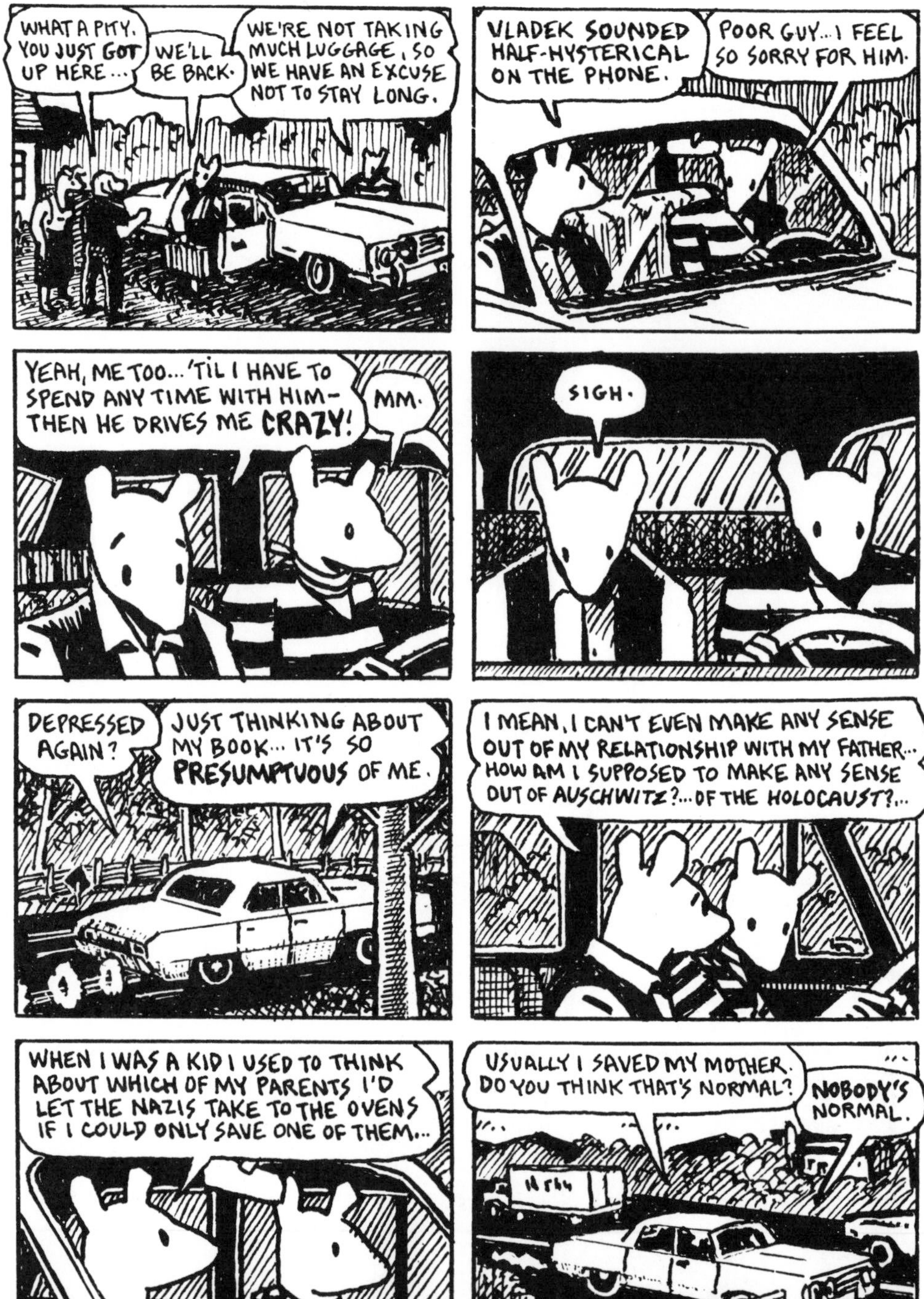
WHAT A PITY. YOU JUST GOT UP HERE...
WE'LL BE BACK.
WE'RE NOT TAKING MUCH LUGGAGE, SO WE HAVE AN EXCUSE NOT TO STAY LONG.
VLADEK SOUNDED HALF-HYSTERICAL ON THE PHONE.
POOR GUY... I FEEL SO SORRY FOR HIM.
YEAH, ME TOO... 'TIL I HAVE TO SPEND ANY TIME WITH HIM- THEN HE DRIVES ME CRAZY!
MM.
SIGH.
DEPRESSED AGAIN?
JUST THINKING ABOUT MY BOOK... IT'S SO PRESUMPTUOUS OF ME.
I MEAN, I CAN'T EVEN MAKE ANY SENSE OUT OF MY RELATIONSHIP WITH MY FATHER... HOW AM I SUPPOSED TO MAKE ANY SENSE OUT OF AUSCHWITZ?... OF THE HOLOCAUST?...
WHEN I WAS A KID I USED TO THINK ABOUT WHICH OF MY PARENTS I'D LET THE NAZIS TAKE TO THE OVENS IF I COULD ONLY SAVE ONE OF THEM...
USUALLY I SAVED MY MOTHER. DO YOU THINK THAT'S NORMAL?
NOBODY'S NORMAL.

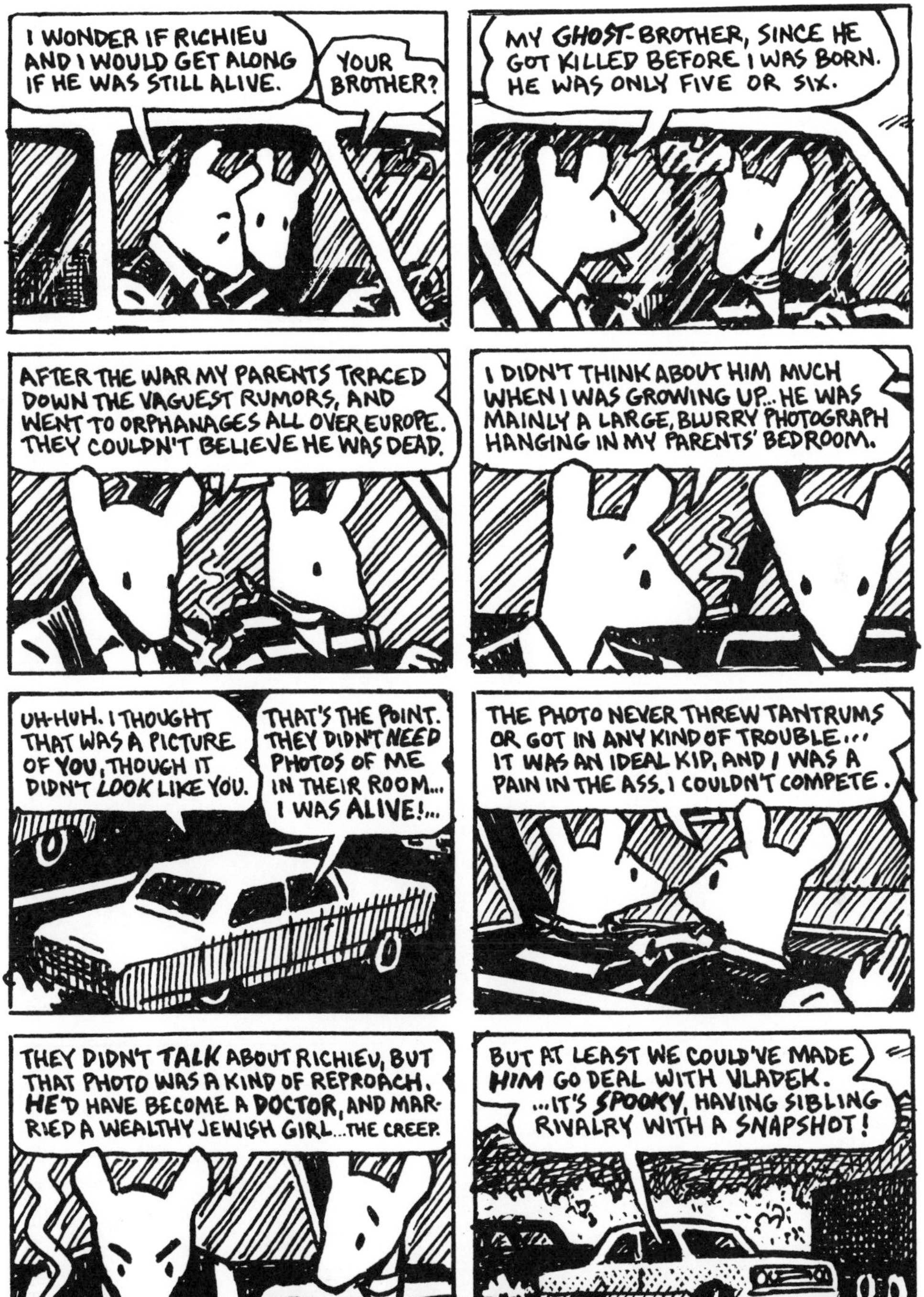
I WONDER IF RICHIEU AND I WOULD GET ALONG IF HE WAS STILL ALIVE.
YOUR BROTHER?
MY GHOST-BROTHER, SINCE HE GOT KILLED BEFORE I WAS BORN. HE WAS ONLY FIVE OR SIX.
AFTER THE WAR MY PARENTS TRACED DOWN THE VAGUEST RUMORS, AND WENT TO ORPHANAGES ALL OVER EUROPE. THEY COULDN'T BELIEVE HE WAS DEAD.
I DIDN'T THINK ABOUT HIM MUCH WHEN I WAS GROWING UP... HE WAS MAINLY A LARGE, BLURRY PHOTOGRAPH HANGING IN MY PARENTS' BEDROOM.
UH-HUH. I THOUGHT THAT WAS A PICTURE OF YOU, THOUGH IT DIDN'T LOOK LIKE YOU.
THAT'S THE POINT. THEY DIDN'T NEED PHOTOS OF ME IN THEIR ROOM... I WAS ALIVE!...
THE PHOTO NEVER THREW TANTRUMS OR GOT IN ANY KIND OF TROUBLE... IT WAS AN IDEAL KID, AND I WAS A PAIN IN THE ASS. I COULDN'T COMPETE.
THEY DIDN'T TALK ABOUT RICHIEU, BUT THAT PHOTO WAS A KIND OF REPROACH. HE'D HAVE BECOME A DOCTOR, AND MARRIED A WEALTHY JEWISH GIRL...THE CREEP.
BUT AT LEAST WE COULD'VE MADE HIM GO DEAL WITH VLADEK. ...IT'S SPOOKY, HAVING SIBLING RIVALRY WITH A SNAPSHOT!

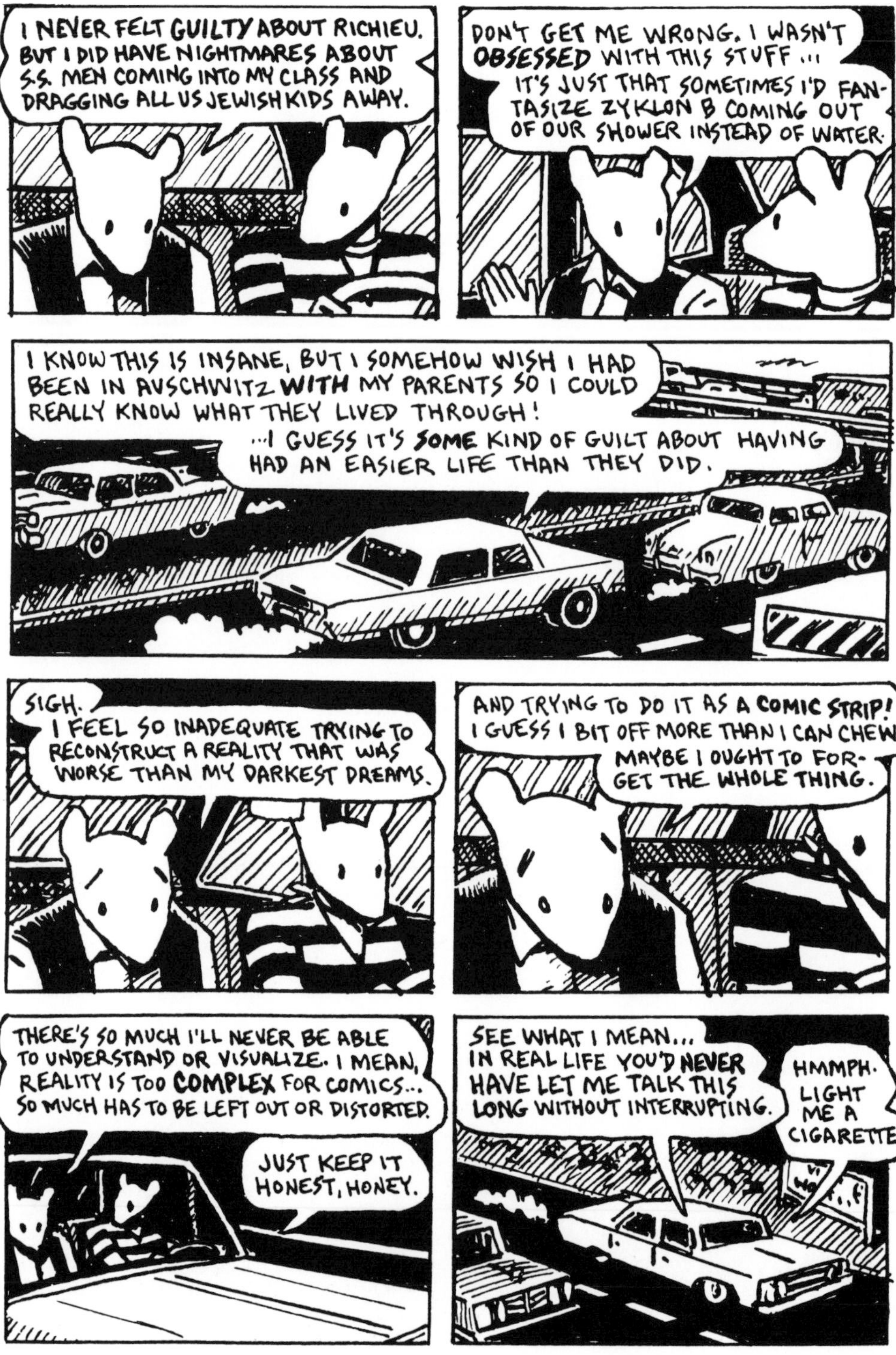
I NEVER FELT GUILTY ABOUT RICHIEU. BUT I DID HAVE NIGHTMARES ABOUT S.S. MEN COMING INTO MY CLASS AND DRAGGING ALL US JEWISH KIDS AWAY.
DON'T GET ME WRONG. I WASN'T OBSESSED WITH THIS STUFF ...
IT'S JUST THAT SOMETIMES I'D FANTASIZE ZYKLON B COMING OUT OF OUR SHOWER INSTEAD OF WATER.
I KNOW THIS IS INSANE, BUT I SOMEHOW WISH I HAD BEEN IN AUSCHWITZ WITH MY PARENTS SO I COULD REALLY KNOW WHAT THEY LIVED THROUGH!
...I GUESS IT'S SOME KIND OF GUILT ABOUT HAVING HAD AN EASIER LIFE THAN THEY DID.
SIGH.
I FEEL SO INADEQUATE TRYING TO RECONSTRUCT A REALITY THAT WAS WORSE THAN MY DARKEST DREAMS.
AND TRYING TO DO IT AS A COMIC STRIP! I GUESS I BIT OFF MORE THAN I CAN CHEW.
MAYBE I OUGHT TO FORGET THE WHOLE THING.
THERE'S SO MUCH I'LL NEVER BE ABLE TO UNDERSTAND OR VISUALIZE. I MEAN, REALITY IS TOO COMPLEX FOR COMICS... SO MUCH HAS TO BE LEFT OUT OR DISTORTED.
JUST KEEP IT HONEST, HONEY.
SEE WHAT I MEAN... IN REAL LIFE YOU'D NEVER HAVE LET ME TALK THIS LONG WITHOUT INTERRUPTING.
HMMPH. LIGHT ME A CIGARETTE.

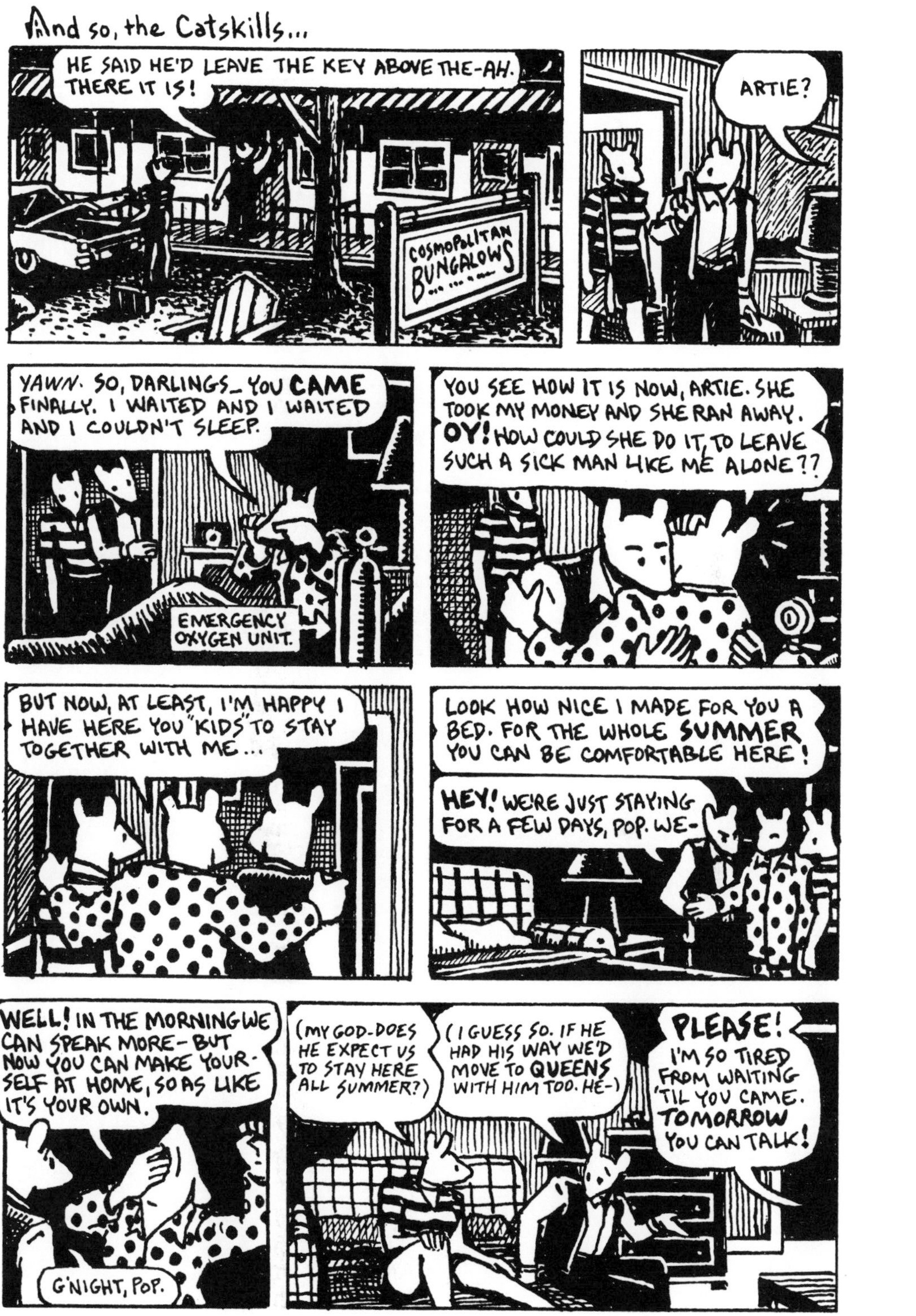
And so, the Catskills...
HE SAID HE'D LEAVE THE KEY ABOVE THE-AH. THERE IT IS!
COSMOPOLITAN BUNGALOWS
ARTIE?
YAWN. SO, DARLINGS_ YOU CAME FINALLY. I WAITED AND I WAITED AND I COULDN'T SLEEP.
EMERGENCY OXYGEN UNIT.
YOU SEE HOW IT IS NOW, ARTIE. SHE TOOK MY MONEY AND SHE RAN AWAY. OY! HOW COULD SHE DO IT, TO LEAVE SUCH A SICK MAN LIKE ME ALONE??
BUT NOW, AT LEAST, I'M HAPPY I HAVE HERE YOU "KIDS" TO STAY TOGETHER WITH ME...
LOOK HOW NICE I MADE FOR YOU A BED. FOR THE WHOLE SUMMER YOU CAN BE COMFORTABLE HERE!
HEY! WE'RE JUST STAYING FOR A FEW DAYS, POP. WE-
WELL! IN THE MORNING WE CAN SPEAK MORE- BUT NOW YOU CAN MAKE YOURSELF AT HOME, SO AS LIKE IT'S YOUR OWN.
G'NIGHT, POP.
(MY GOD-DOES HE EXPECT US TO STAY HERE ALL SUMMER?)
(I GUESS SO. IF HE HAD HIS WAY WE'D MOVE TO QUEENS WITH HIM TOO. HE-)
PLEASE! I'M SO TIRED FROM WAITING 'TIL YOU CAME. TOMORROW YOU CAN TALK!

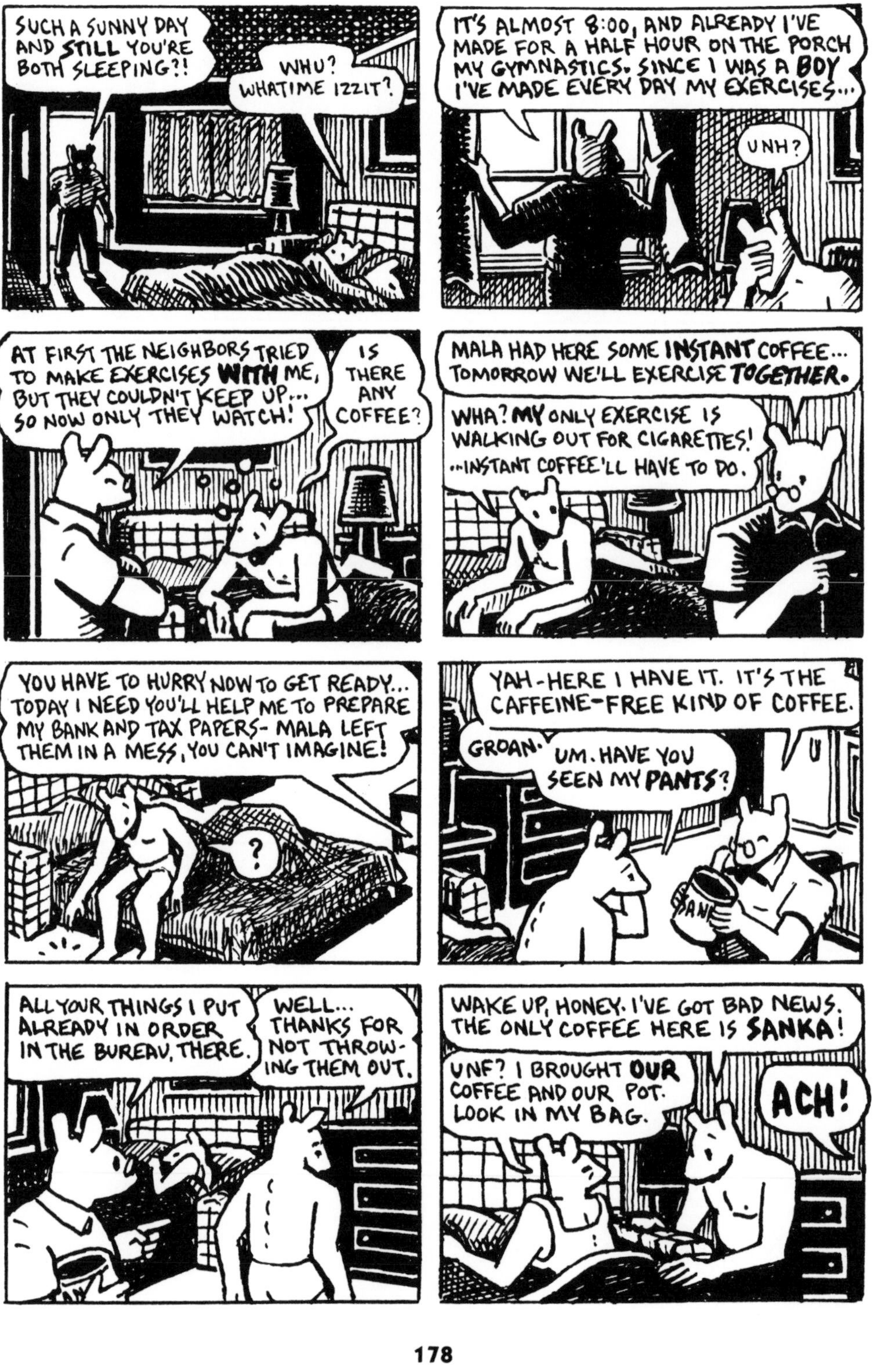
SUCH A SUNNY DAY AND STILL YOU'RE BOTH SLEEPING?!
WHU? WHATIME IZZIT?
IT'S ALMOST 8:00, AND ALREADY I'VE MADE FOR A HALF HOUR ON THE PORCH MY GYMNASTICS. SINCE I WAS A BOY I'VE MADE EVERY DAY MY EXERCISES...
UNH?
AT FIRST THE NEIGHBORS TRIED TO MAKE EXERCISES WITH ME, BUT THEY COULDN'T KEEP UP... SO NOW ONLY THEY WATCH!
IS THERE ANY COFFEE?
MALA HAD HERE SOME INSTANT COFFEE... TOMORROW WE'LL EXERCISE TOGETHER.
WHA? MY ONLY EXERCISE IS WALKING OUT FOR CIGARETTES! ..INSTANT COFFEE'LL HAVE TO DO.
YOU HAVE TO HURRY NOW TO GET READY... TODAY I NEED YOU'LL HELP ME TO PREPARE MY BANK AND TAX PAPERS- MALA LEFT THEM IN A MESS, YOU CAN'T IMAGINE!
?
YAH-HERE I HAVE IT. IT'S THE CAFFEINE-FREE KIND OF COFFEE.
GROAN.
UM. HAVE YOU SEEN MY PANTS?
ALL YOUR THINGS I PUT ALREADY IN ORDER IN THE BUREAU, THERE.
WELL... THANKS FOR NOT THROWING THEM OUT.
WAKE UP, HONEY. I'VE GOT BAD NEWS. THE ONLY COFFEE HERE IS SANKA!
UNF? I BROUGHT OUR COFFEE AND OUR POT. LOOK IN MY BAG.
ACH!

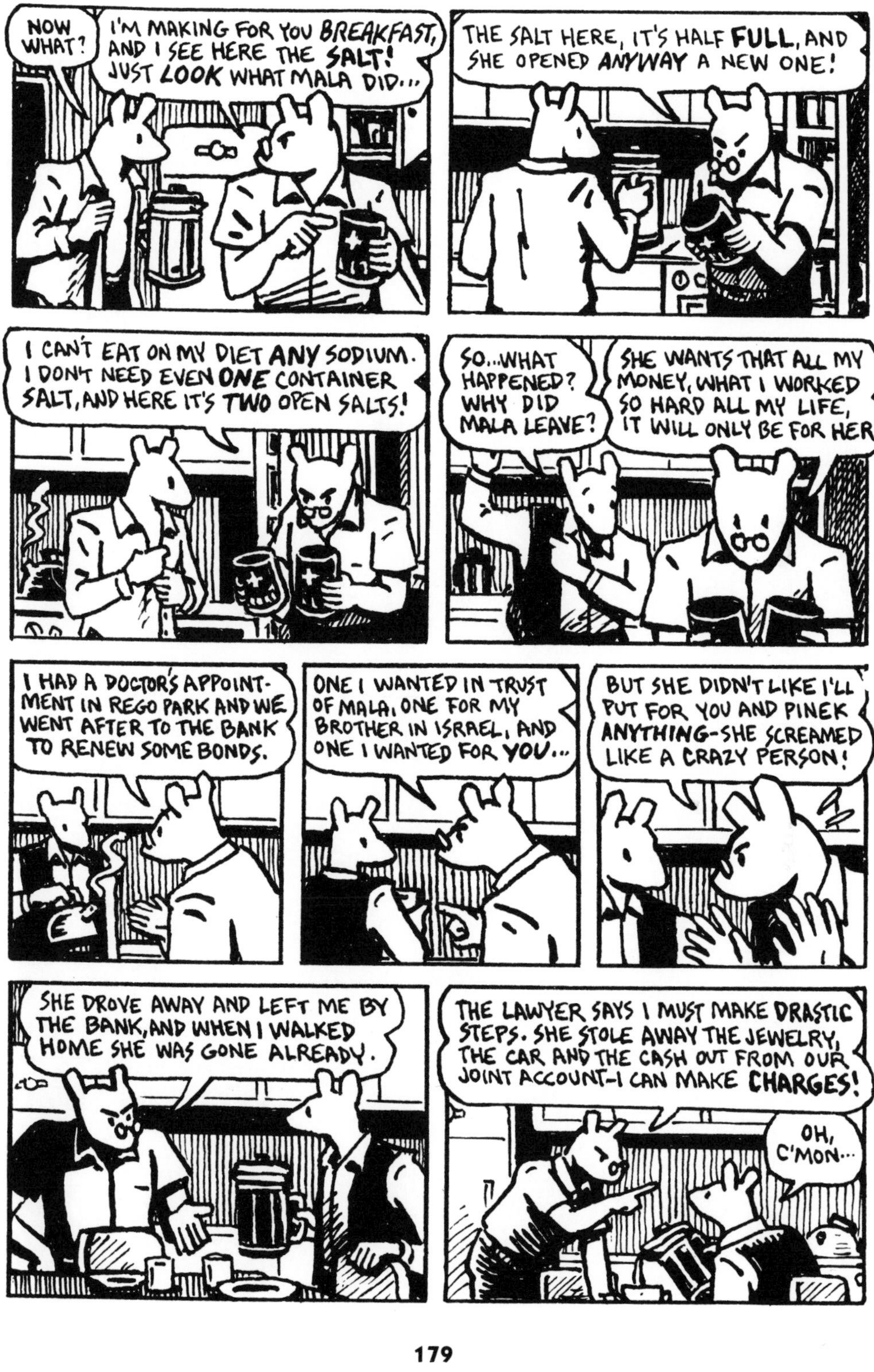
NOW WHAT?
I'M MAKING FOR YOU BREAKFAST, AND I SEE HERE THE SALT! JUST LOOK WHAT MALA DID...
THE SALT HERE, IT'S HALF FULL, AND SHE OPENED ANYWAY A NEW ONE!
I CAN'T EAT ON MY DIET ANY SODIUM. I DON'T NEED EVEN ONE CONTAINER SALT, AND HERE IT'S TWO OPEN SALTS!
SO...WHAT HAPPENED? WHY DID MALA LEAVE?
SHE WANTS THAT ALL MY MONEY, WHAT I WORKED SO HARD ALL MY LIFE, IT WILL ONLY BE FOR HER.
I HAD A DOCTOR'S APPOINTMENT IN REGO PARK AND WE WENT AFTER TO THE BANK TO RENEW SOME BONDS.
ONE I WANTED IN TRUST OF MALA, ONE FOR MY BROTHER IN ISRAEL, AND ONE I WANTED FOR YOU...
BUT SHE DIDN'T LIKE I'LL PUT FOR YOU AND PINEK ANYTHING-SHE SCREAMED LIKE A CRAZY PERSON!
SHE DROVE AWAY AND LEFT ME BY THE BANK, AND WHEN I WALKED HOME SHE WAS GONE ALREADY.
THE LAWYER SAYS I MUST MAKE DRASTIC STEPS. SHE STOLE AWAY THE JEWELRY, THE CAR AND THE CASH OUT FROM OUR JOINT ACCOUNT-I CAN MAKE CHARGES!
OH, C'MON...

181

182

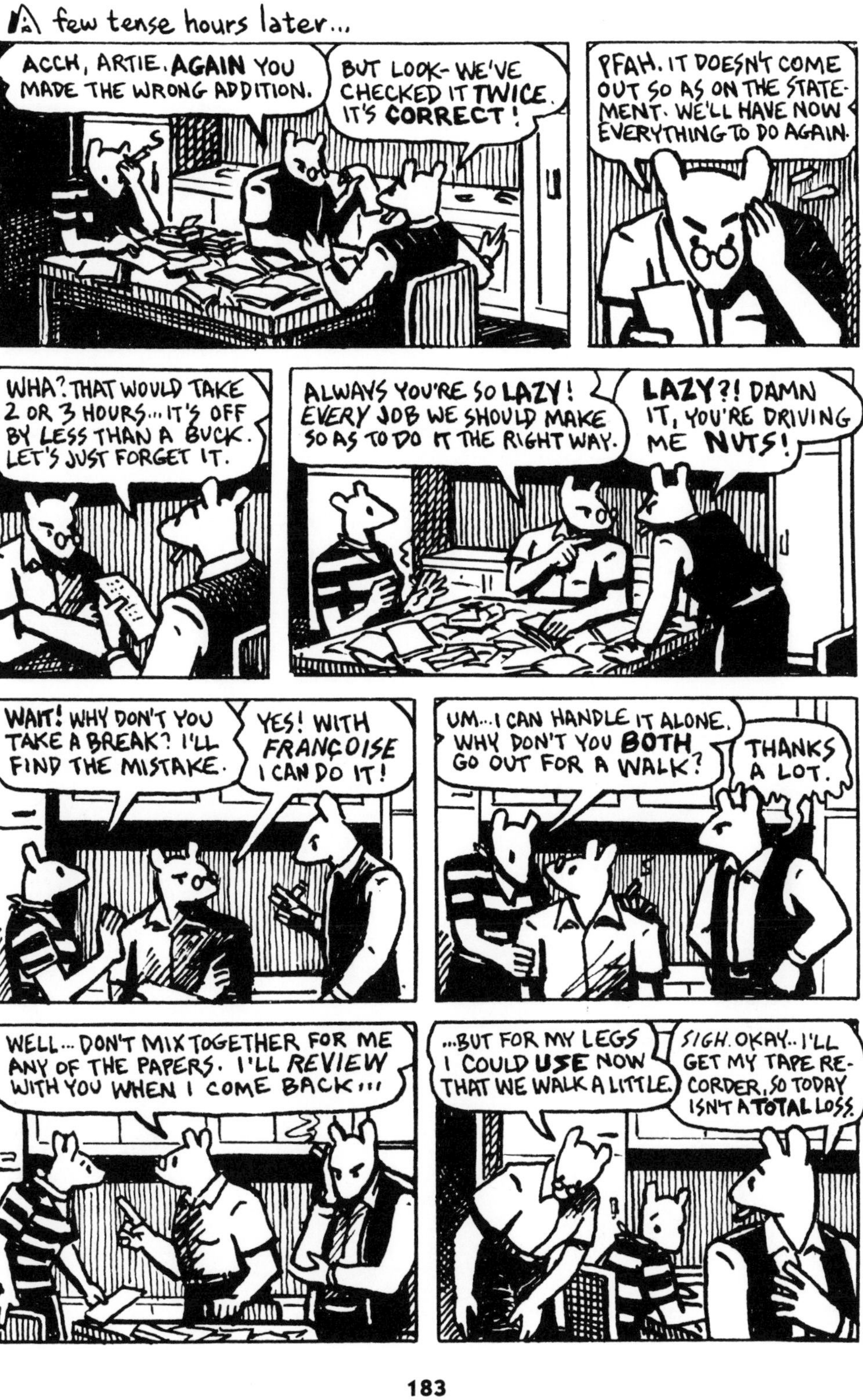
A few tense hours later...
ACCH, ARTIE. AGAIN YOU MADE THE WRONG ADDITION.
BUT LOOK- WE'VE CHECKED IT TWICE. IT'S CORRECT!
PFAH. IT DOESN'T COME OUT SO AS ON THE STATEMENT. WE'LL HAVE NOW EVERYTHING TO DO AGAIN.
WHA? THAT WOULD TAKE 2 OR 3 HOURS... IT'S OFF BY LESS THAN A BUCK. LET'S JUST FORGET IT.
ALWAYS YOU'RE SO LAZY! EVERY JOB WE SHOULD MAKE SO AS TO DO IT THE RIGHT WAY.
LAZY?! DAMN IT, YOU'RE DRIVING ME NUTS!
WAIT! WHY DON'T YOU TAKE A BREAK? I'LL FIND THE MISTAKE.
YES! WITH FRANÇOISE I CAN DO IT!
UM... I CAN HANDLE IT ALONE. WHY DON'T YOU BOTH GO OUT FOR A WALK?
THANKS A LOT.
WELL... DON'T MIX TOGETHER FOR ME ANY OF THE PAPERS. I'LL REVIEW WITH YOU WHEN I COME BACK...
...BUT FOR MY LEGS I COULD USE NOW THAT WE WALK A LITTLE.
SIGH. OKAY.. I'LL GET MY TAPE RECORDER, SO TODAY ISN'T A TOTAL LOSS.

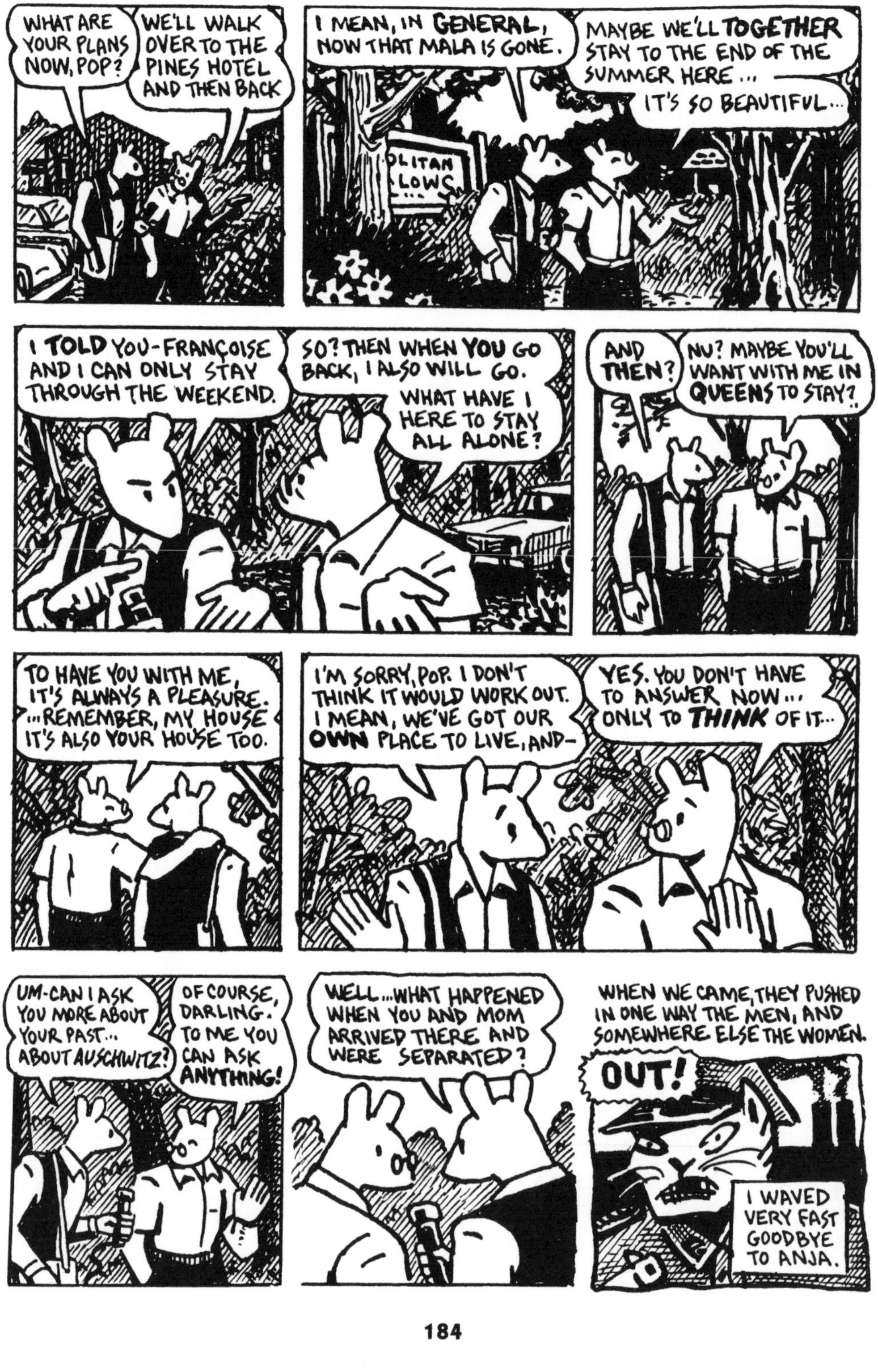
WHAT ARE YOUR PLANS NOW, POP?
WE'LL WALK OVER TO THE PINES HOTEL AND THEN BACK
I MEAN, IN GENERAL, NOW THAT MALA IS GONE.
MAYBE WE'LL TOGETHER STAY TO THE END OF THE SUMMER HERE...
IT'S SO BEAUTIFUL...
I TOLD YOU-FRANÇOISE AND I CAN ONLY STAY THROUGH THE WEEKEND.
SO? THEN WHEN YOU GO BACK, I ALSO WILL GO.
WHAT HAVE I HERE TO STAY ALL ALONE?
AND THEN?
NU? MAYBE YOU'LL WANT WITH ME IN QUEENS TO STAY?
TO HAVE YOU WITH ME, IT'S ALWAYS A PLEASURE. ...REMEMBER, MY HOUSE IT'S ALSO YOUR HOUSE TOO.
I'M SORRY, POP. I DON'T THINK IT WOULD WORK OUT. I MEAN, WE'VE GOT OUR OWN PLACE TO LIVE, AND-
YES. YOU DON'T HAVE TO ANSWER NOW... ONLY TO THINK OF IT...
UM-CAN I ASK YOU MORE ABOUT YOUR PAST... ABOUT AUSCHWITZ?
OF COURSE, DARLING. TO ME YOU CAN ASK ANYTHING!
WELL... WHAT HAPPENED WHEN YOU AND MOM ARRIVED THERE AND WERE SEPARATED?
WHEN WE CAME, THEY PUSHED IN ONE WAY THE MEN, AND SOMEWHERE ELSE THE WOMEN.
OUT!
I WAVED VERY FAST GOODBYE TO ANJA.

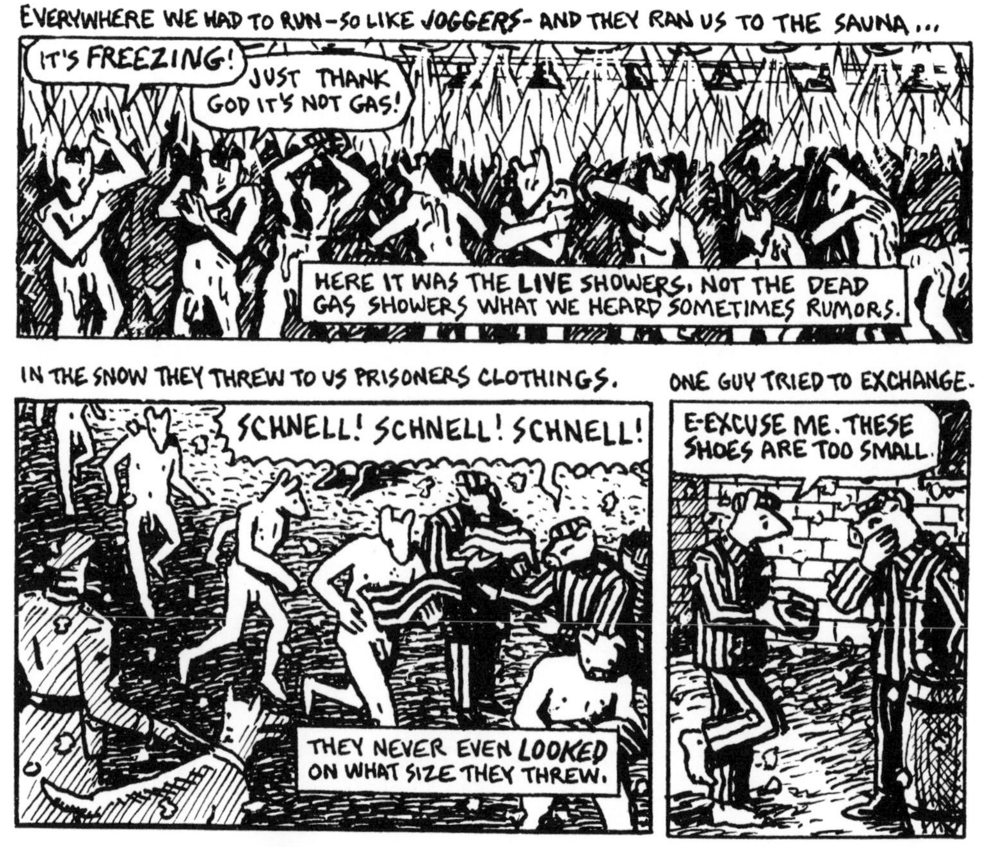
EVERYWHERE WE HAD TO RUN – SO LIKE JOGGERS – AND THEY RAN US TO THE SAUNA...
IT'S FREEZING!
JUST THANK GOD IT'S NOT GAS!
HERE IT WAS THE LIVE SHOWERS, NOT THE DEAD GAS SHOWERS WHAT WE HEARD SOMETIMES RUMORS.
IN THE SNOW THEY THREW TO US PRISONERS CLOTHINGS.
SCHNELL! SCHNELL! SCHNELL!
THEY NEVER EVEN LOOKED ON WHAT SIZE THEY THREW.
ONE GUY TRIED TO EXCHANGE.
E-EXCUSE ME. THESE SHOES ARE TOO SMALL.
MAYBE NOW THEY'LL FIT!
CRAK
THE SHOES WERE WOOD SHOES!
I WAS A LUCKY ONE. EVERYTHING FITTED ME A LITTLE. ONLY THE SHIRT WAS TORN AND TOO BIG FOR ME...
THEY REGISTERED US IN... THEY TOOK FROM US OUR NAMES. AND HERE THEY PUT ME MY NUMBER.
175113

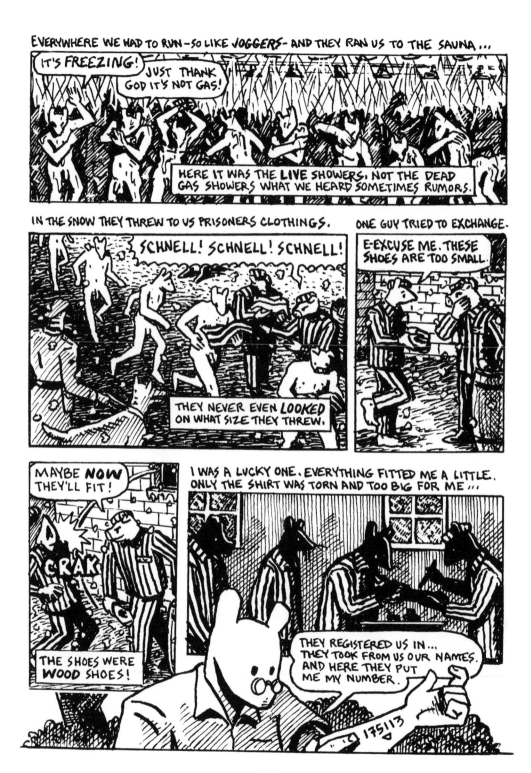

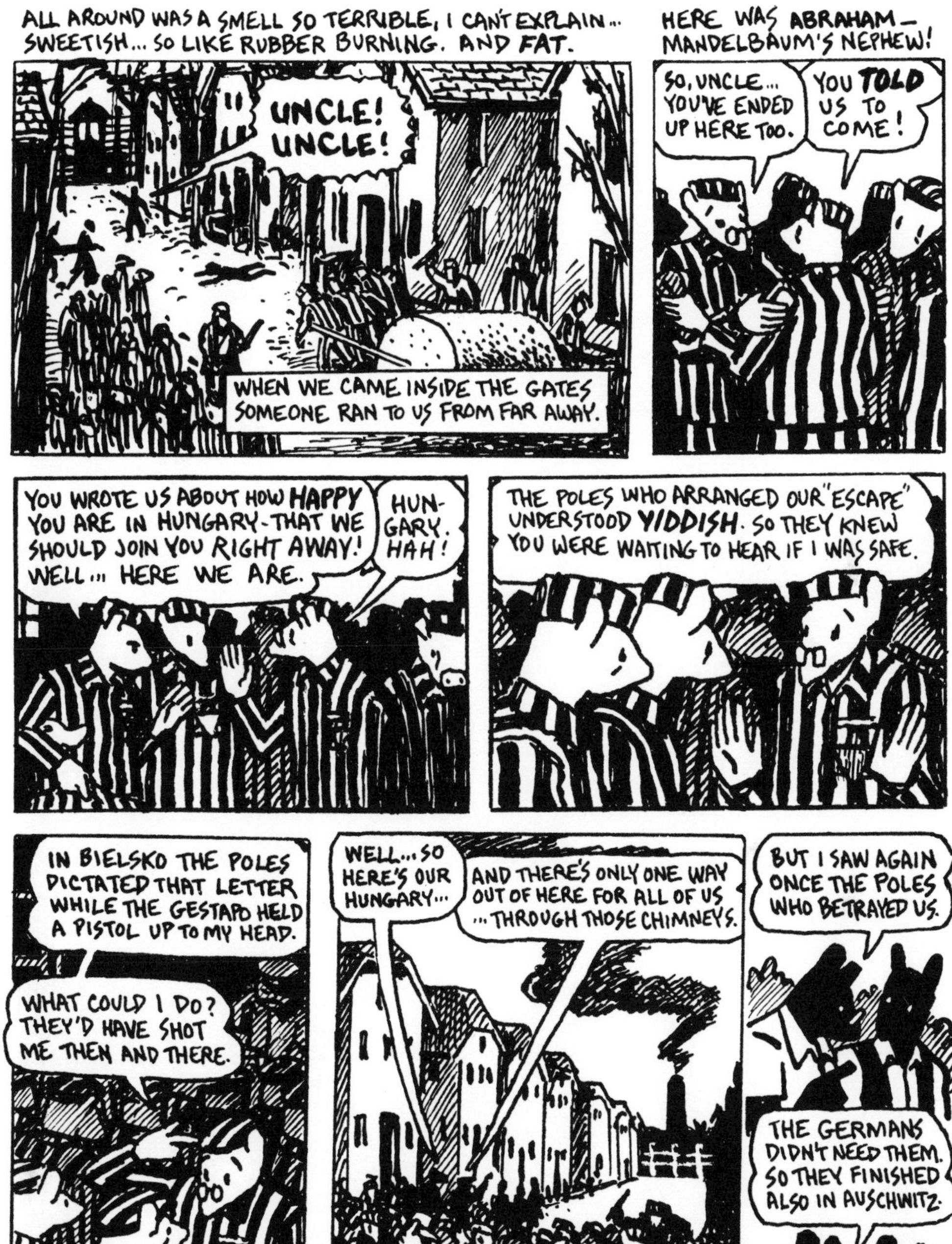
ALL AROUND WAS A SMELL SO TERRIBLE, I CAN'T EXPLAIN... SWEETISH... SO LIKE RUBBER BURNING. AND FAT.
UNCLE! UNCLE!
WHEN WE CAME INSIDE THE GATES SOMEONE RAN TO US FROM FAR AWAY.
HERE WAS ABRAHAM-MANDELBAUM'S NEPHEW!
SO, UNCLE... YOU'VE ENDED UP HERE TOO.
YOU TOLD US TO COME!
YOU WROTE US ABOUT HOW HAPPY YOU ARE IN HUNGARY-THAT WE SHOULD JOIN YOU RIGHT AWAY! WELL... HERE WE ARE.
HUN-GARY. HAH!
THE POLES WHO ARRANGED OUR "ESCAPE" UNDERSTOOD YIDDISH. SO THEY KNEW YOU WERE WAITING TO HEAR IF I WAS SAFE.
IN BIELSKO THE POLES DICTATED THAT LETTER WHILE THE GESTAPO HELD A PISTOL UP TO MY HEAD.
WHAT COULD I DO? THEY'D HAVE SHOT ME THEN AND THERE.
WELL... SO HERE'S OUR HUNGARY...
AND THERE'S ONLY ONE WAY OUT OF HERE FOR ALL OF US ...THROUGH THOSE CHIMNEYS.
ABRAHAM I DIDN'T SEE AGAIN... I THINK HE CAME OUT THE CHIMNEY.
BUT I SAW AGAIN ONCE THE POLES WHO BETRAYED US.
THE GERMANS DIDN'T NEED THEM. SO THEY FINISHED ALSO IN AUSCHWITZ.

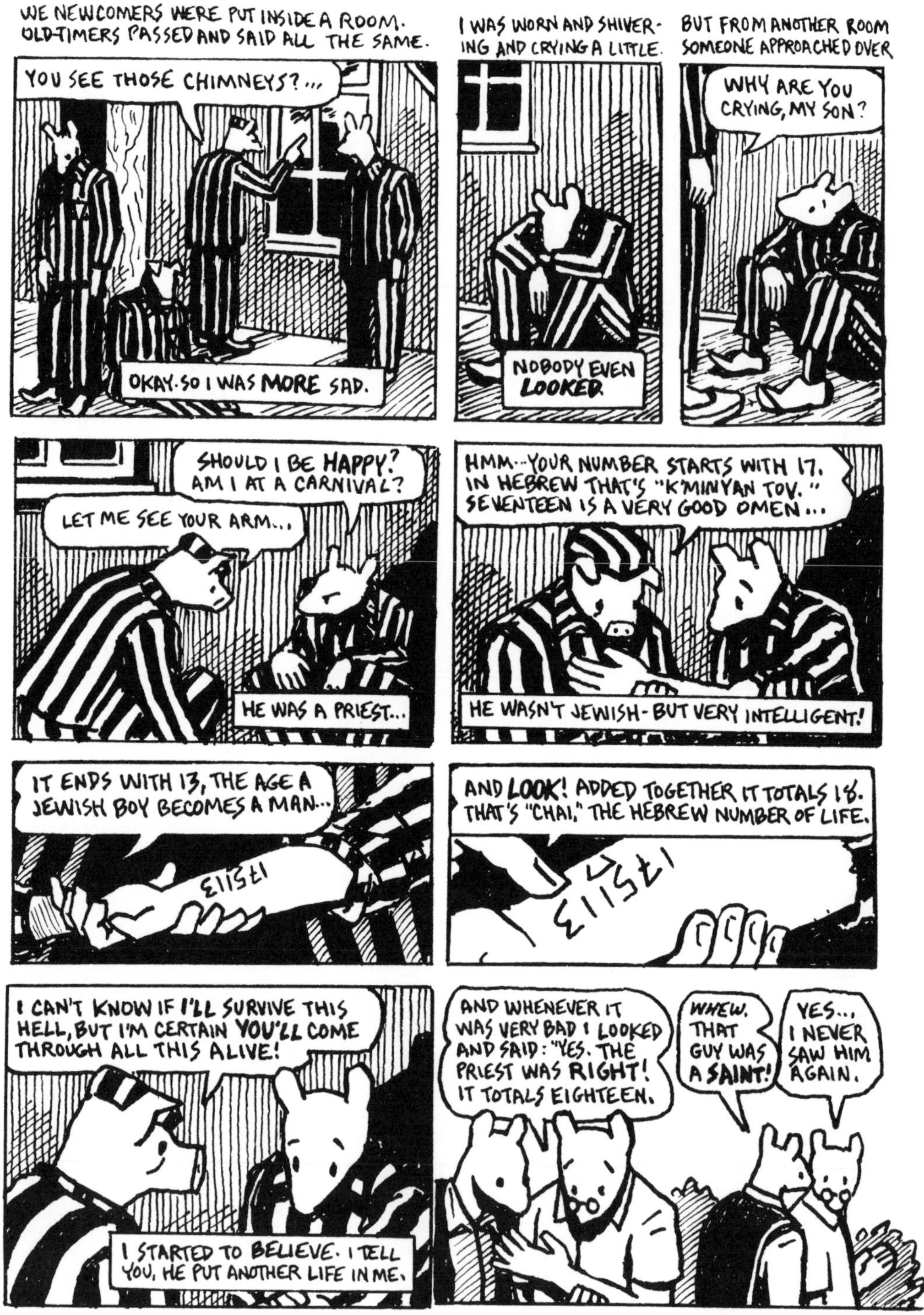
WE NEWCOMERS WERE PUT INSIDE A ROOM. OLD-TIMERS PASSED AND SAID ALL THE SAME.
YOU SEE THOSE CHIMNEYS?...
OKAY. SO I WAS MORE SAD.
I WAS WORN AND SHIVERING AND CRYING A LITTLE.
NOBODY EVEN LOOKED.
BUT FROM ANOTHER ROOM SOMEONE APPROACHED OVER
WHY ARE YOU CRYING, MY SON?
SHOULD I BE HAPPY? AM I AT A CARNIVAL?
LET ME SEE YOUR ARM...
HE WAS A PRIEST...
HMM... YOUR NUMBER STARTS WITH 17. IN HEBREW THAT'S "K'MINYAN TOV." SEVENTEEN IS A VERY GOOD OMEN...
HE WASN'T JEWISH - BUT VERY INTELLIGENT!
IT ENDS WITH 13, THE AGE A JEWISH BOY BECOMES A MAN...
175113
AND LOOK! ADDED TOGETHER IT TOTALS 18. THAT'S "CHAI," THE HEBREW NUMBER OF LIFE.
175113
I CAN'T KNOW IF I'LL SURVIVE THIS HELL, BUT I'M CERTAIN YOU'LL COME THROUGH ALL THIS ALIVE!
I STARTED TO BELIEVE. I TELL YOU, HE PUT ANOTHER LIFE IN ME.
AND WHENEVER IT WAS VERY BAD I LOOKED AND SAID: "YES. THE PRIEST WAS RIGHT! IT TOTALS EIGHTEEN."
WHEW. THAT GUY WAS A SAINT!
YES... I NEVER SAW HIM AGAIN.

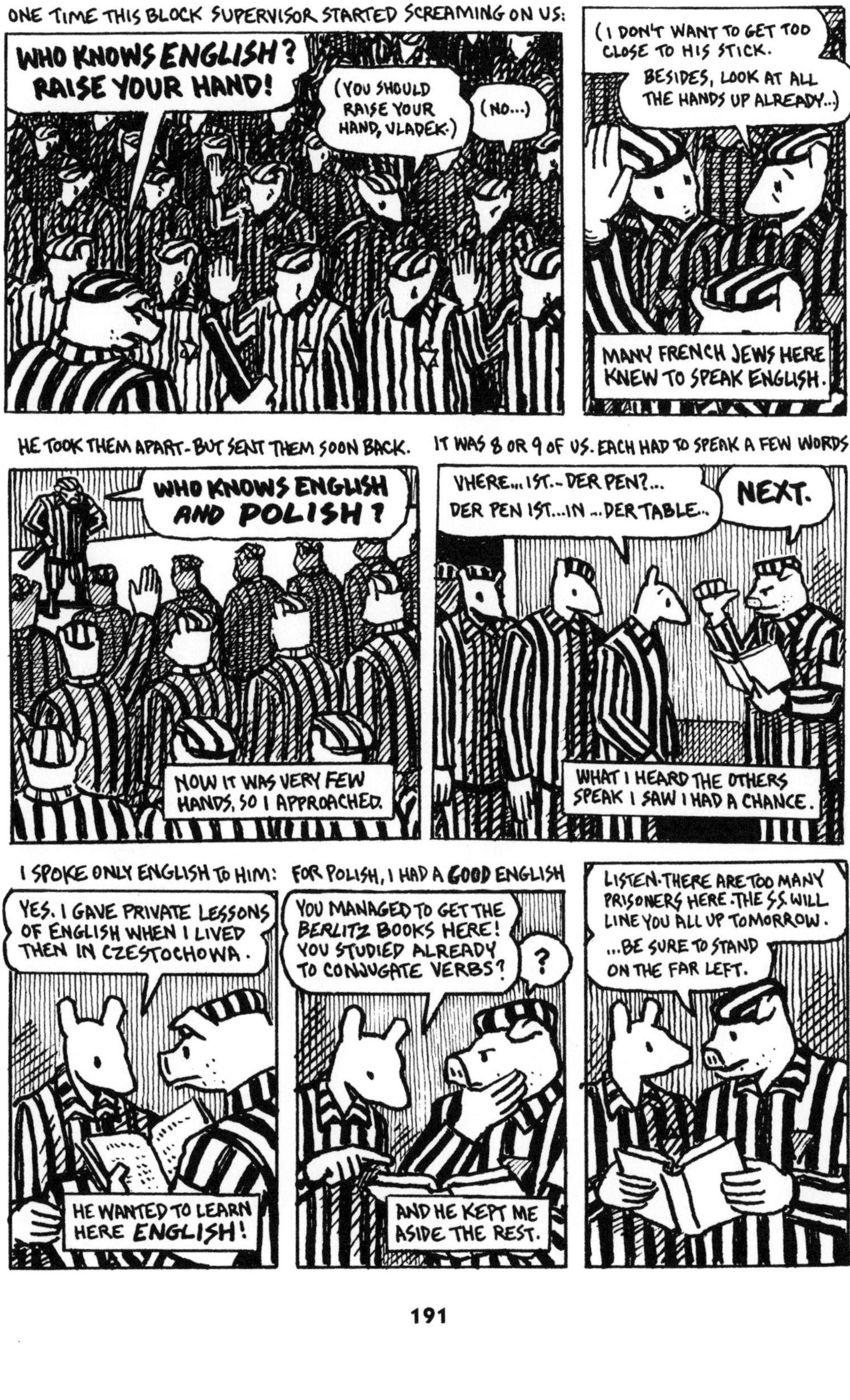
ONE TIME THIS BLOCK SUPERVISOR STARTED SCREAMING ON US:
WHO KNOWS ENGLISH? RAISE YOUR HAND!
(YOU SHOULD RAISE YOUR HAND, VLADEK.)
(NO...)
(I DON'T WANT TO GET TOO CLOSE TO HIS STICK.
BESIDES, LOOK AT ALL THE HANDS UP ALREADY...)
MANY FRENCH JEWS HERE KNEW TO SPEAK ENGLISH.
HE TOOK THEM APART- BUT SENT THEM SOON BACK.
WHO KNOWS ENGLISH AND POLISH?
NOW IT WAS VERY FEW HANDS, SO I APPROACHED.
IT WAS 8 OR 9 OF US. EACH HAD TO SPEAK A FEW WORDS.
VHERE... IST... DER PEN?... DER PEN IST...IN ...DER TABLE...
NEXT.
WHAT I HEARD THE OTHERS SPEAK I SAW I HAD A CHANCE.
I SPOKE ONLY ENGLISH TO HIM:
YES. I GAVE PRIVATE LESSONS OF ENGLISH WHEN I LIVED THEN IN CZESTOCHOWA.
HE WANTED TO LEARN HERE ENGLISH!
FOR POLISH, I HAD A GOOD ENGLISH
YOU MANAGED TO GET THE BERLITZ BOOKS HERE! YOU STUDIED ALREADY TO CONJUGATE VERBS?
?
AND HE KEPT ME ASIDE THE REST.
LISTEN. THERE ARE TOO MANY PRISONERS HERE. THE S.S. WILL LINE YOU ALL UP TOMORROW.
...BE SURE TO STAND ON THE FAR LEFT.

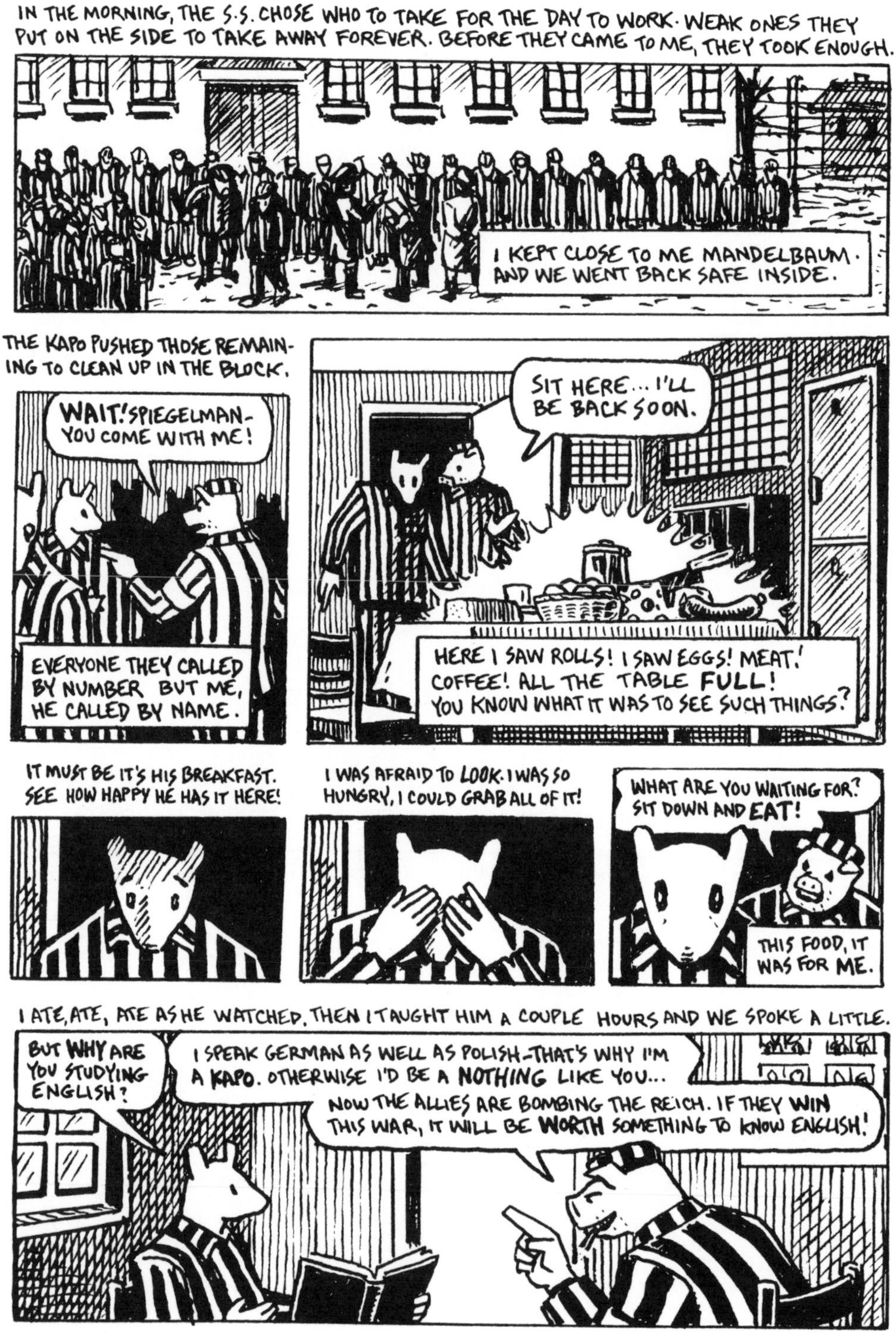
IN THE MORNING, THE S.S. CHOSE WHO TO TAKE FOR THE DAY TO WORK. WEAK ONES THEY PUT ON THE SIDE TO TAKE AWAY FOREVER. BEFORE THEY CAME TO ME, THEY TOOK ENOUGH.
I KEPT CLOSE TO ME MANDELBAUM. AND WE WENT BACK SAFE INSIDE.
THE KAPO PUSHED THOSE REMAINING TO CLEAN UP IN THE BLOCK.
WAIT! SPIEGELMAN-YOU COME WITH ME!
EVERYONE THEY CALLED BY NUMBER BUT ME, HE CALLED BY NAME.
SIT HERE... I'LL BE BACK SOON.
HERE I SAW ROLLS! I SAW EGGS! MEAT! COFFEE! ALL THE TABLE FULL! YOU KNOW WHAT IT WAS TO SEE SUCH THINGS?
IT MUST BE IT'S HIS BREAKFAST. SEE HOW HAPPY HE HAS IT HERE!
I WAS AFRAID TO LOOK. I WAS SO HUNGRY, I COULD GRAB ALL OF IT!
WHAT ARE YOU WAITING FOR? SIT DOWN AND EAT!
THIS FOOD, IT WAS FOR ME.
I ATE, ATE, ATE AS HE WATCHED. THEN I TAUGHT HIM A COUPLE HOURS AND WE SPOKE A LITTLE.
BUT WHY ARE YOU STUDYING ENGLISH?
I SPEAK GERMAN AS WELL AS POLISH-THAT'S WHY I'M A KAPO. OTHERWISE I'D BE A NOTHING LIKE YOU...
NOW THE ALLIES ARE BOMBING THE REICH. IF THEY WIN THIS WAR, IT WILL BE WORTH SOMETHING TO KNOW ENGLISH!

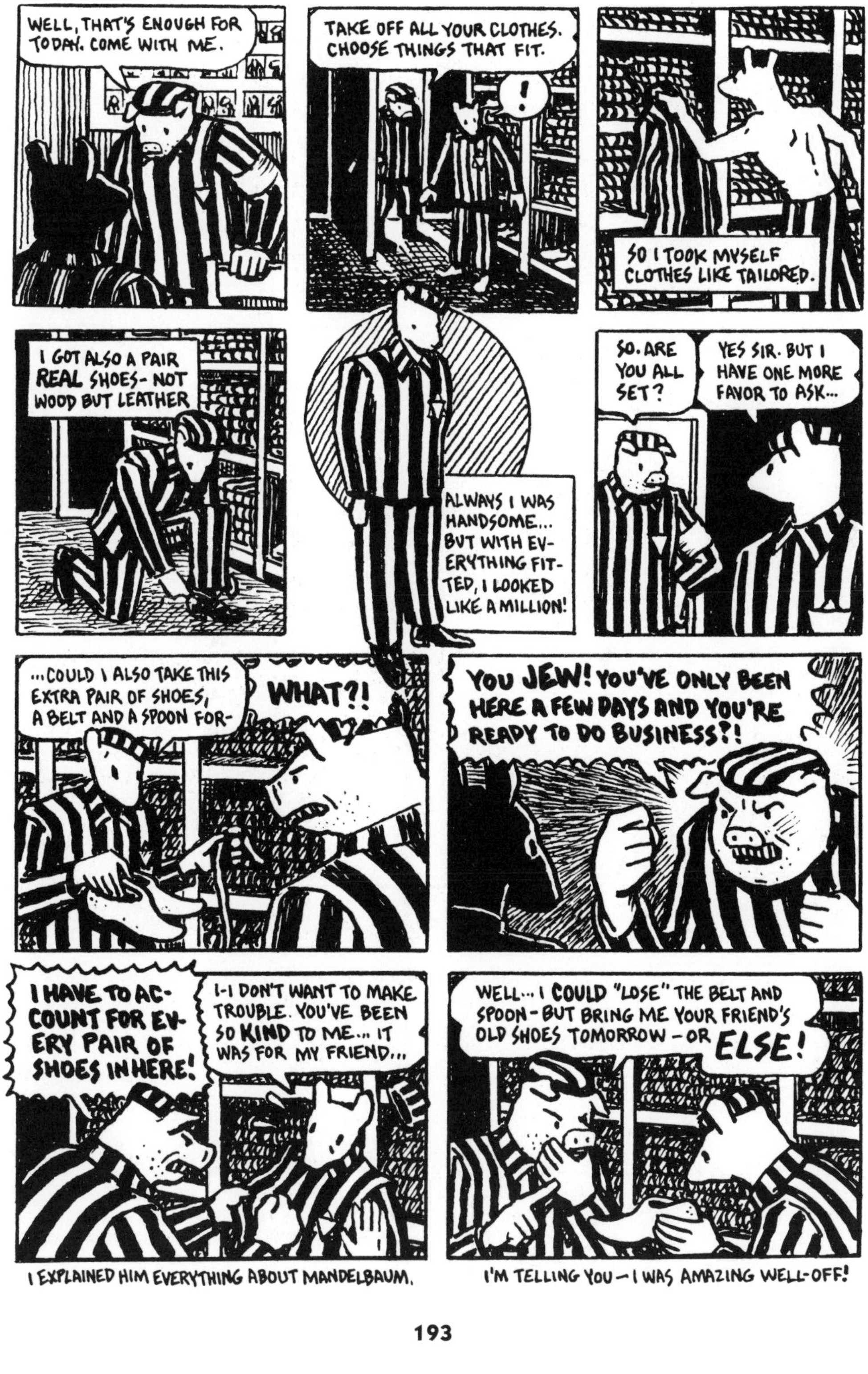
WELL, THAT'S ENOUGH FOR TODAY. COME WITH ME.
TAKE OFF ALL YOUR CLOTHES. CHOOSE THINGS THAT FIT.
!
SO I TOOK MYSELF CLOTHES LIKE TAILORED.
I GOT ALSO A PAIR REAL SHOES- NOT WOOD BUT LEATHER
ALWAYS I WAS HANDSOME... BUT WITH EVERYTHING FITTED, I LOOKED LIKE A MILLION!
SO. ARE YOU ALL SET?
YES SIR. BUT I HAVE ONE MORE FAVOR TO ASK...
...COULD I ALSO TAKE THIS EXTRA PAIR OF SHOES, A BELT AND A SPOON FOR-
WHAT?!
YOU JEW! YOU'VE ONLY BEEN HERE A FEW DAYS AND YOU'RE READY TO DO BUSINESS?!
I HAVE TO ACCOUNT FOR EVERY PAIR OF SHOES IN HERE!
I-I DON'T WANT TO MAKE TROUBLE. YOU'VE BEEN SO KIND TO ME... IT WAS FOR MY FRIEND...
I EXPLAINED HIM EVERYTHING ABOUT MANDELBAUM.
WELL... I COULD "LOSE" THE BELT AND SPOON - BUT BRING ME YOUR FRIEND'S OLD SHOES TOMORROW - OR ELSE!
I'M TELLING YOU - I WAS AMAZING WELL-OFF!

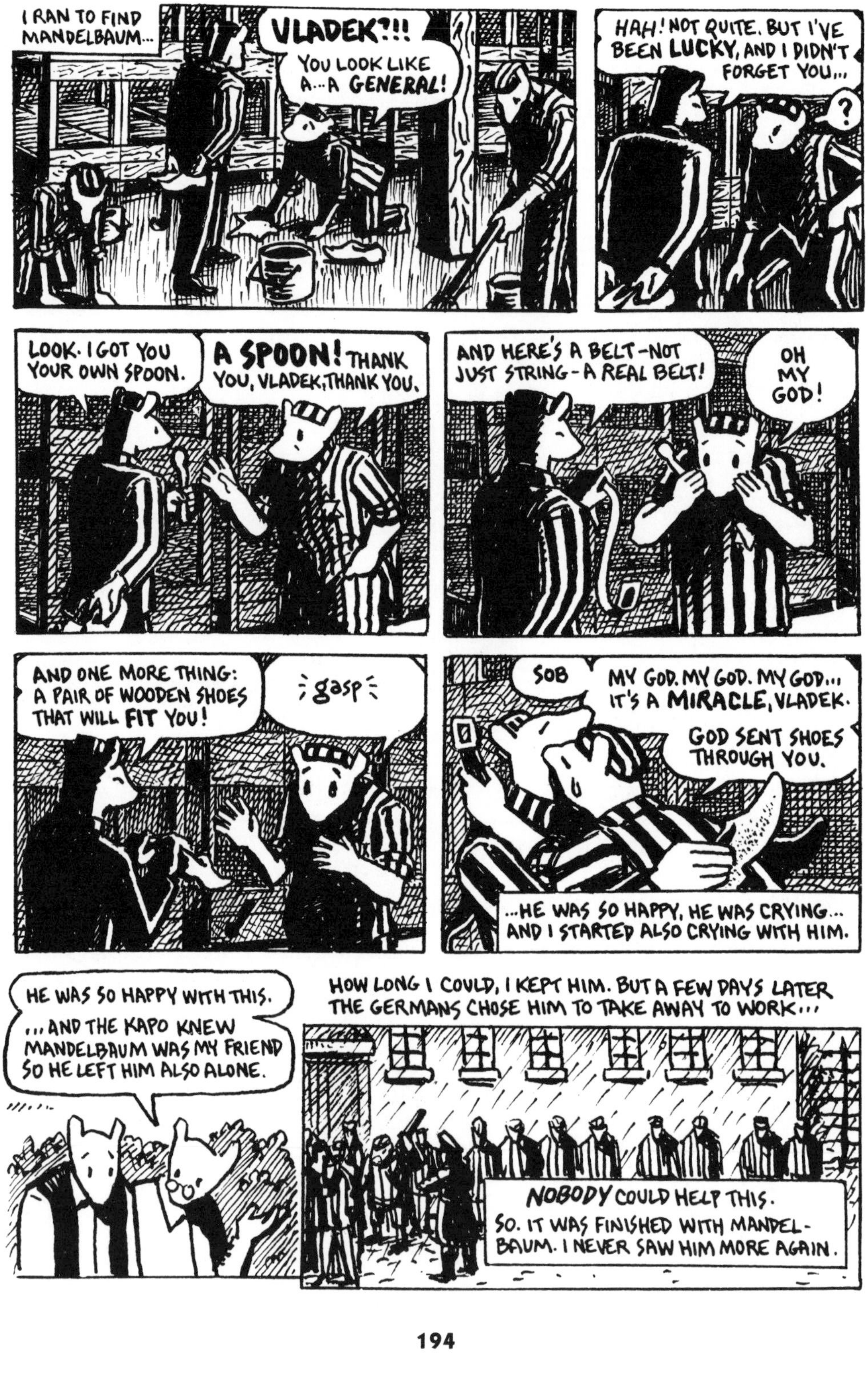

I RAN TO FIND MANDELBAUM...
VLADEK?!! YOU LOOK LIKE A...A GENERAL!
HAH! NOT QUITE. BUT I'VE BEEN LUCKY, AND I DIDN'T FORGET YOU...
?
LOOK. I GOT YOU YOUR OWN SPOON.
A SPOON! THANK YOU, VLADEK, THANK YOU.
AND HERE'S A BELT-NOT JUST STRING-A REAL BELT!
OH MY GOD!
AND ONE MORE THING: A PAIR OF WOODEN SHOES THAT WILL FIT YOU!
gasp
SOB
MY GOD. MY GOD. MY GOD... IT'S A MIRACLE, VLADEK.
GOD SENT SHOES THROUGH YOU.
...HE WAS SO HAPPY, HE WAS CRYING... AND I STARTED ALSO CRYING WITH HIM.
HE WAS SO HAPPY WITH THIS.
...AND THE KAPO KNEW MANDELBAUM WAS MY FRIEND SO HE LEFT HIM ALSO ALONE.
HOW LONG I COULD, I KEPT HIM. BUT A FEW DAYS LATER THE GERMANS CHOSE HIM TO TAKE AWAY TO WORK...
NOBODY COULD HELP THIS.
SO. IT WAS FINISHED WITH MANDELBAUM. I NEVER SAW HIM MORE AGAIN.

CHAPTER TWO

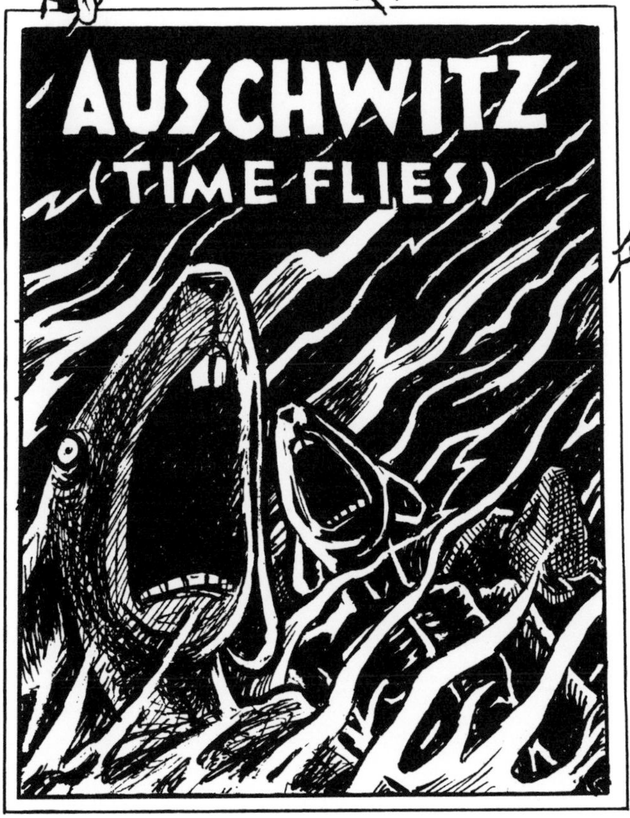
AUSCHWITZ
(TIME FLIES)

Time flies...

And so...

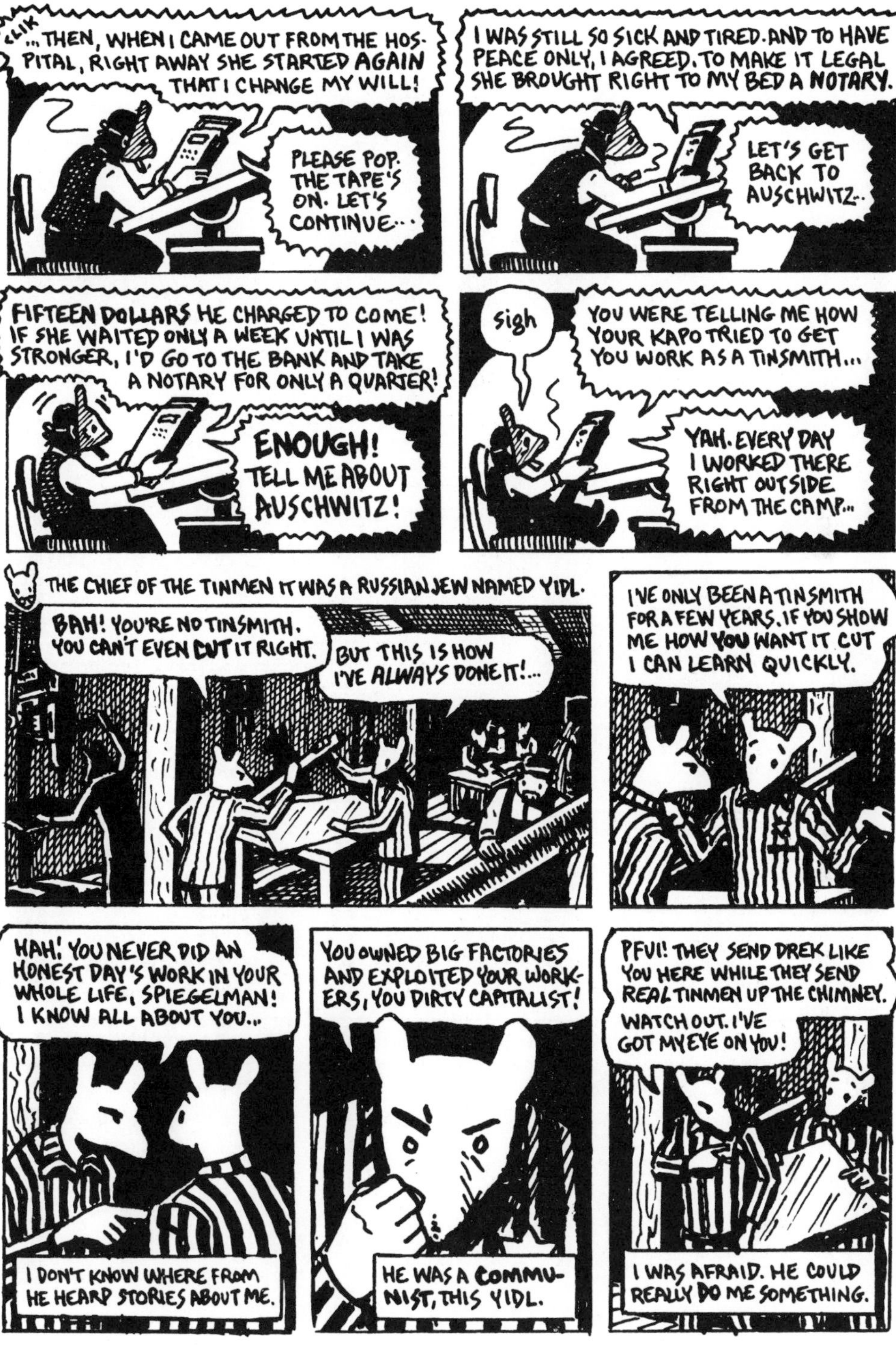
CLIK
...THEN, WHEN I CAME OUT FROM THE HOSPITAL, RIGHT AWAY SHE STARTED AGAIN THAT I CHANGE MY WILL!
PLEASE POP. THE TAPE'S ON. LET'S CONTINUE...
I WAS STILL SO SICK AND TIRED. AND TO HAVE PEACE ONLY, I AGREED. TO MAKE IT LEGAL SHE BROUGHT RIGHT TO MY BED A NOTARY.
LET'S GET BACK TO AUSCHWITZ...
FIFTEEN DOLLARS HE CHARGED TO COME! IF SHE WAITED ONLY A WEEK UNTIL I WAS STRONGER, I'D GO TO THE BANK AND TAKE A NOTARY FOR ONLY A QUARTER!
ENOUGH! TELL ME ABOUT AUSCHWITZ!
Sigh
YOU WERE TELLING ME HOW YOUR KAPO TRIED TO GET YOU WORK AS A TINSMITH...
YAH. EVERY DAY I WORKED THERE RIGHT OUTSIDE FROM THE CAMP...
THE CHIEF OF THE TINMEN IT WAS A RUSSIAN JEW NAMED YIDL.
BAH! YOU'RE NO TINSMITH. YOU CAN'T EVEN CUT IT RIGHT.
BUT THIS IS HOW I'VE ALWAYS DONE IT!...
I'VE ONLY BEEN A TINSMITH FOR A FEW YEARS. IF YOU SHOW ME HOW YOU WANT IT CUT I CAN LEARN QUICKLY.
HAH! YOU NEVER DID AN HONEST DAY'S WORK IN YOUR WHOLE LIFE, SPIEGELMAN! I KNOW ALL ABOUT YOU...
I DON'T KNOW WHERE FROM HE HEARD STORIES ABOUT ME.
YOU OWNED BIG FACTORIES AND EXPLOITED YOUR WORKERS, YOU DIRTY CAPITALIST!
HE WAS A COMMUNIST, THIS YIDL.
PFUI! THEY SEND DREK LIKE YOU HERE WHILE THEY SEND REAL TINMEN UP THE CHIMNEY.
WATCH OUT. I'VE GOT MY EYE ON YOU!
I WAS AFRAID. HE COULD REALLY DO ME SOMETHING.

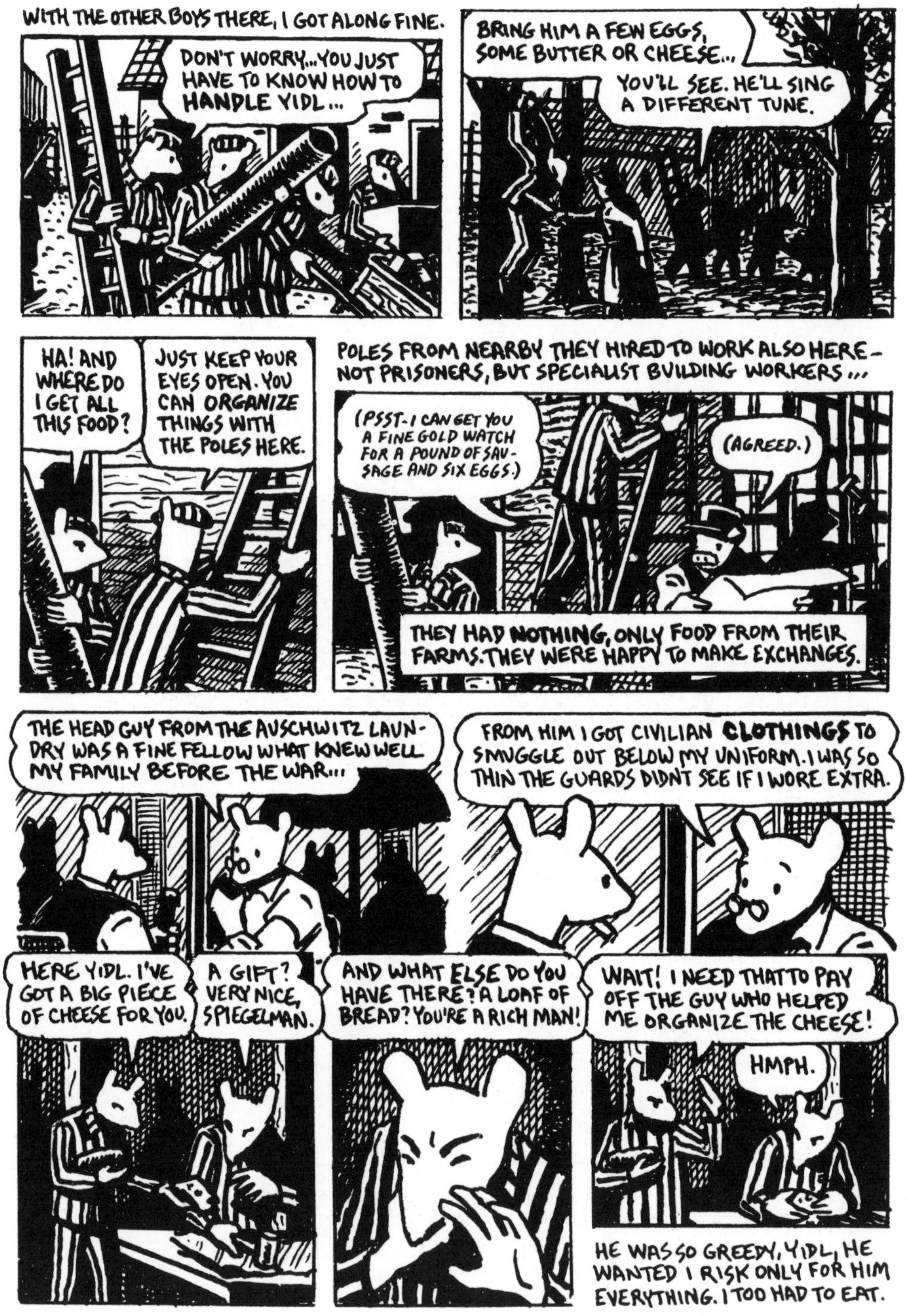

WITH THE OTHER BOYS THERE, I GOT ALONG FINE.
DON'T WORRY... YOU JUST HAVE TO KNOW HOW TO HANDLE YIDL...
BRING HIM A FEW EGGS, SOME BUTTER OR CHEESE...
YOU'LL SEE. HE'LL SING A DIFFERENT TUNE.
HA! AND WHERE DO I GET ALL THIS FOOD?
JUST KEEP YOUR EYES OPEN. YOU CAN ORGANIZE THINGS WITH THE POLES HERE.
POLES FROM NEARBY THEY HIRED TO WORK ALSO HERE - NOT PRISONERS, BUT SPECIALIST BUILDING WORKERS...
(PSST - I CAN GET YOU A FINE GOLD WATCH FOR A POUND OF SAUSAGE AND SIX EGGS.)
(AGREED.)
THEY HAD NOTHING, ONLY FOOD FROM THEIR FARMS. THEY WERE HAPPY TO MAKE EXCHANGES.
THE HEAD GUY FROM THE AUSCHWITZ LAUNDRY WAS A FINE FELLOW WHAT KNEW WELL MY FAMILY BEFORE THE WAR...
FROM HIM I GOT CIVILIAN CLOTHINGS TO SMUGGLE OUT BELOW MY UNIFORM. I WAS SO THIN THE GUARDS DIDN'T SEE IF I WORE EXTRA.
HERE YIDL. I'VE GOT A BIG PIECE OF CHEESE FOR YOU.
A GIFT? VERY NICE, SPIEGELMAN.
AND WHAT ELSE DO YOU HAVE THERE? A LOAF OF BREAD? YOU'RE A RICH MAN!
WAIT! I NEED THAT TO PAY OFF THE GUY WHO HELPED ME ORGANIZE THE CHEESE!
HMPH.
HE WAS SO GREEDY, YIDL, HE WANTED I RISK ONLY FOR HIM EVERYTHING. I TOO HAD TO EAT.

209

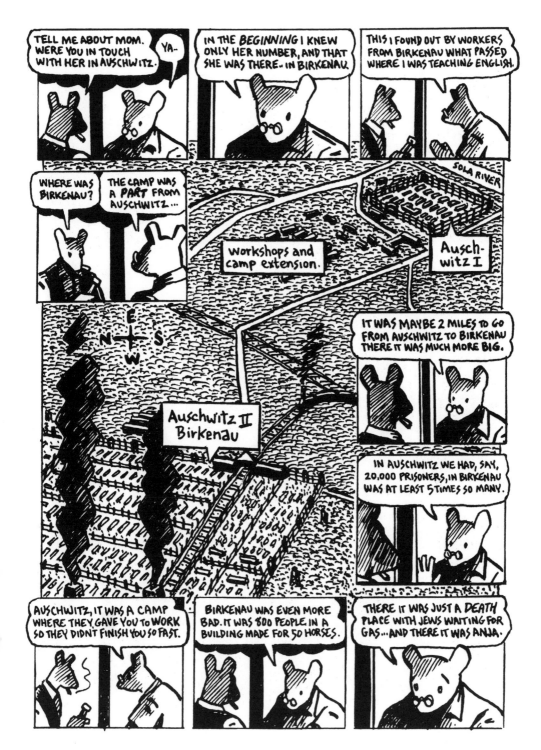

TELL ME ABOUT MOM. WERE YOU IN TOUCH WITH HER IN AUSCHWITZ. YA...

IN THE *BEGINNING* I KNEW ONLY HER NUMBER, AND THAT SHE WAS THERE.. IN BIRKENAU.

THIS I FOUND OUT BY WORKERS FROM BIRKENAU WHAT PASSED WHERE I WAS TEACHING ENGLISH.

WHERE WAS BIRKENAU? THE CAMP WAS A *PART* FROM AUSCHWITZ...

SOLA RIVER

workshops and camp extension.

Auschwitz I

N E S W

Auschwitz II Birkenau

IT WAS MAYBE 2 MILES TO GO FROM AUSCHWITZ TO BIRKENAU THERE IT WAS MUCH MORE BIG.

IN AUSCHWITZ WE HAD, SAY, 20,000 PRISONERS, IN BIRKENAU WAS AT LEAST 5 TIMES SO MANY.

AUSCHWITZ, IT WAS A CAMP WHERE THEY GAVE YOU TO WORK SO THEY DIDN'T FINISH YOU SO FAST.

BIRKENAU WAS EVEN MORE BAD. IT WAS 800 PEOPLE IN A BUILDING MADE FOR 50 HORSES.

THERE IT WAS JUST A *DEATH* PLACE WITH JEWS WAITING FOR GAS... AND THERE IT WAS ANJA.

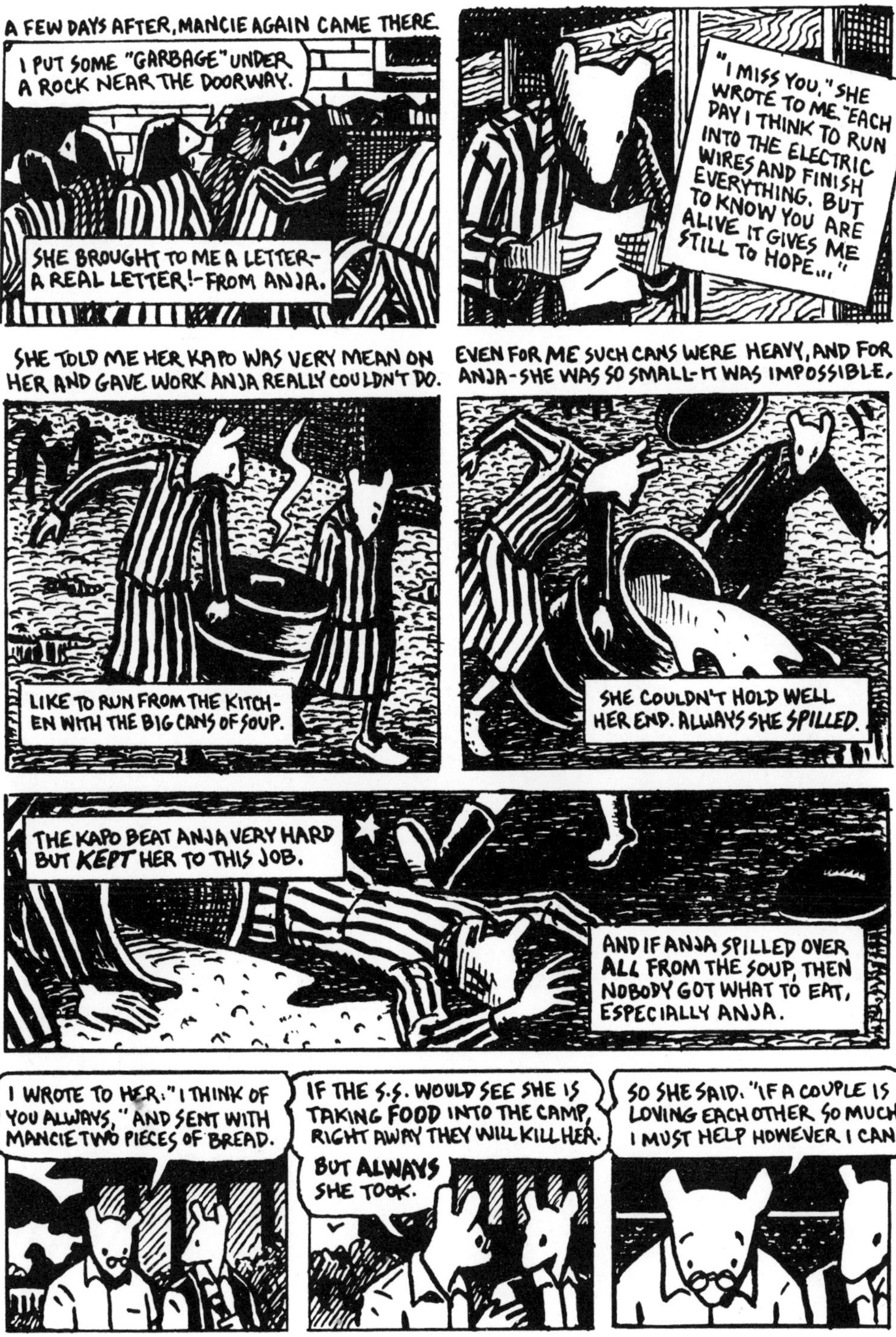
A FEW DAYS AFTER, MANCIE AGAIN CAME THERE.
I PUT SOME "GARBAGE" UNDER A ROCK NEAR THE DOORWAY.
SHE BROUGHT TO ME A LETTER- A REAL LETTER!- FROM ANJA.
"I MISS YOU," SHE WROTE TO ME. "EACH DAY I THINK TO RUN INTO THE ELECTRIC WIRES AND FINISH EVERYTHING. BUT TO KNOW YOU ARE ALIVE IT GIVES ME STILL TO HOPE..."
SHE TOLD ME HER KAPO WAS VERY MEAN ON HER AND GAVE WORK ANJA REALLY COULDN'T DO.
LIKE TO RUN FROM THE KITCHEN WITH THE BIG CANS OF SOUP.
EVEN FOR ME SUCH CANS WERE HEAVY, AND FOR ANJA - SHE WAS SO SMALL - IT WAS IMPOSSIBLE.
SHE COULDN'T HOLD WELL HER END. ALWAYS SHE SPILLED.
THE KAPO BEAT ANJA VERY HARD BUT KEPT HER TO THIS JOB.
AND IF ANJA SPILLED OVER ALL FROM THE SOUP, THEN NOBODY GOT WHAT TO EAT, ESPECIALLY ANJA.
I WROTE TO HER: "I THINK OF YOU ALWAYS," AND SENT WITH MANCIE TWO PIECES OF BREAD.
IF THE S.S. WOULD SEE SHE IS TAKING FOOD INTO THE CAMP, RIGHT AWAY THEY WILL KILL HER.
BUT ALWAYS SHE TOOK.
SO SHE SAID: "IF A COUPLE IS LOVING EACH OTHER SO MUCH, I MUST HELP HOWEVER I CAN."

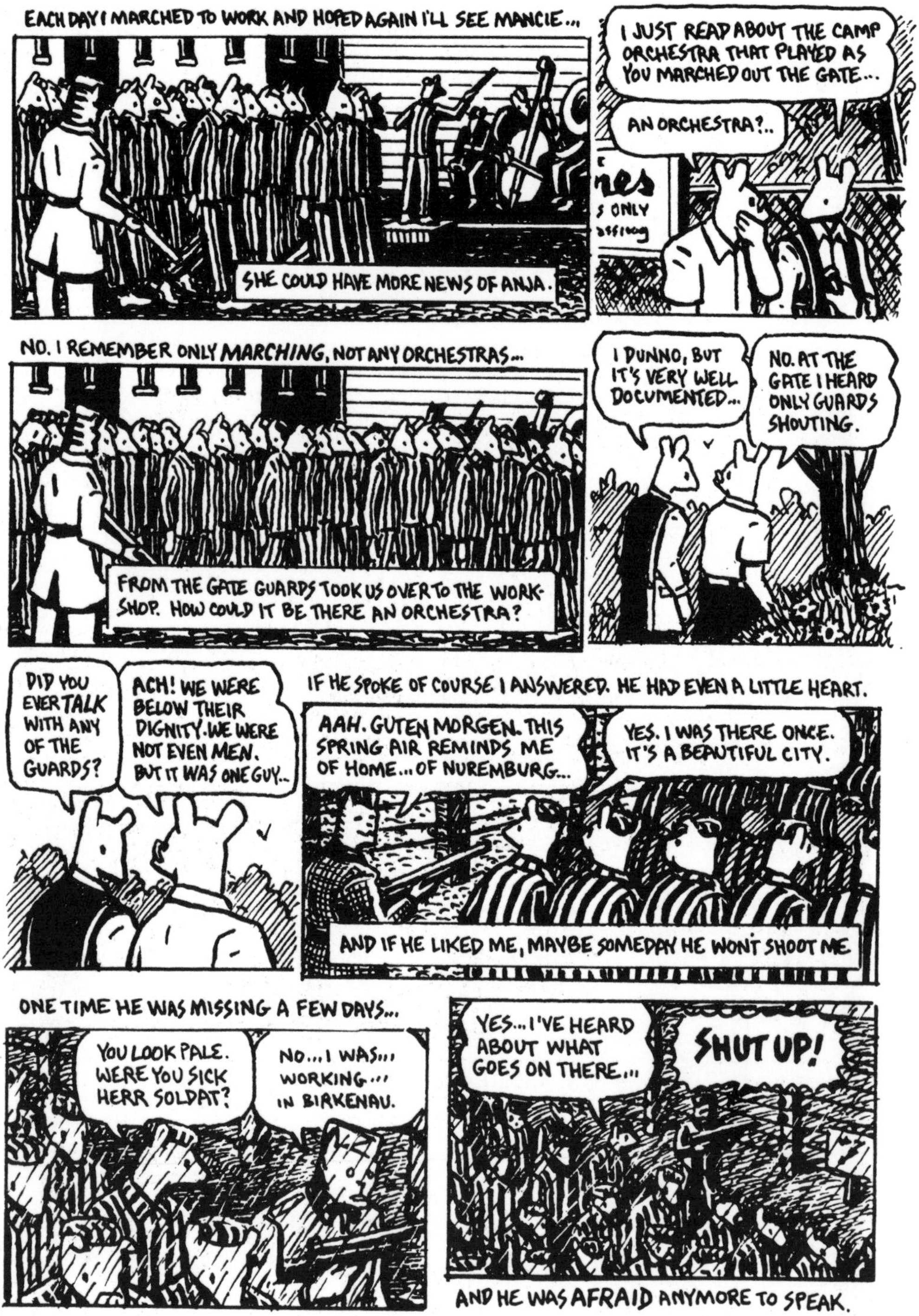
EACH DAY I MARCHED TO WORK AND HOPED AGAIN I'LL SEE MANCIE...
SHE COULD HAVE MORE NEWS OF ANJA.
I JUST READ ABOUT THE CAMP ORCHESTRA THAT PLAYED AS YOU MARCHED OUT THE GATE...
AN ORCHESTRA?..
NO. I REMEMBER ONLY MARCHING, NOT ANY ORCHESTRAS...
FROM THE GATE GUARDS TOOK US OVER TO THE WORKSHOP. HOW COULD IT BE THERE AN ORCHESTRA?
I DUNNO, BUT IT'S VERY WELL DOCUMENTED...
NO. AT THE GATE I HEARD ONLY GUARDS SHOUTING.
DID YOU EVER TALK WITH ANY OF THE GUARDS?
ACH! WE WERE BELOW THEIR DIGNITY. WE WERE NOT EVEN MEN. BUT IT WAS ONE GUY...
IF HE SPOKE OF COURSE I ANSWERED. HE HAD EVEN A LITTLE HEART.
AAH. GUTEN MORGEN. THIS SPRING AIR REMINDS ME OF HOME... OF NUREMBURG...
YES. I WAS THERE ONCE. IT'S A BEAUTIFUL CITY.
AND IF HE LIKED ME, MAYBE SOMEDAY HE WON'T SHOOT ME
ONE TIME HE WAS MISSING A FEW DAYS...
YOU LOOK PALE. WERE YOU SICK HERR SOLDAT?
NO... I WAS... WORKING... IN BIRKENAU.
YES... I'VE HEARD ABOUT WHAT GOES ON THERE...
SHUT UP!
AND HE WAS AFRAID ANYMORE TO SPEAK.

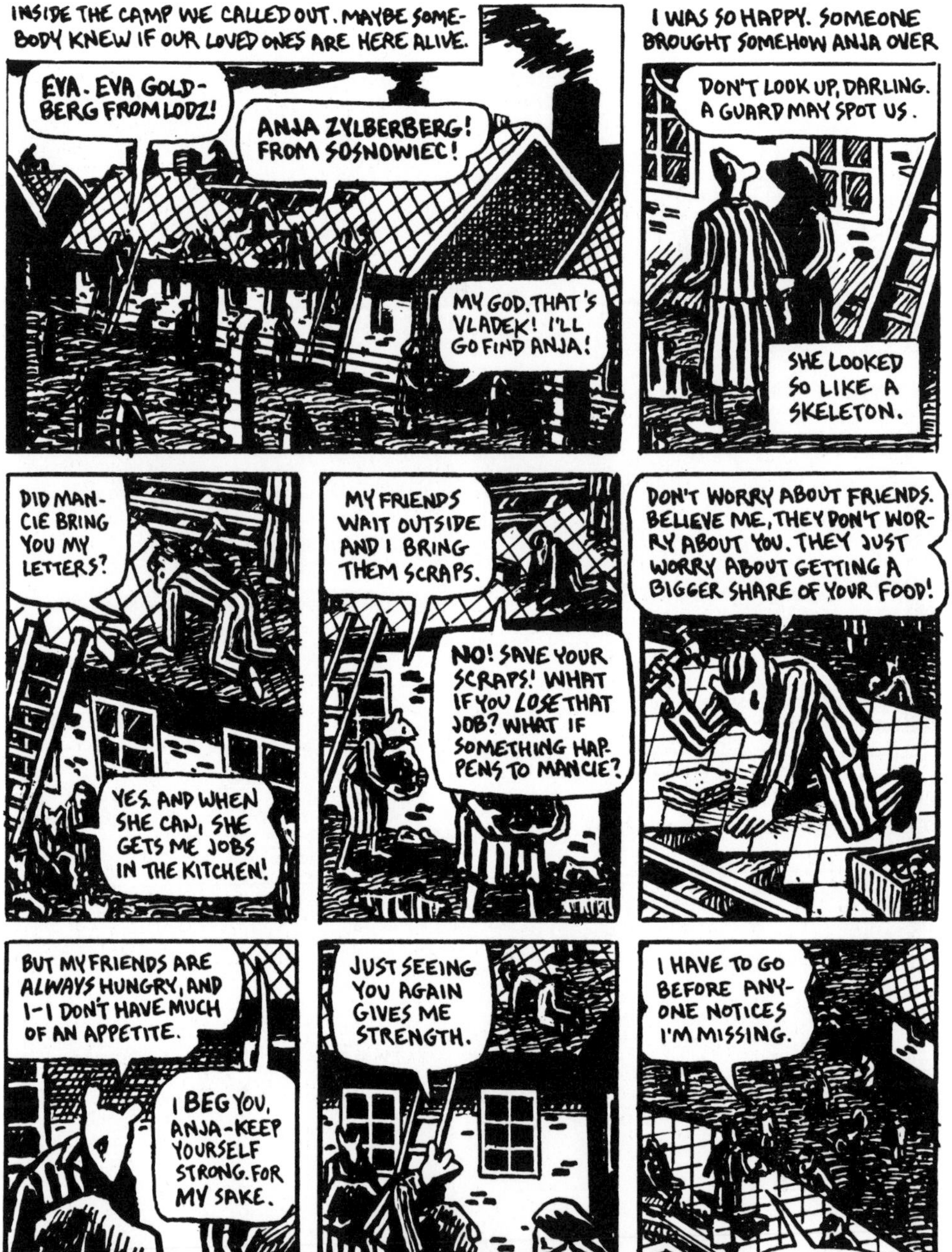
INSIDE THE CAMP WE CALLED OUT. MAYBE SOMEBODY KNEW IF OUR LOVED ONES ARE HERE ALIVE.
EVA. EVA GOLDBERG FROM LODZ!
ANJA ZYLBERBERG! FROM SOSNOWIEC!
MY GOD. THAT'S VLADEK! I'LL GO FIND ANJA!
I WAS SO HAPPY. SOMEONE BROUGHT SOMEHOW ANJA OVER
DON'T LOOK UP, DARLING. A GUARD MAY SPOT US.
SHE LOOKED SO LIKE A SKELETON.
DID MANCIE BRING YOU MY LETTERS?
YES. AND WHEN SHE CAN, SHE GETS ME JOBS IN THE KITCHEN!
MY FRIENDS WAIT OUTSIDE AND I BRING THEM SCRAPS.
NO! SAVE YOUR SCRAPS! WHAT IF YOU LOSE THAT JOB? WHAT IF SOMETHING HAPPENS TO MANCIE?
DON'T WORRY ABOUT FRIENDS. BELIEVE ME, THEY DON'T WORRY ABOUT YOU. THEY JUST WORRY ABOUT GETTING A BIGGER SHARE OF YOUR FOOD!
BUT MY FRIENDS ARE ALWAYS HUNGRY, AND I-I DON'T HAVE MUCH OF AN APPETITE.
I BEG YOU, ANJA-KEEP YOURSELF STRONG. FOR MY SAKE.
JUST SEEING YOU AGAIN GIVES ME STRENGTH.
I HAVE TO GO BEFORE ANYONE NOTICES I'M MISSING.
I... I THINK ABOUT YOU ...ALWAYS.

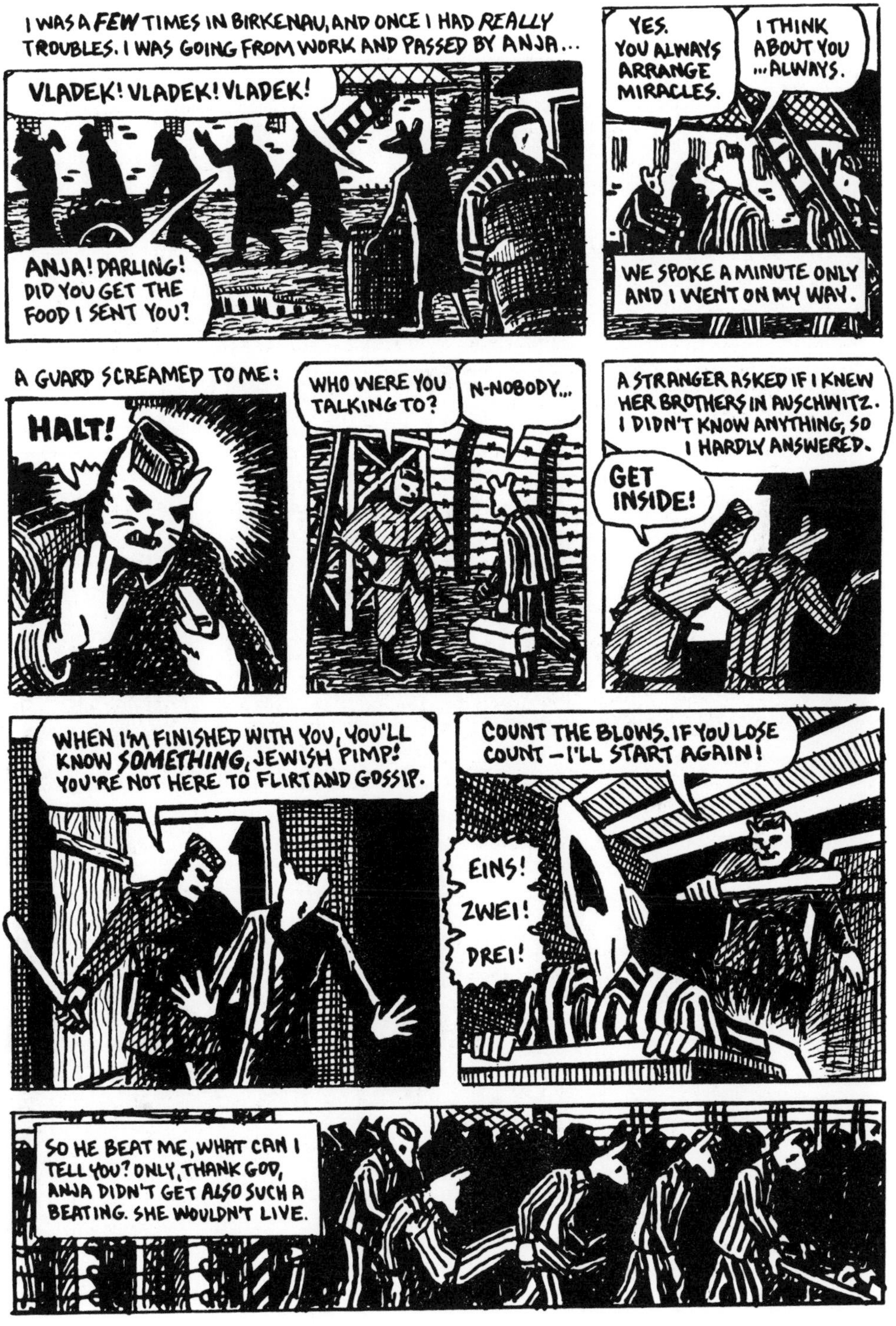
I WAS A FEW TIMES IN BIRKENAU, AND ONCE I HAD REALLY TROUBLES. I WAS GOING FROM WORK AND PASSED BY ANJA...
VLADEK! VLADEK! VLADEK!
ANJA! DARLING! DID YOU GET THE FOOD I SENT YOU?
YES. YOU ALWAYS ARRANGE MIRACLES.
I THINK ABOUT YOU ...ALWAYS.
WE SPOKE A MINUTE ONLY AND I WENT ON MY WAY.
A GUARD SCREAMED TO ME:
HALT!
WHO WERE YOU TALKING TO?
N-NOBODY...
A STRANGER ASKED IF I KNEW HER BROTHERS IN AUSCHWITZ. I DIDN'T KNOW ANYTHING, SO I HARDLY ANSWERED.
GET INSIDE!
WHEN I'M FINISHED WITH YOU, YOU'LL KNOW SOMETHING, JEWISH PIMP! YOU'RE NOT HERE TO FLIRT AND GOSSIP.
COUNT THE BLOWS. IF YOU LOSE COUNT – I'LL START AGAIN!
EINS!
ZWEI!
DREI!
SO HE BEAT ME, WHAT CAN I TELL YOU? ONLY, THANK GOD, ANJA DIDN'T GET ALSO SUCH A BEATING. SHE WOULDN'T LIVE.

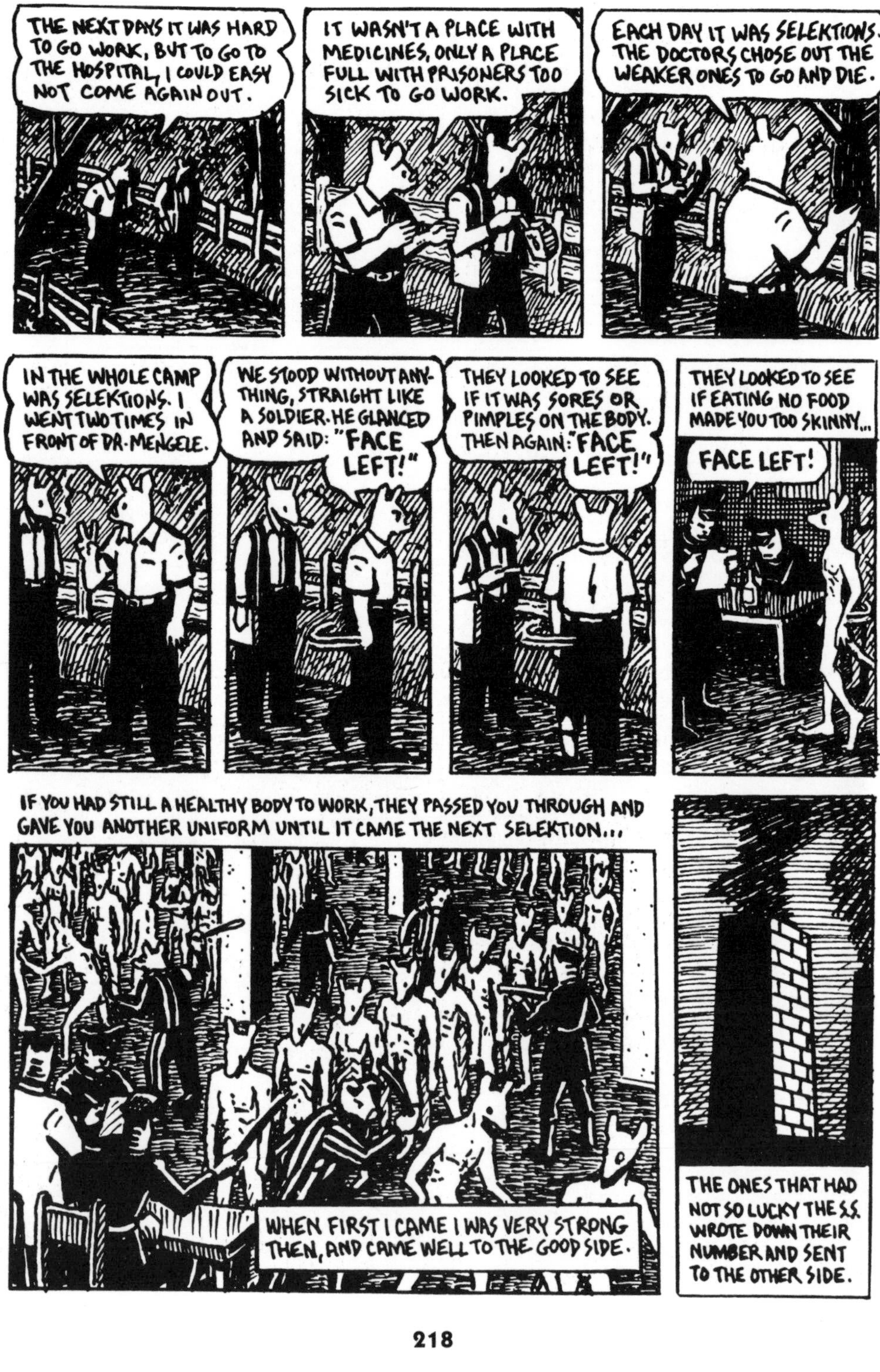
THE NEXT DAYS IT WAS HARD TO GO WORK, BUT TO GO TO THE HOSPITAL, I COULD EASY NOT COME AGAIN OUT.
IT WASN'T A PLACE WITH MEDICINES, ONLY A PLACE FULL WITH PRISONERS TOO SICK TO GO WORK.
EACH DAY IT WAS SELEKTIONS. THE DOCTORS CHOSE OUT THE WEAKER ONES TO GO AND DIE.
IN THE WHOLE CAMP WAS SELEKTIONS. I WENT TWO TIMES IN FRONT OF DR. MENGELE.
WE STOOD WITHOUT ANYTHING, STRAIGHT LIKE A SOLDIER. HE GLANCED AND SAID: "FACE LEFT!"
THEY LOOKED TO SEE IF IT WAS SORES OR PIMPLES ON THE BODY. THEN AGAIN: "FACE LEFT!"
THEY LOOKED TO SEE IF EATING NO FOOD MADE YOU TOO SKINNY...
FACE LEFT!
IF YOU HAD STILL A HEALTHY BODY TO WORK, THEY PASSED YOU THROUGH AND GAVE YOU ANOTHER UNIFORM UNTIL IT CAME THE NEXT SELEKTION...
WHEN FIRST I CAME I WAS VERY STRONG THEN, AND CAME WELL TO THE GOOD SIDE.
THE ONES THAT HAD NOT SO LUCKY THE S.S. WROTE DOWN THEIR NUMBER AND SENT TO THE OTHER SIDE.

219

SO...IN THE TINSHOP I HAD STILL THE SAME STORY WITH YIDL.

ONLY ONE APPLE FOR ME TODAY? IS BUSINESS BAD, MR. CAPITALIST?

WHAT HAPPENED TO THE SHOEMAKER WHO WORKED IN THERE?

A LOT OF THE POLISH PRISONERS WERE SENT TO CAMPS INSIDE THE REICH. THEY TOOK SOME OF MY BOYS TOO.

I RAN TO THE KAPO IN CHARGE FROM ALL THE SHOP.

DO YOU NEED A NEW SHOEMAKER?

SURE. THE S.S. TOOK THE OLD ONE AWAY, BUT THEY'RE STILL BRINGING SHOES IN!

I LEARNED A LITTLE SHOE FIXING WATCHING HOW THEY WORKED WHEN I WAS WITH MY COUSIN MILOCH, THERE IN THE GHETTO SHOE SHOP.

TO FIX SUCH AN OPENED SOLE I KNEW TO TAKE A DOUBLE THREAD SMEARED WITH WAX.

...MAKE THEN A HOLE AND PUSH THE THREAD HALF WAY ONLY.

YOU KNOW, I'VE BEEN A SHOEMAKER SINCE CHILDHOOD.

YOU DON'T *LOOK* LIKE A SHOEMAKER TO ME... YOU'RE A *TINMAN*!

AND ON THE UPPER PART PUT TWO HOLES EVEN TO THE SOLE...

BRING THE THREAD THEN THROUGH *THESE* HOLES.

CROSS THE THREAD FROM THE TOP AND BOTTOM, *BOTH* ENDS THROUGH A NEW HOLE IN THE SOLE AND REPEAT SO UNTIL THE SHOE IS CLOSED.

DO I HAVE TO HAVE IT WRITTEN ON MY FOREHEAD?

ALRIGHT, THEN... FIX *THIS*!

...AND SO IT'S MADE, YOU CAN'T EVEN *SEE* IT HAS STITCHES!

YOU'RE BETTER THAN OUR *LAST* SHOEMAKER!

YOU SEE? IT'S GOOD TO KNOW HOW TO DO *EVERYTHING*!

220

EVEN PAPER WAS HARD TO HAVE THERE. MY FRIENDS CAME ALWAYS TO ME WHEN THEY NEEDED.

I FOUND AND SAVED. FOR THE TOILET MOST USED A PIECE FROM THEIR CLOTHES OR THEIR HAND.

WHY DIDN'T OTHER PEOPLE SAVE PAPER?

ACH! YOU KNOW HOW MOST PEOPLE ARE!

SO... I WROTE OVER TO ANJA THAT NOW I AM A SHOEMAKER, AND I HEARD HERE ABOUT THESE NEW BARRACKS...

AND MANCIE TOOK IT. SHE WAS SO GOOD, ALWAYS SHE TOOK.

ON THE BACK FROM MY LETTER ANJA WROTE HOW MUCH SHE WANTED ONLY TO COME TO SUCH A BARRACK NEAR TO ME.

ANJA'S BARRACK WAS MAYBE 1000 GIRLS WITH A BAD KAPO WHAT HIT ANYBODY WHAT CAME NEAR.

SNEAK! I SAW YOU TAKE A SECOND PIECE OF BREAD!

NO. I—

N-NICE BOOTS—IT'S A PITY THE SOLES ARE COMING APART.

SO! WHAT DO YOU CARE?

YOU COULD SEND THEM TO MY HUSBAND, HE'S A SHOEMAKER IN AUSCHWITZ....

OH, REALLY

SHE HAD LEATHER BOOTS—NOT WOOD. THEY WERE IN A VERY BAD SHAPE, BUT REALLY LEATHER.

SO, SHE ARRANGED THE BOOTS OVER TO ME.

OF COURSE I FIXED VERY NICE THE SHOES, AND THE KAPO THEN WAS VERY DIFFERENT WITH ANJA.

THAT SOUP CAN IS TOO HEAVY FOR YOU. COME REST IN MY ROOM UNTIL THE APPEL.

...VERY DIFFERENT.

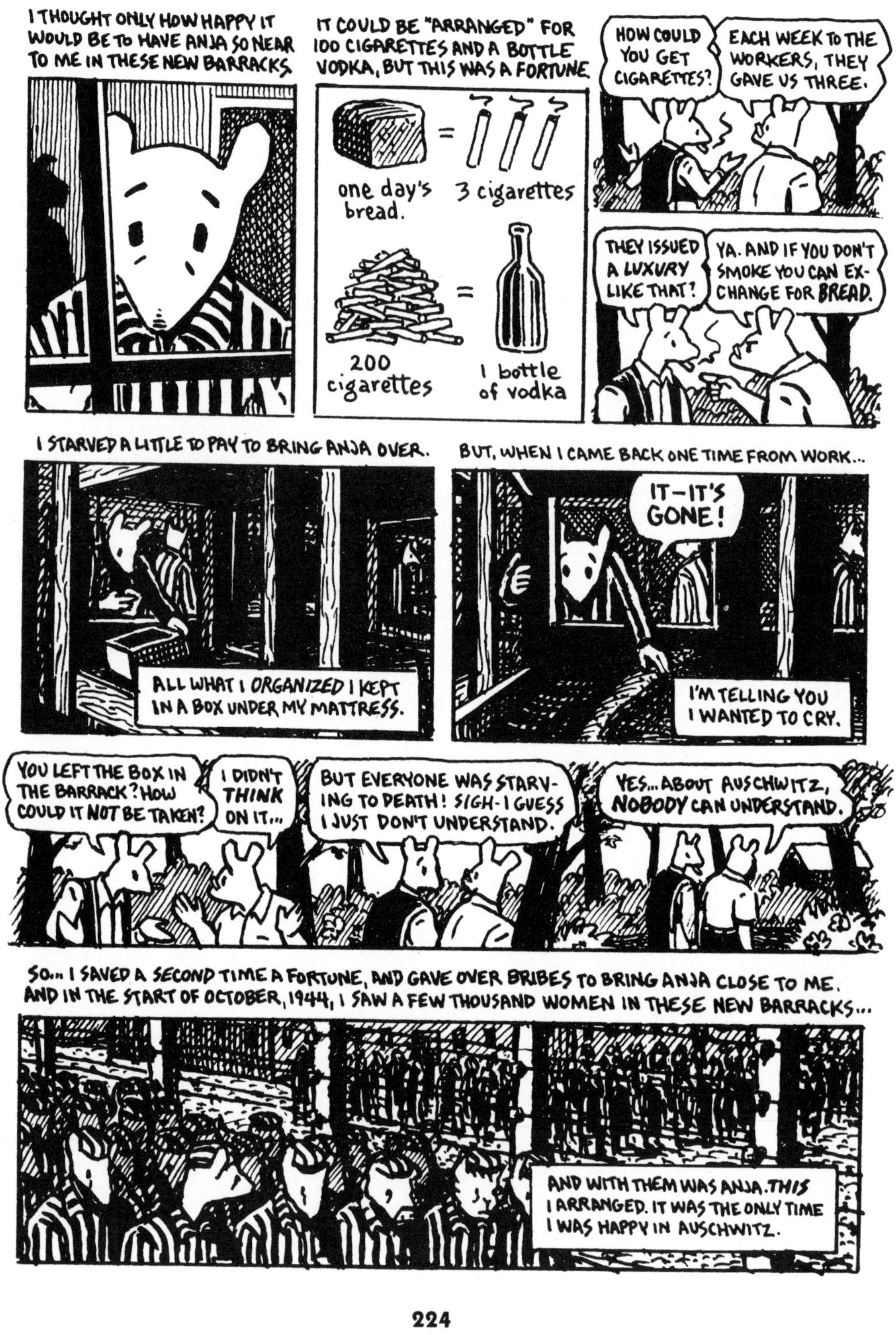
I THOUGHT ONLY HOW HAPPY IT WOULD BE TO HAVE ANJA SO NEAR TO ME IN THESE NEW BARRACKS.
IT COULD BE "ARRANGED" FOR 100 CIGARETTES AND A BOTTLE VODKA, BUT THIS WAS A FORTUNE.
one day's bread.
=
3 cigarettes
200 cigarettes
=
1 bottle of vodka
HOW COULD YOU GET CIGARETTES?
EACH WEEK TO THE WORKERS, THEY GAVE US THREE.
THEY ISSUED A LUXURY LIKE THAT?
YA. AND IF YOU DON'T SMOKE YOU CAN EXCHANGE FOR BREAD.
I STARVED A LITTLE TO PAY TO BRING ANJA OVER.
ALL WHAT I ORGANIZED I KEPT IN A BOX UNDER MY MATTRESS.
BUT, WHEN I CAME BACK ONE TIME FROM WORK...
IT—IT'S GONE!
I'M TELLING YOU I WANTED TO CRY.
YOU LEFT THE BOX IN THE BARRACK? HOW COULD IT NOT BE TAKEN?
I DIDN'T THINK ON IT...
BUT EVERYONE WAS STARVING TO DEATH! SIGH—I GUESS I JUST DON'T UNDERSTAND.
YES... ABOUT AUSCHWITZ, NOBODY CAN UNDERSTAND.
SO... I SAVED A SECOND TIME A FORTUNE, AND GAVE OVER BRIBES TO BRING ANJA CLOSE TO ME. AND IN THE START OF OCTOBER, 1944, I SAW A FEW THOUSAND WOMEN IN THESE NEW BARRACKS...
AND WITH THEM WAS ANJA. THIS I ARRANGED. IT WAS THE ONLY TIME I WAS HAPPY IN AUSCHWITZ.

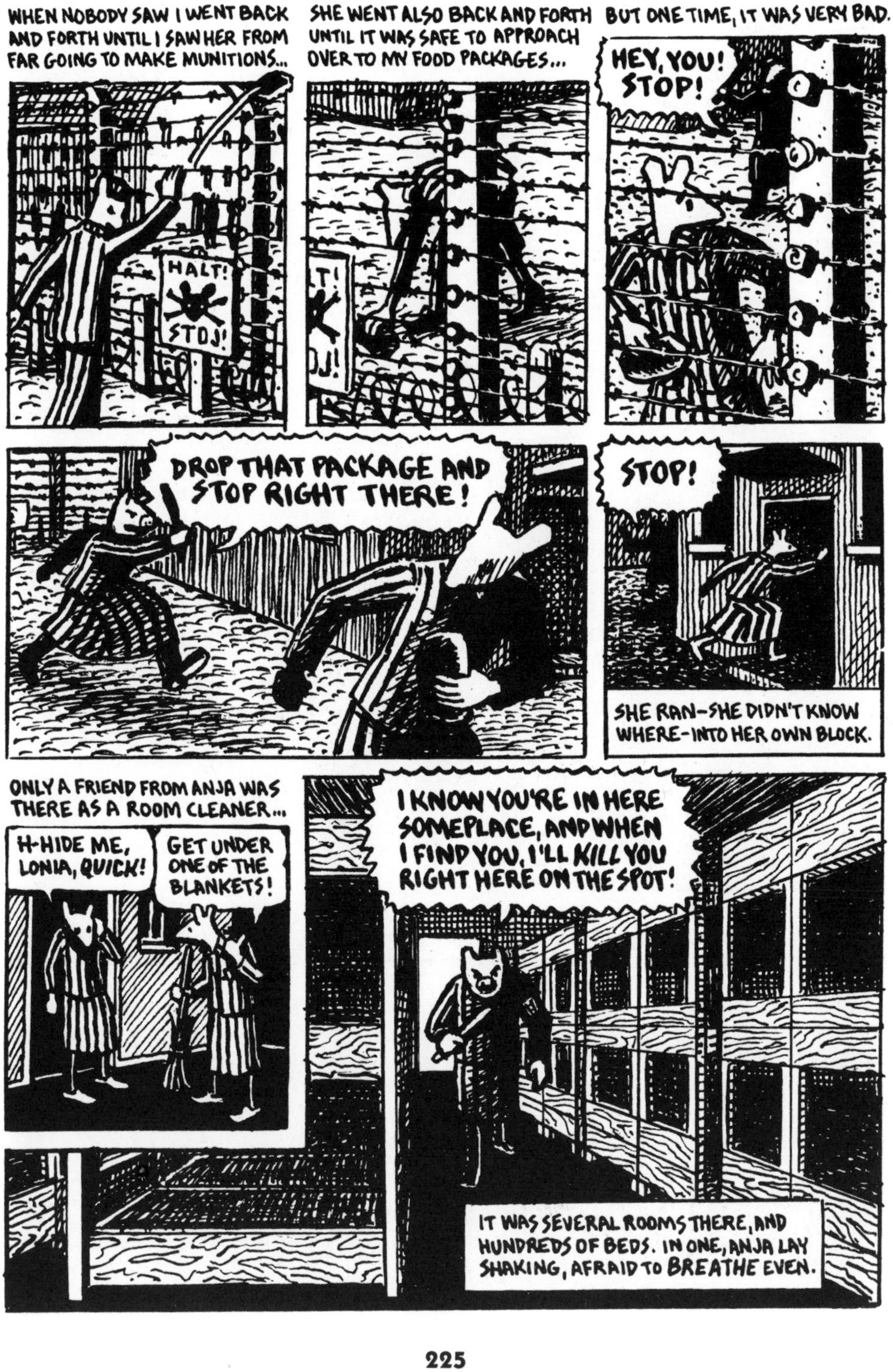
WHEN NOBODY SAW I WENT BACK AND FORTH UNTIL I SAW HER FROM FAR GOING TO MAKE MUNITIONS...
HALT!
STOJ!
SHE WENT ALSO BACK AND FORTH UNTIL IT WAS SAFE TO APPROACH OVER TO MY FOOD PACKAGES...
BUT ONE TIME, IT WAS VERY BAD.
HEY, YOU! STOP!
DROP THAT PACKAGE AND STOP RIGHT THERE!
STOP!
SHE RAN–SHE DIDN'T KNOW WHERE–INTO HER OWN BLOCK.
ONLY A FRIEND FROM ANJA WAS THERE AS A ROOM CLEANER...
H-HIDE ME, LONIA, QUICK!
GET UNDER ONE OF THE BLANKETS!
I KNOW YOU'RE IN HERE SOMEPLACE, AND WHEN I FIND YOU, I'LL KILL YOU RIGHT HERE ON THE SPOT!
IT WAS SEVERAL ROOMS THERE, AND HUNDREDS OF BEDS. IN ONE, ANJA LAY SHAKING, AFRAID TO BREATHE EVEN.

228

FOR THIS I WAS AN *EYEWITNESS*.

I CAME TO ONE OF THE FOUR CREMO BUILDINGS. IT LOOKED SO LIKE A BIG BAKERY...

FROM BELOW GROUND, IN THE GAS ROOM, WE TINMEN HAD TO TAKE OUT THE PIPES AND FANS FOR VENTILATING.

EXE- CUTION ROOM

UNDRESS- ING ROOM

RM. FOR MELTING GOLD FILLINGS

CORPSE LIFT

GAS CHAMBER

INCINERATION RM. W. OVENS

CHIMNEY

TOILET

COAL STORAGE

CREMATORIUM II.

THIS WAS A FACTORY TO MAKE —ONE, TWO, THREE— ASHES AND SMOKE FROM ALL WHAT CAME HERE.

underground undressing room

ovens

underground gas chamber

SPECIAL PRISONERS WORKED HERE SEPARATE. THEY GOT BETTER BREAD, BUT EACH FEW MONTHS THEY ALSO WERE SENT UP THE CHIMNEY. ONE FROM THEM SHOWED ME EVERYTHING HOW IT WAS.

DISINFEKTION
DEZYNFEKCIE
DISINFECTION

PEOPLE BELIEVED **REALLY** IT WAS HERE A PLACE FOR SHOWERS. SO THEY WERE TOLD.

THEY CAME TO A BIG ROOM TO UNDRESS THEIR CLOTHES WHAT LOOKS SO, YES-HERE IS A PLACE SO LIKE THEY SAY.

Sauber

ein Ges

IMPORTANT REMEMBER YOUR HOOK NUMBER

PLEASE TIE YOUR SHOES TO- GETH- ER

IF I SAW A COUPLE MONTHS BEFORE HOW IT WAS ALL ARRANGED HERE, ONLY **ONE** TIME I COULD SEE IT!

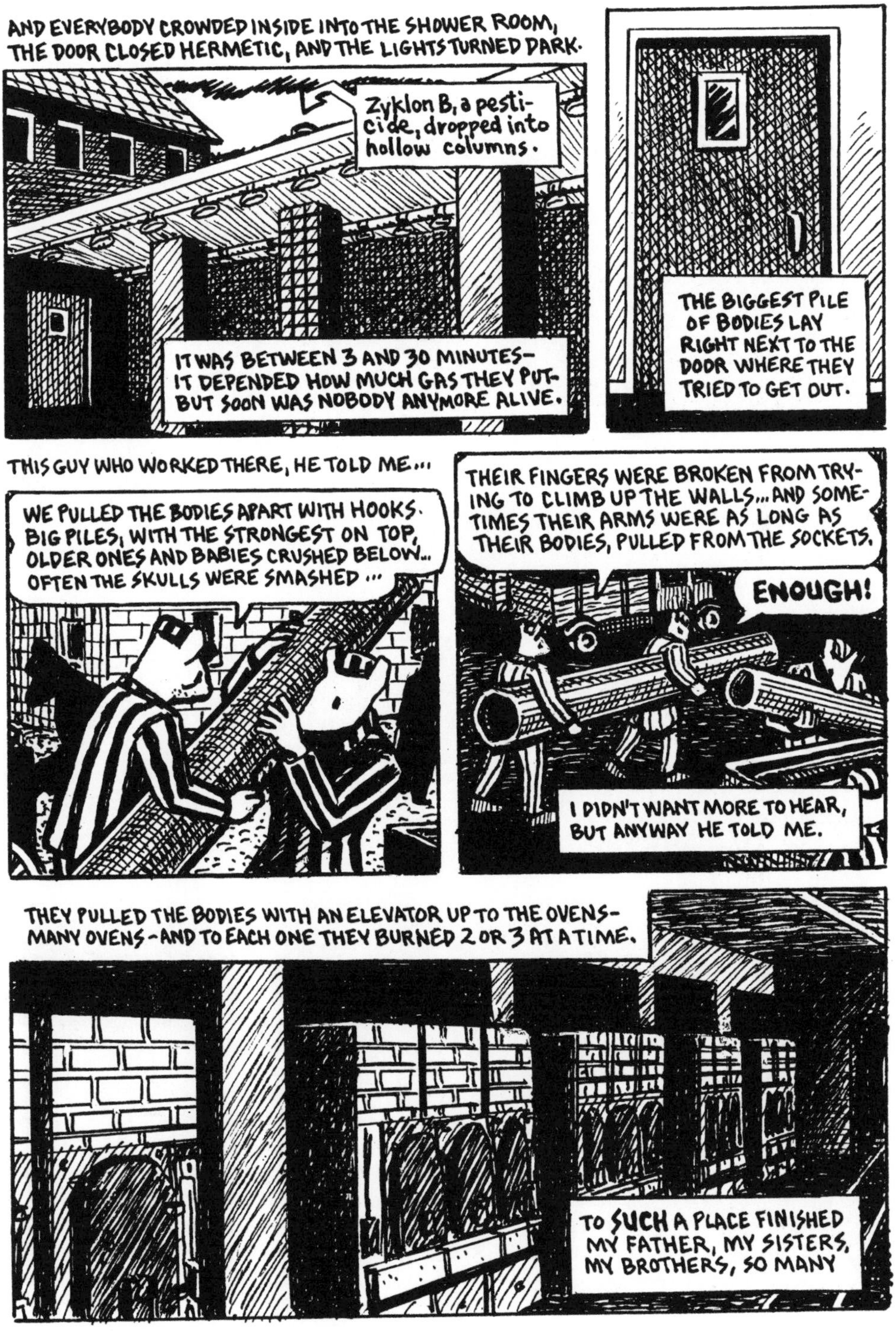
AND EVERYBODY CROWDED INSIDE INTO THE SHOWER ROOM, THE DOOR CLOSED HERMETIC, AND THE LIGHTS TURNED DARK.
Zyklon B, a pesticide, dropped into hollow columns.
IT WAS BETWEEN 3 AND 30 MINUTES- IT DEPENDED HOW MUCH GAS THEY PUT- BUT SOON WAS NOBODY ANYMORE ALIVE.
THE BIGGEST PILE OF BODIES LAY RIGHT NEXT TO THE DOOR WHERE THEY TRIED TO GET OUT.
THIS GUY WHO WORKED THERE, HE TOLD ME...
WE PULLED THE BODIES APART WITH HOOKS. BIG PILES, WITH THE STRONGEST ON TOP, OLDER ONES AND BABIES CRUSHED BELOW... OFTEN THE SKULLS WERE SMASHED ...
THEIR FINGERS WERE BROKEN FROM TRYING TO CLIMB UP THE WALLS... AND SOMETIMES THEIR ARMS WERE AS LONG AS THEIR BODIES, PULLED FROM THE SOCKETS.
ENOUGH!
I DIDN'T WANT MORE TO HEAR, BUT ANYWAY HE TOLD ME.
THEY PULLED THE BODIES WITH AN ELEVATOR UP TO THE OVENS- MANY OVENS - AND TO EACH ONE THEY BURNED 2 OR 3 AT A TIME.
TO SUCH A PLACE FINISHED MY FATHER, MY SISTERS, MY BROTHERS, SO MANY

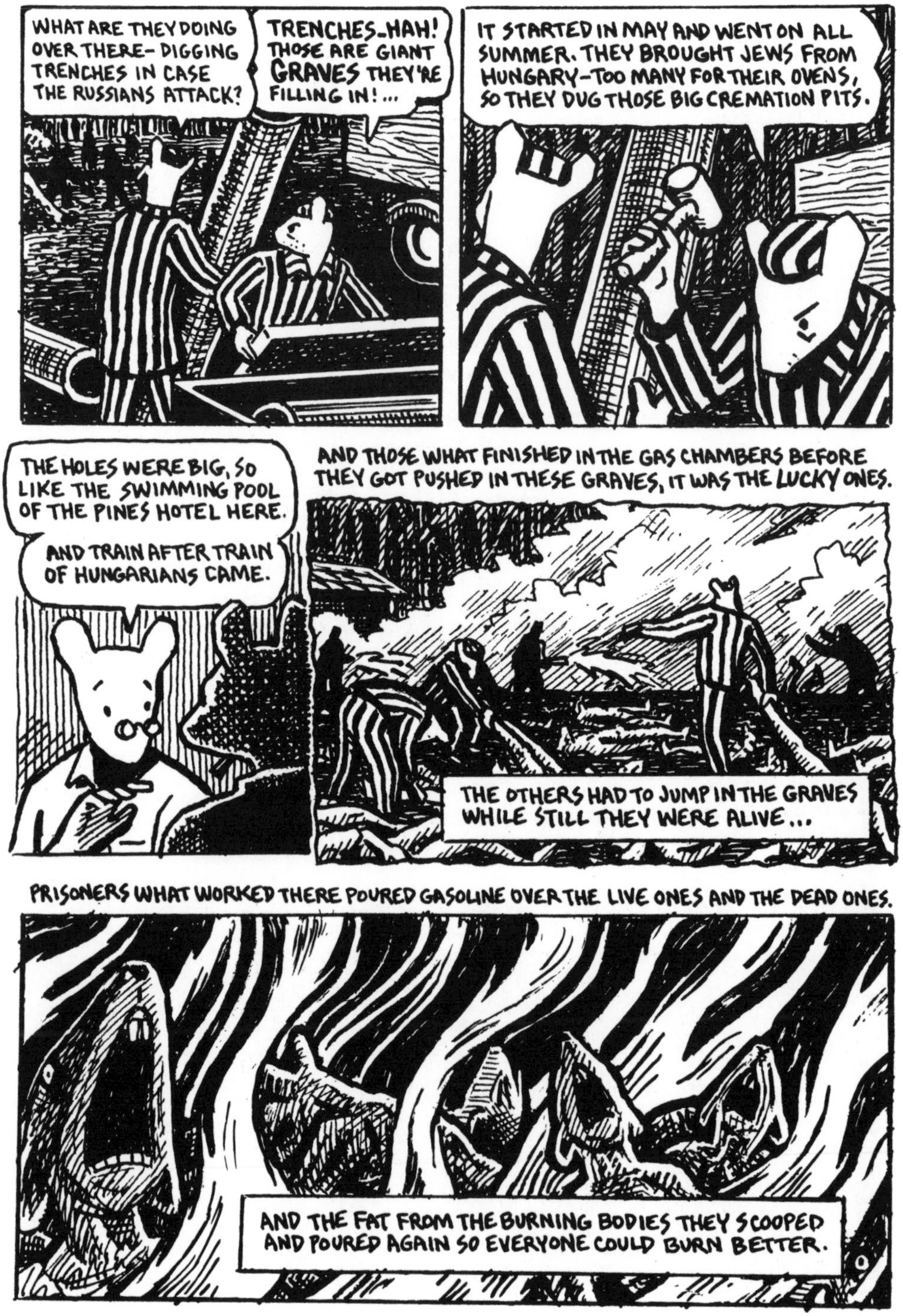
WHAT ARE THEY DOING OVER THERE- DIGGING TRENCHES IN CASE THE RUSSIANS ATTACK?
TRENCHES-HAH! THOSE ARE GIANT GRAVES THEY'RE FILLING IN!...
IT STARTED IN MAY AND WENT ON ALL SUMMER. THEY BROUGHT JEWS FROM HUNGARY-TOO MANY FOR THEIR OVENS, SO THEY DUG THOSE BIG CREMATION PITS.
THE HOLES WERE BIG, SO LIKE THE SWIMMING POOL OF THE PINES HOTEL HERE.
AND TRAIN AFTER TRAIN OF HUNGARIANS CAME.
AND THOSE WHAT FINISHED IN THE GAS CHAMBERS BEFORE THEY GOT PUSHED IN THESE GRAVES, IT WAS THE LUCKY ONES.
THE OTHERS HAD TO JUMP IN THE GRAVES WHILE STILL THEY WERE ALIVE...
PRISONERS WHAT WORKED THERE POURED GASOLINE OVER THE LIVE ONES AND THE DEAD ONES.
AND THE FAT FROM THE BURNING BODIES THEY SCOOPED AND POURED AGAIN SO EVERYONE COULD BURN BETTER.

233

That night...

CHAPTER THREE

237

And so...

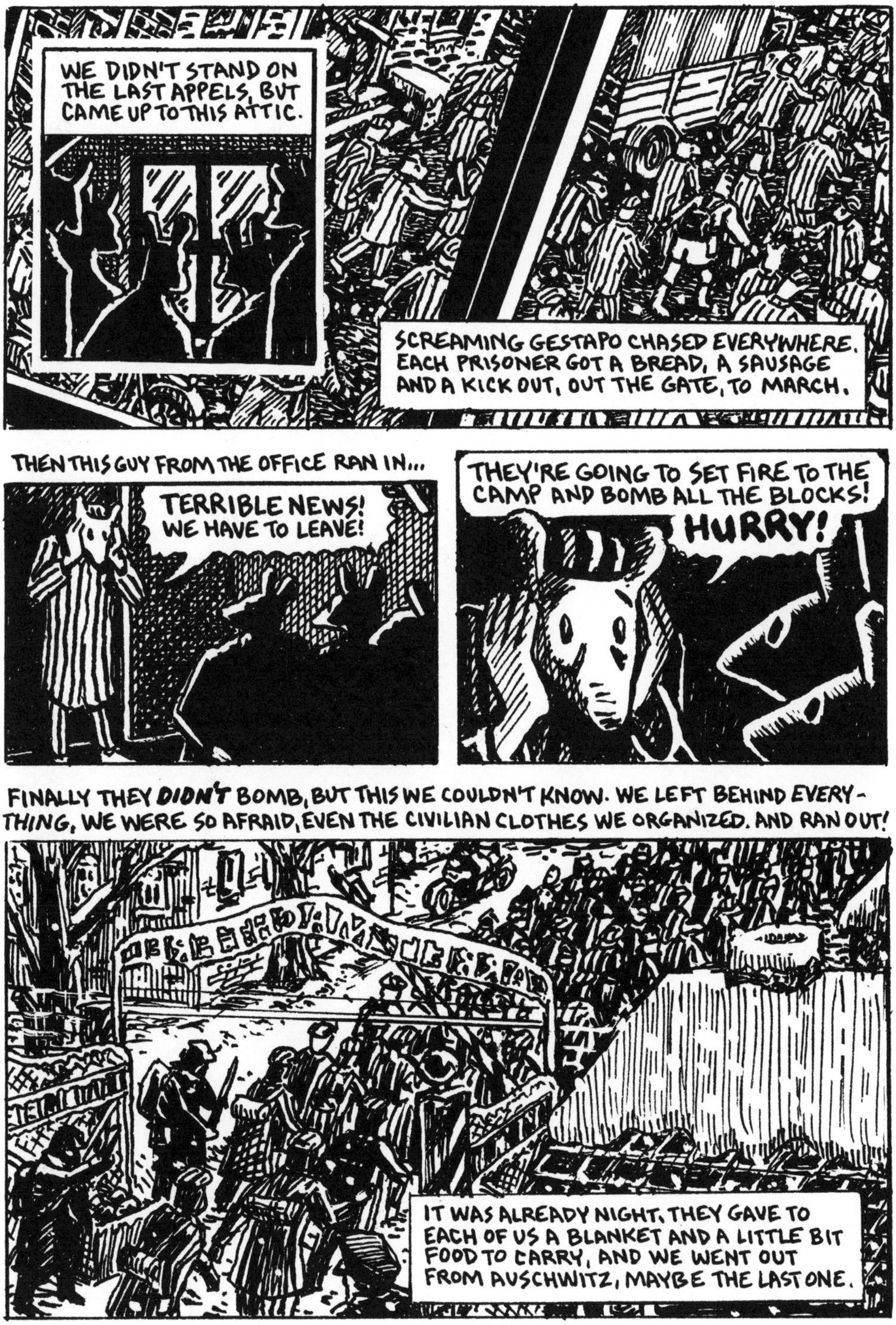
WE DIDN'T STAND ON THE LAST APPELS, BUT CAME UP TO THIS ATTIC.
SCREAMING GESTAPO CHASED EVERYWHERE. EACH PRISONER GOT A BREAD, A SAUSAGE AND A KICK OUT, OUT THE GATE, TO MARCH.
THEN THIS GUY FROM THE OFFICE RAN IN...
TERRIBLE NEWS! WE HAVE TO LEAVE!
THEY'RE GOING TO SET FIRE TO THE CAMP AND BOMB ALL THE BLOCKS!
HURRY!
FINALLY THEY ***DIDN'T*** BOMB, BUT THIS WE COULDN'T KNOW. WE LEFT BEHIND EVERYTHING, WE WERE SO AFRAID, EVEN THE CIVILIAN CLOTHES WE ORGANIZED. AND RAN OUT!
IT WAS ALREADY NIGHT, THEY GAVE TO EACH OF US A BLANKET AND A LITTLE BIT FOOD TO CARRY, AND WE WENT OUT FROM AUSCHWITZ, MAYBE THE LAST ONE.

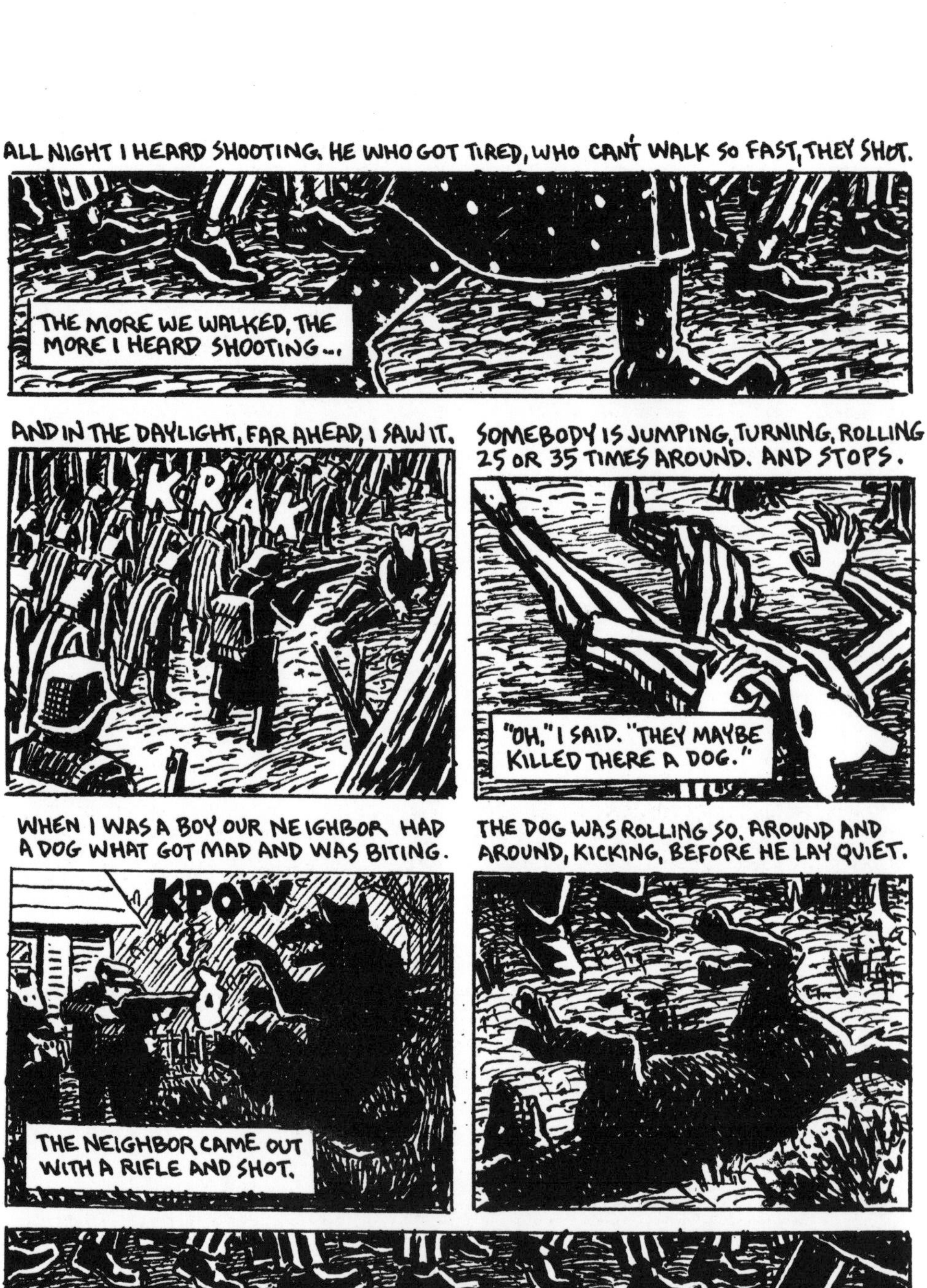
ALL NIGHT I HEARD SHOOTING. HE WHO GOT TIRED, WHO CAN'T WALK SO FAST, THEY SHOT.
THE MORE WE WALKED, THE MORE I HEARD SHOOTING...
AND IN THE DAYLIGHT, FAR AHEAD, I SAW IT.
KRAK
SOMEBODY IS JUMPING, TURNING, ROLLING 25 OR 35 TIMES AROUND. AND STOPS.
"OH," I SAID. "THEY MAYBE KILLED THERE A DOG."
WHEN I WAS A BOY OUR NEIGHBOR HAD A DOG WHAT GOT MAD AND WAS BITING.
KPOW
THE NEIGHBOR CAME OUT WITH A RIFLE AND SHOT.
THE DOG WAS ROLLING SO, AROUND AND AROUND, KICKING, BEFORE HE LAY QUIET.
AND NOW I THOUGHT: "HOW AMAZING IT IS THAT A HUMAN BEING REACTS THE SAME LIKE THIS NEIGHBOR'S DOG."

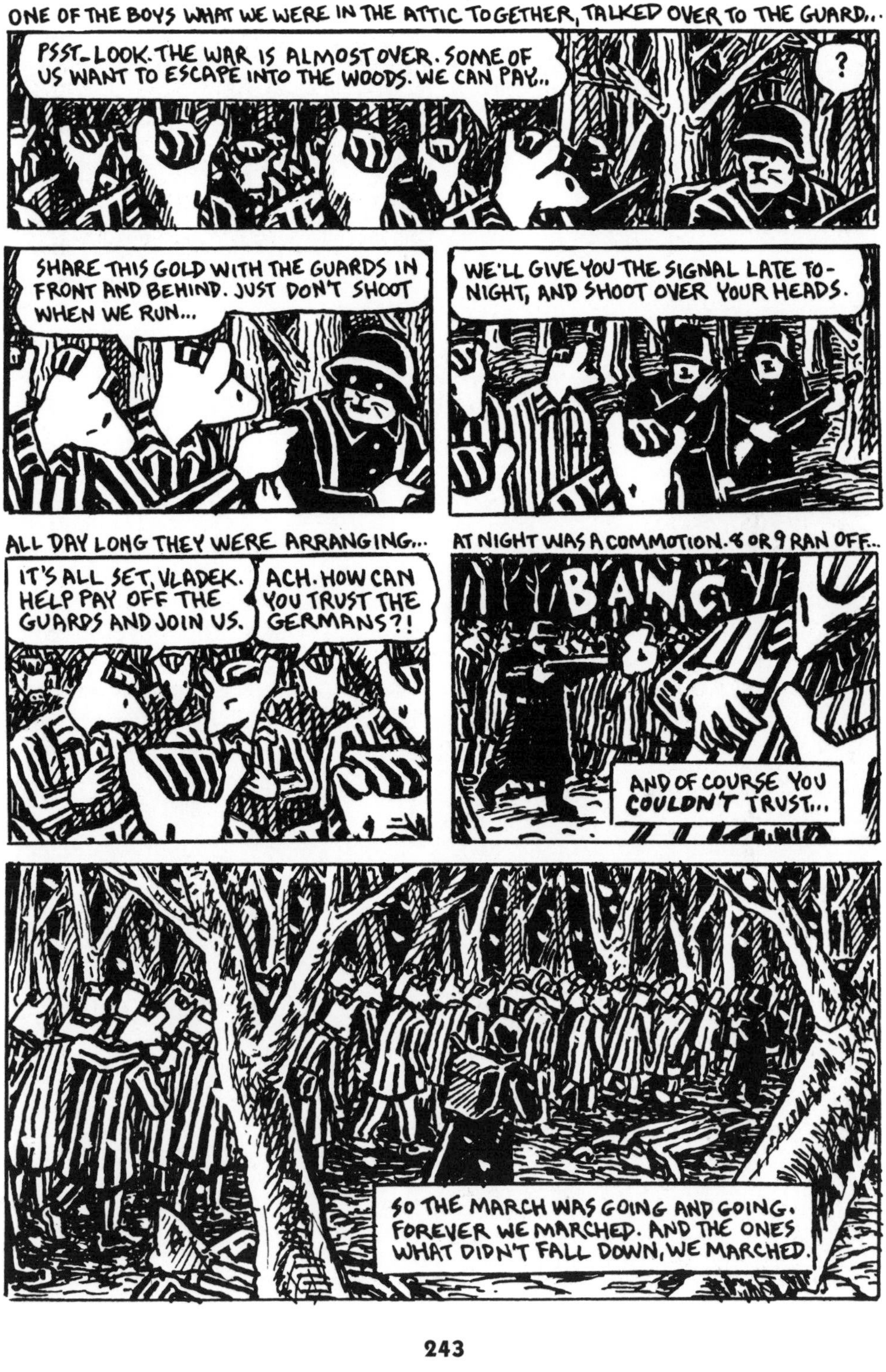
ONE OF THE BOYS WHAT WE WERE IN THE ATTIC TOGETHER, TALKED OVER TO THE GUARD...
PSST_LOOK. THE WAR IS ALMOST OVER. SOME OF US WANT TO ESCAPE INTO THE WOODS. WE CAN PAY..
?
SHARE THIS GOLD WITH THE GUARDS IN FRONT AND BEHIND. JUST DON'T SHOOT WHEN WE RUN...
WE'LL GIVE YOU THE SIGNAL LATE TO-NIGHT, AND SHOOT OVER YOUR HEADS.
ALL DAY LONG THEY WERE ARRANGING...
IT'S ALL SET, VLADEK. HELP PAY OFF THE GUARDS AND JOIN US.
ACH. HOW CAN YOU TRUST THE GERMANS?!
AT NIGHT WAS A COMMOTION. 8 OR 9 RAN OFF...
BANG
AND OF COURSE YOU COULDN'T TRUST...
SO THE MARCH WAS GOING AND GOING. FOREVER WE MARCHED. AND THE ONES WHAT DIDN'T FALL DOWN, WE MARCHED.

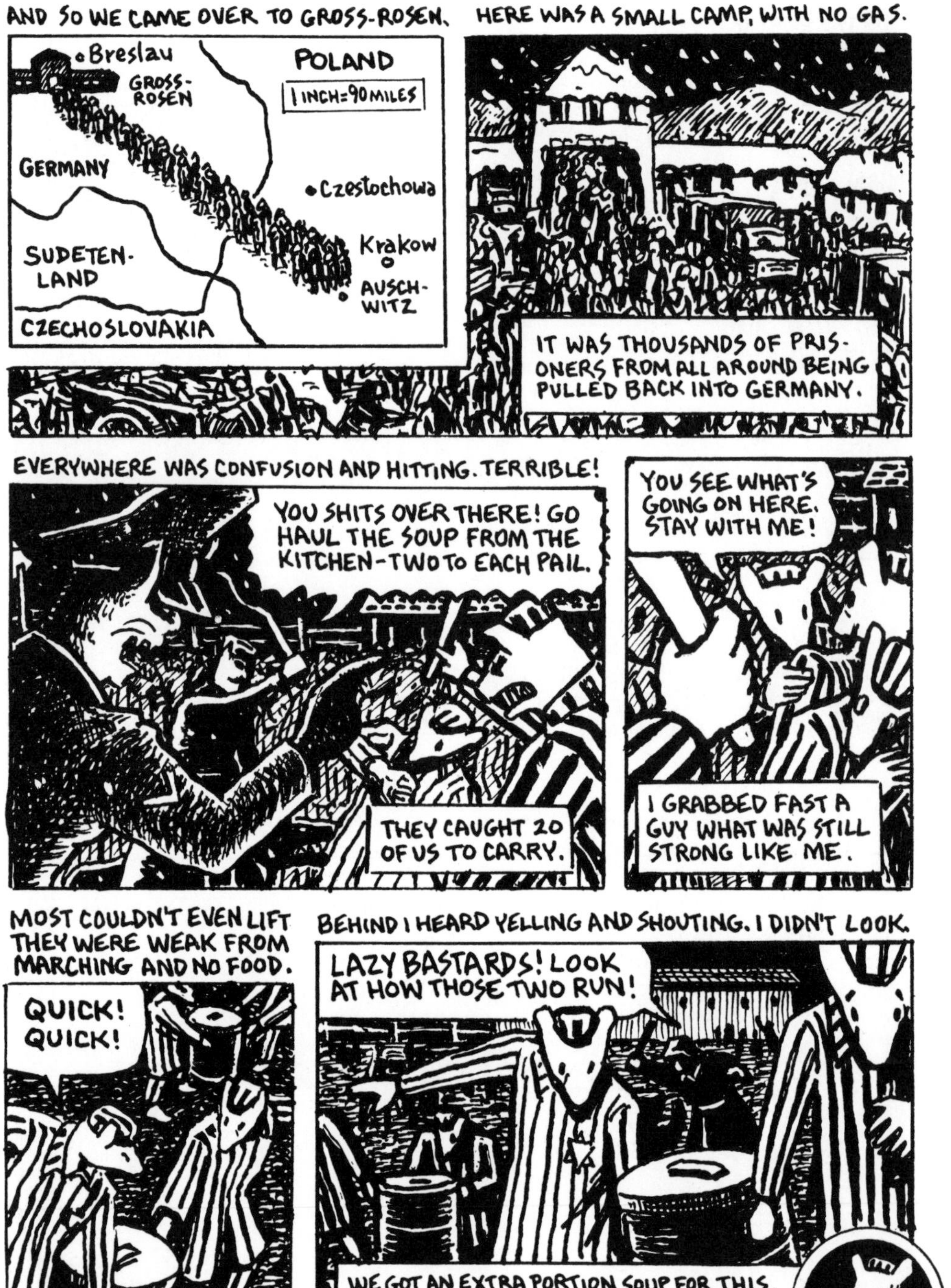
AND SO WE CAME OVER TO GROSS-ROSEN.
Breslau
GROSS-ROSEN
POLAND
1 INCH=90 MILES
GERMANY
Czestochowa
SUDETEN-LAND
Krakow
AUSCH-WITZ
CZECHOSLOVAKIA
HERE WAS A SMALL CAMP, WITH NO GAS.
IT WAS THOUSANDS OF PRISONERS FROM ALL AROUND BEING PULLED BACK INTO GERMANY.
EVERYWHERE WAS CONFUSION AND HITTING. TERRIBLE!
YOU SHITS OVER THERE! GO HAUL THE SOUP FROM THE KITCHEN-TWO TO EACH PAIL.
THEY CAUGHT 20 OF US TO CARRY.
YOU SEE WHAT'S GOING ON HERE. STAY WITH ME!
I GRABBED FAST A GUY WHAT WAS STILL STRONG LIKE ME.
MOST COULDN'T EVEN LIFT THEY WERE WEAK FROM MARCHING AND NO FOOD.
QUICK! QUICK!
BEHIND I HEARD YELLING AND SHOUTING. I DIDN'T LOOK.
LAZY BASTARDS! LOOK AT HOW THOSE TWO RUN!
WE GOT AN EXTRA PORTION SOUP FOR THIS. MOST WERE NOT LUCKY TO BE STILL STRONG.

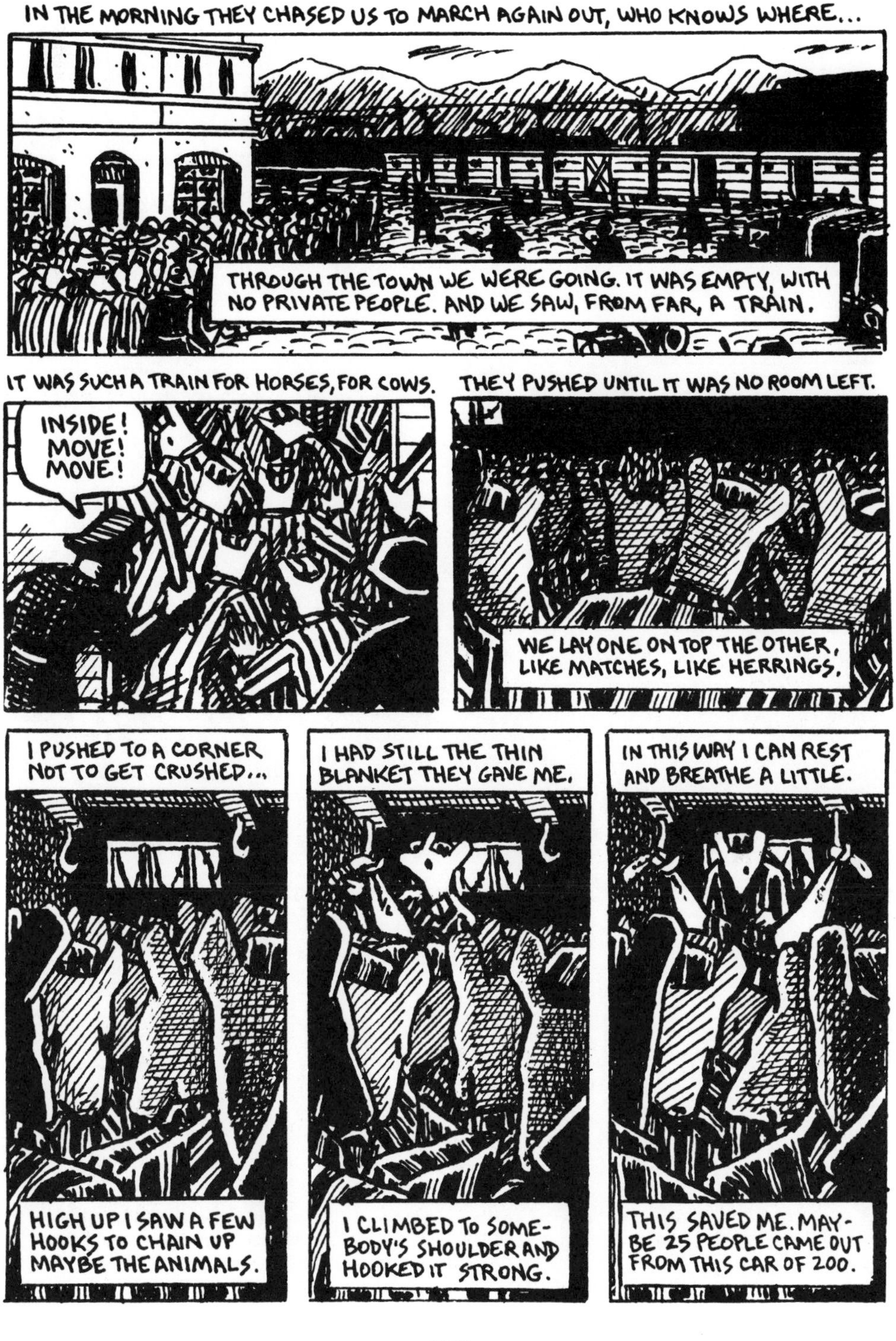
IN THE MORNING THEY CHASED US TO MARCH AGAIN OUT, WHO KNOWS WHERE...
THROUGH THE TOWN WE WERE GOING. IT WAS EMPTY, WITH NO PRIVATE PEOPLE. AND WE SAW, FROM FAR, A TRAIN.
IT WAS SUCH A TRAIN FOR HORSES, FOR COWS.
INSIDE! MOVE! MOVE!
THEY PUSHED UNTIL IT WAS NO ROOM LEFT.
WE LAY ONE ON TOP THE OTHER, LIKE MATCHES, LIKE HERRINGS.
I PUSHED TO A CORNER NOT TO GET CRUSHED...
HIGH UP I SAW A FEW HOOKS TO CHAIN UP MAYBE THE ANIMALS.
I HAD STILL THE THIN BLANKET THEY GAVE ME.
I CLIMBED TO SOME-BODY'S SHOULDER AND HOOKED IT STRONG.
IN THIS WAY I CAN REST AND BREATHE A LITTLE.
THIS SAVED ME. MAY-BE 25 PEOPLE CAME OUT FROM THIS CAR OF 200.

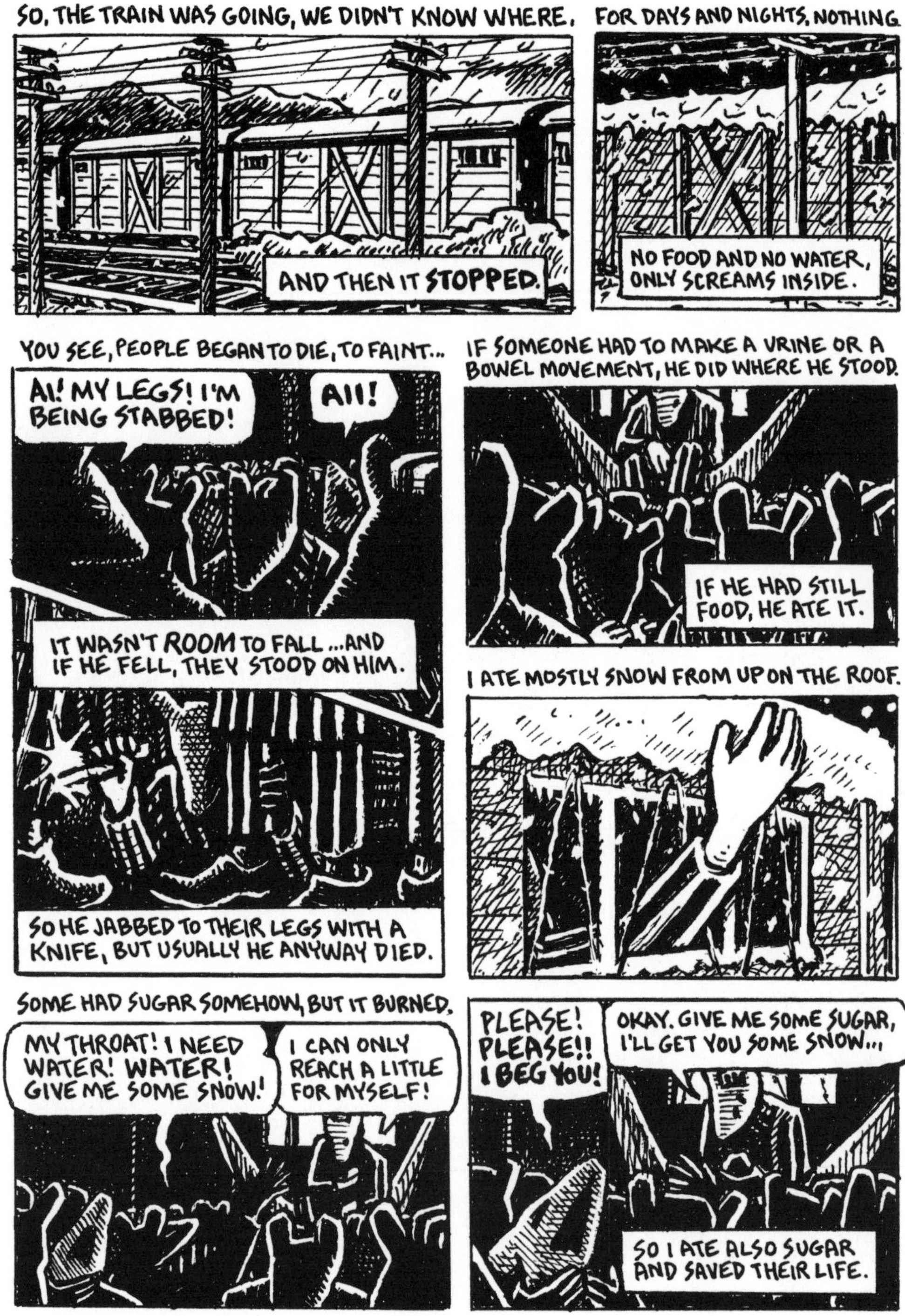

SO, THE TRAIN WAS GOING, WE DIDN'T KNOW WHERE.
AND THEN IT STOPPED.
FOR DAYS AND NIGHTS, NOTHING
NO FOOD AND NO WATER, ONLY SCREAMS INSIDE.
YOU SEE, PEOPLE BEGAN TO DIE, TO FAINT...
AI! MY LEGS! I'M BEING STABBED!
AII!
IT WASN'T ROOM TO FALL ...AND IF HE FELL, THEY STOOD ON HIM.
SO HE JABBED TO THEIR LEGS WITH A KNIFE, BUT USUALLY HE ANYWAY DIED.
IF SOMEONE HAD TO MAKE A URINE OR A BOWEL MOVEMENT, HE DID WHERE HE STOOD.
IF HE HAD STILL FOOD, HE ATE IT.
I ATE MOSTLY SNOW FROM UP ON THE ROOF.
SOME HAD SUGAR SOMEHOW, BUT IT BURNED.
MY THROAT! I NEED WATER! WATER! GIVE ME SOME SNOW!
I CAN ONLY REACH A LITTLE FOR MYSELF!
PLEASE! PLEASE!! I BEG YOU!
OKAY. GIVE ME SOME SUGAR, I'LL GET YOU SOME SNOW...
SO I ATE ALSO SUGAR AND SAVED THEIR LIFE.

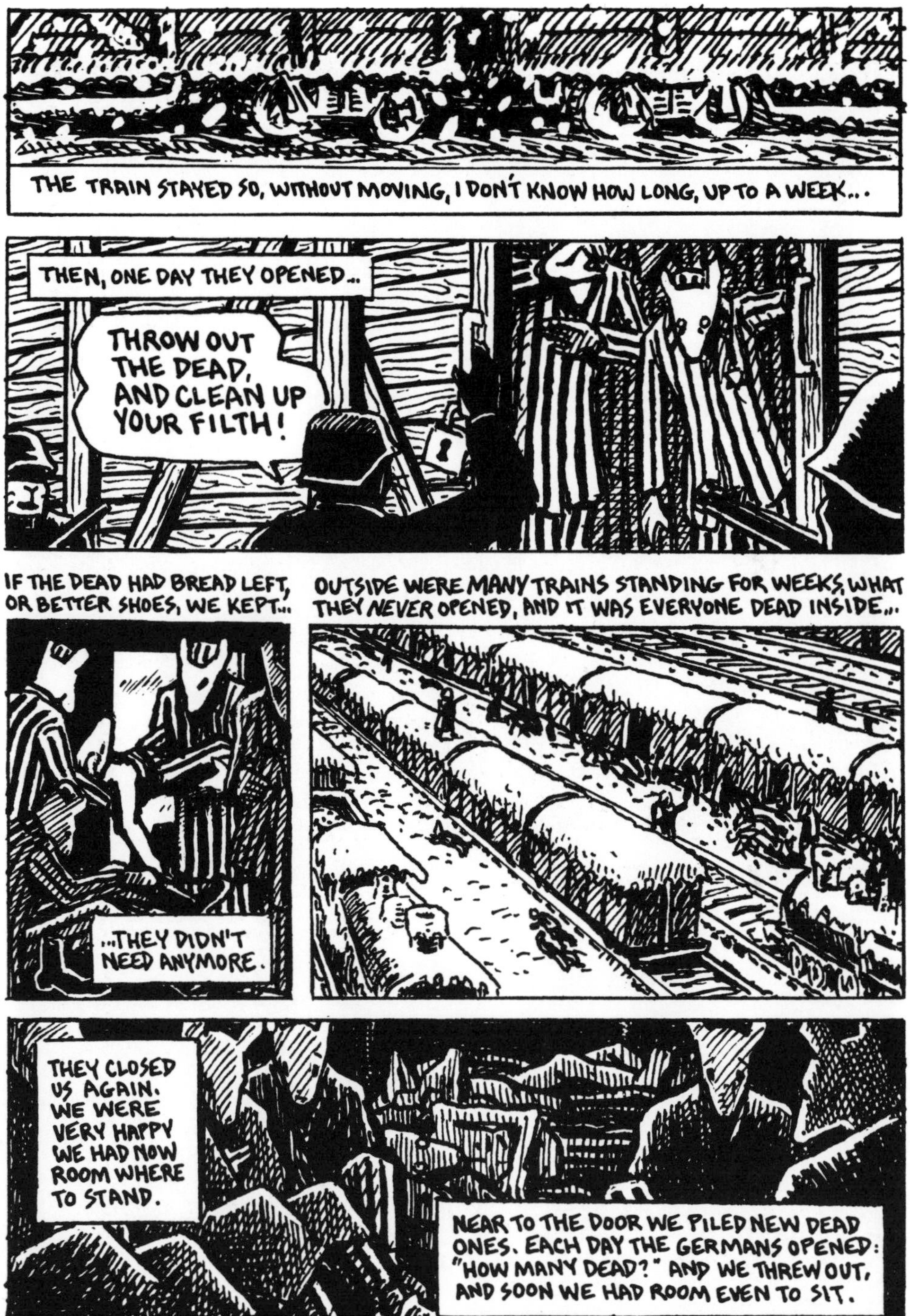
THE TRAIN STAYED SO, WITHOUT MOVING, I DON'T KNOW HOW LONG, UP TO A WEEK...
THEN, ONE DAY THEY OPENED...
THROW OUT THE DEAD, AND CLEAN UP YOUR FILTH!
IF THE DEAD HAD BREAD LEFT, OR BETTER SHOES, WE KEPT...
...THEY DIDN'T NEED ANYMORE.
OUTSIDE WERE MANY TRAINS STANDING FOR WEEKS, WHAT THEY NEVER OPENED, AND IT WAS EVERYONE DEAD INSIDE...
THEY CLOSED US AGAIN. WE WERE VERY HAPPY WE HAD NOW ROOM WHERE TO STAND.
NEAR TO THE DOOR WE PILED NEW DEAD ONES. EACH DAY THE GERMANS OPENED: "HOW MANY DEAD?" AND WE THREW OUT, AND SOON WE HAD ROOM EVEN TO SIT.

250

WE WERE CLOSED IN BARRACKS, SITTING ON STRAW, WAITING ONLY TO DIE.

IN THE STRAW, IT WAS LICE... FROM THE LICE WAS TYPHUS.

IF IT WAS ANY LICE, YOU GOT NO SOUP. THIS WAS IMPOSSIBLE. EVERYWHERE WAS LICE!

YOU CAN'T KNOW WHAT IT IS, TO BE HUNGRY.

252

254

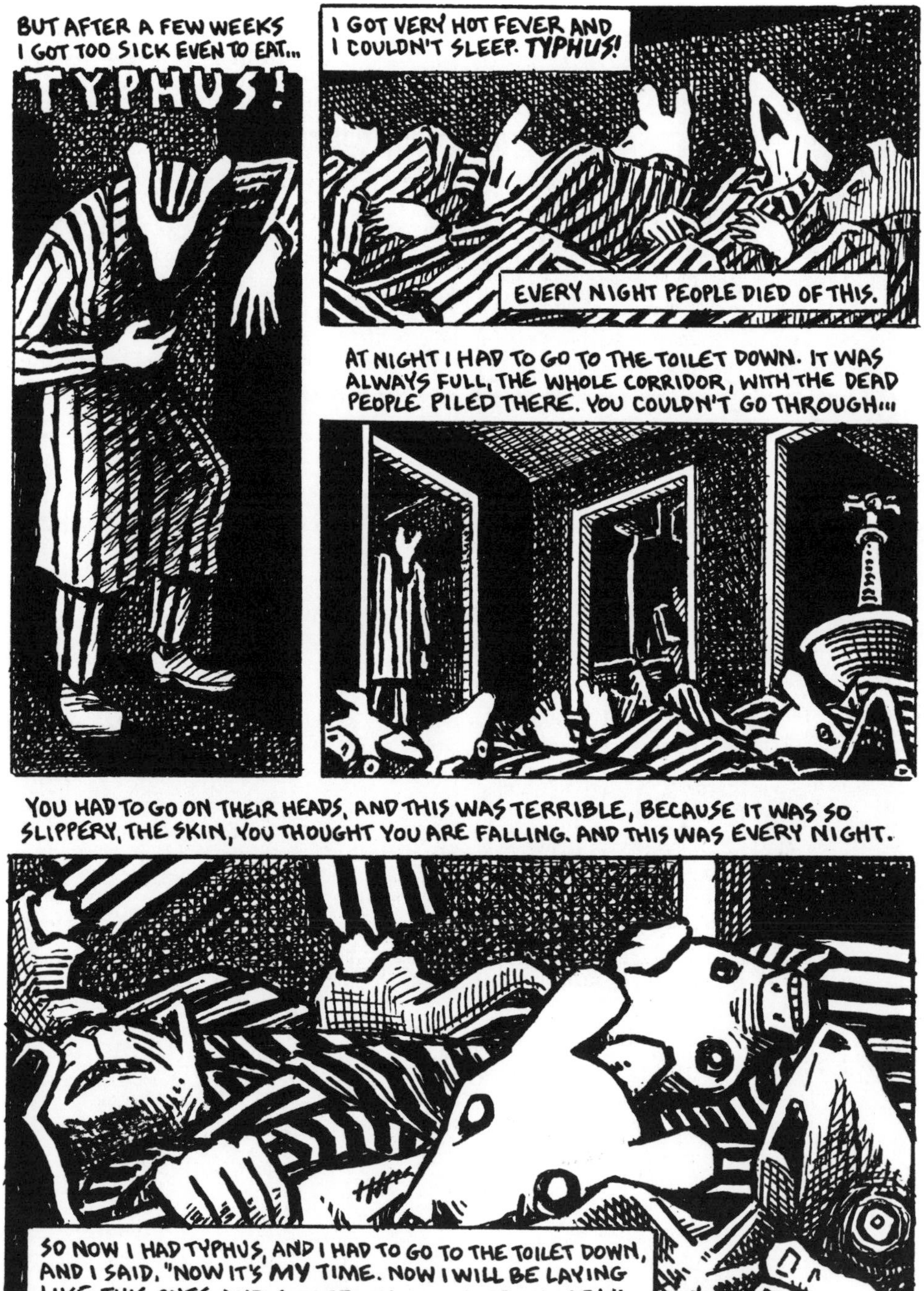
BUT AFTER A FEW WEEKS I GOT TOO SICK EVEN TO EAT...
TYPHUS!
I GOT VERY HOT FEVER AND I COULDN'T SLEEP. TYPHUS!
EVERY NIGHT PEOPLE DIED OF THIS.
AT NIGHT I HAD TO GO TO THE TOILET DOWN. IT WAS ALWAYS FULL, THE WHOLE CORRIDOR, WITH THE DEAD PEOPLE PILED THERE. YOU COULDN'T GO THROUGH...
YOU HAD TO GO ON THEIR HEADS, AND THIS WAS TERRIBLE, BECAUSE IT WAS SO SLIPPERY, THE SKIN, YOU THOUGHT YOU ARE FALLING. AND THIS WAS EVERY NIGHT.
SO NOW I HAD TYPHUS, AND I HAD TO GO TO THE TOILET DOWN, AND I SAID, "NOW IT'S MY TIME. NOW I WILL BE LAYING LIKE THIS ONES AND SOMEBODY WILL STEP ON ME!"

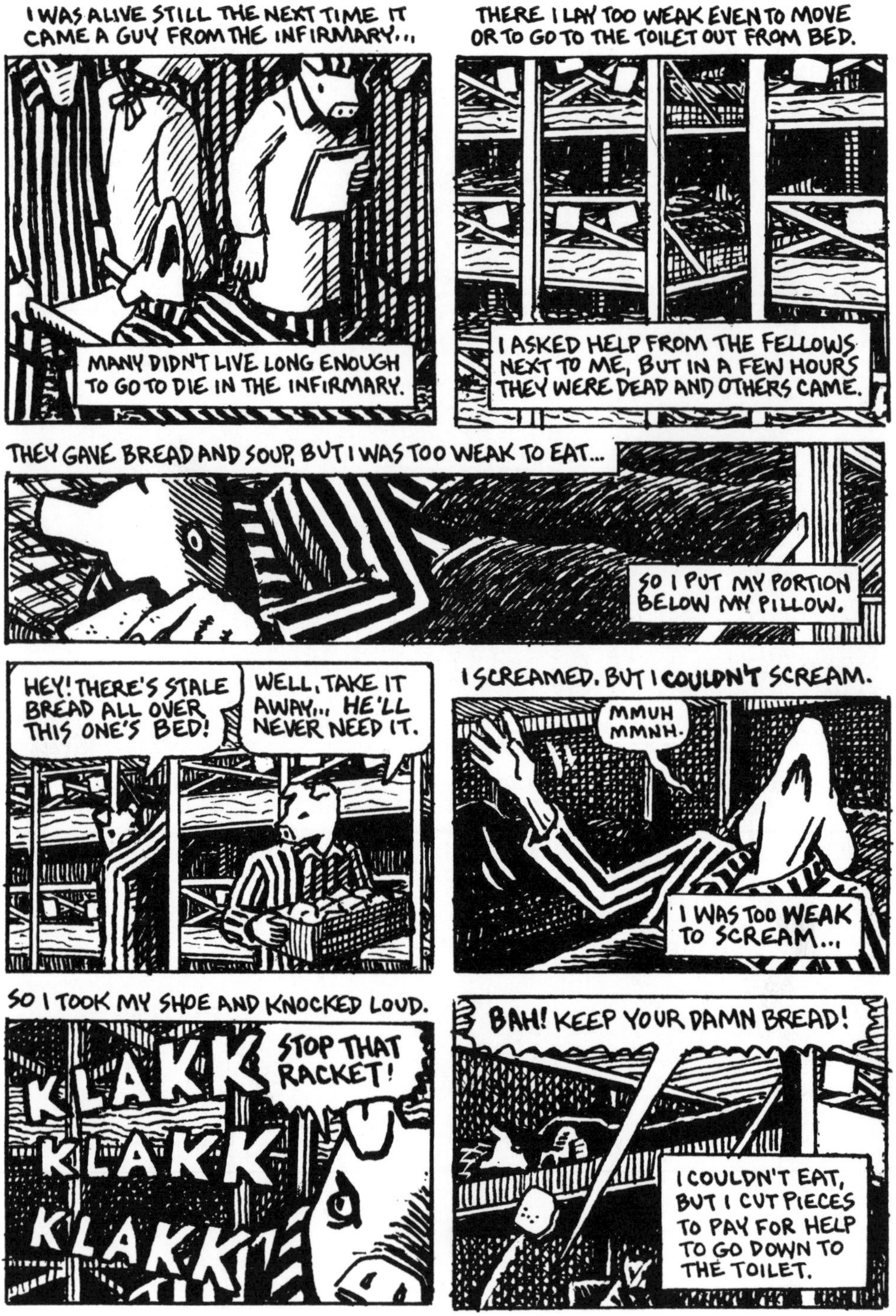
I WAS ALIVE STILL THE NEXT TIME IT CAME A GUY FROM THE INFIRMARY...
MANY DIDN'T LIVE LONG ENOUGH TO GO TO DIE IN THE INFIRMARY.
THERE I LAY TOO WEAK EVEN TO MOVE OR TO GO TO THE TOILET OUT FROM BED.
I ASKED HELP FROM THE FELLOWS NEXT TO ME, BUT IN A FEW HOURS THEY WERE DEAD AND OTHERS CAME.
THEY GAVE BREAD AND SOUP, BUT I WAS TOO WEAK TO EAT...
SO I PUT MY PORTION BELOW MY PILLOW.
HEY! THERE'S STALE BREAD ALL OVER THIS ONE'S BED!
WELL, TAKE IT AWAY... HE'LL NEVER NEED IT.
I SCREAMED. BUT I COULDN'T SCREAM.
MMUH MMNH.
I WAS TOO WEAK TO SCREAM...
SO I TOOK MY SHOE AND KNOCKED LOUD.
KLAKK
KLAKK
KLAKK
STOP THAT RACKET!
BAH! KEEP YOUR DAMN BREAD!
I COULDN'T EAT, BUT I CUT PIECES TO PAY FOR HELP TO GO DOWN TO THE TOILET.

259

CHAPTER FOUR

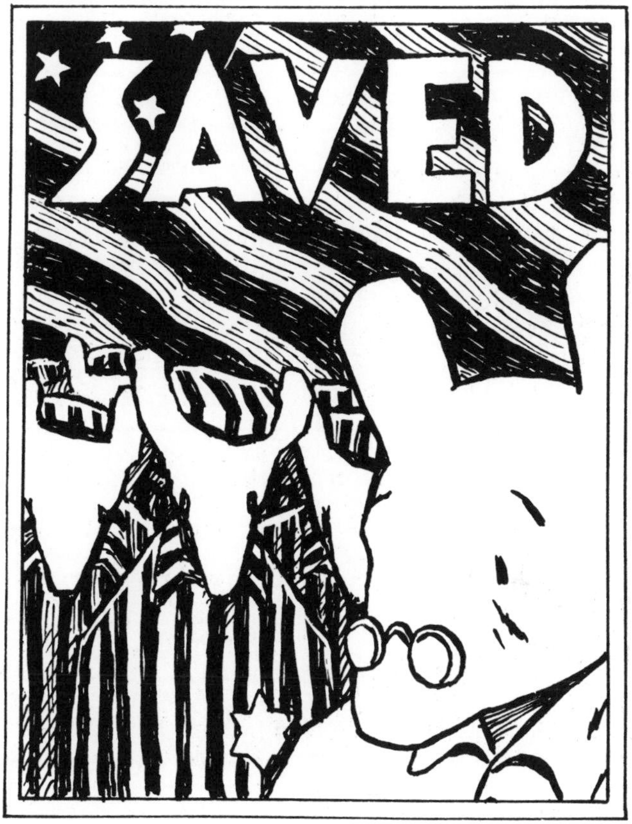
SAVED

BUT HOW DID ANJA SURVIVE?

MANCIE-THE HUNGARIAN GIRL WHAT I KNEW THERE IN AUSCHWITZ-SHE KEPT ANJA CLOSE BY TO HER.

AFTER THE WAR I LOOKED ALWAYS FOR MANCIE, TO GIVE A NICE REWARD, BUT I DIDN'T KNOW EVEN HER FULL NAME, AND I NEVER FOUND!

MOM USED TO MENTION RAVENSBRÜCK. WAS MANCIE WITH HER THERE?

YAH... MAYBE IT WAS THERE...

I KNOW ONLY THAT ANJA CAME OUT FREE BY THE RUSSIAN SIDE AND SHE CAME BACK TO SOSNOWIEC BEFORE ME. MY LIBERATION, IT TOOK LONGER...

IT WAS THE LAST MINUTES OF THE WAR, I LEFT DACHAU...

I WENT TO BE EXCHANGED FOR GERMAN PRISONERS ON THE SWISS BORDER BUT WE NEVER CAME.

I REMEMBER WE GOT EACH A TREASURE BOX FROM THE SWISS RED CROSS: SARDINES! BISCUITS! CHOCOLATE!

SOME ATE RIGHT AWAY EVERYTHING. I KEPT, OF COURSE, TO HAVE LATER.

SO, AT NIGHT, SOME TRIED TO STEAL FROM ME...

HEY!

WITH MY TYPHUS I NEEDED STILL MUCH TO REST, BUT THIS TREASURE WAS MORE TO ME THAN SLEEPING.

264

271

273

C H A P T E R   F I V E

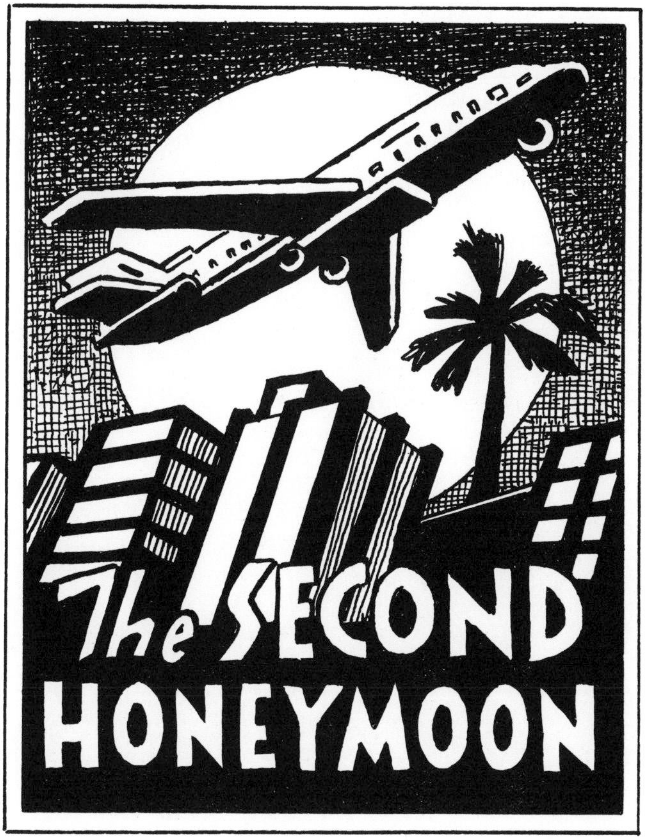

The SECOND
HONEYMOON

Winter...

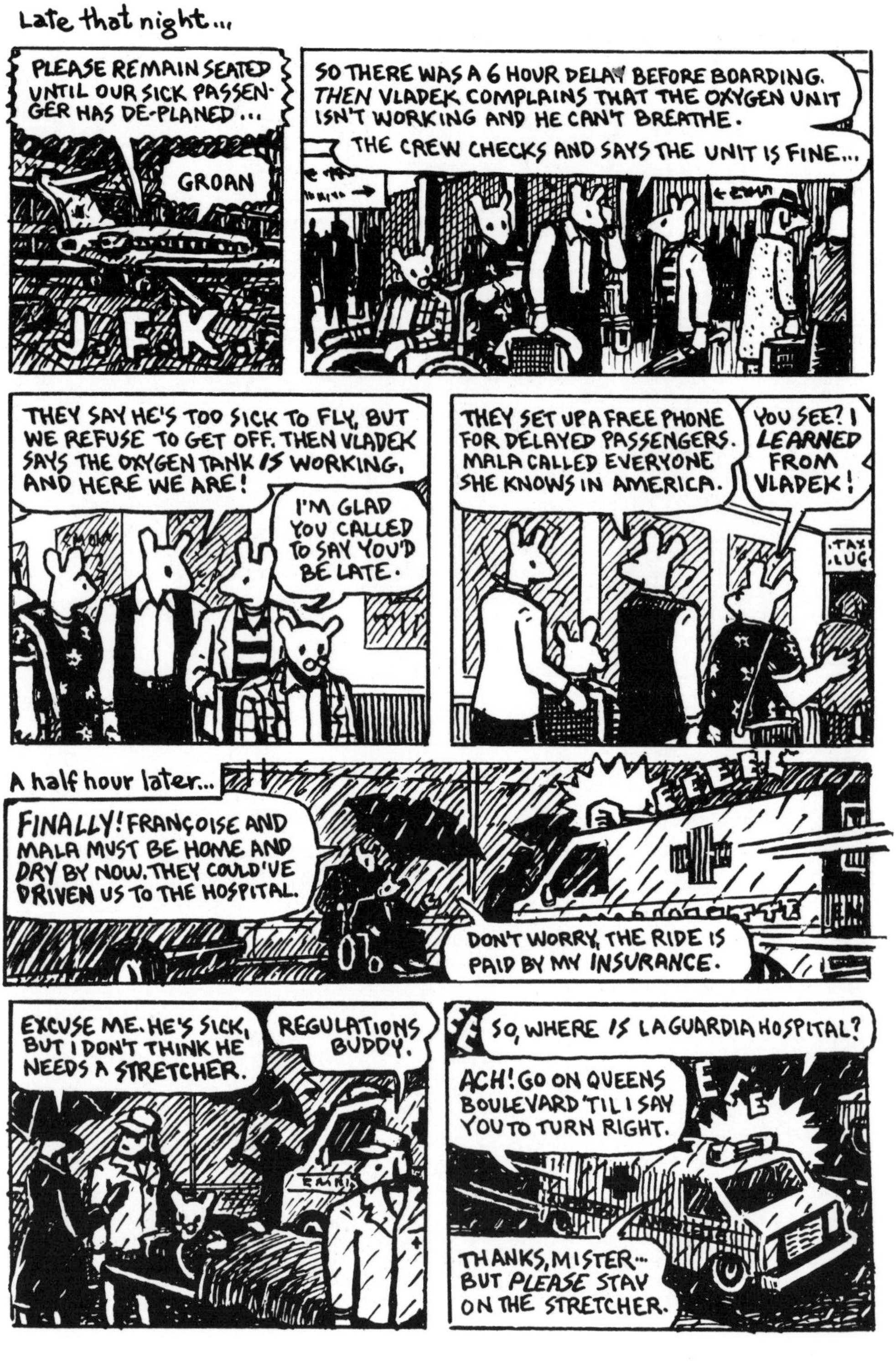
Late that night...
PLEASE REMAIN SEATED UNTIL OUR SICK PASSENGER HAS DE-PLANED...
GROAN
J.F.K.
SO THERE WAS A 6 HOUR DELAY BEFORE BOARDING. THEN VLADEK COMPLAINS THAT THE OXYGEN UNIT ISN'T WORKING AND HE CAN'T BREATHE.
THE CREW CHECKS AND SAYS THE UNIT IS FINE...
THEY SAY HE'S TOO SICK TO FLY, BUT WE REFUSE TO GET OFF. THEN VLADEK SAYS THE OXYGEN TANK IS WORKING, AND HERE WE ARE!
I'M GLAD YOU CALLED TO SAY YOU'D BE LATE.
THEY SET UP A FREE PHONE FOR DELAYED PASSENGERS. MALA CALLED EVERYONE SHE KNOWS IN AMERICA.
YOU SEE? I LEARNED FROM VLADEK!
A half hour later...
FINALLY! FRANÇOISE AND MALA MUST BE HOME AND DRY BY NOW. THEY COULD'VE DRIVEN US TO THE HOSPITAL.
DON'T WORRY, THE RIDE IS PAID BY MY INSURANCE.
EXCUSE ME. HE'S SICK, BUT I DON'T THINK HE NEEDS A STRETCHER.
REGULATIONS BUDDY.
SO, WHERE IS LAGUARDIA HOSPITAL?
ACH! GO ON QUEENS BOULEVARD 'TIL I SAY YOU TO TURN RIGHT.
THANKS, MISTER... BUT PLEASE STAY ON THE STRETCHER.

A month or so later...

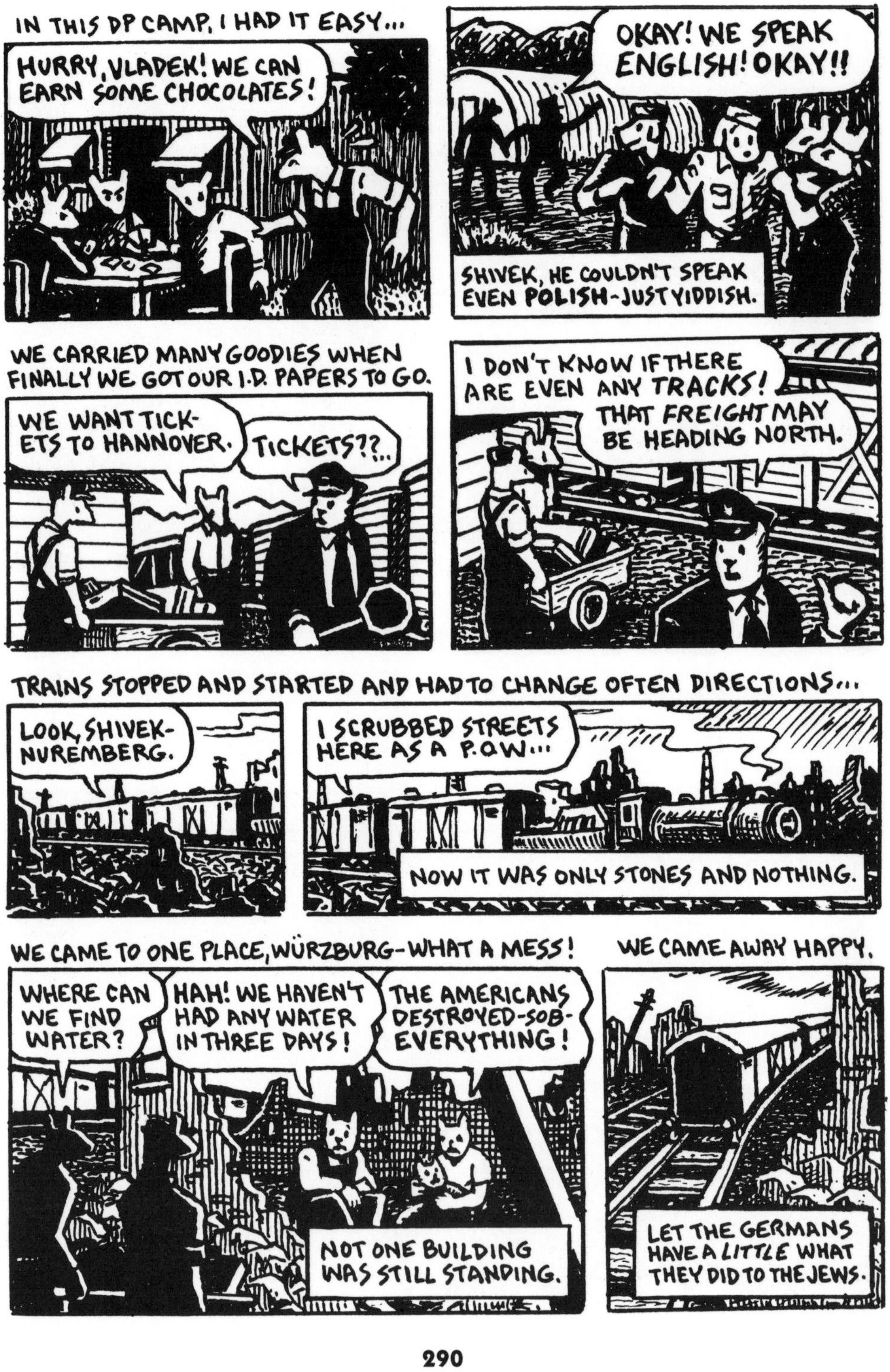
IN THIS DP CAMP, I HAD IT EASY...
HURRY, VLADEK! WE CAN EARN SOME CHOCOLATES!
OKAY! WE SPEAK ENGLISH! OKAY!!
SHIVEK, HE COULDN'T SPEAK EVEN POLISH-JUST YIDDISH.
WE CARRIED MANY GOODIES WHEN FINALLY WE GOT OUR I.D. PAPERS TO GO.
WE WANT TICKETS TO HANNOVER.
TICKETS??...
I DON'T KNOW IF THERE ARE EVEN ANY TRACKS!
THAT FREIGHT MAY BE HEADING NORTH.
TRAINS STOPPED AND STARTED AND HAD TO CHANGE OFTEN DIRECTIONS...
LOOK, SHIVEK-NUREMBERG.
I SCRUBBED STREETS HERE AS A P.O.W...
NOW IT WAS ONLY STONES AND NOTHING.
WE CAME TO ONE PLACE, WÜRZBURG-WHAT A MESS!
WHERE CAN WE FIND WATER?
HAH! WE HAVEN'T HAD ANY WATER IN THREE DAYS!
THE AMERICANS DESTROYED-SOB-EVERYTHING!
NOT ONE BUILDING WAS STILL STANDING.
WE CAME AWAY HAPPY.
LET THE GERMANS HAVE A LITTLE WHAT THEY DID TO THE JEWS.

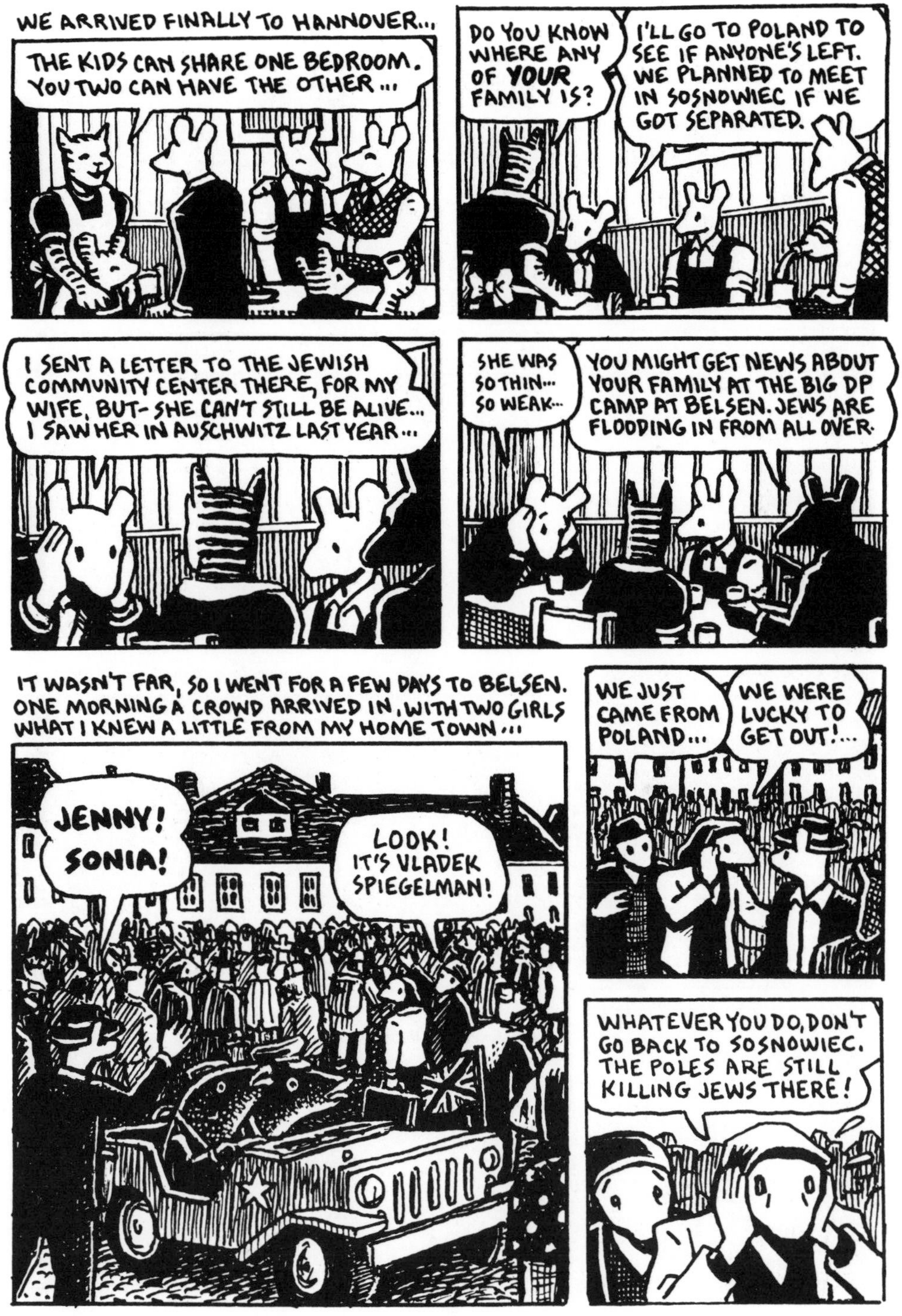
WE ARRIVED FINALLY TO HANNOVER...
THE KIDS CAN SHARE ONE BEDROOM. YOU TWO CAN HAVE THE OTHER...
DO YOU KNOW WHERE ANY OF YOUR FAMILY IS?
I'LL GO TO POLAND TO SEE IF ANYONE'S LEFT. WE PLANNED TO MEET IN SOSNOWIEC IF WE GOT SEPARATED.
I SENT A LETTER TO THE JEWISH COMMUNITY CENTER THERE, FOR MY WIFE, BUT- SHE CAN'T STILL BE ALIVE... I SAW HER IN AUSCHWITZ LAST YEAR...
SHE WAS SO THIN... SO WEAK...
YOU MIGHT GET NEWS ABOUT YOUR FAMILY AT THE BIG DP CAMP AT BELSEN. JEWS ARE FLOODING IN FROM ALL OVER.
IT WASN'T FAR, SO I WENT FOR A FEW DAYS TO BELSEN. ONE MORNING A CROWD ARRIVED IN, WITH TWO GIRLS WHAT I KNEW A LITTLE FROM MY HOME TOWN...
JENNY! SONIA!
LOOK! IT'S VLADEK SPIEGELMAN!
WE JUST CAME FROM POLAND...
WE WERE LUCKY TO GET OUT!...
WHATEVER YOU DO, DON'T GO BACK TO SOSNOWIEC. THE POLES ARE STILL KILLING JEWS THERE!

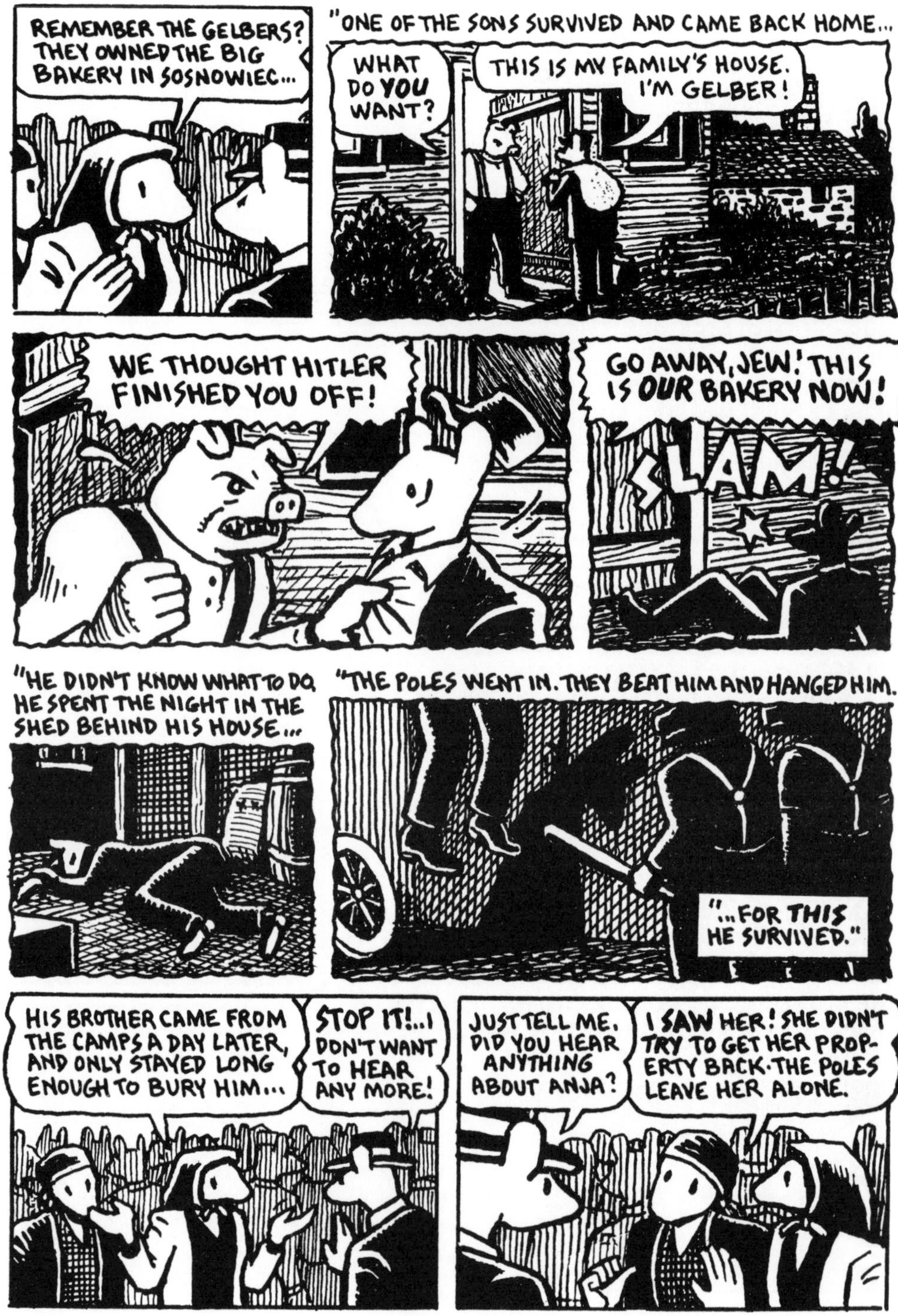
REMEMBER THE GELBERS? THEY OWNED THE BIG BAKERY IN SOSNOWIEC...
"ONE OF THE SONS SURVIVED AND CAME BACK HOME...
WHAT DO YOU WANT?
THIS IS MY FAMILY'S HOUSE. I'M GELBER!
WE THOUGHT HITLER FINISHED YOU OFF!
GO AWAY, JEW! THIS IS OUR BAKERY NOW!
SLAM!
"HE DIDN'T KNOW WHAT TO DO. HE SPENT THE NIGHT IN THE SHED BEHIND HIS HOUSE...
"THE POLES WENT IN. THEY BEAT HIM AND HANGED HIM.
"...FOR THIS HE SURVIVED."
HIS BROTHER CAME FROM THE CAMPS A DAY LATER, AND ONLY STAYED LONG ENOUGH TO BURY HIM...
STOP IT!..I DON'T WANT TO HEAR ANY MORE!
JUST TELL ME. DID YOU HEAR ANYTHING ABOUT ANJA?
I SAW HER! SHE DIDN'T TRY TO GET HER PROPERTY BACK. THE POLES LEAVE HER ALONE.

293

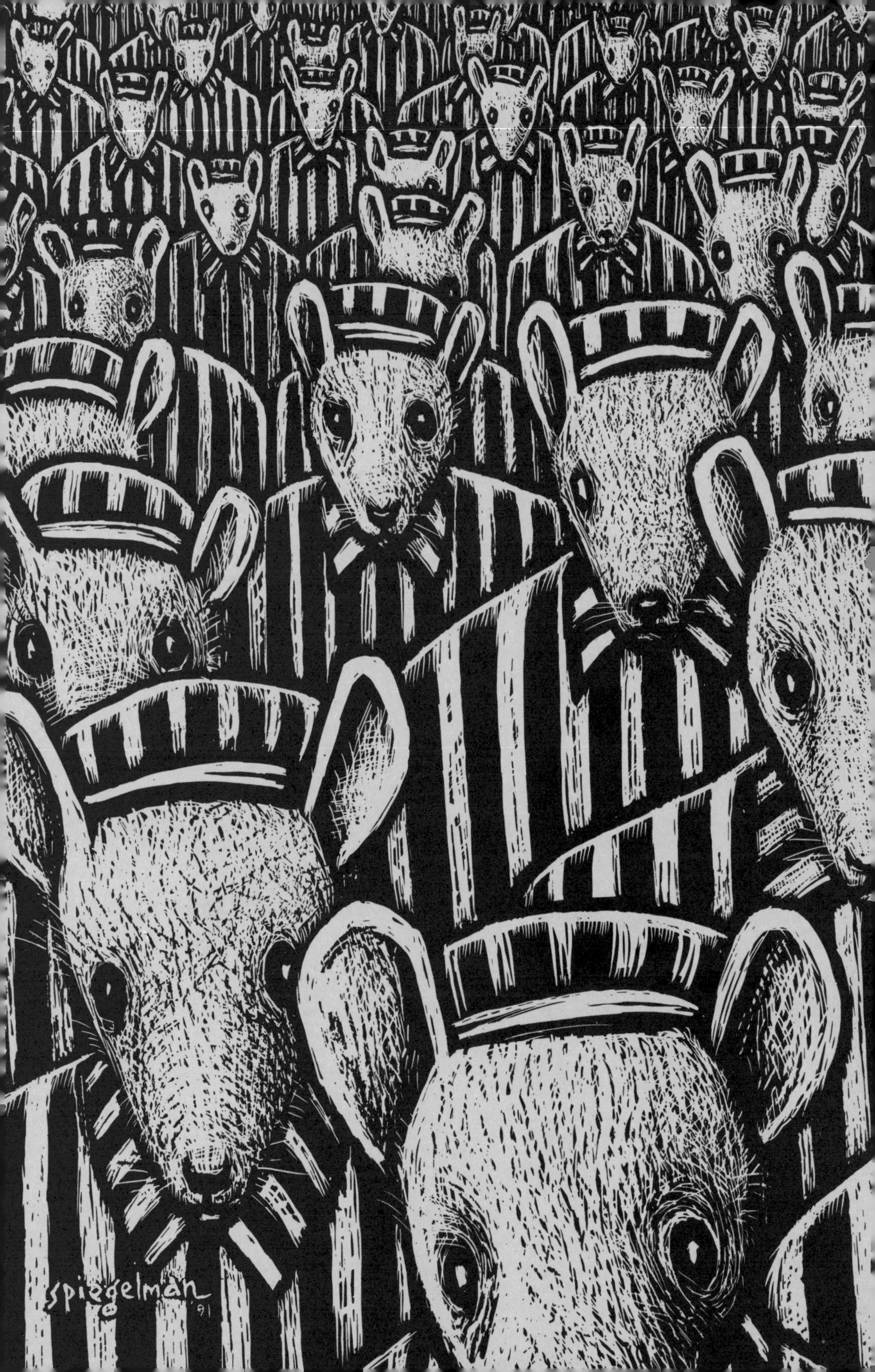
spiegelman
'91